The Expositor's Bible
The Epistle To The Galatians

by

George G. Findlay

Double9
BOOKS

The Expositor's Bible
The Epistle To The Galatians
by George G. Findlay

ISBN: 978-93-61154-48-5

Published by

DOUBLE 9 BOOKS

2/13-B, Ansari Road
Daryaganj, New Delhi – 110002
info@double9books.com
www.double9books.com
Tel. 011-40042856

ABOUT THE AUTHOR

George G. Findlay, a fantastic Scottish theologian, became an important parent inside the past due nineteenth and early 20th a long time. Findlay, famous for his scholarly contributions, wrote "The Expositor's Bible: The Epistle to the Galatians." This masterpiece, demonstrates Findlay's profound theological insights and exegetical skills. In "The Expositor's Bible," Findlay focuses on the Epistle to the Galatians, imparting a thorough and perceptive analysis of this sizable biblical textual be counted. The book is part of the wider "Expositor's Bible" collection, which ambitions to offer handy however scholarly interpretations of the Scriptures for each clergy and lay readers. Findlay's artwork on Galatians discover the theological subject matters of justification by religion, Christian freedom, and the relationship between regulation and style. His assertion is distinguished through an intensive investigation of the Greek text, historical context, and theological implications, making it an invaluable useful resource for college college students, pastors, and instructors alike. "The Expositor's Bible: The Epistle to the Galatians" demonstrates George G. Findlay's dedication to authentic biblical take a look at and his lasting effect on the sphere of theological literature.

CONTENTS

THE DOCTRINAL POLEMIC

THE ETHICAL APPLICATION

CHAPTER I
THE ADDRESS

"Paul, an apostle (not from men, neither through man, but through Jesus Christ, and God the Father, who raised Him from the dead), and all the brethren which are with me, unto the Churches of Galatia."[1]—Gal. i. 1, 2.

Antiquity has nothing to show more notable in its kind, or more precious, than this letter of Paul to the Churches of Galatia. It takes us back, in some respects nearer than any other document we possess, to the beginnings of Christian theology and the Christian Church. In it the spiritual consciousness of Christianity first reveals itself in its distinctive character and its full strength, free from the trammels of the past, realizing the advent of the new kingdom of God that was founded in the death of Christ. It is the voice of the Church testifying "God hath sent forth the Spirit of His Son into our hearts." Buried for a thousand years under the weight of the Catholic legalism, the teaching of this Epistle came to life again in the rise of Protestantism. Martin Luther put it to his lips as a trumpet to blow the reveillé of the Reformation. His famous Commentary summoned enslaved Christendom to recover "the liberty wherewith Christ hath made us free." Of all the great Reformer's writings this was the widest in its influence and the dearest to himself. For the spirit of Paul lived again in Luther, as in no other since the Apostle's day. The Epistle to the Galatians is the charter of Evangelical faith.

The historical criticism of the present century has brought this writing once more to the front of the conflict of faith. Born in controversy, it seems inevitably to be born for controversy. Its interpretation forms the pivot of the most thoroughgoing recent discussions touching the beginnings of Christian history and the authenticity of the New Testament record. The Galatian Epistle is, in fact, the key of New Testament Apologetics. Round it the Roman and Corinthian Letters group themselves, forming together a solid, impregnable quaternion, and supplying a fixed starting-point and an indubitable test for the examination of the critical questions belonging to the Apostolic age. Whatever else may be disputed, it is agreed that there was an apostle Paul, who wrote these four Epistles to certain Christian societies gathered out of heathenism, communities numerous, widely scattered, and containing men of advanced intelligence; and this within thirty years of the death of Jesus Christ. Every critic must reckon with this fact. The most sceptical criticism makes a respectful pause before our Epistle. Hopeless of destroying its testimony, Rationalism treats it with an even exaggerated deference; and seeks to extract evidence from it against its companion witnesses amongst the New Testament writings. This attempt, however misdirected, is a signal tribute to the importance of the document, and to the force with which the personality of the writer and the conditions of the time have stamped themselves upon it. The deductions of the Baurian criticism appear to us to rest on a narrow and arbitrary examination of isolated passages; they spring from a mistaken *à priori* view of the historical situation. Granting however to these inferences, which will meet us as we proceed, their utmost weight, they still leave the testimony of Paul to the supernatural character of Christianity substantially intact.

Of the four major Epistles, this one is superlatively characteristic of its author. It is *Paulinissima Paulinarum*—most Pauline of Pauline things. It is largely autobiographical; hence its peculiar value. Reading it, we watch history in the making. We trace the rise of the new religion in the typical man of the epoch. The master-builder of the Apostolic Church stands before us, at the crisis of his work. He lets us look into his heart, and learn the secret of his power. We come to know the Apostle Paul as we know scarcely any other of the world's great minds. We find in him a man of the highest intellectual and spiritual powers, equally great in passion and in action, as a thinker and a leader of men. But at every step of our acquaintance the Apostle points us beyond himself; he says, "It is not I: it is Christ that lives in me." If this Epistle teaches us the greatness of Paul, it teaches us all the more the Divine greatness of Jesus Christ, before whom that kingly intellect and passionate heart bowed in absolute devotion.

The situation which the Epistle reveals and the personal references in which it abounds are full of interest at every point. They furnish quite essential data to the historian of the Early Church. We could wish that the Apostle, telling us so much, had told us more. His allusions, clear enough, we must suppose, to the first readers, have lent themselves subsequently to very conflicting interpretations. But as they stand, they are invaluable. The fragmentary narrative of the Acts requires, especially in its earlier sections, all the illustration that can be obtained from other sources. The conversion of Paul, and the Council at Jerusalem, events of capital importance for the history of Apostolic times, are thereby set in a light certainly more complete and satisfactory than is furnished in Luke's narrative, taken by itself. And

Paul's references to the Judean Church and its three "pillars," touch the crucial question of New Testament criticism, namely that concerning the relation of the Gentile Apostle to Jewish Christianity and the connection between his theology and the teaching of Jesus. Our judgement respecting the conflict between Peter and Paul at Antioch in particular will determine our whole conception of the legalist controversy, and consequently of the course of Church history during the first two centuries. Around these cursory allusions has gathered a contest only less momentous than that from which they sprung.

The personal and the doctrinal element are equally prominent in this Epistle; and appear in a combination characteristic of the writer. Paul's theology is the theology of experience. "It pleased God," he says, "to reveal His Son in me" (ch. i. 16). His teaching is cast in a psychological mould. It is largely a record of the Apostle's spiritual history; it is the expression of a living, inward process—a personal appropriation of Christ, and a growing realization of the fulness of the Godhead in Him. The doctrine of Paul was as far as possible removed from being the result of abstract deduction, or any mere combination of data externally given. In his individual consciousness, illuminated by the vision of Christ and penetrated by the Spirit of God, he found his message for the world. "We believe, and therefore speak. We have received the Spirit of God, that we may know the things freely given us of God:" sentences like these show us very clearly how the Apostle's doctrine formed itself in his mind. His apprehension of Christ, above all of the cross, was the focus, the creative and governing centre, of all his thoughts concerning God and man, time and eternity. In the light of this knowledge he read the Old Testament, he interpreted the earthly life and teaching of Jesus. On the ground of this personal sense of salvation he confronted Peter at Antioch; on the same ground he appeals to the vacillating Galatians, sharers with himself in the new life of the Spirit. Here lies the nerve of his argument in this Epistle. The theory of the relation of the Law to the Abrahamic promise developed in the third chapter, is the historical counterpart of the relation of the legal to the evangelical consciousness, as he had experienced the two states in turn within his own breast. The spirit of Paul was a microcosm, in which the course of the world's religious evolution was summed up, and brought to the knowledge of itself.

The Apostle's influence over the minds of others was due in great part to the extraordinary force with which he apprehended the facts of his own spiritual nature. Through the depth and intensity of his personal experience he touched the experience of his fellows, he seized on those universal truths that are latent in the consciousness of mankind, "by manifestation of the truth commending himself to every man's conscience in the sight of God."

But this knowledge of the things of God was not the mere fruit of reflection and self-searching; it was "the ministration of the Spirit." Paul did not simply *know* Christ; he was one with Christ, "joined to the Lord, one spirit" with Him. He did not therefore speak out of the findings of his own spirit; the absolute Spirit, the Spirit of truth and of Christ, spoke in him. Truth, as he knew it, was the self-assertion of a Divine life. And so this handful of old letters, broken and casual in form, with their "rudeness of speech," their many obscurities, their rabbinical logic, have stirred the thoughts of men and swayed their lives with a power greater perhaps than belongs to any human utterances, saving only those of the Divine Master.

The features of Paul's style show themselves here in their most pronounced form. "The style is the man." And the whole man is in this letter. Other Epistles bring into relief this or that quality of the Apostle's disposition and of his manner as a writer; here all are present. The subtlety and trenchant vigour of Pauline dialectic are nowhere more conspicuous than in the discussion with Peter in ch. ii. The discourse on Promise and Law in ch. iii. is a master-piece of exposition, unsurpassed in its keenness of insight, breadth of view, and skill of application. Such passages as ch. i. 15, 16; ii. 19, 20; vi. 14, take us into the heart of the Apostle's teaching, and reveal its mystical depth of intuition. Behind the masterful dialectician we find the spiritual seer, the man of contemplation, whose fellowship is with the eternal and unseen. And the emotional temperament of the writer has left its impress on this Epistle not less distinctly than his mental and spiritual gifts. The denunciations of ch. i. 6-10; ii. 4, 5; iv. 9; v. 7-12; vi. 12-14, burn with a concentrated intensity of passion, a sublime and holy scorn against the enemies of the cross, such as a nature like Paul's alone is capable of feeling. Nor has the Apostle penned anything on the other hand more amiable and touching, more winningly frank and tender in appeal, than the entreaty of ch. iv. 11-20. His last sentence, in ch. vi. 17, is an irresistible stroke of pathos. The ardour of his soul, his vivacity of mind and quick sensibility, are apparent throughout. Those sudden turns of thought and bursts of emotion that occur in all his Epistles and so much perplex their interpreters, are especially numerous in this. And yet we find that these interruptions are never allowed to divert the writer from his purpose, nor to destroy the sequence of his thought. They rather carry it forward with greater vehemence along the chosen course, as storms will a strong and well-manned ship. The Epistle is strictly a unity. It is written, as one might say, at a single breath, as if under pressure and in stress of mind. There is little of the amplitude of expression and the delight in lingering over some favourite idea that characterize the later Epistles. Nor is there any passage of sustained eloquence to compare with those that are found in the Roman and

Corinthian letters. The business on which the Apostle writes is too urgent, his anxiety too great, to allow of freedom and discursiveness of thought. Hence this Epistle is to an unusual degree closely packed in matter, rapid in movement, and severe in tone.

In its construction the Epistle exhibits an almost dramatic character. It is full of action and animation. There is a gradual unfolding of the subject, and a skilful combination of scene and incident brought to bear on the solution of the crucial question. The Apostle himself, the insidious Judaizers, and the wavering Galatians, — these are the protagonists of the action; with Peter and the Church at Jerusalem playing a secondary part, and Abraham and Moses, Isaac and Ishmael, appearing in the distance. The first Act conducts us rapidly from scene to scene till we behold Paul labouring amongst the Gentiles, and the Churches of Judea listening with approval to the reports of his success. The Council of Jerusalem opens a new stage in the history. Now Gentile liberties are at stake; but Titus' circumcision is successfully resisted, and Paul as the Apostle of the Uncircumcised is acknowledged by "the pillars" as their equal; and finally Peter, when he betrays the truth of the Gospel at Antioch, is corrected by the Gentile Apostle. The third chapter carries us away from the present conflict into the region of first principles, — to the Abrahamic Covenant with its spiritual blessing and world-wide promise, opposed by the condemning Mosaic Law, an opposition finally resolved by the coming of Christ and the gift of His Spirit of adoption. At this point the Apostle turns the gathered force of his argument upon his readers, and grapples with them front to front in the expostulation carried on from ch. iv. 8 to v. 12, in which the story of Hagar forms a telling episode. The fifth and closing Act, extending to the middle of ch. vi., turns on the antithesis of Flesh and Spirit, bringing home the contention to the region of ethics, and exhibiting to the Galatians the practical effect of their following the Pauline or the Judaistic leadership. Paul and the Primitive Church; Judaism and Gentile-Christian liberties; the Covenants of Promise and of Law; the circumcision or non-circumcision of the Galatians; the dominion of Flesh or Spirit: these are the contrasts through which the Epistle advances. Its centre lies in the decisive question given in the *fourth* of these antitheses. If we were to fix it in a single point, ver. 2 of ch. v. is the sentence we should choose: —

"Behold, I Paul say unto you,

If ye be circumcised, Christ will profit you nothing."

The above analysis may be reduced to the common threefold division, followed in this exposition: — viz. (1) *Personal History*, ch. i. 11-ii. 21; (2) *Doctrinal Polemic*, ch. iii. 1-v. 12; (3) *Ethical Application*, ch. v. 13-vi. 10.

The epistolary Introduction forms the *Prologue*, ch. i. 1-10; and an *Epilogue* is appended, by way of renewed warning and protestation, followed by the concluding signature and benediction, — ch. vi. 11-18.

The Address occupies the first two verses of the Epistle.

I. On the one side is *the writer*: "Paul, an Apostle." In his earliest Letters (to Thessalonica) the title is wanting; so also in Philippians and Philemon. The last instance explains the other two. To the Macedonian Churches Paul writes more in the style of friendship than authority: "for love's sake he rather entreats." With the Galatians it is different. He proceeds to define his apostleship in terms that should leave no possible doubt respecting its character and rights: "not from men," he adds, "nor through man; but through Jesus Christ, and God the Father, that raised Him from the dead."

This reads like a contradiction of some statement made by Paul's opposers. Had they insinuated that he *was* "an apostle from men," that his office was derived, like their own, only from the mother Church in Jerusalem? Such insinuations would very well serve their purpose; and if they were made, Paul would be sure not to lose a moment in meeting them.

The word *apostle* had a certain latitude of meaning.[2] It was already, there is reason to believe, a term of Jewish official usage when our Lord applied it to His chosen Twelve. It signified a *delegate* or *envoy*, accredited by some public authority, and charged with a special message. We can understand therefore its application to the emissaries of particular Churches—of Jerusalem or Antioch, for example—despatched as their messengers to other Churches, or with a general commission to proclaim the Gospel. The recently discovered "Teaching of the Apostles" shows that this use of the title continued in Jewish-Christian circles to the end of the first century, alongside of the restricted and higher use. The lower apostleship belonged to Paul in common with Barnabas and Silas and many others.

In the earlier period of his ministry, the Apostle was seemingly content to rank in public estimation with his companions in the Gentile mission. But a time came when he was compelled to arrogate to himself the higher dignity. His right thereto was acknowledged at the memorable conference in Jerusalem by the leaders of the Jewish Church. So we gather from the language of ch. ii. 7-9. But the full exercise of his authority was reserved for the present emergency, when all his energy and influence were required to stem the tide of the Judaistic reaction. We can well imagine that Paul "gentle in the midst" of his flock and "not seeking to be of weight" (1 Thess. ii. 6, 7), had hitherto said as little as need be on the subject of his official rights. His modesty had exposed him to misrepresentations both in Corinth and in Galatia. He will "have" these people "to know" that his gospel is in the strictest sense Divine, and that he received his commission, as certainly as any of the Twelve, from the lips of Jesus Christ Himself (ver. 11).

"Not from men" excludes human derivation; "not through man," human intervention in the conferment of Paul's office. The singular number (*man*) replaces the plural in the latter phrase, because it stands immediately opposed to "Jesus Christ" (a striking witness this to His Divinity). The second clause carries the negation farther than the first; for a call from God may be, and commonly is, imposed by human hands. There are, says Jerome, four kinds of Christian ministers: first, those sent neither from men nor through man, like the prophets of old time and the Apostles; secondly, those who are from God, but through man, as it is with their legitimate successors; thirdly, those who are from men, but not from God, as when one is ordained through mere human favour and flattery; the fourth class consists of such as have their call neither from God nor man, but wholly from themselves, as with false prophets and the false apostles of whom Paul speaks. His vocation, the Apostle declares, was superhuman, alike in its origin and in the channel by which it was conveyed. It was no voice of man that summoned Saul of Tarsus from the ranks of the enemies to those of the servants of Christ, and gave him the message he proclaimed. Damascus and Jerusalem in turn acknowledged the grace given unto him; Antioch had sent him forth on her behalf to the regions beyond: but he was conscious of a call anterior to all this, and that admitted of no earthly validation. "Am I not an apostle?" he exclaims, "have I not seen Jesus our Lord?" (1 Cor. ix. 1). "Truly the signs of the Apostle were wrought in him," both in the miraculous powers attending his office, and in those moral and spiritual qualities of a minister of God in which he was inferior to none.[3] For the exercise of his ministry he was responsible neither to "those of repute" at Jerusalem, nor to his censurers at Corinth; but to Christ who had bestowed it (1 Cor. iv. 3, 4).

The call of the Apostle proceeded also from "God the Father, who raised Jesus Christ from the dead." Christ was in this act the mediator, declaring the Supreme will. In other places, more briefly, he styles himself "Apostle by the will of God." His appointment took place by a Divine intervention, in which the ordinary sequence of events was broken through. Long after the Saviour in His bodily presence had ascended to heaven, when in the order of nature it was impossible that another Apostle should be elected, and when the administration of His Church had been for several years carried on by human hands, He appeared once more on earth for the purpose of making this man His "minister and witness;" He appeared in the name of "the Father, who had raised Him from the dead." This interposition gave to Paul's ministry an exceptional character. While the mode of his election was in one aspect humbling, and put him in the position of "the untimely one," the "least of the Apostles," whose appearance in that capacity was unlooked for and necessarily open to suspicion; on the other hand, it was glorious and exalting, since it so richly displayed the Divine mercy and the transforming power of grace.

But why does he say, *who raised Him from the dead*? Because it was the *risen Jesus* that he saw, and that he was conscious of seeing in the moment of the vision. The revelation that arrested him before Damascus, in the same moment convinced him that Jesus was risen, and that he himself was called to be His servant. These two convictions were inseparably linked in Paul's recollections. As surely as God the Father had raised His Son Jesus from the dead and given Him glory, so surely had the glorified Jesus revealed Himself to Saul his persecutor to make him His Apostle. He was, not less truly than Peter or John, a witness of His resurrection. The message of the Resurrection was the burden of the Apostleship.

He adds, "and all the brethren which are with me." For it was Paul's custom to associate with himself in these official letters his fellow-labourers, present at the time. From this expression we gather that he was attended just now by a considerable band of companions, such as we find enumerated in Acts xx. 2-6, attending him on his journey from Ephesus to Corinth during the third missionary tour. This circumstance has some bearing on the date of the letter. Bishop Lightfoot (in his Commentary) shows reason for believing that it was written, not from Ephesus as commonly supposed, but at a somewhat later time, from *Macedonia*. It is connected by numerous and close links of internal association with the Epistle to the Romans, which on this supposition speedily followed, and with 2 Corinthians, immediately preceding it. And the allusion of the text, though of no decisive weight taken by itself, goes to support this reasoning. Upon this hypothesis, our Epistle was composed in Macedonia, during the autumn of 57 (or possibly, 58) A.D. The emotion which surcharges 2 Corinthians runs over into Galatians: while the theology which labours for expression in Galatians finds ampler and calmer development in Romans.

II. Of *the readers*, "the churches of Galatia," it is not necessary to say much at present. The character of the Galatians, and the condition of their Churches, will speak for themselves as we proceed. *Galatian* is equivalent to *Gaul*, or *Kelt*. This people was a detached fragment of the great Western-European race, which forms the basis of our own Irish and West-British populations, as well as of the French nationality. They had conquered for themselves a home in the north of Asia Minor during the Gaulish invasion that poured over South-eastern Europe and into the Asiatic peninsula some three and a half centuries before. Here the Gallic intruders stubbornly held their ground; and only succumbed to the irresistible power of Rome. Defeated by the Consul Manlius in 189 B.C., the Galatians retained their autonomy, under the rule of native princes, until in the year 25 B.C., on the death of Amyntas, the country was made a province of the Empire. The people maintained their distinctive character and speech despite these changes. At the same time they readily acquired Greek culture, and were by no means barbarians; indeed they were noted for their intelligence. In religion they seem to have largely imbibed the Phrygian idolatry of the earlier inhabitants.

The Roman Government had annexed to Galatia certain districts lying to the south, in which were situated most of the cities visited by Paul and Barnabas in their first missionary tour. This has led some scholars to surmise that Paul's "Galatians" were really Pisidians and Lycaonians, the people of Derbe, Lystra, and Pisidian Antioch. But this is improbable. The inhabitants of these regions were never called Galatians in common speech; and Luke distinguishes "the Galatic country" quite clearly from its southern borderlands. Besides, the Epistle contains no allusions, such as we should expect in the case supposed, to the Apostle's earlier and memorable associations with these cities of the South. Elsewhere he mentions them by name (2 Tim. iii. 11); and why not here, if he were addressing this circle of Churches?

The Acts of the Apostles relates nothing of Paul's sojourn in Galatia, beyond the fact that he twice "passed through the Galatic country" (Acts xvi. 6; xviii. 23), on the first occasion during the second missionary journey, in travelling north and then westwards from Pisidia; the second time, on his way from Antioch to Ephesus, in the course of the third tour. Galatia lay outside the main line of Paul's evangelistic career, as the historian of the Acts describes it, outside the Apostle's own design, as it would appear from ch. iv. 13. In the first instance Galatia follows (in the order of the Acts), in the second precedes Phrygia, a change which seems to indicate some new importance accruing to this region: the further clause in Acts xviii. 23, "strengthening all the disciples," shows that the writer was aware that by this time a number of Christian societies were in existence in this neighbourhood.

No *city* is mentioned in the address, but the *country* of Galatia only— the single example of the kind in Paul's Epistles. The Galatians were countryfolk rather than townsfolk. And the Church seems to have spread over the district at large, without gathering itself into any one centre, such as the Apostle had occupied in other parts of his Gentile field.

Still more significant is the curtness of this designation. Paul does not say, "To the Churches *of God* in Galatia," or "to the saints and faithful brethren in Christ," as in other Epistles. He is in no mood for compliments. These Galatians are, he fears, "removing from God who had called them" (ver. 6). He stands in doubt of them. It is a question whether they are now, or will long continue, "Churches of God" at all. He would gladly commend them if he could; but he must instead begin with reproaches. And yet we shall find that, as the Apostle proceeds, his sternness gradually relaxes. He remembers that these "foolish Galatians" are his "children," once ardently attached to him (ch. iv. 12-20). His heart yearns towards them; he travails over them in birth again. Surely they will not forsake him, and renounce the gospel of whose blessings they had enjoyed so rich an experience (ch. iii. 3; v. 10). He calls them "brethren" once and again; and with this kindly word, holding out the hand of forgiveness, he concludes the letter.

CHAPTER II
THE SALUTATION

"Grace to you and peace from God the Father, and our Lord
Jesus Christ, who gave Himself for our sins, that He might
deliver us out of this present evil world, according to the
will of our God and Father: to whom be the glory for ever
and ever. Amen." —Gal. i. 3-5.

The greetings and benedictions of the Apostolic Letters deserve more
attention from us than they sometimes receive. We are apt to pass over them
as if they were a kind of pious formality, like the conventional phrases of
our own epistles. But to treat them in such fashion is to do injustice to the
seriousness and sincerity of Holy Scripture. This salutation of "Grace and
Peace" comes from Paul's very heart. It breathes the essence of his gospel.

This formula appears to be of the Apostle's coining. Other writers, we
may believe, borrowed it from him. *Grace* represents the common Greek
salutation, —*joy to you*, χαίρειν changing to the kindred χάρις; while the
more religious *peace* of the Hebrew, so often heard from the lips of Jesus,
remains unaltered, only receiving from the New Covenant a tenderer
significance. It is as though East and West, the old world and the new, met
here and joined their voices to bless the Church and people of Jesus Christ.

Grace is the sum of all blessing bestowed by God; *peace*, in its wide
Hebraic range of meaning, the sum of all blessing experienced by man. *Grace*
is the Father's goodwill and bounty in Christ to His undeserving children;
peace, the rest and reconcilement, the recovered health and gladness of
the child brought home to the Father's house, dwelling in the light of his
Father's face. *Grace* is the fountain of redeeming love; *peace* is the "river of
life proceeding from the throne of God and of the Lamb," that flows calm
and deep through each believing soul, the river whose "streams make glad
the city of God."

What could a pastor wish better for his people, or friend for the friend
he loves most, than this double blessing? Paul's letters are perfumed with
its fragrance. Open them where you will, they are breathing out, "Grace
to you and peace." Paul has hard things to write in this Epistle, sorrowful

complaints to make, grievous errors to correct; but still with "Grace and peace" he begins, and with "Peace and grace" he will end! And so this stern and reproachful letter to these "foolish Galatians" is all embalmed and folded up in grace and peace. That is the way to "be angry and sin not." So mercy rejoices over judgement.

These two benedictions, we must remember, go together. Peace comes through grace. The proud heart never knows peace; it will not yield to God the glory of His grace. It scorns to be a debtor, even to Him. The proud man stands upon his rights, upon his merits. And he will have them; for God is just. But peace is not amongst them. No sinful child of man deserves that. Is there wrong between your soul and God, iniquity hidden in the heart? Till that wrong is confessed, till you submit to the Almighty and your spirit bows at the Redeemer's cross, what hast thou to do with peace? No peace in this world, or in any world, for him who will not be at peace with God. "When I kept silence," so the ancient confession runs (Ps. xxxii. 3-5), "my bones waxed old through my moaning all the day long"—that is why many a man is old before his time! because of this continual inward chafing, this secret, miserable war of the heart against God. "Day and night Thy hand was heavy upon me; my moisture was turned into the drought of summer"—the soul withered like grass, all the freshness and pure delight of life wasted and perishing under the steady, unrelenting heat of the Divine displeasure. "Then I said"—I could bear it no longer—"I said, I will confess my transgression unto the Lord; and Thou forgavest the iniquity of my sin." And then peace came to the weary soul. The bitterness and hardness of life were gone; the heart was young again. The man was new born, a child of God.

But while Paul gives this salutation to all his Churches, his greeting is extended and qualified here in a peculiar manner. The Galatians were falling away from faith in Christ to Jewish ritualism. He does not therefore wish them "Grace and peace" in a general way, or as objects to be sought from any quarter or by any means that they might choose; but only "from God our Father, and our Lord Jesus Christ, who gave Himself for our sins." Here is already a note of warning and a tacit contradiction of much that they were tempted to believe. It would have been a mockery for the Apostle to desire for these fickle Galatians grace and peace on other terms. As at Corinth, so in Galatia, he is "determined to know nothing save Jesus Christ and Him crucified." Above the puerilities of their Jewish ritual, above the pettiness of their wrangling factions, he directs his readers' gaze once more to the sacrifice of Calvary and the sublime purpose of God which it reveals.

Do *we* not need to be recalled to the same sight? We live in a distracted and distracting age. Even without positive unbelief, the cross is too frequently thrust out of view by the hurry and press of modern life. Nay, in the Church itself is it not in danger of being practically set on one side, amidst the throng of competing interests which solicit, and many of them justly solicit, our attention? We visit Calvary too seldom. We do not haunt in our thoughts the sacred spot, and linger on this theme, as the old saints did. We fail to attain "the fellowship of Christ's sufferings;" and while the cross is outwardly exalted, its inward meaning is perhaps but faintly realised. "Tell us something new," they say; "that story of the cross, that evangelical doctrine of yours we have heard it so often, we know it all so well!" If men are saying this, if the cross of Christ is made of none effect, its message staled by repetition, we must be strangely at fault either in the hearing or the telling. Ah, if we knew the cross of Christ, it would crucify us; it would possess our being. Its supremacy can never be taken from it. That cross is still the centre of the world's hope, the pillar of salvation. Let the Church lose her hold of it, and she loses everything. She has no longer any reason to exist.

I. So the Apostle's greeting invites his readers to contemplate anew *the Divine gift bestowed upon sinful men*. It invokes blessing upon them "from our Lord Jesus Christ, who gave Himself for our sins."

To see this gift in its greatness, let us go a little farther back; let us consider who the Christ is that thus "gives Himself." He is, we are taught, the almoner of all the Divine bounties. He is not the object alone, but the depositary and dispenser of the Father's good pleasure to all worlds and all creatures. Creation is rooted in "the Son of God's love" (Col. i. 15-18). Universal life has its fountain in "the Only-begotten, which is in the bosom of the Father." The light that dispelled the weltering gloom of chaos, the more wondrous light that shone in the dawn of human reason, came from this "outbeaming of the Father's glory." Countless gifts had He, "the life of men, the Word that was from the beginning," bestowed on a world that knew Him not. Upon the chosen race, the people whom on the world's behalf he formed for Himself, He showered His blessings. He had given them promise and law, prophet and priest and king, gifts of faith and hope, holy obedience and brave patience and deep wisdom and prophetic fire and heavenly rapture; and His gifts to them have come through them to us, "partakers with them of the root and fatness of the olive tree."

But now, to crown all, *He gave Himself!* "The Word became flesh." The Son of God planted Himself into the stock of human life, made Himself over to mankind; He became the Son of man. So in the fulness of time came the fulness of blessing. Earlier bestowments were instalments and prophecies of this; later gifts are its outcome and its application. What could He have done more than this? What could the Infinite God do more, even for the most worthy, than He has done for us in "sending His Son, the Only-begotten, that we might live through Him!" Giving us Him, surely He will give us grace and peace.

And if our Lord Jesus Christ "gave Himself," is not that sufficient? What could Jewish ritual and circumcision add to this "fulness of the Godhead?" Why hunt after the shadows, when one has the substance? Such were the questions which the Apostle has to ask his Judaizing readers. And what, pray, do *we* want with modern Ritualism, and its scenic apparatus, and its priestly offices? Are these things designed to eke out the insufficiency of Christ? Will they recommend Him better than His own gospel and the pure influence of His Spirit avail to do in these latter days? Or has modern thought, to be sure, and the progress of the 19th century carried us beyond Jesus Christ, and created spiritual wants for which He has no supply? Paul at least had no anticipation of this failure. All the need of hungry human hearts and searching minds and sorrowing spirits, to the world's latest ages, the God of Paul, the Father of our Lord Jesus Christ, is able to supply in Him. "We are complete in Him,"—if we but knew our completeness. The most advanced thinkers of the age will still find Jesus Christ in advance of them. Those who draw the most largely from His fulness, leave its depths unsounded. There are resources stored for the times to come in the revelation of Christ, which our age is too slight, too hasty of thought, to comprehend. We are straitened in ourselves; never in Him.

From this supreme gift we can argue down to the humblest necessities, the commonest trials of our daily lot. It adapts itself to the small anxieties of a struggling household, equally with the largest demands of our exacting age. "Thou hast given us Thy Son," says some one, "and wilt Thou not give us bread?" We have a generous Lord. His only complaint is that we do not ask enough. "Ye are My friends," He says: "I have given My life for you. Ask what ye will, and it shall be done unto you." Giving us Himself, He has given us all things. Abraham and Moses, David and Isaiah, "Paul and Apollos and Cephas—yea the world itself, life and death, things present and to come—all are ours; and we are Christ's and Christ is God's" (1 Cor. iii. 22, 23). Such is the chain of blessing that hangs on this single gift.

Great as the gift is, it is not greater than our need. Wanting a Divine Son of man, human life remains a baffled aspiration, a pathway leading to no goal. Lacking Him, the race is incomplete, a body without its head, a flock that has no master. By the coming of Christ in the flesh human life finds its ideal realized; its haunting dream of a Divine helper and leader in the midst of men, of a spiritual and immortal perfection brought within its reach, has attained fulfilment. "God hath raised up a horn of salvation for us in the house of His servant David; as He spake by the mouth of His holy prophets, which have been since the world began." Jacob's vision has come true. There is the golden ladder, with its foot resting on the cold, stony earth, and its top on heaven's starry platform, with its angels ascending and descending through the darkness; and you may climb its steps, high as you will! So humanity receives its crown of life. Heaven and earth are linked, God and man reunited in the person of Jesus Christ.

But Paul will not suffer us to linger at Bethlehem. He hastens on to Calvary. The Atonement, not the Incarnation, is in his view the centre of Christianity. To the cross of Jesus, rather than to His cradle, he attaches our salvation. "Jesus Christ gave Himself"—what for, and in what way? What was the errand that brought Him here, in such a guise, and at such a time? Was it to meet our *need*, to fulfil our human aspirations, to crown the moral edifice, to lead the race onward to the goal of its development? Yes—ultimately, and in the final issue, for "as many as receive Him"; it was to "present every man perfect in Christ." But that was not the primary object of His coming, of such a coming. Happy for us indeed, and for Him, if it could have been so. To come to a world waiting for Him, hearkening for the cry, "Behold thy God, O Israel," would have been a pleasant and a fitting thing. But to find Himself rejected by His own, to be spit upon, to hear the multitude shout, "Away with Him!" was this the welcome that He looked for? Yea surely, nothing else but this. For He gave Himself *for our sins*. He came to a world steeped in wickedness, seething with rebellion against God, hating Him because it hated the Father that sent Him, sure to say as soon as it saw Him, "We will not have this man to reign over us." Not therefore by way of incarnation and revelation alone, as it might have been for an innocent race; but by way of *sacrifice*, as a victim on the altar of expiation, "a lamb led to the slaughter," He gave Himself up for us all. "To deliver us from an evil world," says the Apostle; to mend a faulty and imperfect world, something less and other would have sufficed.

Extreme diseases call for extreme remedies. The case with which our good Physician had to deal was a desperate one. The world was sick at heart; its moral nature rotting to the core. Human life was shattered to its foundation. If it was to be saved, if the race was to escape perdition, the fabric must be reconstructed upon another basis, on the ground of a new righteousness, outside ourselves and yet akin to us, near enough to take hold of us and grow into us, which should draw to itself the broken elements of human life, and as a vital organic force refashion them, "creating" men "anew in Christ Jesus"—a righteousness availing before God, and in its depth and width sufficient to bear a world's weight. Such a new foundation Jesus Christ has laid in His death. "He laid down His life for us," the Shepherd for the sheep, the Friend for His perishing friends, the Physician for sufferers who had no other remedy. It had come to this,—either He must die, or we must die for ever. Such was the sentence of the All-wise Judge; on that judgement the Redeemer acted. "His judgements are a great deep"; and in this sentence there are depths of mystery into which we tremble to look, "secret things that belong unto the Lord our God." But so it was. There was no way but this, no moral possibility of saving the world, and yet saving Him the accursed death.

If there had been, would not the Almighty Father have found it out? would He not have "taken away the cup" from those white, quivering lips? No; He must *die*. He must consent to be "made sin, made a curse" for us. He must humble His stainless innocence, humble His glorious Godhead down to the dust of death. He must die, at the hands of the men He created and loved, with the horror of the world's sin fastened on Him; die under a blackened heaven, under the averting of the Father's face. And He did it. He said, "Father, Thy will be done. Smite the Shepherd; but let the sheep escape." So He "gave Himself for our sins."

Ah, it was no easy march, no holiday pageant, the coming of the Son of God into this world of ours. He "came to *save sinners*." Not to help good men—this were a grateful task; but to redeem bad men—the hardest work in God's universe. It tasked the strength and the devotion of the Son of God. Witness Gethsemane. And it will cost His Church something, more haply than we dream of now, if the work of the Redeemer is to be made effectual, and "the travail of His soul satisfied."

In pity and in sorrow was that gift bestowed; in deep humility and sorrow must it be accepted. It is a very humbling thing to "receive the atonement," to be made righteous on such terms as these. A man who has done well, can with satisfaction accept the help given him to do better. But to know that one has done very ill, to stand in the sight of God and truth condemned, marked with the disgrace that the crucifixion of the Son of God has branded on our human nature, with every stain of sin in ourselves revealed in the light of His sacrifice, is a sore abasement. When one has been compelled to cry out, "Lord, save; or I perish!" he has not much left to plume himself upon. There was Saul himself, a perfect moralist, "blameless in the righteousness of the law." Yet he must confess, "How to perform that which is good I find not. In me, that is in my flesh, dwelleth no good thing. Wretch that I am, who shall deliver me?" Was not this mortifying to the proud young Pharisee, the man of strict conscience and high-souled moral endeavour? It was like death. And whoever has with sincerity made the same attempt to attain in the strength of his will to a true virtue, has tasted of this bitterness.

This however is what many cannot understand. The proud heart says, "No; I will not stoop to that. I have my faults, my defects and errors, not a few. But as for what you call *sin*, as for guilt and inborn depravity, I am not going to tax myself with anything of the kind. Leave me a little self-respect." So with the whole herd of the self-complacent, half-religious Laodiceans. Once a week they confess themselves "miserable sinners," but their sins against God never yet cost them one half hour of misery. And Paul's "gospel is hid to them." If they read this Epistle, they cannot tell what it is all about; why Paul makes so much ado, why these thunderings of judgement, these cries of indignation, these beseechings and protestings and redoubled arguments,—all because a parcel of foolish Galatians wanted to play at being Jews! They are inclined to think with Festus, that this good Paul was a little beside himself. Alas! to such men, content with the world's good opinion and their own, the death of Christ is made of none effect. Its moral grandeur, its infinite pathos, is lost upon them. They pay it a conventional respect, but as for *believing* in it, as for making it their own, and dying with Christ to live in Him—they have no idea what it means. That, they will tell you, is "mysticism," and they are practical men of the world. They have never gone out of themselves, never discovered their moral insufficiency. These are they of whom Jesus said, "The publicans and the harlots go into the kingdom of God before you." It is our human independence, our moral self-conceit, that robs us of the Divine bounty. How should God give His righteousness to men so well furnished with their own? "Blessed" then "are the poor in spirit"; blessed are the broken in heart—poor enough, broken enough, bankrupt enough to stoop to a Saviour "who gave Himself for our sins."

II. Sinful men have made an *evil world*. The world, as Paul knew it, was evil indeed. "The existing evil age," he says, the world as it then was, in contrast with the glory of the perfected Messianic kingdom.

This was a leading distinction of the rabbinical schools; and the writers of the New Testament adopt it, with the necessary modification, that "the coming age," in their view, commences with the *Parousia*, the full advent of the Messiah King.[4] The period that intervenes since His first appearing is transitional, belonging to both eras. It is the conclusion of "this world,"[5] to which it appertains in its outward and material relations;[6] but under the perishing form of the present there lies hidden for the Christian believer the seed of immortality, "the earnest" of his future and complete inheritance.[7] Hence the different and seemingly contradictory ways in which Scripture speaks of the world that now is.

To Paul at this time the world wore its darkest aspect. There is a touching emphasis in the order of this clause. "The present world, *evil as it is:"* the words are a sigh for deliverance. The Epistles to Corinth show us how the world just now was using the Apostle. The wonder is that one man could bear so much. "We are made as the filth of the world," he says, "the offscouring of all things."[8] So the world treated its greatest living benefactor. And as for his Master—"the princes of this world crucified the Lord of glory." Yes, it was a bad old world, that in which Paul and the Galatians lived—false, licentious, cruel. And that "evil world" still exists.

True, the world, as we know it, is vastly better than that of Paul's day. Not in vain have Apostles taught, and martyrs bled, and the Church of Christ witnessed and toiled through so many ages. "Other men have laboured; we enter into their labours." An English home of to-day is the flower of the centuries. To those cradled in its pure affections, endowed with health and honourable work and refined tastes, the world must be, and was meant to be, in many aspects a bright and pleasant world. Surely the most sorrowful have known days in which the sky was all sunshine and the very air alive with joy, when the world looked as when it came forth fresh from its Creator's hand, "and behold, it was very good." There is nothing in the Bible, nothing in the spirit of true religion to damp the pure joy of such days as these. But there are "the days of darkness;" and they are many. The Serpent has crept into our Paradise. Death breathes on it his fatal blast.

And when we look outside the sheltered circles of home-life and Christian brotherhood, what a sea of misery spreads around us. How limited and partial is the influence of religion. What a mass of unbelief and godlessness surges up to the doors of our sanctuaries. What appalling depths of iniquity exist in modern society, under the brilliant surface of our material civilization. And however far the dominance of sin in human society may be broken—as, please God, it shall be broken, still evil is likely to remain in many tempting and perilous forms until the world is burnt to ashes in the fires of the Last Judgement. Is it not an evil world, where every morning newspaper serves up to us its miserable tale of disaster and of crime, where the Almighty's name is "all the day blasphemed," and every night drunkenness holds its horrid revels and the daughters of shame walk the city streets, where great Christian empires tax the poor man's bread and make his life bitter to maintain their huge standing armies and their cruel engines of war, and where, in this happy England and its cities teeming with wealth, there are thousands of patient, honest working women, whose life under the fierce stress of competition is a veritable slavery, a squalid, dreary struggle just to keep hunger from the door? Ay, it is a world so evil that no good and right-thinking man who knows it, would care to live in it for a single day, but for the hope of helping to make it better.

Now it was the purpose of Jesus Christ, that for those who believe in Him this world's evil should be brought absolutely to an end. He promises a full deliverance from all that tempts and afflicts us here. With sin, the root of evil, removed, its bitter fruits at last will disappear. We shall rise to the life immortal. We shall attain our perfect consummation and bliss both in body and soul. Kept from the evil of the world while they remain in it, enabled by His grace to witness and contend against it, Christ's servants shall then be lifted clean out for it of ever. "Father, I will," prayed Jesus, "that they also whom Thou hast given Me, may be with Me where I am." To that final salvation, accomplished in the redemption of our body and the setting up of Christ's heavenly kingdom, the Apostle's words look forward: "that He might deliver us *out of* this present evil world." This was the splendid hope which Paul offered to the dying and despairing world of his day. The Galatians were persuaded of it and embraced it; he entreats them not to let it go.

The self-sacrifice of Christ, and the deliverance it brings, are both, the Apostle concludes, "according to the will of God, even our Father." The wisdom and might of the Eternal are pledged to the work of human redemption. The cross of Jesus Christ is the manifesto of Infinite Love. Let him therefore who rejects it, know against Whom he is contending. Let him who perverts and falsifies it, know with what he is trifling. He who receives and obeys it, may rest assured that all things are working for his good. For all things are in the hands of our God and Father; "to Whom," let us say with Paul, "be glory for ever. Amen."

CHAPTER III
THE ANATHEMA

"I marvel that ye are so quickly removing from him that called you in the grace of Christ unto a different gospel; which is not another *gospel*: only there are some that trouble you, and would pervert the gospel of Christ. But though we, or an angel from heaven, should preach unto you any gospel other than that which we preached unto you, let him be anathema. As we have said before, so say I now again, If any man preacheth unto you any gospel other than that which ye received, let him be anathema. For am I now persuading men, or God? or am I seeking to please men? if I were still pleasing men, I should not be a servant of Christ." — Gal. i. 6-10.

After the Salutation in Paul's Epistles comes the Thanksgiving. Εὐχαριστῶ or Εὐλογητός — these are the words we expect first to meet. Even in writing to Corinth, where there was so much to censure and deplore, he begins, "I give thanks to my God always for you." This letter deviates from the Apostle's devout and happy usage. Not "I give thanks," but "I marvel;" not blessing, but *anathema* is coming from his lips: a surprise that jars all the more upon one's ears, because it follows on the sublime doxology of the preceding verse. "I marvel to see you so quickly falling away to another gospel.... But if any one preach unto you any gospel other than that ye received — ay, though it were ourselves, or an angel from heaven — I have said once, and I say again, Let him be Anathema."

These words were well calculated to startle the Galatians out of their levity. They are like a lightning-flash which shows one to be standing on the edge of a precipice. We see at once the infinite seriousness of the Judaic controversy, the profound gulf that lies between Paul and his opposers. He is for open war. He is in haste to fling his gage of defiance against these enemies of the cross. With all his tact and management, his readiness to consult the susceptibilities and accommodate the scruples of sincere consciences, the Apostle can find no room for conciliation here. He knows the sort of men he has to deal with. He perceives that the whole truth of the Gospel is at stake. Not circumstantials, but essentials; not his personal authority, but the honour of Christ, the doctrine of the cross, is involved in this defection. He must speak plainly; he must act strongly, and at once; or the cause of the Gospel is lost. "If I continued any longer to please men," he says, "I should not be a servant of Christ." To stand on terms with such opponents, to palter with this "other gospel," would be treason against Him. There is but one tribunal at which this quarrel can be decided. To Him "who had called" the Galatian believers "in Christ's grace," who by the same grace had called the Apostle to His service and given him the message he had preached to them—to *God* he appeals. In His name, and by the authority conferred upon him and for which he must give account, he pronounces these troublers "anathema." They are enemies of Christ, by their treachery excluded from His kingdom.

However unwelcome, however severe the course the Apostle takes, he has no alternative. "For now," he cries, "is it *men* that I persuade, or *God*?" He must do his duty, let who will condemn. Paul was ready to go all lengths in pleasing men in consistence with loyalty to Christ, where he could do it "for their good, unto edification." But if their approval clashed with God's, then it became "a very small thing:"[9] he did not heed it one jot. Such is the temper of mind which the Epistles to Corinth disclose in Paul at this juncture. In the same spirit he indites these trenchant and displeasing words.

With a heavy heart Paul has taken up his pen. If we judge rightly of the date of this letter, he had just passed through the darkest hour of his experience, when not his life alone, but the fate of his Gentile mission hung in the balance. His expulsion from Ephesus, coming at the same time as the Corinthian revolt, and followed by a prostrating attack of sickness, had shaken his soul to its depths. Never had his heart been so torn with anxiety, never had he felt himself so beaten down and discomfited, as on that melancholy journey from Ephesus to Macedonia.[10] "Out of anguish of heart and with many tears" and after-relentings (2 Cor. ii. 4; vii. 8) he wrote his First letter to Corinth. And this Epistle is even more severe. There runs through it a peculiar mental tension, an exaltation of feeling such as prolonged and deep suffering leaves behind in a nature like Paul's. "The marks of Jesus" (ch. vi. 17) are visible, impressed on his spirit no less than on his body. The Apostle's heart is full to overflowing. Its warm glow is felt under the calmer course of narrative and argument: while at the beginning and end of the Epistle it breaks forth in language of burning indignation and melting pathos. Before advancing a single step, before entering on any sort of explanation or discussion, his grief at the fickleness of his Galatian children and his anger against their seducers must find expression.

These sentences demand, before we proceed further, a few words of exegetical definition. For the reference of "so quickly" it is needless to go beyond the verb it qualifies. The Apostle cannot surely mean, "*so soon falling away (after your conversion).*" For the Galatian Churches had been founded five, if not seven, years before this time; and the backsliding of recent converts is less, and not more, surprising than of established believers. What astonishes Paul is the *suddenness* of this movement, the facility with which the Galatians yielded to the Judaizing "persuasion," the rapid spread of this new leaven. As to the double "other" (ἕτερον, *different*, R.V.—ἄλλο) of vv. 6 and 7, and the connection of the idiomatic "only" (εἰ μή, *except*),—we regard the second *other* as an abrupt correction of the first; while the *only* clause, extending to the end of ver. 7, mediates between the two, qualifying the statement "There is no other gospel," by showing in what sense the writer at first had spoken of "another." "Ye are falling away," says he, "to another sort of gospel—which is not another, except that there are certain that trouble you and would fain pervert the gospel of Christ." The word *gospel* is therefore in the first instance applied ironically. Paul yields the sacred title up to his opponents, only to snatch it out of their false hands. "*Another* gospel! there is only one; although there are men that falsify it, and seek to foist something else upon you in its name." Seven times in this context (vv. 6-11) does the Apostle reiterate, in noun or verb, this precious word, as though he could not let it go. A strange sort of "good news" for the Galatians, that they must be circumcised forsooth, and observe the Jewish Kalender! (ch. v. 2, 3; vi. 12; iv. 9, 10.)

I. In Paul's view, there is but one gospel for mankind. *The gospel of Jesus Christ bears a fixed, inviolable character.*

On this position the whole teaching of Paul rests,—and with it, may we not add, Christianity itself? However variously we may formulate the essentials of a Christian man's faith, we are generally agreed that there are such essentials, and that they are found in Paul's gospel to the Gentiles. With him the good tidings about Christ constituted a very definite and, as we should say, *dogmatic* body of truth. In whatever degree his gospel has been confused and overlaid by later teachings, to his own mind its terms were perfectly clear, and its authority incontestable. With all its breadth, there is nothing nebulous, nothing limp or hesitating about the theology of Paul. In its main doctrines it is fixed and hard as adamant; and at the challenge of this Judaistic perversion it rings out an instant and peremptory denial. It was the ark of God on which the Jewish troublers laid their unholy hands. "Christ's grace" is lodged in it. God's call to mankind was conveyed by these "good tidings." The Churches which the Apostle had planted were "God's husbandry, God's building;" and woe to the man who tampered with the work, or sought to lay another foundation than that which had been laid (1 Cor. iii. 5-11). To distort or mutilate "the word of the truth of the gospel," to make it mean now one thing and now another, to disturb the faith of half-instructed Christians by captious reasonings and self-interested perversions, was a capital offence, a sin against God and a crime against humanity. Paul possesses in his gospel truth of unspeakable value to mankind, the supreme revelation of God's mercy to the world. And he is prepared to launch his anathema against every wilful impugner, no matter what his pretensions, or the quarter from which he comes.

"Well," it may be said, "this is sheer religious intolerance. Paul is doing what every dogmatist, every ecclesiastical bigot has done in his turn. His beliefs are, to be sure, *the* truth; and accordingly he unchurches and anathematizes those who cannot agree with him. With all his nobility of mind, there is in Paul a leaven of Jewish rancour. He falls short of the sweet reasonableness of Jesus." So some will say, and in saying claim to represent the mild and tolerant spirit of our age. But is there not in every age an intolerance that is just and necessary? There is a logical intolerance of sophistry and trifling. There is a moral intolerance of impurity and deceit. And there is a religious intolerance, which includes both these and adds to them a holy jealousy for the honour of God and the spiritual welfare of mankind. It is mournful indeed to think how many crimes have been perpetrated under the cloak of pious zeal. *Tantum Religio potuit suadere malorum.* The corruption of Christianity by human pride and cruelty has furnished copious illustrations of the terrible line of Lucretius. But the perversion of this noblest instinct of the soul does not take away either its reasonableness or its use. The quality of a passion is one thing; the mode of its expression is another. The hottest fires of bigotry are cold when compared with the scorching intolerance of Christ's denunciations of the Pharisees. The anathemas of Jesus and of Paul are very different from those of arrogant pontiffs, or of narrow sectaries, inflamed with the idolatry of their own opinions. After all, the zeal of the rudest fanatic in religion has more in it of manly worth and moral capability than the languors of a blasé scepticism, that sits watching with amused contempt the strife of creeds and the search of human hearts after the Living God. There is an idle, listless, cowardly tolerance, as there is an intolerance that is noble and just.

The *one gospel* has had many interpreters. Their voices, it must be confessed, sound strangely discordant. While the teachings of Christianity excite so intensely a multitude of different minds, of every variety of temper and capacity, contradiction will inevitably arise. Nothing is easier than to scoff at "the Babel of religious opinions." Christian truth is necessarily refracted and discoloured in passing through disordered natures and defective minds. And, alas, that Church which claims to hold the truth without possibility of error or variation, has perverted Christ's gospel most of all.

But notwithstanding all differences, there exists a large and an increasing measure of agreement amongst the great body of earnest Christians. Slowly, yet surely, one debate after another comes to its settlement. The noise and publicity with which discussion on matters of faith is carried on in an age of religious freedom, and when liberty of thought has outrun mental discipline, should not lead us to exaggerate the extent of our disagreements. In the midst of human controversy and error, the Spirit of truth is carrying on His work. He is the supreme witness of Jesus Christ. And He abides with us for ever. The newly awakened historical conscience of our times is visibly making for unity. The Church is going back to the New Testament. And the more thoroughly she does this, the more directly and truthfully she addresses herself to the original record and comes face to face with Christ and His Apostles there, so much the more shall we realize the oneness and certainty of "the faith once delivered to the saints." Beneath the many superstructures, faulty and changing in their form, we reach the one "foundation of the apostles and prophets, Jesus Christ Himself being the chief corner-stone." There we touch solid rock. "The unity of the faith" lies in "the knowledge of the Son of God." Of Him we shall learn most from those who knew Him best. Let us transport ourselves into the fellowship of His first disciples; and listen to His gospel as it came fresh from the lips of Peter and John and Paul, and the Divine Master Himself. Let us bid the voices of the centuries be silent, that we may *hear Him.*

For the Galatian readers, as for Paul, there could be but *one gospel.* By his voice the call of God had reached their hearts, (ver. 6; ch. v. 8). The witness of the Spirit of God and of Christ in the supernatural gifts they had received, and in the manifold fruit of a regenerate life (ch. iii. 2-5; v. 22, 23), was evidence to them that the Apostle's message was "the true gospel of the grace of God." This they had gratefully acknowledged at the time of his first visit (ch. iv. 15). The proclamation of the crucified and risen Christ had brought to them unspeakable blessing. Through it they received the knowledge of God; they were made consciously sons of God, heirs of life eternal (ch. iii. 26; iv. 6-9; vi. 8). To entertain any other gospel, after this experience and all these professions, was an act of apostasy. "Ye are deserting (like runaway soldiers), *turning renegades* from God:" such is the language in which Paul taxes his readers. In listening to the persuasion of the Judaists, they were "disobeying the truth" (ch. v. 7, 8). They were disloyal to conscience; they were trifling with the most sacred convictions of their lives, and with the testimony of the Spirit of God. They were forgetting the cross of Christ, and making His death of none effect. Surely they must have been "bewitched" to act thus; some deadly spell was upon them, which had laid memory and conscience both to sleep (ch. ii. 21-iii. 3).

The nature and the contents of the two "gospels" current in Galatia will be made clear in the further course of the Epistle. They were the gospels of Grace and of Law respectively; of Salvation by Faith, and by Works; of life in the Spirit, and in the Flesh; of the Cross and the Resurrection on the one hand, and of Circumcision and the Kalendar and "Clean meats" on the other; the gospels of inwardness, and of externalism—of Christ, and of self. The conflict between these two was the great struggle of Paul's life. His success was, historically speaking, the salvation of Christianity.

But this contention did not end with his victory. The Judaistic perversion appealed to tendencies too persistent in our nature to be crushed at one blow. The gospel of externalism is dear to the human heart. It may take the form of culture and moralities; or of "services" and sacraments and churchly order; or of orthodoxy and philanthropy. These and such things make themselves our idols; and trust in them takes the place of Faith in the living Christ. It is not enough that the eyes of our heart should once have seen the Lord, that we should in other days have experienced "the renewing of the Holy Ghost." It is possible to forget, possible to "remove from Him that called us in the grace of Christ." With little change in the form of our religious life, its inward reality of joy in God, of conscious sonship, of fellowship in the Spirit, may be utterly departed. The gospel of formalism will spring up and flourish on the most evangelical soil, and in the most strictly Pauline Churches. Let it be banned and barred out never so completely, it knows how to find entrance, under the simplest modes of worship and the soundest doctrine. The serried defence of Articles and Confessions constructed against it will not prevent its entrance, and may even prove its cover and intrenchment. Nothing avails, as the Apostle says, but a constant "new creation." The life of God in human souls is sustained by the energy of His Spirit, perpetually renewed, ever proceeding from the Father and the Son. "The life that I live in the flesh, I live by the Faith of the Son of God, who loved me and gave Himself for me." This is the true orthodoxy. The vitality of his personal faith in Christ kept Paul safe from error, faithful in will and intellect to the *one gospel*.

II. We have still to consider the import of *the judgement pronounced by Paul upon those who pervert the gospel of Christ.* "Let him be anathema. Even should it be ourselves, or an angel from heaven, *let him be anathema.*"

These are tremendous words. Commentators have been shocked at the Apostle's damning his opponents after this fashion, and have sought to lighten the weight of this awful sentence. It has been sometimes toned down into an act of excommunication or ecclesiastical censure. But this explanation will not hold. Paul could not think of subjecting "an angel" to a penalty like that. He pronounced excommunication against disorderly members of the Thessalonian Church; and in 1 Cor. v. 1-8 he gives directions for the carrying out of a similar decree, attended with severe bodily affliction supernaturally adjudged, against a sinner whose presence grossly stained the purity of the Church. But this sentence goes beyond either of those. It contemplates the exclusion of the offenders from the Covenant of grace, their loss of final salvation.

Thrice besides has Paul used this ominous word. The cry "Jesus is anathema," in 1 Cor. xii. 3, reveals with a lurid effect the frenzied malignity towards Christ of which the spirit of evil is sometimes capable. In a very different connection the word appears in Rom. ix. 3; where Paul "could wish himself anathema from Christ," if that were possible, for his brethren's sake; he could find it in his heart to be cut off for ever from that love of God in Christ of which he has just spoken in terms of unbounded joy and confidence (Rom. viii. 31-39), and banished from the heavenly kingdom, if through his exclusion his Jewish kindred might be saved. Self-sacrifice can go no further. No heavier loss than this could be conceived for any human being. Nearest to our passage is the imprecation at the end of 1 Corinthians: "If any man love not the Lord, let him be anathema,"—a judgement proclaimed against cold and false hearts, knowing His love, bearing His name, but with no true love to Him.

This Greek word in its Biblical use has grown out of the *chérem* of the Old Testament, the *ban* declared against that which was cut off from the Divine mercies and exposed to the full sweep of judgement. Thus in Deut. xiii. 12-18, the city whose people should "go and serve other gods," is declared *chérem (anathema)*, an "accursed," or "devoted thing" (R.V.), on which ensues its destruction by sword and fire, leaving it to remain "a ruin-heap for ever." Similarly in Joshua vi., vii., the spoil of Jericho is *anathema*, Achan's theft is therefore *anathema*, and Israel is made by it *anathema* until "the accursed thing is destroyed" from among the people. Such were the recollections associated with this word in the Mosaic law, which it would inevitably carry with it to the minds of those against whom it was now directed. And there is nothing in later Jewish usage to mitigate its force.

Now the Apostle is not writing like a man in a passion, who flings out his words as missiles, eager only to wound and confound his opponents. He repeats the sentence. He quotes it as one that he had already affirmed in the hearing of his readers. The passage bears the marks of well-weighed thought and judicial solemnity. In pronouncing this judgement on "the troublers," Paul acts under the sense of Apostolic responsibility. We must place the sentence in the same line as that of Peter against Ananias and Sapphira, and of Paul himself against Elymas the Cypriot sorcerer, and against the incestuous Corinthian. In each case there is a supernatural insight and authorization, "the authority which the Lord gave" and which is wielded by His inspired Apostle. The exercise of this judicial function was one of "the signs of the Apostle." This was the proof of "Christ speaking in him" which Paul was so loth to give at Corinth,[11] but which at this crisis of his ministry he was compelled to display. And if he "reckons to be bold against" his adversaries in Galatia, he knows well the ground on which he stands.

His anathema struck at men who were the worst enemies of Christ. "We can do nothing against the truth," he says; "but for the truth" he was ready to do and dare everything,—to "come with a rod," as he tells the proud Corinthians. There was no authority, however lofty, that he was not warranted to use on Christ's behalf, no measure, however severe, from which he would shrink, if it were required in defence of the truth of the Gospel. "He possesses weapons, not fleshly, but mighty through God"; and he is prepared to bring them all into play rather than see the gospel perverted or overthrown. Paul will hurl his anathema at the prince of the archangels, should He come "preaching another gospel," tempting his children from their allegiance to Christ. This bolt was not shot a moment too soon. Launched against the legalist conspiracy, and followed up by the arguments of this and the Roman Epistle, it saved the Church from being overpowered by reactionary Judaism. The Apostle's judgement has marked the gospel of the cross for all time as God's inviolable truth, guarded by lightnings.

The sentences of judgement pronounced by the Apostles present a striking contrast to those that have fulminated from the Chair of their self-styled successors. In the Canons of the Council of Trent, for example, we have counted one hundred and thirty-five anathemas. A large proportion of these are concerned with the rights of the priesthood; others with complicated and secondary points of doctrine; some are directed virtually against the teaching of Paul himself. Here is one specimen: "If any one shall say that justifying faith is nothing else but a trust in the Divine mercy, remitting sins for Christ's sake, or that it is this trust alone by which we are justified: let him be anathema."[12] Again, "If any one shall say that the Canon of the Mass contains errors, and therefore should be abrogated: let him be anathema."[13] In the closing session, the final act of the presiding Cardinal was to pronounce, "Anathema to all heretics;" to which the assembled prelates shouted in response, "Anathema, anathema." With this imprecation on their lips the Fathers of the Church concluded their pious labours. It was the Reformation, it was "the liberty of the sons of God" that Rome anathematized. Paul's censure holds good against all the Conciliar Canons and Papal Bulls that contravene it. But twice has he pronounced this awful word; once against any that "love not the Lord," a second time upon those who wilfully pervert His gospel. The Papal anathemas sound like the maledictions of an angry priesthood, jealous for its prerogatives; here we have the holy severity of an inspired Apostle, concerned only for the truth, and for his Master's honour. There speaks the conscious "lord over God's heritage," wearing the triple crown, wielding the powers of Interdict and Inquisition, whose word sets armies in motion and makes kings tremble on their seats. Here a feeble, solitary man, "his bodily presence weak, his speech contemptible," hunted from place to place, scourged and stoned, shut up for years in prison, who could not, except for love's sake, command the meanest service. How conspicuous in the one case, how wanting in the other, is the might of the Spirit and the dignity of the inspired word, the transcendence of moral authority.

It is *the moral conduct* of those he judges that determines in each case the sentence passed by the Apostle. For a man knowing Jesus Christ, as we presume the members of the Corinthian Church did know Him, not to love Him, argues a bad heart. Must not we count *ourselves* accursed, if with our knowledge of Christ we had no love for Him? Such a man is already virtually *anathema*. He is severed as a branch from its vine, ready to be gathered for the burning (John xv. 6). And these Galatian disturbers were something worse than mere mistaken enthusiasts for their native Jewish rites. Their policy was dishonourable (ch. iv. 17). They made the gospel of Christ subservient to factious designs. They sought to win credit with their fellow-countrymen and to escape the reproach of the cross by imposing circumcision on the Gentiles (ch. ii. 4; vi. 12, 13). They prostituted religion to selfish and party purposes. They sacrificed truth to popularity, the glory of Christ and the cross to their own. They were of those whom the Apostle describes as "walking in craftiness and handling the word of God deceitfully," who "traffic" in the gospel, peddling with it as with petty wares, cheapening and adulterating it like dishonest hucksters to make their own market by it (2 Cor. ii. 17; iv. 2). Did not Paul do well to smite them with the rod of his mouth? Justly has he marked with the brand of this fiery anathema the false minister, "who serves not the Lord Christ, but his own belly."

But does this declaration preclude in such a case the possibility of repentance? We trow not. It declares the doom which is due to any, be he man or angel, who should do what these "troublers" are doing. It is a general sentence, and has for the individuals concerned the effect of a warning, like the announcement made concerning the Traitor at the Last Supper. However unlikely repentance might be in either instance, there is nothing to forbid it. So when Peter said to Simon Magus, "Thy money perish with thee!" he nevertheless continued, "Repent, therefore, of this thy wickedness, and pray the Lord, if perhaps the thought of thy heart shall be forgiven thee" (Acts viii. 20-22). To his worst opponents, on any sign of contrition, Paul, we may be sure, would have gladly said the same.

THE PERSONAL HISTORY

CHAPTER IV
PAUL'S GOSPEL REVEALED BY CHRIST

"For I make known to you, brethren, as touching the gospel
which was preached by me, that it is not after man. For
neither did I receive it from man, nor was I taught it, but *it
came to me* through revelation of Jesus Christ. For ye have
heard of my manner of life in time past in the Jews' religion,
how that beyond measure I persecuted the church of God,
and made havock of it: and I advanced in the Jews' religion
beyond many of mine own age among my countrymen,
being more exceedingly zealous for the traditions of my
fathers." —Gal. i. 11-14.

Here the Epistle begins in its main purport. What has gone before is
so much exordium. The sharp, stern sentences of vv. 6-10 are like the roll
of artillery that ushers in the battle. The mists rise from the field. We see
the combatants arrayed on either side. In due order and with cool self-
command the Apostle proceeds to marshal and deploy his forces. His
truthful narrative corrects the misrepresentations of his opponents, and
repels their attack upon himself. His powerful dialectic wrests from their
hands and turns against them their weapons of Scriptural proof. He wins
the citadel of their position, by establishing the claim of the men of faith to
be the sons of Abraham. On the ruins of confuted legalism he builds up an
impregnable fortress for Christian liberty, an immortal vindication of the
gospel of the grace of God.

The cause of Gentile freedom at this crisis was bound up with the
person of the Apostle Paul. His Gospel and his Apostleship must stand or
fall together. The former was assailed through the latter. He was himself just
now "the pillar and stay of the truth." If his character had been successfully
attacked and his influence destroyed, nothing, humanly speaking, could
have saved Gentile Christendom at this decisive moment from falling under

the assaults of Judaism. When he begins his crucial appeal with the words, "Behold, *I Paul* say unto you" (ch. v. 2), we feel that the issue depends upon the weight which his readers may attach to his personal affirmation. He pits his own truthfulness, his knowledge of Christ, his spiritual discernment and authority, and the respect due to himself from the Galatians, against the pretensions of the new teachers. The comparison is not indeed so open and express as that made in 2 Corinthians; none the less it tacitly runs through this Epistle. Paul is compelled to put himself in the forefront of his argument. In the eyes of his children in the faith, he is bound to vindicate his Apostolic character, defamed by Jewish malice and untruth.

The first two chapters of this Epistle are therefore Paul's *Apologia pro vita sua*. With certain chapters in 2 Corinthians, and scattered passages in other letters, they form the Apostle's autobiography, one of the most perfect self-portraitures that literature contains. They reveal to us the man more effectively than any ostensible description could have done. They furnish an indispensable supplement to the external and cursory delineations given in the Acts of the Apostles. While Luke skilfully presents the outward framework of Paul's life and the events of his public career, it is to the Epistles that we turn—to none more frequently than this—for the necessary subjective data, for all that belongs to his inner character, his motives and principles. This Epistle brings into bold relief the Apostle's moral physiognomy. Above all, it throws a clear and penetrating light on the event which determined his career—the greatest event in the history of Christianity after the Day of Pentecost—Paul's conversion to faith in the Lord Jesus.

This was at once the turning-point in the Apostle's life, and the birth-hour of his gospel. If the Galatians were to understand his teaching, they must understand this occurrence; they must know why he became a Christian, how he had received the message which he brought to them. They would, he felt sure, enter more sympathetically into his doctrine, if they were better acquainted with the way in which he had arrived at it. They would see how well-justified was the authority, how needful the severity with which he writes. Accordingly he begins with a brief relation of the circumstances of his call to the service of Christ, and his career from the days of his Judaistic zeal, when he made havoc of the faith, till the well-known occasion on which he became its champion against Peter himself, the chief of the Twelve (ch. i. 11-ii. 21.) His object in this recital appears to be threefold: to refute the misrepresentations of the Circumcisionists; to vindicate his independent authority as an Apostle of Christ; and further, to unfold the nature and terms of his gospel, so as to pave the way for the theological argument which is to follow, and which forms the body of the Epistle.

I. *Paul's gospel was supernaturally conveyed to him, by a personal intervention of Jesus Christ.* This assertion is the Apostle's starting-point. "My gospel is not after man. I received it as Jesus Christ revealed it to me."

That the initial revelation was made to him by Christ in person, was a fact of incalculable importance for Paul. This had made him an Apostle, in the august sense in which he claims the title (ver. 1). This accounts for the vehemence with which he defends his doctrine, and for the awful sentence which he has passed upon its impugners. The Divine authorship of the gospel he preached made it impossible for him to temporize with its perverters, or to be influenced by human favour or disfavour in its administration. Had his teaching been "according to man," he might have consented to a compromise; he might reasonably have tried to humour and accommodate Jewish prejudices. But the case is far otherwise. "I am not at liberty to please men," he says, "for my gospel comes directly from Jesus Christ" (vv. 10, 11). So he "gives" his readers "to know," as if by way of formal notification.[14]

The gospel of Paul was inviolable, then, because of its superhuman character. And this character was impressed upon it by its superhuman origin: "not according to man, for neither *from man* did I receive it, nor was I taught it, but by a revelation of Jesus Christ." The Apostle's knowledge of Christianity did not come through the ordinary channel of tradition and indoctrination; Jesus Christ had, by a miraculous interposition, taught him the truth about Himself. He says, "Neither did *I*," with an emphasis that points tacitly to the elder Apostles, whom he mentions a few sentences later (ver. 17). To this comparison his adversaries forced him, making use of it as they freely did to his disparagement.[15] But it comes in by implication rather than direct assertion. Only by putting violence upon himself, and with strong expressions of his unworthiness, can Paul be brought to set his official claims in competition with those of the Twelve. Notwithstanding, it is perfectly clear that he puts his ministry on a level with theirs. He is no Apostle at second-hand, no disciple of Peter's or dependant of the "pillars" at Jerusalem. "Neither did I," he declares, "any more than they, take my instructions from other lips than those of Jesus our Lord."

But what of this "revelation of Jesus Christ," on which Paul lays so much stress? Does he mean a revelation made *by* Christ, or *about* Christ? Taken by itself, the expression, in Greek as in English, bears either interpretation. In favour of the second construction—viz. that Paul speaks of a revelation by which Christ was made known to him—the language of ver. 16 is adduced: "It pleased God to reveal His Son in me." Paul's general usage points in the same direction. With him Christ is the *object* of manifestation, preaching, and the like. 2 Cor. xii. 1 is probably an instance to the contrary: "I will come to visions and revelations of the Lord."[16] But it should be observed that wherever this genitive is objective (a revelation revealing Christ), *God* appears in the context, just as in ver. 16 below, to Whom the authorship of the revelation is ascribed. In this instance, *the gospel* is the object revealed; and *Jesus Christ*, in contrast with man, is claimed for its Author. So at the outset (ver. 1) Christ, in His Divine character, was the *Agent* by whom Paul, as veritably as the Twelve, had received his Apostleship. We therefore assent to the ordinary view, reading this passage in the light of the vision of Jesus thrice related in the Acts.[17] We understand Paul to say that no *mere man* imparted to him the gospel he preached, but *Jesus Christ revealed it.*

On the Damascus road the Apostle Paul found his mission. The vision of the glorified Jesus made him a Christian, and an Apostle. The act was a *revelation*—that is, in New Testament phrase, a supernatural, an immediately Divine communication of truth. And it was a revelation not conveyed in the first instance, as were the ordinary prophetic inspirations, through the Spirit; "Jesus Christ," in His Divine-human person, made Himself known to His persecutor. Paul had "seen that Just One and heard a voice from His mouth."

The appearance of Jesus to Saul of Tarsus was in itself a gospel, an earnest of the good tidings he was to convey to the world. "Why persecutest thou Me?" that Divine voice said, in tones of reproach, yet of infinite pity. The sight of Jesus the Lord, meeting Saul's eyes, revealed His grace and truth to the persecutor's heart. He was brought in a moment to the obedience of faith; he said, "Lord, what wilt Thou have me to do?" He "confessed with his mouth the Lord Jesus"; he "believed in his heart that God had raised Him from the dead." It was true, after all, that "God had made" the crucified Nazarene "both Lord and Christ;" for this was He!

The cross, which had been Saul's stumbling-block, deeply affronting his Jewish pride, from this moment was transformed. The glory of the exalted Redeemer cast back its light upon the tree of shame. The curse of the Law visibly resting upon Him, the rejection of men, marked Him out as God's chosen sacrifice for sin. This explanation at once presented itself to an instructed and keenly theological mind like Saul's, so soon as it was evident that Jesus was not accursed, as he had supposed, but approved by God. So Paul's gospel was given him at a stroke. Jesus Christ dying for our sins, Jesus Christ living to save and to rule—behold "the good news"! The Apostle had it on no less authority than that of the risen Saviour. From Him he received it to publish wide as the world.

Thus Saul of Tarsus was born again. And with the Christian man, the Christian thinker, the theologian, was born in him. The Pauline doctrine has its root in Paul's conversion. It was a single, organic growth, the seed of which was this "revelation of Jesus Christ." Its creative impulse was given in the experience of the memorable hour, when "God who said, Light shall shine out of darkness, in the face of Jesus Christ shined" into Saul's heart. As the light of this revelation penetrated his spirit, he recognised, step by step, the fact of the resurrection, the import of the crucifixion, the Divinity of Jesus, His human mediatorship, the virtue of faith, the office of the Holy Spirit, the futility of Jewish ritual and works of law, and all the essential principles of his theology. Given the genius of Saul and his religious training, and the Pauline system of doctrine was, one might almost say, *a necessary deduction* from the fact of the appearance to him of the glorified Jesus. If that form of celestial splendour was Jesus, then He was risen indeed; then He was the Christ; He was, as He affirmed, the Son of God. If He was Lord and Christ, and yet died by the Father's will on the cross of shame, then His death could only be a propitiation, accepted by God, for the sins of men, whose efficacy had no limit, and whose merit left no room for legal works of righteousness. If this Jesus was the Christ, then the assumptions of Saul's Judaism, which had led him into blasphemous hatred and outrage towards Him, were radically false; he will purge himself from the "old leaven," that his life may become "a new lump." From that moment a world of life and thought began for the future Apostle, the opposite in all respects of that in which hitherto he had moved. "The old things," he cries, "passed away; lo, they have become new" (2 Cor. v. 17). Paul's conversion was as complete as it was sudden.

This intimate relation of doctrine and experience gives to Paul's teaching a peculiar warmth and freshness, a vividness of human reality which it everywhere retains, despite its lofty intellectualism and the scholastic form in which it is largely cast. It is theology alive, trembling with emotion, speaking words like flames, forming dogmas hard as rock, that when you touch them are yet glowing with the heat of those central depths of the human spirit from which they were cast up. The collision of the two great Apostles at Antioch shows how the strength of Paul's teaching lay in his inward realization of the truth. There was *life* behind his doctrine. He was, and for the time the Jewish Apostle was not, acting and speaking out of the reality of spiritual conviction, of truth personally verified. Of the Apostle Paul above all divines the saying is true, *Pectus facit theologum*. And this personal knowledge of Christ, "the master light of all his seeing," began when on the way to Damascus his eyes beheld Jesus our Lord. His farewell charge to the Church through Timothy (2 Tim. i. 9-12), while referring to the general manifestation of Christ to the world, does so in language coloured by the recollection of the peculiar revelation made at the beginning to himself:

"God," he says, "called us with a holy calling, according to His purpose and grace, which hath now been manifested by the appearing[18] of our Saviour Christ Jesus, who abolished death and brought life and immortality to light[19] through the gospel, whereunto I was appointed a preacher and apostle. For which cause I also suffer these things. But I am not ashamed: for I *know* Him in whom I have believed." This manifestation of the celestial Christ shed its brightness along all his path.

II. His assertion of the Divine origin of his doctrine Paul sustains by referring to *the previous course of his life.* There was certainly nothing in that to account for his preaching Christ crucified. "For you have heard," he continues, "of my manner of life aforetime, when I followed Judaism."

Here ends the chain of *fors* reaching from ver. 10 to 13—a succession of explanations linking Paul's denunciation of the Christian Judaizers to the fact that he had himself been a violent anti-Christian Judaist. The seeming contradiction is in reality a consistent sequence. Only one who had imbibed the spirit of legalism as Saul of Tarsus had done, could justly appreciate the hostility of its principles to the new faith, and the sinister motives actuating the men who pretended to reconcile them. Paul knew Judaism by heart. He understood the sort of men who opposed him in the Gentile Churches. And if his anathema appear needlessly severe, we must remember that no one was so well able to judge of the necessities of the case as the man who pronounced it.

"You have heard"—from whom? In the first instance, probably, from Paul himself. But on this matter, we may be pretty sure, his opponents would have something to say. They did not scruple to assert that he "still preached circumcision"[20] and played the Jew even now when it suited him, charging him with insincerity. Or they might say, "Paul is a renegade. Once the most ardent of zealots for Judaism, he has passed to the opposite extreme. He is a man you cannot trust. Apostates are proverbially bitter against their old faith." In these and in other ways Paul's Pharisaic career was doubtless thrown in his teeth.

The Apostle sorrowfully confesses "that above measure he persecuted the Church of God and laid it waste." His friend Luke makes the same admission in similar language.[21] There is no attempt to conceal or palliate this painful fact, that the famous Apostle of the Gentiles had been a persecutor, the deadliest enemy of the Church in its infant days. He was the very type of a determined, pitiless oppressor, the forerunner of the Jewish fanatics who afterwards sought his life, and of the cruel bigots of the Inquisition and the Star-chamber in later times. His restless energy, his indifference to the feelings of humanity in this work of destruction, were due to religious zeal. "I thought," he says, "I ought to do many things contrary to the name of Jesus of Nazareth." In him, as in so many others, the saying of Christ was fulfilled: "The time cometh, when whoso killeth you will think that he is offering a sacrifice to God." These Nazarenes were heretics, traitors to Israel, enemies of God. Their leader had been crucified, branded with the extremest mark of Divine displeasure. His followers must perish. Their success meant the ruin of Mosaism. God willed their destruction. Such were Saul's thoughts, until he heard the protesting voice of Jesus as he approached Damascus to ravage His little flock. No wonder that he suffered remorse to the end of his days.

Saul's persecution of the Church was the natural result of his earlier training, of the course to which in his youth he committed himself. The Galatians had heard also "how proficient he was in Judaism, beyond many of his kindred and age; that he was surpassed by none in zeal for their ancestral traditions." His birth (Phil. iii. 4, 5), education (Acts xxii. 3), temperament, circumstances, all combined to make him a zealot of the first water, the pink and pattern of Jewish orthodoxy, the rising hope of the Pharisaic party, and an instrument admirably fitted to crush the hated and dangerous sect of the Nazarenes. These facts go to prove, not that Paul is a traitor to his own people, still less that he is a Pharisee at heart, preaching Gentile liberty from interested motives; but that it must have been some extraordinary occurrence, quite out of the common run of human influences and probabilities, that set him on his present course. What could have turned this furious Jewish persecutor all at once into the champion of the cross? What indeed but the revelation of Christ which he received at the Damascus gate? His previous career up to that hour had been such as to make it impossible that he should have received his gospel through human means. The chasm between his Christian and pre-Christian life had only been bridged by a supernatural interposition of the mercy of Christ.

Our modern critics, however, think that they know Paul better than he knew himself. They hold that the problem raised by this passage is capable of a natural solution. Psychological analysis, we are told, sets the matter in a different light. Saul of Tarsus had a tender conscience. Underneath his fevered and ambitious zeal, there lay in the young persecutor's heart a profound misgiving, a mortifying sense of his failure, and the failure of his people, to attain the righteousness of the Law. The seventh chapter of his Epistle to the Romans is a leaf taken out of the inner history of this period of the Apostle's life. Through what a stern discipline the Tarsian youth had passed in these legal years! How his haughty spirit chafed and tortured itself under the growing consciousness of its moral impotence! The Law had been truly his παιδαγωγός (ch. iii. 24), a severe tutor, preparing him unconsciously "for Christ." In this state of mind such scenes as the martyrdom of Stephen could not but powerfully affect Saul, in spite of himself. The bearing of the persecuted Nazarenes, the words of peace and forgiveness that they uttered under their sufferings, stirred questionings in his breast not always to be silenced. Self-distrust and remorse were secretly undermining the rigour of his Judaic faith. They acted like a "goad" (Acts xxvi. 14), against which he "kicked in vain." He rode to Damascus—a long and lonely journey—in a state of increasing disquiet and mental conflict. The heat and exhaustion of the desert march, acting on a nervous temperament naturally excitable and overwrought, hastened the crisis. Saul fell from his horse in an access of fever, or catalepsy. His brain was on fire. The convictions that haunted him suddenly took form and voice in the apparition of the glorified Jesus, whom Stephen in his dying moments had addressed. From that figure seemed to proceed the reproachful cry which the persecutor's conscience had in vain been striving to make him hear. A flash of lightning, or, if you like, a sunstroke, is readily imagined to fire this train of circumstances,— and the explanation is complete! When, besides, M. Renan is good enough to tell us that he has himself "experienced an attack of this kind at Byblos," and "with other principles would certainly have taken the hallucinations he then had for visions,"[22] what more can we desire? Nay, does not Paul himself admit, in ver. 16 of this chapter, that his conversion was essentially a spiritual and subjective event?

Such is the diagnosis of Paul's conversion offered us by rationalism; and it is not wanting in boldness nor in skill. But the corner-stone on which it rests, the hinge of the whole theory, is imaginary and in fatal contradiction with the facts of the case. Paul himself *knows nothing* of the remorse imputed to him previously to the vision of Jesus. The historian of the Acts knows nothing of it. In a nature so upright and conscientious as that of Saul, this misgiving would at least have induced him to desist from persecution. From first to last his testimony is, "I did it *ignorantly*, in unbelief." It was this ignorance, this absence of any sense of wrong in the violence he used against the followers of Jesus, that, in his view, accounted for his "obtaining mercy" (1 Tim. i. 13). If impressions of an opposite kind were previously struggling in his mind, with such force that on a mere nervous shock they were ready to precipitate themselves in the shape of an over-mastering hallucination, changing instantly and for ever the current of his life, how comes it that the Apostle has told us nothing about them? That he should have *forgotten* impressions so poignant and so powerful, is inconceivable. And if he has of set purpose ignored, nay, virtually denied this all-important fact, what becomes of his sincerity?

The Apostle was manifestly innocent of any such predisposition to Christian faith as the above theory imputes to him. True, he was conscious in those Judaistic days of his failure to attain righteousness, of the disharmony existing between "the law of his reason" and that which wrought "in his members." His conviction of sin supplied the moral precondition necessary in every case to saving faith in Christ. But this negative condition does not help us in the least to explain the vision of the glorified Jesus. By no psychological process whatever could the experience of Rom. vii. 7-24 be made to project itself in such an apparition. With all his mysticism and emotional susceptibility, Paul's mind was essentially sane and critical. To call him *epileptic* is a calumny. No man so diseased could have gone through the Apostle's labours, or written these Epistles. His discussion of the subject of supernatural gifts, in 1 Cor. xii. and xiv., is a model of shrewdness and good sense. He had experience of trances and ecstatic visions; and he knew, perhaps as well as M. Renan, how to distinguish them from objective realities.[23] The manner in which he speaks of this appearance allows of no reasonable doubt as to the Apostle's full persuasion that "in sober certainty of waking sense" he had seen Jesus our Lord.

It was this sensible and outward revelation that led to the inward revelation of the Redeemer to his soul, of which Paul goes on to speak in ver. 16. Without the latter the former would have been purposeless and useless. The objective vision could only have revealed a "Christ after the flesh," had it not been the means of opening Saul's closed heart to the influence of the Spirit of Christ. It was the means to this, and in the given circumstances the indispensable means.

To a history that "knows no miracles," the Apostle Paul must remain an enigma. His faith in the crucified Jesus is equally baffling to naturalism with that of the first disciples, who had laid Him in the grave. When the Apostle argues that his antecedent relations to Christianity were such as to preclude his conversion having come about by natural human means, we are bound to admit both the sincerity and the conclusiveness of his appeal.

CHAPTER V
PAUL'S DIVINE COMMISSION

"But when it was the good pleasure of God, who separated
me, *even* from my mother's womb, and called me through
His grace, to reveal His Son in me, that I might preach Him
among the Gentiles; immediately I conferred not with flesh
and blood: neither went I up to Jerusalem to them which
were apostles before me: but I went away into Arabia; and
again I returned unto Damascus." —Gal. i. 15-17.

It pleased God to reveal His Son in me: this is after all the essential
matter in Paul's conversion, as in that of every Christian. The outward
manifestation of Jesus Christ served in his case to bring about this result,
and was necessary to qualify him for his extraordinary vocation. But of itself
the supernatural vision had no redeeming virtue, and gave Saul of Tarsus
no message of salvation for the world. Its glory blinded and prostrated the
persecutor; his heart might notwithstanding have remained rebellious and
unchanged. "I am Jesus," said the heavenly Form, — "Go, and it shall be told
thee what thou shalt do"; — that was all! And that was not salvation. "Even
though one rose from the dead," still it is possible not to believe. And faith
is possible in its highest degree, and is exercised to-day by multitudes, with
no celestial light to illumine, no audible voice from beyond the grave to
awaken. The sixteenth verse gives us the inward counterpart of that exterior
revelation in which Paul's knowledge of Christ had its beginning, — but only
its beginning.

The Apostle does not surely mean by "in me," *in my case, through me
(to others)*. This gives a sense true in itself, and expressed by Paul elsewhere
(ver. 24; 1 Tim. i. 16), but unsuitable to the word "reveal," and out of place
at this point of the narrative. In the next clause—"that I might preach Him
among the Gentiles" —we learn what was to be the issue of this revelation
for the world. But in the first place it was a Divine certainty *within the breast
of Paul himself*. His Gentile Apostleship rested upon the most assured basis of
inward conviction, upon a spiritual apprehension of the Redeemer's person.
He says, laying emphasis on the last two words, "to reveal His Son *within
me*." So Chrysostom: Why did he not say *to me*, but *in me*? Showing that not

by words alone he learned the things concerning faith; but that he was also filled with the abundance of the Spirit, the revelation shining through his very soul; and that he had Christ speaking in himself.

I. *The substance of Paul's gospel was, therefore, given him by the unveiling of the Redeemer to his heart.*

The "revelation" of ver. 16 takes up and completes that of ver. 12. The dazzling appearance of Christ before his eyes and the summons of His voice addressed to Saul's bodily ears formed the special mode in which it pleased God to "call him by His grace." But "whom He called, He also justified." In this further act of grace salvation is first personally realised, and the gospel becomes the man's individual possession. This experience ensued upon the acceptance of the fact that the crucified Jesus was the Christ. But this was by no means all. As the revelation penetrated further into the Apostle's soul, he began to apprehend its deeper significance. He knew already that the Nazarene had claimed to be the Son of God, and on that ground had been sentenced to death by the Sanhedrim. His resurrection, now a demonstrated fact, showed that this awful claim, instead of being condemned, was acknowledged by God Himself. The celestial majesty in which He appeared, the sublime authority with which He spoke, witnessed to His Divinity. To Paul equally with the first Apostles, He "was declared Son of God in power, by the resurrection of the dead." But this persuasion was borne in upon him in his after reflections, and could not be adequately realised in the first shock of his great discovery. The language of this verse throws no sort of suspicion on the reality of the vision before Damascus. Quite the opposite. The inward presupposes the outward. Understanding follows sight. The subjective illumination, the inward conviction of Christ's Divinity, in Paul's case as in that of the first disciples, was brought about by the appearance of the risen, Divine Jesus. That appearance furnishes in both instances the explanation of the astounding change that took place in the men. The heart full of blasphemy against His name has learnt to own Him as "the Son of God, who loved me and gave Himself for me." Through the bodily eyes of Saul of Tarsus the revelation of Jesus Christ had entered and transformed his spirit.

Of this interior revelation *the Holy Spirit*, according to the Apostle's doctrine, had been the organ. The Lord on first meeting the gathered Apostles after His resurrection "breathed upon them, saying, Receive ye the Holy Ghost" (John xx. 22). This influence was in truth "the power of His resurrection"; it was the inspiring breath of the new life of humanity issuing from the open grave of Christ. The baptism of Pentecost, with its "mighty rushing wind," was but the fuller effusion of the power whose earnest the Church received in that gentle breathing of peace on the day of the resurrection. By His Spirit Christ made Himself a dwelling in the hearts of His disciples, raised at last to a true apprehension of His nature. All this was recapitulated in the experience of Paul. In his case the common experience was the more sharply defined because of the suddenness of his conversion, and the startling effect with which this new consciousness projected itself upon the background of his earlier Pharisaic life. Paul had his Resurrection-vision on the road to Damascus. He received his Pentecostal baptism in the days that followed.

It is not necessary to fix the precise occasion of the second revelation, or to connect it specifically with the visit of Ananias to Saul in Damascus, much less with his later "ecstasy" in the temple (Acts ix. 10-19; xxii. 12-21). When Ananias, sent by Christ, brought him the assurance of forgiveness from the injured Church, and bade him "recover his sight, and be filled with the Holy Ghost," this message greatly comforted his heart, and pointed out to him more clearly the way of salvation along which he was groping. But it is the office of the Spirit of God to reveal the Son of God; so Paul teaches everywhere in his Epistles, taught first by his own experience. Not from Ananias, nor from any man had he received this knowledge; *God* revealed His Son in the soul of the Apostle—"sent forth the Spirit of His Son into his heart" (ch. iv. 6). The language of 2 Cor. iii. 12-iv. 6 is the best commentary on this verse. A veil rested on the heart of Saul the Pharisee. He read the Old Covenant only in the condemning letter. Not yet did he know "the Lord" who is "the spirit." This veil was done away in Christ. "The glory of the Lord" that burst upon him in his Damascus journey, rent it once and for ever from his eyes. God, the Light-giver, had "shined in his heart, in the face of Jesus Christ." Such was the further scope of the revelation which effected Paul's conversion. As he writes afterwards to Ephesus, "the God of our Lord Jesus Christ, the Father of glory, had given him a spirit of wisdom and revelation in the knowledge of Christ; eyes of the heart enlightened to know the hope of His calling, and His exceeding power to usward, according to that He wrought in Christ when He raised Him from the dead, and set Him at His own right hand" (Eph. i. 17-21). In these words we hear an echo of the thoughts that passed through the Apostle's mind when first "it pleased God in him to reveal His Son."

II. *In the light of this inner revelation Paul received his Gentile mission.*

He speedily perceived that this was the purpose with which the revelation was made: "that I should preach Him among the Gentiles." The three accounts of his conversion furnished by the Acts witness to the same effect. Whether we should suppose that the Lord Jesus gave Saul this commission directly, at His first appearance, as seems to be implied in Acts xxvi., or infer from the more detailed narrative of chapters ix. and xxii., that the announcement was sent by Ananias and afterwards more urgently repeated in the vision at the Temple, in either case the fact remains the same; from the beginning Paul knew that he was appointed to be Christ's witness to the Gentiles. This destination was included in the Divine call which brought him to faith in Jesus. His Judaic prejudices were swept away. He was ready to embrace the universalism of the Gospel. With his fine logical instinct, sharpened by hatred, he had while yet a Pharisee discerned more clearly than many Jewish Christians the bearing of the doctrine of the cross upon the legal system. He saw that the struggle was one of life and death. The vehemence with which he flung himself into the contest was due to this perception. But it followed from this, that, once convinced of the Messiahship of Jesus, Paul's faith at a bound overleaped all Jewish barriers. "Judaism—or the religion of the Crucified," was the alternative with which his stern logic pursued the Nazarenes. Judaism *and* Christianity—this was a compromise intolerable to his nature. Before Saul's conversion he had left that halting-place behind; he apprehended already, in some sense, the truth up to which the elder Apostles had to be educated, that "in Christ Jesus there is neither Greek nor Jew." He passed at a step from the one camp to the other. In this there was consistency. The enlightened, conscientious persecutor, who had debated with Stephen and helped to stone him, was sure, if he became a Christian, to become a Christian of Stephen's school. When he entered the Church, Paul left the Synagogue. He was ripe for his world-wide commission. There was no surprise, no unpreparedness in his mind when the charge was given him, "Go; for I will send thee far hence among the Gentiles."

In the Apostle's view, his personal salvation and that of the race were objects united from the first. Not as a privileged Jew, but as a sinful man, the Divine grace had found him out. The righteousness of God was revealed to him on terms which brought it within the reach of every human being. The Son of God whom he now beheld was a personage vastly greater than his national Messiah, the "Christ after the flesh" of his Jewish dreams, and His gospel was correspondingly loftier and larger in its scope. "God was in Christ, reconciling," not a nation, but *a world* unto Himself." The "grace" conferred on him was given that he might "preach among the Gentiles Christ's unsearchable riches, and make all men see the mystery" of the counsel of redeeming love (Eph. iii. 1-11). It was the world's redemption of which Paul partook; and it was his business to let the world know it. He had fathomed the depths of sin and self-despair; he had tasted the uttermost of pardoning grace. God and the world met in his single soul, and were reconciled. He felt from the first what he expresses in his latest Epistles, that "the grace of God which appeared" to him, was "for the salvation of all men" (Tit. ii. 11). "Faithful is the saying, and worthy of all acceptation, that Christ Jesus came into the world to save sinners, of whom I am chief" (1 Tim. i. 15). The same revelation that made Paul a Christian, made him the Apostle of mankind.

III. *For this vocation the Apostle had been destined by God from the beginning.* "It pleased God to do this," he says, "who had marked me out from my mother's womb, and called me by His grace."

While "Saul was yet breathing out threatening and slaughter" against the disciples of Jesus, how different a future was being prepared for him! How little can we forecast the issue of our own plans, or of those we form for others. His Hebrew birth, his rabbinical proficiency, the thoroughness with which he had mastered the tenets of Legalism, had fitted him like no other to be the bearer of the Gospel to the Gentiles. This Epistle proves the fact. Only a graduate of the best Jewish schools could have written it. Paul's master, Gamaliel, if he had read the letter, must perforce have been proud of his scholar; he would have feared more than ever that those who opposed the Nazarene might "haply be found fighting against God." The Apostle foils the Judaists with their own weapons. He knows every inch of the ground on which the battle is waged. At the same time, he was a born Hellenist and a citizen of the Empire, native "of no mean city." Tarsus, his birthplace, was the capital of an important Roman province, and a centre of Greek culture and refinement. In spite of the Hebraic conservatism of Saul's family, the genial atmosphere of such a town could not but affect the early development of so sensitive a nature. He had sufficient tincture of Greek letters and conversance with Roman law to make him a true cosmopolitan, qualified to be "all things to all men." He presents an admirable example of that versatility and suppleness of genius which have distinguished for so many ages the sons of Jacob, and enable them to find a home and a market for their talents in every quarter of the world. Paul was "a chosen vessel, to bear the name of Jesus before Gentiles and kings, and the sons of Israel."

But his mission was concealed till the appointed hour. Thinking of his personal election, he reminds himself of the words spoken to Jeremiah touching his prophetic call. "Before I formed thee in the belly I knew thee; and before thou camest out of the womb I sanctified thee. I appointed thee a prophet unto the nations" (Jer. i. 5). Or like the Servant of the Lord in Isaiah he might say, "The Lord hath called me from the womb; from the bowels of my mother hath He made mention of my name. And He hath made my mouth like a sharp sword, in the shadow of His hand hath He hid me; and He hath made me a polished shaft, in His quiver hath He kept me close" (Isa. xlix. 1, 2). This belief in a fore-ordaining Providence, preparing in secret its chosen instruments, so deeply rooted in the Old Testament faith, was not wanting to Paul. His career is a signal illustration of its truth. He applies it, in his doctrine of Election, to the history of every child of grace. "Whom He foreknew, He did predestinate. Whom He did predestinate, He called." Once more we see how the Apostle's theology was moulded by his experience.

The manner in which Saul of Tarsus had been prepared all his life long for the service of Christ, magnified to his eyes the sovereign grace of God. "He called me *through His grace*." The call came at precisely the fit time; it came at a time and in a manner calculated to display the Divine compassion in the highest possible degree. This lesson Paul could never forget. To the last he dwells upon it with deep emotion. "In me," he writes to Timothy, "Jesus Christ first showed forth all His longsuffering. I was a blasphemer, a persecutor, insolent and injurious; but I obtained mercy" (1 Tim. i. 13-16). He was so dealt with from the beginning, he had been called to the knowledge of Christ under such circumstances that he felt he had a right to say, above other men, "By the grace of God I am what I am." The predestination under which his life was conducted "from his mother's womb," had for its chief purpose, to exhibit God's mercy to mankind, "that in the ages to come He might show the exceeding riches of His grace in kindness toward us in Christ Jesus" (Eph. ii. 7). To this purpose, so soon as he discerned it, he humbly yielded himself. The Son of God, whose followers he had hunted to death, whom in his madness he would have crucified afresh, had appeared to him to save and to forgive. The *grace* of it, the infinite kindness and compassion such an act revealed in the Divine nature, excited new wonder in the Apostle's soul till his latest hour. Henceforth he was the bondman of grace, the celebrant of grace. His life was one act of thanksgiving "to the praise of the glory of His grace!"

IV. From Jesus Christ in person Paul had received his knowledge of the Gospel, without human intervention. In the revelation of Christ to his soul he possessed the substance of the truth he was afterwards to teach; and with the revelation there came the commission to proclaim it to all men. His gospel-message was in its essence complete; the Apostleship was already his. Such are the assertions the Apostle makes in reply to his gainsayers. And he goes on to show that *the course he took after his conversion sustains these lofty claims*: "When God had been pleased to reveal His Son in me, immediately (right from the first) I took no counsel with flesh and blood. I avoided repairing to Jerusalem, to the elder Apostles; I went away into Arabia, and back again to Damascus. It was three years before I set foot in Jerusalem."

If that were so, how could Paul have received his doctrine or his commission from the Church of Jerusalem, as his traducers alleged? He acted from the outset under the sense of a unique Divine call, that allowed of no human validation or supplement. Had the case been otherwise, had Paul come to his knowledge of Christ by ordinary channels, his first impulse would have been to go up to the mother city to report himself there, and to gain further instruction. Above all, if he intended to be a minister of Christ, it would have been proper to secure the approval of the Twelve, and to be accredited from Jerusalem. This was the course which "flesh and blood" dictated, which Saul's new friends at Damascus probably urged upon him. It was insinuated that he had actually proceeded in this way, and put himself under the direction of Peter and the Judean Church. But he says, "I did nothing of the sort. I kept clear of Jerusalem for three years; and then I only went there to make private acquaintance with Peter, and stayed in the city but a fortnight." Although Paul did not for many years make public claim to rank with the Twelve, from the commencement he acted in conscious independence of them. He calls them "Apostles *before me*," by this phrase assuming the matter in dispute. He tacitly asserts his equality in official status with the Apostles of Jesus, assigning to the others precedence only in point of time. And he speaks of this equality in terms implying that it was already present to his mind at this former period. Under this conviction he held aloof from human guidance and approbation. Instead of "going up to Jerusalem," the centre of publicity, the head-quarters of the rising Church, Paul "went off into Arabia."

There were, no doubt, other reasons for this step. Why did he choose *Arabia* for his sojourn? and what, pray, was he doing there? The Apostle leaves us to our own conjectures. *Solitude*, we imagine, was his principal object. His Arabian retreat reminds us of the Arabian exile of Moses, of the wilderness discipline of John the Baptist, and the "forty days" of Jesus in the wilderness. In each of these instances, the desert retirement followed upon a great inward crisis, and was preparatory to the entrance of the Lord's servant on his mission to the world. Elijah, at a later period of his course, sought the wilderness under motives not dissimilar. After such a convulsion as Paul had passed through, with a whole world of new ideas and emotions pouring in upon him, he felt that he must be alone; he must get away from the voices of men. There are such times in the history of every earnest soul. In the silence of the Arabian desert, wandering amid the grandest scenes of ancient revelation, and communing in stillness with God and with his own heart, the young Apostle will think out the questions that press upon him; he will be able to take a calmer survey of the new world into which he has been ushered, and will learn to see clearly and walk steadily in the heavenly light that at first bewildered him. So "the Spirit immediately driveth him out into the wilderness." In Arabia one confers, not with flesh and blood, but with the mountains and with God. From Arabia Saul returned in possession of himself, and of his gospel.

The Acts of the Apostles omits this Arabian episode (Acts ix. 19-25). But for what Paul tells us here, we should have gathered that he began at once after his baptism to preach Christ in Damascus, his preaching after no long time[24] exciting Jewish enmity to such a pitch that his life was imperilled, and the Christian brethren compelled him to seek safety by flight to Jerusalem. The reader of Luke is certainly surprised to find a period of three years,[25] with a prolonged residence in Arabia, interpolated between Paul's conversion and his reception in Jerusalem. Luke's silence, we judge, is *intentional*. The Arabian retreat formed no part of the Apostle's public life, and had no place in the narrative of the Acts. Paul only mentions it here in the briefest terms, and because the reference was necessary to put his relations to the first Apostles in their proper light. For the time the converted Saul had dropped out of sight; and the historian of the Acts respects his privacy.

The place of the Arabian journey seems to us to lie between vv. 21 and 22 of Acts ix. That passage gives a twofold description of Paul's preaching in Damascus, in its earlier and later stages, with a double note of time (vv. 19 and 23). Saul's first testimony, taking place "straightway," was, one would presume, a mere declaration of faith in Jesus: "In the synagogues he proclaimed Jesus, (saying) that He is the Son of God" (R.V.), language in striking harmony with that of the Apostle in the text (vv. 12, 16). Naturally this recantation caused extreme astonishment in Damascus, where Saul's reputation was well-known both to Jews and Christians, and his arrival was expected in the character of Jewish inquisitor-in-chief. Ver. 22 presents a different situation. Paul is now preaching in his established and characteristic style; as we read it, we might fancy we hear him debating in the synagogues of Pisidian Antioch or Corinth or Thessalonica: "He was confounding the Jews, *proving* that this is the Christ." Neither Saul himself nor his Jewish hearers in the first days after his conversion would be in the mood for the sustained argumentation and Scriptural dialectic thus described. The explanation of the change lies behind the opening words of the verse: "But Saul increased in strength" — a growth due not only to the prolonged opposition he had to encounter, but still more, as we conjecture from this hint of the Apostle, to the period of rest and reflection which he enjoyed in his Arabian seclusion. The two marks of time given us in vv. 19 and 23 of Luke's narrative, may be fairly distinguished from each other — "certain days," and "sufficient days" (or "a considerable time") — as denoting a briefer and a longer season respectively: the former so short that the excitement caused by Saul's declaration of his new faith had not yet subsided when he withdrew from the city into the desert — in which case

Luke's note of time does not really conflict with Paul's "immediately"; the latter affording a lapse of time sufficient for Saul to develope his argument for the Messiahship of Jesus, and to provoke the Jews, worsted in logic, to resort to other weapons. From Luke's point of view the sojourn in Arabia, however extended, was simply an incident, of no public importance, in Paul's early ministry in Damascus.

The disappearance of Saul during this interval helps however, as we think, to explain a subsequent statement in Luke's narrative that is certainly perplexing (Acts ix. 26, 27). When Saul, after his escape from Damascus, "was come to Jerusalem," and "essayed to join himself to the disciples," they, we are told, "were all afraid of him, not believing that he was a disciple!" For while the Church at Jerusalem had doubtless heard at the time of Saul's marvellous conversion three years before, his long retirement and avoidance of Jerusalem threw an air of mystery and suspicion about his proceedings, and revived the fears of the Judean brethren; and his reappearance created a panic. In consequence of his sudden departure from Damascus, it is likely that no public report had as yet reached Judæa of Saul's return to that city and his renewed ministry there. Barnabas now came forward to act as sponsor for the suspected convert. What induced him to do this—whether it was that his largeness of heart enabled him to read Saul's character better than others, or whether he had some earlier private acquaintance with the Tarsian—we cannot tell. The account that Barnabas was able to give of his friend's conversion and of his bold confession in Damascus, won for Paul the place in the confidence of Peter and the leaders of the Church at Jerusalem which he never afterwards lost.

The two narratives—the history of Luke and the letter of Paul—relate the same series of events, but from almost opposite standpoints. Luke dwells upon *Paul's connection with the Church at Jerusalem and its Apostles.* Paul is maintaining *his independence of them.* There is no contradiction; but there is just such discrepancy as will arise where two honest and competent witnesses are relating identical facts in a different connection.

CHAPTER VI
PAUL AND THE PRIMITIVE CHURCH

"Then after three years I went up to Jerusalem to visit Cephas, and tarried with him fifteen days. But other of the apostles saw I none, but only James the Lord's brother. Now touching the things which I write unto you, behold, before God, I lie not. Then I came into the regions of Syria and Cilicia And I was still unknown by face unto the churches of Judæa which were in Christ: but they only heard say, He that once persecuted us now preacheth the faith of which he once made havock; and they glorified God in me."—Gal. i. 18-24.

For the first two years of his Christian life, Paul held no intercourse whatever with the Church at Jerusalem and its chiefs. His relation with them was commenced by the visit he paid to Peter in the third year after his conversion. And that relation was more precisely determined and made public when, after successfully prosecuting for fourteen years his mission to the heathen, the Apostle again went up to Jerusalem to defend the liberty of the Gentile Church (ch. ii. 1-10).

A clear understanding of this course of events was essential to the vindication of Paul's position in the eyes of the Galatians. The "troublers" told them that Paul's doctrine was not that of the mother Church; that his knowledge of the gospel and authority to preach it came from the elder Apostles, with whom since his attack upon Peter at Antioch he was at open variance. They themselves had come down from Judæa on purpose to set his pretensions in their true light, and to teach the Gentiles the way of the Lord more perfectly.

Modern rationalism has espoused the cause of these "deceitful workers" (2 Cor. xi. 13-15). It endeavours to rehabilitate the Judaistic party. The "critical" school maintain that the opposition of the Circumcisionists to the Apostle Paul was perfectly legitimate. They hold that the "pseudapostles" of Corinth, the "certain from James," the "troublers" and "false brethren privily brought in" of this Epistle, did in truth represent, as they claimed to do, the principles of the Jewish Christian Church; and that there was a radical divergence between the Pauline and Petrine gospels, of which the two Apostles were fully aware from the time of their encounter at Antioch. However Paul may have wished to disguise the fact to himself, the teaching of the Twelve was identical, we are told, with that "other gospel" on which he pronounces his anathema; the original Church of Jesus never emancipated itself from the trammels of legalism; the Apostle Paul, and not his Master, was in reality the author of evangelical doctrine, the founder of the catholic Church. The conflict between Peter and Paul at Antioch, related in this Epistle, supplies, in the view of Baur and his followers, the key to the history of the Early Church. The Ebionite assumption of a personal rivalry between the two Apostles and an intrinsic opposition in their doctrine, hitherto regarded as the invention of a desperate and decaying heretical sect, these ingenious critics have adopted for the basis of their "scientific" reconstruction of the New Testament. Paul's Judaizing hinderers and troublers are to be canonized; and the pseudo-Clementine writings, forsooth, must take the place of the discredited Acts of the Apostles. Verily "the whirligig of time hath its revenges." To empanel Paul on his accusers' side, and to make this Epistle above all convict him of heterodoxy, is an attempt which dazzles by its very daring.

Let us endeavour to form a clear conception of the facts touching Paul's connection with the first Apostles and his attitude and feeling towards the Jewish Church, as they are in evidence in the first two chapters of this Epistle.

I. On the one hand, it is clear that the Gentile Apostle's relations to Peter and the Twelve were those of *personal independence and official equality*.

This is the aspect of the case on which Paul lays stress. His sceptical critics argue that under his assertion of independence there is concealed an opposition of principle, a "radical divergence." The sense of independence is unmistakable. It is on that side that the Apostle seeks to guard himself. With this aim he styles himself at the outset "an Apostle not from men, nor by man"—neither man-made nor man-sent. Such apostles there were; and in this character, we imagine, the Galatian Judaistic teachers, like those of Corinth,[26] professed to appear, as the emissaries of the Church in Jerusalem and the authorised exponents of the teaching of the "pillars" there. Paul is an Apostle at first-hand, taking his commission directly from Jesus Christ. In that quality he pronounces his benediction and his anathema. To support this assumption he has shown how impossible it was in point of time and circumstances that he should have been beholden for his gospel to the Jerusalem Church and the elder Apostles. So far as regarded the manner of his conversion and the events of the first decisive years in which his Christian principles and vocation took their shape, his position had been altogether detached and singular; the Jewish Apostles could in no way claim him for their son in the gospel.

But at last, "after three years," Saul "did go up to Jerusalem." What was it for? To report himself to the authorities of the Church and place himself under their direction? To seek Peter's instruction, in order to obtain a more assured knowledge of the gospel he had embraced? Nothing of the kind. Not even *"to question* Cephas," as some render ἱστορῆσαι, following an older classical usage—"to gain information" from him; but "I went up *to . make acquaintance with* Cephas." Saul went to Jerusalem carrying in his heart the consciousness of his high vocation, seeking, as an equal with an equal, to make personal acquaintance with the leader of the Twelve. *Cephas* (as he was called at Jerusalem) must have been at this time to Paul a profoundly interesting personality. He was the one man above all others whom the Apostle felt he must get to know, with whom it was necessary for him to have a thorough understanding.

How momentous was this meeting! How much we could wish to know what passed between these two in the conversations of the fortnight they spent together. One can imagine the delight with which Peter would relate to his listener the scenes of the life of Jesus; how the two men would weep together at the recital of the Passion, the betrayal, trial and denial, the agony of the Garden, the horror of the cross; with what mingled awe and triumph he would describe the events of the Resurrection and the Forty Days, the Ascension, and the baptism of fire. In Paul's account of the appearances of the risen Christ (1 Cor. xv. 4-8), written many years afterwards, there are statements most naturally explained as a recollection of what he had heard privately from Peter, and possibly also from James, at this conference. For it is in his gospel message and doctrine, and his Apostolic commission, not in regard to the details of the biography of Jesus, that Paul claims to be independent of tradition. And with what deep emotion would Peter receive in turn from Paul's lips the account of his meeting with Jesus, of the three dark days that followed, of the message sent through Ananias, and the revelations made and purposes formed during the Arabian exile. Between two such men, met at such a time, there would surely be an entire frankness of communication and a brotherly exchange of convictions and of plans. In that case Paul could not fail to inform the elder Apostle of the extent of the commission he had received from their common Master; although he does not appear to have made any public and formal assertion of his Apostolic dignity for a considerable time afterwards. The supposition of a private cognizance on Peter's part of Paul's true status makes the open recognition which took place fourteen years later easy to understand (ch. ii. 6-10).

"But other of the Apostles," Paul goes on to say, "saw I none, but only James the brother of the Lord." James, *no Apostle* surely; neither in the higher sense, for he cannot be reasonably identified with "James the son of Alphæus;" nor in the lower, for he was, as far as we can learn, stationary at Jerusalem. But he stood so near the Apostles, and was in every way so important a person, that if Paul had omitted the name of James in this connection, he would have seemed to pass over a material fact. The reference to James in 1 Cor. xv. 7—a hint deeply interesting in itself, and lending so much dignity to the position of James—suggests that Paul had been at this time in confidential intercourse with James as well as Peter, each relating to the other how he had "seen the Lord."

So cardinal are the facts just stated (vv. 15-19), as bearing on Paul's apostleship, and so contrary to the representations made by the Judaizers, that he pauses to call God to witness his veracity: "Now in what I am writing to you, lo, before God, I lie not." The Apostle never makes this appeal lightly; but only in support of some averment in which his personal honour and his strongest feelings are involved.[27] It was alleged, with some show of proof, that Paul was an underling of the authorities of the Church at Jerusalem, and that all he knew of the gospel had been learned from the Twelve. From ver. 11 onwards he has been making a circumstantial contradiction of these assertions. He protests that up to the time when he commenced his Gentile mission, he had been under no man's tutelage or tuition in respect to his knowledge of the gospel. He can say no more to prove his case. Either his opposers or himself are uttering falsehood. The Galatians know, or ought to know, how incapable he is of such deceit. Solemnly therefore he avouches, closing the matter so far, as if drawing himself up to his utmost height: "Behold, before God, I do not lie!"

But now we are confronted with the narrative of the Acts (chap. ix. 26-30), which renders a very different account of this passage in the Apostle's life. (To vv. 26, 27 of Luke's narrative we have already alluded in the concluding paragraphs of Chapter V). We are told there that Barnabas introduced Saul "to the Apostles"; here, that he saw none of them but Cephas, and only James besides. The *number* of the Apostolate present in Jerusalem at the time is a particular that does not engage Luke's mind; while it is of the essence of Paul's affirmation. What the Acts relates is that Saul, through Barnabas' intervention, was now received by the Apostolic fellowship as a Christian brother, and as one who "had seen the Lord." The object which Saul had in coming to Jerusalem, and the fact that just then Cephas was the only one of the Twelve to be found in the city, along with James—these are matters which only come into view from the private and personal standpoint to which Paul admits us. For the rest, there is certainly no contradiction when we read in the one report that Paul "went up to make acquaintance with Cephas," and in the other, that he "was with them going in and out at Jerusalem, preaching boldly in the name of the Lord;" that "he spake and disputed against the Hellenists," moving their anger so violently that his life was again in danger, and he had to be carried down to Cæsarea and shipped off to Tarsus. Saul was not the man to hide his head in Jerusalem. We can understand how greatly his spirit was stirred by his arrival there, and by the recollection of his last passage through the city gates. In these very synagogues of the Hellenists he had himself confronted Stephen; outside those walls he had assisted to stone the martyr. Paul's address delivered many years later to the Jewish mob that attempted his life in Jerusalem, shows how deeply these remembrances troubled his soul (Acts xxii. 17-22). And they would not suffer him now to be silent. He hoped that his testimony to Christ, delivered in the spot where he had been so notorious as a persecutor, would produce a softening effect on his old companions. It was sure to affect them powerfully, one way or the other. As the event proved, it did not take many words from Saul's lips to awaken against him the same fury that hurried Stephen to his death. A fortnight was time quite sufficient, under the circumstances, to make Jerusalem, as we say, too hot to hold Saul. Nor can we wonder, knowing his love for his kindred, that there needed a special command from heaven (Acts xxii. 21), joined to the friendly compulsion of the Church, to induce him to yield ground and quit the city. But he had accomplished something; he had "made acquaintance with Cephas."

This brief visit to the Holy City was a second crisis in Paul's career. He was now thrust forth upon his mission to the heathen. It was evident that he was not to look for success among his Jewish brethren. He lost no opportunity of appealing to them; but it was commonly with the same result as at Damascus and Jerusalem. Throughout life he carried with him this "great sorrow and unceasing pain of heart," that to his "kinsmen according to the flesh," for whose salvation he could consent to forfeit his own, his gospel was hid. In their eyes he was a traitor to Israel, and must count upon their enmity. Everything conspired to point in one direction: "Depart," the Divine voice had said, "for I will send thee far hence unto the Gentiles." And Paul obeyed. "I went," he relates here, "into the regions of Syria and Cilicia" (ver. 21).

To Tarsus, the Cilician capital, Saul voyaged from Judæa. So we learn from Acts ix. 30. His native place had the first claim on the Apostle after Jerusalem, and afforded the best starting-point for his independent mission. Syria, however, precedes Cilicia in the text; it was the leading province of these two, in which Paul was occupied during the fourteen years ensuing, and became the seat of distinguished Churches. In Antioch, the Syrian capital, Christianity was already planted (Acts xi. 19—21). The close connection of the Churches of these provinces, and their predominantly Gentile character, are both evident from the letter addressed to them subsequently by the Council of Jerusalem (Acts xv. 23, 24). Acts xv. 41 shows that a number of Christian societies owning Paul's authority were found at a later time in this region. And there was a highroad direct from Syro-Cilicia to Galatia, which Paul traversed in his second visit to the latter country (Acts xviii. 22, 23); so that the Galatians would doubtless be aware of the existence of these older Gentile Churches, and of their relation to Paul. He has no need to dwell on this first chapter of his missionary history. After but a fortnight's visit to Jerusalem, Paul went into these Gentile regions, and there for twice seven years—with what success was known to all—"preached the faith of which once he made havoc."

This period was divided into two parts. For five or six years the Apostle laboured alone; afterwards in conjunction with Barnabas, who invited his help at Antioch (Acts xi. 25, 26). Barnabas was Paul's senior, and had for some time held the leading position in the Church of Antioch; and Paul was personally indebted to this generous man (p. 82). He accepted the position of helper to Barnabas without any compromise of his higher authority, as yet held in reserve. He accompanied Barnabas to Jerusalem in 44 (or 45) A.D., with the contribution made by the Syrian Church for the relief of the famine-stricken Judean brethren—a visit which Paul seems here to forget. [28] But the Church at Jerusalem was at that time undergoing a severe persecution; its leaders were either in prison or in flight. The two delegates can have done little more than convey the moneys entrusted to them, and that with the utmost secrecy. Possibly Paul on this occasion never set foot inside the city. In any case, the event had no bearing on the Apostle's present contention.

Between this journey and the really important visit to Jerusalem introduced in chap. ii. 1, Barnabas and Paul undertook, at the prompting of the Holy Spirit expressed through the Church of Antioch (Acts xiii. 1-4), the missionary expedition described in Acts xiii., xiv. Under the trials of this journey the ascendancy of the younger evangelist became patent to all. Paul was marked out in the eyes of the Gentiles as their born leader, the Apostle of heathen Christianity. He appears to have taken the chief part in the discussion with the Judaists respecting circumcision, which immediately ensued at Antioch; and was put at the head of the deputation sent up to Jerusalem concerning this question. This was a turning-point in the Apostle's history. It brought about the public recognition of his leadership in the Church. The seal of man was now to be set upon the secret election of God.

During this long period, the Apostle tells us, he "remained unknown by face to the Churches of Judæa." Absent for so many years from the metropolis, after a fortnight's flying visit, spent in private intercourse with Peter and James, and in controversy in the Hellenistic synagogues where few Christians of the city would be likely to follow him,[29] Paul was a stranger to the bulk of the Judean disciples. But they watched his course, notwithstanding, with lively interest and with devout thanksgiving to God (vv. 22, 23). Throughout this first period of his ministry the Apostle acted in complete independence of the Jewish Church, making no report to its chiefs, nor seeking any direction from them. Accordingly, when afterwards he did go up to Jerusalem and laid before the authorities there his gospel to the heathen, they had nothing to add to it; they did not take upon themselves to give him any advice or injunction, beyond the wish that he and Barnabas should "remember the poor," as he was already forward to do (ch. ii. 1-10). Indeed the three famous Pillars of the Jewish Church at this time openly acknowledged Paul's equality with Peter in the Apostleship, and resigned to his direction the Gentile province. Finally at Antioch, the head-quarters of Gentile Christianity, when Peter compromised the truth of the gospel by yielding to Judaistic pressure, Paul had not hesitated publicly to reprove him (ch. ii. 11-21). He had been compelled in this way to carry the vindication of his gospel to the furthest lengths; and he had done this successfully. It is only when we reach the end of the second chapter that we discover how much the Apostle meant when he said, "My gospel is not according to man."

If there was any man to whom as a Christian teacher he was bound to defer, any one who might be regarded as his official superior, it was the Apostle Peter. Yet against this very Cephas he had dared openly to measure himself. Had he been a disciple of the Jewish Apostle, a servant of the Jerusalem Church, how would this have been possible? Had he not possessed an authority derived immediately from Christ, how could he have stood out alone, against the prerogative of Peter, against the personal friendship and local influence of Barnabas, against the example of all his Jewish brethren? Nay, he was prepared to rebuke all the Apostles, and anathematize all the angels, rather than see Christ's gospel set at nought. For it was in his view "the gospel of the glory of the blessed God, *committed to my trust!*" (1 Tim. i. 11).

II. But while Paul stoutly maintains his independence, he does this in such a way as to show that there was no hostility or personal rivalry between himself and the first Apostles. His relations to the Jewish Church were all the while those of *friendly acquaintance and brotherly recognition.*

That Nazarene sect which he had of old time persecuted, was "the Church of God" (ver. 13). To the end of his life this thought gave a poignancy to the Apostle's recollection of his early days. To "the Churches of Judæa"[30] he attaches the epithet *in Christ,* a phrase of peculiar depth of meaning with Paul, which he could never have conferred as matter of formal courtesy, nor by way of mere distinction between the Church and the Synagogue. From Paul's lips this title is a guarantee of orthodoxy. It satisfies us that the "other gospel" of the Circumcisionists was very far from being the gospel of the Jewish Christian Church at large. Paul is careful to record the sympathy which the Judean brethren cherished for his missionary work in its earliest stages, although their knowledge of him was comparatively distant: "Only they continued to hear that our old persecutor is preaching the faith which once he sought to destroy. And in me they glorified God." Nor does he drop the smallest hint to show that the disposition of the Churches in the mother country toward himself, or his judgement respecting them, had undergone any change up to the time of his writing this Epistle.

He speaks of the elder Apostles in terms of unfeigned respect. In his reference in ch. ii. 11-21 to the error of Peter, there is great plainness of speech, but no bitterness. When the Apostle says that he "went up to Jerusalem to see Peter," and describes James as "the Lord's brother," and when he refers to both of them, along with John, as "those accounted to be pillars," can he mean anything but honour to these honoured men? To read into these expressions a covert jealousy and to suppose them written by way of disparagement, seems to us a strangely jaundiced and small-minded sort of criticism. The Apostle testifies that Peter held a Divine trust in the Gospel, and that God had "wrought for Peter" to this effect, as for himself. By claiming the testimony of the Pillars at Jerusalem to his vocation, he shows his profound respect for theirs. When the unfortunate difference arose between Peter and himself at Antioch, Paul is careful to show that the Jewish Apostle on that occasion was influenced by the circumstances of the moment, and nevertheless remained true in his real convictions to the common gospel.

In view of these facts, it is impossible to believe, as the *Tendency* critics would have us do, that Paul when he wrote this letter was at feud with the Jewish Church. In that case, while he taxes Peter with "dissimulation" (ch. ii. 11-13), he is himself the real dissembler, and has carried his dissimulation to amazing lengths. If he is in this Epistle contending against the Primitive Church and its leaders, he has concealed his sentiments toward them with an art so crafty as to overreach itself. He has taught his readers to reverence those whom on this hypothesis he was most concerned to discredit. The terms under which he refers to Cephas and the Judean Churches would be just so many testimonies against himself, if their doctrine was the "other gospel" of the Galatian troublers, and if Paul and the Twelve were rivals for the suffrages of the Gentile Christians.

The one word which wears a colour of detraction is the parenthesis in ver. 6 of ch. ii.: "whatever aforetime[31] they (those of repute) were, makes no difference to me. God accepts no man's person." But this is no more than Paul has already said in ch. i. 16, 17. At the first, after receiving his gospel from the Lord in person, he felt it to be out of place for him to "confer with flesh and blood." So now, even in the presence of the first Apostles, the earthly companions of his Master, he cannot abate his pretensions, nor forget that his ministry stands on a level as exalted as theirs. This language is in precise accord with that of 1 Cor. xv. 10. The suggestion that the repeated οἱ δοκοῦντες conveys a sneer against the leaders at Jerusalem, as "seeming" to be more than they were, is an insult to Paul that recoils upon the critics who utter it. The phrase denotes "those of repute," "reputed to be pillars," the acknowledged heads of the mother Church. Their position was recognised on all hands; Paul assumes it, and argues upon it. He desires to magnify, not to minify, the importance of these illustrious men. They were pillars of his own cause. It is a maladroit interpretation that would have Paul cry down James and the Twelve. By so much as he impaired their worth, he must assuredly have impaired his own. If their status was mere *seeming*, of what value was their endorsement of his? But for a preconceived opinion, no one, we may safely affirm, reading this Epistle would have gathered that Peter's "gospel of the circumcision" was the "other gospel" of Galatia, or that the "certain from James" of ch. ii. 12 represented the views and the policy of the first Apostles. The assumption that Peter's dissimulation at Antioch expressed the settled doctrine of the Jewish Apostolic Church, is unhistorical. The Judaizers *abused* the authority of Peter and James when they pleaded it in favour of their agitation. So we are told expressly in Acts xv.; and a candid interpretation of this letter bears out the statements of Luke. In James and Peter, Paul and John, there were indeed "diversities of gifts and operations," but they had received the same Spirit; they served the same Lord. They held alike the one and only gospel of the grace of God.

CHAPTER VII
PAUL AND THE FALSE BRETHREN

"Then after the space of fourteen years I went up again to
Jerusalem with Barnabas, taking Titus also with me. And
I went up by revelation; and I laid before them the gospel
which I preach among the Gentiles, but privately before them
who were of repute, [*asking them* whether I am running, or
had run, in vain: but not even Titus who was with me, being
a Greek, was compelled to be circumcised. But *it was* [32]]
because of the false brethren privily brought in, who came in
privily to spy out our liberty which we have in Christ Jesus,
that they might bring us into bondage: to whom we gave
place in the way of subjection, no, not for an hour; that the
truth of the gospel might continue with you."—Gal. ii. 1-5.

"Fourteen years" had elapsed since Paul left Jerusalem for Tarsus, and
commenced his Gentile mission.[33] During this long period—a full half
of his missionary course—the Apostle was lost to the sight of the Judean
Churches. For nearly half this time, until Barnabas brought him to Antioch,
we have no further trace of his movements. But these years of obscure
labour had, we may be sure, no small influence in shaping the Apostle's
subsequent career. It was a kind of Apostolic apprenticeship. Then his
evangelistic plans were laid; his powers were practised; his methods of
teaching and administration formed and tested. This first, unnoted period
of Paul's missionary life held, we imagine, much the same relation to his
public ministry that the time of the Arabian retreat did to his spiritual
development.

We are apt to think of the Apostle Paul only as we see him in the full
tide of his activity, carrying "from Jerusalem round about unto Illyricum"
the standard of the cross and planting it in one after another of the great
cities of the Empire, "always triumphing in every place;" or issuing those
mighty Epistles whose voice shakes the world. We forget the earlier term
of preparation, these years of silence and patience, of unrecorded toil in a
comparatively narrow and humble sphere, which had after all their part
in making Paul the man he was. If Christ Himself would not "clutch" at

His Divine prerogatives (Phil. ii. 5-11), nor win them by self-assertion and before the time, how much more did it become His servant to rise to his great office by slow degrees. Paul served first as a private missionary pioneer in his native land, then as a junior colleague and assistant to Barnabas, until the summons came to take a higher place, when "the signs of an Apostle" had been fully "wrought in him." Not in a day, nor by the effect of a single revelation did he become the fully armed and all-accomplished Apostle of the Gentiles whom we meet in this Epistle. "After the space of fourteen years" it was time for him to stand forth the approved witness and minister of Jesus Christ, whom Peter and John publicly embraced as their equal.

Paul claims here the initiative in the momentous visit to Jerusalem undertaken by himself and Barnabas, of which he is going to speak. In Acts xv. 2 he is similarly placed at the head of the deputation sent from Antioch about the question of circumcision. The account of the preceding missionary tour in Acts xiii., xiv., shows how the headship of the Gentile Church had come to devolve on Paul. In Luke's narrative they are "Barnabas and Saul" who set out; "Paul and Barnabas" who return.[34] Under the trials and hazards of this adventure—at Paphos, Pisidian Antioch, Lystra—Paul's native ascendancy and his higher vocation irresistibly declared themselves. Age and rank yielded to the fire of inspiration, to the gifts of speech, the splendid powers of leadership which the difficulties of this expedition revealed in Paul. Barnabas returned to Antioch with the thought in his heart, "He must increase; I must decrease." And Barnabas was too generous a man not to yield cheerfully to his companion the precedence for which God thus marked him out. Yet the "sharp contention" in which the two men parted soon after this time (Acts xv. 36-40), was, we may conjecture, due in some degree to a lingering soreness in the mind of Barnabas on this account.

The Apostle expresses himself with modesty, but in such a way as to show that *he* was regarded in this juncture as the champion of the Gentile cause. The "revelation" that prompted the visit came to him. The "taking up of Titus" was his distinct act (ver. 1). Unless Paul has deceived himself, he was quite the leading figure in the Council; it was his doctrine and his Apostleship that exercised the minds of the chiefs at Jerusalem, when the delegates from Antioch appeared before them. Whatever Peter and James may have known or surmised previously concerning Paul's vocation, it was only now that it became a public question for the Church. But as matters stood, it was a vital question. The status of uncircumcised Christians, and the Apostolic rank of Paul, constituted the twofold problem placed before the chiefs of the Jewish Church. At the same time, the Apostle, while fixing our attention mainly on his own position, gives to Barnabas his meed of honour; for he says, "I went up with Barnabas,"—"*we* never yielded for an hour to the false brethren,"—"the Pillars gave *to me and Barnabas* the right hand of fellowship, that we might go to the Gentiles." But it is evident that the elder Gentile missionary stood in the background. By the action that he takes Paul unmistakably declares, "I am the Apostle of the Gentiles;"[35] and that claim is admitted by the consenting voice of both branches of the Church. The Apostle stepped to the front at this solemn crisis, not for his own rank or office' sake, but at the call of God, in defence of the truth of the gospel and the spiritual freedom of mankind.

This meeting at Jerusalem took place in 51, or it may be, 52 A.D. We make no doubt that it is the same with the Council of Acts xv. The identification has been controverted by several able scholars, but without success. The two accounts are different, but in no sense contradictory. In fact, as Dr: Pfleiderer acknowledges,[36] they "admirably supplement each other. The agreement as to the chief points is in any case greater than the discrepancies in the details; and these discrepancies can for the most part be explained by the different standpoint of the relaters." A difficulty lies, however, in the fact that the historian of the Acts makes this the *third* visit of Paul to Jerusalem subsequently to his conversion; whereas, from the Apostle's statement, it appears to have been the *second*. This discrepancy has already come up for discussion in the last Chapter (p. 92). Two further observations may be added on this point. In the first place, Paul does not say that he had never been to Jerusalem since the visit of ch. i. 18; he does say, that on this occasion he "went up again," and that meanwhile he "remained unknown by face" to the Christians of Judæa (ch. i. 22)—a fact quite compatible, as we have shown, with what is related in Acts xi. 29, 30. And further, the request addressed at this conference to the Gentile missionaries, that they should "remember the poor," and the reference made by the Apostle to his previous zeal in the same business (vv. 9, 10), are in agreement with the earlier visit of charity mentioned by Luke.

I. The emphasis of ver. 1 rests upon its last clause,—*taking along with me also Titus*. Not "Titus as well as Barnabas"—this cannot be the meaning of the "also"—for Barnabas was Paul's colleague, deputed equally with himself by the Church of Antioch; nor "Titus as well as others"—there were other members of the deputation (Acts xv. 2), but Paul makes no reference to them. The *also* (καὶ) calls attention to the fact of Paul's taking *Titus*, in view of the sequel; as though he said, "I not only went up to Jerusalem at this particular time, under Divine direction, but I took along with me Titus besides." The prefixed *with* (συν-) of the Greek participle refers to Paul himself: compare ver. 3, "Titus who was with me." As for the "certain others" referred to in Acts xv. 2, they were most likely Jews; or if any of them were Gentiles, still it was Titus whom Paul had chosen for his companion;

and his case stood out from the rest in such a way that it became the decisive one, the *test-case* for the matter in dispute.

The mention of *Titus'* name in this connection was calculated to raise a lively interest in the minds of the Apostle's readers. He is introduced as known to the Galatians; indeed by this time his name was familiar in the Pauline Churches, as that of a fellow-traveller and trusted helper of the Apostle. He was with Paul in the latter part of the third missionary tour—so we learn from the Corinthian letters—and therefore probably in the earlier part of the same journey, when the Apostle paid his second visit to Galatia. He belonged to the heathen mission, and was Paul's "true child after a common faith" (Tit. i. 4), an uncircumcised man, of Gentile birth equally with the Galatians. And now they read of his "going up to Jerusalem with Paul," to the mother-city of believers, where are the pillars of the Church— the Jewish teachers would say—the true Apostles of Jesus, where His doctrine is preached in its purity, and where every Christian is circumcised and keeps the Law. Titus, the unclean Gentile, at Jerusalem! How could he be admitted or tolerated there, in the fellowship of the first disciples of the Lord? This question Paul's readers, after what they had heard from the Circumcisionists, would be sure to ask. He will answer it directly.

But the Apostle goes on to say, that he "went up in accordance with a revelation." For this was one of those supreme moments in his life when he looked for and received the direct guidance of heaven. It was a most critical step to carry this question of Gentile circumcision up to Jerusalem, and to take Titus with him there, into the enemies' stronghold. Moreover, on the settlement of this matter Paul knew that his Apostolic status depended, so far as human recognition was concerned. It would be seen whether the Jewish Church would acknowledge the converts of the Gentile mission as brethren in Christ; and whether the first Apostles would receive him, "the untimely one," as a colleague of their own. Never had he more urgently needed or more implicitly relied upon Divine direction than at this hour.

"And I put before them (the Church at Jerusalem) the gospel which I preach among the Gentiles—but privately to those of repute: am I running (said I), or have I run, in vain?" The latter clause we read *interrogatively*, along with such excellent grammatical interpreters as Meyer, Wieseler, and Hofmann. Paul had not come to Jerusalem *in order to solve any doubt in his own mind*; but he wished the Church of Jerusalem *to declare its mind* respecting the character of his ministry. He was not "running as uncertainly;" nor in view of the "revelation" just given him could he have any fear for the result of his appeal. But it was in every way necessary that the appeal should be made.

The interjected words, "but privately," etc., indicate that there were *two* meetings during the conference, such as those which seem to be distinguished in Acts xv. 4 and 6; and that the Apostle's statement and the question arising out of it were addressed more pointedly to "those of repute." By this term we understand, here and in ver. 6, "the apostles and elders" (Acts xv.), headed by Peter and James, amongst whom "those reputed to be pillars" are distinguished in ver. 9. Paul dwells upon the phrase οἱ δοκοῦντες, because, to be sure, it was so often on the lips of the Judaizers, who were in the habit of speaking with an imposing air, and by way of contrast with Paul, of "the authorities" (at Jerusalem)—as the designation might appropriately be rendered. These very men whom the Legalists were exalting at Paul's expense, the venerated chiefs of the mother Church, had on this occasion, Paul is going to say, given their approval to his doctrine; they declined to impose circumcision on Gentile believers. The Twelve were not stationary at Jerusalem, and therefore could not form a fixed court of reference there; hence a greater importance accrued to the Elders of the city Church, with the revered James at their head, the brother of the Lord.

The Apostle, in bringing Titus, had brought up the subject-matter of the controversy. The "gospel of the uncircumcision" stood before the Jewish authorities, an accomplished fact. Titus was there, by the side of Paul, a sample—and a noble specimen, we can well believe—of the Gentile Christendom which the Jewish Church must either acknowledge or repudiate. How will they treat him? Will they admit this foreign protege of Paul to their communion? Or will they require him first to be circumcised? The question at issue could not take a form more crucial for the prejudices of the mother Church. It was one thing to acknowledge uncircumcised fellow-believers in the abstract, away yonder at Antioch or Iconium, or even at Cæsarea; and another thing to see Titus standing amongst them in his heathen uncleanness, on the sacred soil of Jerusalem, under the shadow of the Temple, and to hear Paul claiming for him—for this "dog" of a Gentile—equally with himself the rights of Christian brotherhood! The demand was most offensive to the pride of Judaism, as no one knew better than Paul; and we cannot wonder that a revelation was required to justify the Apostle in making it. The case of *Trophimus*, whose presence with the Apostle at Jerusalem many years afterwards proved so nearly fatal (Acts xxi. 27-30), shows how exasperating to the legalist party his action in this instance must have been. Had not Peter and the better spirits of the Church in Jerusalem laid to heart the lesson of the vision of Joppa, that "no man must be called common or unclean," and had not the wisdom of the Holy Spirit eminently guided this first Council of the Church,[37] Paul's challenge would have received a negative answer; and Jewish and Gentile Christianity must have been driven asunder.

The answer, the triumphant answer, to Paul's appeal comes in the next verse: "Nay, not even[38] Titus who was with me, being a Greek, was compelled to be circumcised." Titus *was not circumcised*, in point of fact—how can we doubt this in view of the language of ver. 5: "Not even for an hour did we yield in subjection?" And he "was *not compelled* to be circumcised"—a mode of putting the denial which implies that in refusing his circumcision urgent solicitation had to be withstood, solicitation addressed to Titus himself, as well as to the leaders of his party. The kind of pressure brought to bear in the case and the quarter from which it proceeded, the Galatians would understand from their own experience (ch. vi. 12; comp. ii. 14).

The attempt made to bring about Titus' circumcision signally failed. Its failure was the practical reply to the question which Paul tells us (ver. 2) he had put to the authorities in Jerusalem; or, according to the more common rendering of ver. 2*b*, it was the answer to the apprehension under which he addressed himself to them. On the former of these views of the connection, which we decidedly prefer, the authorities are clear of any share in the "compulsion" of Titus. When the Apostle gives the statement that his Gentile companion "was not compelled to be circumcised" as the reply to his appeal to "those of repute," it is as much as to say: "The chiefs at Jerusalem did not require Titus' circumcision. They repudiated the attempt of certain parties to force this rite upon him." This testimony precisely accords with the terms of the rescript of the Council, and with the speeches of Peter and James, given in Acts xv. But it was a great point gained to have the liberality of the Jewish Christian leaders put to the proof in this way, to have the generous sentiments of speech and letter made good in this example of uncircumcised Christianity brought to their doors.

To the authorities at Jerusalem the question put by the delegates from Antioch on the one side, and by the Circumcisionists on the other, was perfectly clear. If they insist on Titus' circumcision, they disown Paul and the Gentile mission: if they accept Paul's gospel, they must leave Titus alone. Paul and Barnabas stated the case in a manner that left no room for doubt or compromise. Their action was marked, as ver. 5 declares, with the utmost decision. And the response of the Jewish leaders was equally frank and definite. We have no business, says James (Acts xv. 19), "to trouble those from the Gentiles that turn to God." Their judgement is virtually affirmed in ver. 3, in reference to Titus, in whose person the Galatians could not fail to see that their own case had been settled by anticipation. "Those of repute" disowned the Circumcisionists; the demand that the yoke of circumcision should be imposed on the Gentiles had no sanction from them. If the Judaizers claimed their sanction, the claim was false.

Here the Apostle pauses, as his Gentile readers must have paused and drawn a long breath of relief or of astonishment at what he has just alleged. If Titus was not compelled to be circumcised, even at Jerusalem, who, they might ask, was going to compel *them*?—The full stop should therefore be placed at the end of ver. 3, not ver. 2. Vv. 1-3 form a paragraph complete in itself. Its last sentence resolves the decisive question raised in this visit of Paul's to Jerusalem, when he "took with him also Titus."

II. The opening words of ver. 4 have all the appearance of commencing a new sentence. This sentence, concluded in ver. 5, is grammatically incomplete; but that is no reason for throwing it upon the previous sentence, to the confusion of both. There is a transition of thought, marked by the introductory *But*,[39] from the issue of Paul's second critical visit to Jerusalem (vv. 1-3) to *the cause which made it necessary*. This was the action of "false brethren," to whom the Apostle made a determined and successful resistance (vv. 4, 5). The opening "But" does not refer to ver. 3 in particular, rather to the entire foregoing paragraph. The ellipsis (after "But") is suitably supplied in the marginal rendering of the Revisers, where we take *it was* to mean, not "Because of the false brethren *Titus was not* (or *was not compelled to be*) *circumcised*," but "Because of the false brethren *this meeting came about, or, I took the course aforesaid*."

To know what Paul means by "false brethren," we must turn to ch. i. 6-9, iii. 1, iv. 17, v. 7-12, vi. 12-14, in this Epistle; and again to 2 Cor. ii. 17-iii. 1, iv. 2, xi. 3, 4, 12-22, 26; Rom. xvi. 17, 18; Phil. iii. 2. They were men bearing the name of Christ and professing faith in Him, but Pharisees at heart, self-seeking, rancorous, unscrupulous men, bent on exploiting the Pauline Churches for their own advantage, and regarding Gentile converts to Christ as so many possible recruits for the ranks of the Circumcision.

But where, and how, were these traitors "privily brought in?" Brought in, we answer, to the field of the Gentile mission; and doubtless by local Jewish sympathisers, who introduced them without the concurrence of the officers of the Church. They "came in privily"—slipped in by stealth—"to spy out our liberty which we have in Christ Jesus." Now it was at Antioch and in the pagan Churches that this liberty existed in its normal exercise— the liberty for which our Epistle contends, the enjoyment of Christian privileges independently of Jewish law—in which Paul and his brother missionaries had identified themselves with their Gentile followers. The "false brethren" were Jewish spies in the Gentile Christian camp. We do not see how the Galatians could have read the Apostle's words otherwise; nor how it could have occurred to them that he was referring to the way in which these men had been originally "brought into" the Jewish Church. That concerned neither him nor them. But *their getting into the Gentile fold* was the serious thing. They are the "certain who came down from Judæa, and taught the (Gentile) brethren, saying, Except ye be circumcised after the custom of Moses, ye cannot be saved;" and whom their own Church afterwards repudiated (Acts xv. 24). With Antioch for the centre of their operations, these mischief-makers disturbed the whole field of Paul and Barnabas' labours in Syria and Cilicia (Acts xv. 23; comp. Gal. i. 21). For the Galatian readers, the terms of this sentence, coming after the anathema of ch. i. 6-9, threw a startling light on the character of the Judean emissaries busy in their midst. This description of the former "troublers" strikes at the Judaic opposition in Galatia. It is as if the Apostle said: "These false brethren, smuggled in amongst us, to filch away our liberties in Christ, wolves in sheep's clothing—I know them well; I have encountered them before this. I never yielded to their demands a single inch. I carried the struggle with them to Jerusalem. There, in the citadel of Judaism, and before the assembled chiefs of the Judean Church, I vindicated once and for all, under the person of Titus, your imperilled Christian rights."

But as the Apostle dilates on the conduct of these Jewish intriguers, the precursors of such an army of troublers, his heart takes fire; in the rush of his emotion he is carried away from the original purport of his sentence, and breaks it off with a burst of indignation: "To whom," he cries, "not even for an hour did we yield by subjection, that the truth of the gospel might abide with you." A breakdown like this—an *anacoluthon*, as the grammarians call it—is nothing strange in Paul's style. Despite the shipwrecked grammar, the sense comes off safely enough. The clause, "we did not yield," etc., describes in a negative form, and with heightened effect, the course the Apostle had pursued from the first in dealing with the false brethren. In this unyielding spirit he had acted, without a moment's wavering, from the hour when, guided by the Holy Spirit, he set out for Jerusalem with the uncircumcised Titus by his side, until he heard his Gentile gospel vindicated by the lips of Peter and James, and received from them the clasp of fellowship as Christ's acknowledged Apostle to the heathen.

It was therefore the action of Jewish interlopers, men of the same stamp as those infesting the Galatian Churches, which occasioned Paul's second, public visit to Jerusalem, and his consultation with the heads of the Judean Church. This decisive course he was himself inspired to take; while at the same time it was taken on behalf and under the direction of the Church of Antioch, the metropolis of Gentile Christianity. He had gone up with Barnabas and "certain others"—including the Greek Titus chosen by himself—the company forming a representative deputation, of which Paul was the leader and spokesman. This measure was the boldest and the only effectual means of combatting the Judaistic propaganda. It drew from the authorities at Jerusalem the admission that "Circumcision is nothing," and that Gentile Christians are free from the ritual law. This was a victory gained over Jewish prejudice of immense significance for the future of Christianity. The ground was already cut from under the feet of the Judaic teachers in Galatia, and of all who should at any time seek to impose external rites as things essential to salvation in Christ. To all his readers Paul can now say, so far as his part is concerned: *The truth of the gospel abides with you.*

CHAPTER VIII
PAUL AND THE THREE PILLARS

"But from those who were reputed to be somewhat (what they once were, it maketh no matter to me: God accepteth not man's person)—they, I say, who were of repute imparted nothing to me: but contrariwise, when they saw that I had been intrusted with the gospel of the uncircumcision, even as Peter with *the gospel* of the circumcision (for he that wrought for Peter unto the apostleship of the circumcision wrought for me also unto the Gentiles); and when they perceived the grace that was given unto me, James and Cephas and John, they who were reputed to be pillars, gave to me and Barnabas the right hands of fellowship, that we should go unto the Gentiles, and they unto the circumcision; only *they would* that we should remember the poor; which very thing I was also zealous to do."—Gal. ii. 6-10.

We have dealt by anticipation, in Chapter VI., with several of the topics raised in this section of the Epistle—touching particularly the import of the phrase "those of repute," and the tone of disparagement in which these dignitaries appear to be spoken of in ver. 6. But there still remains in these verses matter in its weight and difficulty more than sufficient to occupy another Chapter.

The grammatical connection of the first paragraph, like that of vv. 2, 3, is involved and disputable. We construe its clauses in the following way:— (1) Ver. 6 begins with a *But*, contrasting "those of repute" with the "false brethren" dealt with in the last sentence. It contains another *anacoluthon* (or incoherence of language), due to the surge of feeling remarked in ver. 4, which still disturbs the Apostle's grammar. He begins: "But from those reputed to be something"—as though he intended to say, "I received on my part nothing, no addition or qualification to my gospel." But he has no sooner mentioned "those of repute" than he is reminded of the studied attempt that was made to set up their authority in opposition to his own, and accordingly throws in this protest: "what they were aforetime,[40] makes no difference to me: man's person God doth not accept." But in saying this,

Paul has laid down one of his favourite axioms, a principle that filled a large place in his thoughts;[41] and its enunciation deflects the course of the main sentence, so that it is resumed in an altered form: "For to me those of repute imparted nothing." Here the *me* receives a greater emphasis; and *for* takes the place of *but*. The fact that the first Apostles had nothing to impart to Paul, signally illustrates the Divine impartiality, which often makes the last and least in human eyes equal to the first.

(2) Vv. 7-9 state the *positive*, as ver. 6 the *negative* side of the relation between Paul and the elder Apostles, still keeping in view the principle laid down in the former verse. "Nay, on the contrary, when they saw that I have in charge the gospel of the uncircumcision, as Peter that of the circumcision (ver. 7)—and when they perceived the grace that had been given me, James and Cephas and John, those renowned pillars of the Church, gave the right hand of fellowship to myself and Barnabas, agreeing that we should go to the Gentiles, while they laboured amongst the Jews" (ver. 9).

(3) Ver. 8 comes in as a parenthesis, explaining how the authorities at Jerusalem came to see that this trust belonged to Paul. "For," he says, "He that in Peter's case displayed His power in making him (above all others) Apostle of the Circumcision, did as much for me in regard to the Gentiles." It is not human ordination, but Divine inspiration that makes a minister of Jesus Christ. The noble Apostles of Jesus had the wisdom to see this. It had pleased God to bestow this grace on their old Tarsian persecutor; and they frankly acknowledged the fact.

Thus Paul sets forth, in the first place, *the completeness of his Apostolic qualifications*, put to proof at the crisis of the circumcision controversy; and in the second place, *the judgement formed respecting him and his office by the first Apostles and companions of the Lord*.

I. "To me those of repute added nothing." Paul had spent but a fortnight in the Christian circle of Jerusalem, fourteen years ago. Of its chiefs he had met at that time only Peter and James, and them in the capacity of a visitor, not as a disciple or a candidate for office. He had never sought the opportunity, nor felt the need, of receiving instruction from the elder Apostles during all the years in which he had preached Christ amongst the heathen. It was not likely he would do so now. When he came into conference and debate with them at the Council, he showed himself their equal, neither in knowledge nor authority "a whit behind the very chiefest." And they were conscious of the same fact.

On the essentials of the gospel Paul found himself in agreement with the Twelve. This is implied in the language of ver. 6. When one writes, "A adds nothing to B," one assumes that B has already what belongs to A, and not something different. Paul asserts in the most positive terms he can command, that his intercourse with the holders of the primitive Christian tradition left him as a minister of Christ exactly where he was before. "On me," he says, "they conferred nothing"—rather, perhaps, "*addressed no communication to me.*" The word used appears to deny their having made any motion of the kind. The Greek verb is the same that was employed in ch. i. 16, a rare and delicate compound.[42] Its meaning varies, like that of our *confer, communicate,* as it is applied in a more or less active sense. In the former place Paul had said that he "did not confer with flesh and blood"; now he adds, that flesh and blood did not confer anything upon him. Formerly he did not bring his commission to lay it before men; now they had nothing to bring on their part to lay before him. The same word affirms the Apostle's independence at both epochs, shown in the first instance by his reserve toward the dignitaries at Jerusalem, and in the second by their reserve toward him. Conscious of his Divine call, he sought no patronage from the elder Apostles then; and they, recognising that call, offered him no such patronage now. Paul's gospel for the Gentiles was complete, and sufficient unto itself. His ministry showed no defect in quality or competence. There was nothing about it that laid it open to correction, even on the part of those wisest and highest in dignity amongst the personal followers of Jesus.

So Paul declares; and we can readily believe him. Nay, we are tempted to think that it was rather the Pillars who might need to learn from him, than he from them. In doctrine, Paul holds the primacy in the band of the Apostles. While all were inspired by the Spirit of Christ, the Gentile Apostle was in many ways a more richly furnished man than any of the rest. The Paulinism of Peter's First Epistle goes to show that the debt was on the other side. Their earlier privileges and priceless store of recollections of "all that Jesus did and taught," were matched on Paul's side by a penetrating logic, a breadth and force of intellect applied to the facts of revelation, and a burning intensity of spirit, which in their combination were unique. The Pauline teaching, as it appears in the New Testament, bears in the highest degree the marks of original genius, the stamp of a mind whose inspiration is its own.

Modern criticism even exaggerates Paul's originality. It leaves the other Apostles little more than a negative part to play in the development of Christian truth. In some of its representations, the figure of Paul appears to overshadow even that of the Divine Master. It was Paul's creative genius, it is said, his daring idealism, that deified the human Jesus, and transformed the scandal of the cross into the glory of an atonement reconciling the world to God. Such theories Paul himself would have regarded with horror. "I received *of the Lord* that which I delivered unto you:" such is his uniform testimony. If he owed so little as a minister of Christ to his brother Apostles, he felt with the most sincere humility that he owed everything to Christ. The agreement of Paul's teaching with that of the other New Testament writers, and especially with that of Jesus in the Gospels, proves that, however distinct and individual his conception of the common gospel, none the less there was a common gospel of Christ, and he did not speak of his own mind. The attempts made to get rid of this agreement by postdating the New Testament documents, and by explaining away the larger utterances of Jesus found in the Gospels as due to Paulinist interpolation, are unavailing. They postulate a craftiness of ingenuity on the part of the writers of the incriminated books, and an ignorance in those who first received them, alike inconceivable. Paul did not build up the splendid and imperishable fabric of his theology on some speculation of his own. Its foundation lies in the person and the teaching of Jesus Christ, and was common to Paul with James and Cephas and John. "Whether I or they," he testifies, "so we preach, and so ye believed" (1 Cor. xv. 11). Paul satisfied himself at this conference that he and the Twelve taught the same gospel. Not in its primary data, but in their logical development and application, lies the specifically *Pauline* in Paulinism. The harmony between Paul and the other Apostolic leaders has the peculiar value which belongs to the agreement of minds of different orders, working independently.

The Judaizers, however, persistently asserted Paul's dependence on the elder Apostles. "The authority of the Primitive Church, the Apostolic tradition of Jerusalem"—this was the fulcrum of their argument. Where could Paul, they asked, have derived his knowledge of Christ, but from this fountain-head? And the power that made him, could unmake him. Those who commissioned him had the right to overrule him, or even to revoke his commission. Was it not known that he had from time to time resorted to Jerusalem; that he had once publicly submitted his teaching to the examination of the heads of the Church there? The words of ver. 6 contradict these malicious insinuations. Hence the positiveness of the Apostle's self-assertion. In the Corinthian Epistles his claim to independence is made in gentler style, and with expressions of humility that might have been misunderstood here. But the position Paul takes up is the same in either case: "I am an Apostle. I have seen Jesus our Lord. You—Corinthians, Galatians—are my work in the Lord." That Peter and the rest were in the old days so near to the Master, "makes no difference" to Paul. They are what they are—their high standing is universally acknowledged, and Paul has no need or wish to question it; but, by the grace of God, *he* also is what he is (1 Cor. xv. 10). Their Apostleship does not exclude or derogate from his.

The self-depreciation, the keen sense of inferiority in outward respects, so evident in Paul's allusions to this subject elsewhere, is after all not wanting here. For when he says, "God regards not *man's person*," it is evident that in respect of visible qualifications Paul felt that he had few pretensions to make. Appearances were against him. And those who "glory in appearance" were against him too (2 Cor. v. 12). Such men could not appreciate the might of the Spirit that wrought in Paul, nor the sovereignty of Divine election. They "reckoned" of the Apostle "as though he walked according to flesh" (2 Cor. x. 2). It seemed to them obvious, as a matter of course, that he was far below the Twelve. With men of worldly wisdom the Apostle did not expect that his arguments would prevail. His appeal was to "the spiritual, who judge all things."

So we come back to the declaration of the Apostle in ch. i. 11: "I give you to know, brethren, that my gospel is not according to man." Man had no hand either in laying its foundation or putting on the headstone. Paul's predecessors in Apostolic office did not impart the gospel to him at the outset; nor at a later time had they attempted to make any addition to the doctrine he had taught far and wide amongst the heathen. His Apostleship was from first to last a supernatural gift of grace.

II. Instead, therefore, of assuming to be his superiors, or offering to bestow something of their own on Paul, *the three renowned pillars of the faith at Jerusalem acknowledged him as a brother Apostle.*

"They saw that I am intrusted with the gospel of the uncircumcision." The form of the verb implies a trust given in the past and taking effect in the present, a settled fact. Once for all, this charge had devolved on Paul. He is "appointed herald and apostle" of "Christ Jesus, who gave Himself a ransom for all,—teacher of the Gentiles in faith and truth" (1 Tim. ii. 6, 7). That office Paul still holds. He is the leader of Christian evangelism. Every new movement in heathen missionary enterprise looks to his teaching for guidance and inspiration.

The conference at Jerusalem in itself furnished conclusive evidence of Paul's Apostolic commission. The circumcision controversy was a test not only for Gentile Christianity, but at the same time for its Apostle and champion. Paul brought to this discussion a knowledge and insight, a force of character, a conscious authority and unction of the Holy Spirit, that powerfully impressed the three great men who listened to him. The triumvirate at Jerusalem well knew that Paul had not received his marvellous gifts through their hands. Nor was there anything lacking to him which they felt themselves called upon to supply. They could only say, "This is the Lord's doing; and it is marvellous in our eyes." Knowing, as Peter at least, we presume, had done for many years,[43] the history of Paul's conversion, and seeing as they now did the conspicuous Apostolic signs attending his ministry, James and Cephas and John could only come to one conclusion. The gospel of the uncircumcision, they were convinced, was committed to Paul, and his place in the Church was side by side with Peter. Peter must have felt as once before on a like occasion: "If God gave unto him a gift equal to that He gave to me, who am I, that I should be able to hinder God?" (Acts xi. 17). It was not for them because of their elder rank and dignity to debate with God in this matter, and to withhold their recognition from His "chosen vessel."

John had not forgotten his Master's reproof for banning the man that "followeth not with us" (Luke ix. 49; Mark ix. 38). They "recognised," Paul says, "the grace that had been given me;" and by that he means, to be sure, the undeserved favour that raised him to his Apostolic office.[44] This recognition was given to *Paul*. Barnabas shared the "fellowship." His hand was clasped by the three chiefs at Jerusalem, not less warmly than that of his younger comrade. But it is in the singular number that Paul speaks of "the grace that was given *me*," and of the "trust in the gospel" and the "working of God *unto Apostleship*."

Why then does not Paul say outright, "they acknowledged me an Apostle, the equal of Peter?" Some are bold enough to say—*Holsten* in particular—"Because this is just what the Jerusalem chiefs never did, and never could have done."[45] We will only reply, that if this were the case, the passage is a continued *suggestio falsi*. No one could write the words of vv. 7-9, without intending his readers to believe that such a recognition took place. Paul avoids the point-blank assertion, with a delicacy that any man of tolerable modesty will understand. Even the appearance of "glorying" was hateful to him (2 Cor. x. 17; xi. 1; xii. 1-5, 11).

The Church at Jerusalem, as we gather from vv. 7, 8, observed in Paul "signs of the Apostle" resembling those borne by Peter. His Gentile commission ran parallel with Peter's Jewish commission. The labours of the two men were followed by the same kind of success, and marked by similar displays of miraculous power. The like seal of God was stamped on both. This correspondence runs through the Acts of the Apostles. Compare, for example, Paul's sermon at Antioch in Pisidia with that of Peter on the Day of Pentecost; the healing of the Lystran cripple and the punishment of Elymas, with the case of the lame man at the Temple gate and the encounter of Peter and Simon Magus. The conjunction of the names of Peter and Paul was familiar to the Apostolic Church. The parallelism between the course of these great Apostles was no invention of second-century orthodoxy, set up in the interests of a "reconciling hypothesis;" it attracted public attention as early as 51 A.D., while they were still in their mid career. If this idea so strongly possessed the minds of the Jewish Christian leaders and influenced their action at the Council of Jerusalem, we need not be surprised that it should dominate Luke's narrative to the extent that it does. The allusions to Peter in 1 Corinthians[46] afford further proof that in the lifetime of the two Apostles it was a common thing to link their names together.

But had not Peter also a share in the Gentile mission? Does not the division of labour made at this conference appear to shut out the senior Apostle from a field to which he had the prior claim? "Ye know," said Peter at the Council, "how that a good while ago God made choice among you, that by my mouth the Gentiles should hear the word of the gospel, and believe" (Acts xv. 7). To Peter was assigned the double honour of "opening the door of faith" both to Jew and Gentile. This experience made him the readier to understand Paul's position, and gave him the greater weight in the settlement of the question at issue. And not Peter alone, but Philip the evangelist and other Jewish Christians had carried the gospel across the line of Judaic prejudice, before Paul appeared on the scene. Barnabas and Silas were both emissaries of Jerusalem. So that the mother Church, if she could not claim Paul as her son, had nevertheless a large stake in the heathen mission. But when Paul came to the front, when his miraculous call, his incomparable gifts and wonderful success had made themselves known, it was evident to every discerning mind that he was the man chosen by God to direct this great work. Peter had *opened* the door of faith to the heathen, and had bravely kept it open; but it was for Paul to lead the Gentile nations through the open door, and to make a home for them within the fold of Christ. The men who had laboured in this field hitherto were Paul's forerunners. And Peter does not hesitate to acknowledge the younger Apostle's special fitness for this wider province of their common work; and with the concurrence of James and John he yields the charge of it to him.

Let us observe that it is two different *provinces*, not different gospels, that are in view. When the Apostle speaks of "the gospel of the uncircumcision" as committed to himself, and that "of the circumcision" to Peter, he never dreams of any one supposing, as some of his modern critics persist in doing, that he meant two different *doctrines*. How can that be possible, when he has declared those *anathema* who preach any other gospel? He has laid his gospel before the heads of the Jerusalem Church. Nothing has occurred there, nothing is hinted here, to suggest the existence of a "radical divergence." If James and the body of the Judean Church really sympathised with the Circumcisionists, with those whom the Apostle calls "false brethren," how could he with any sincerity have come to an agreement with them, knowing that this tremendous gulf was lying all the while between the

Pillars and himself? Zeller argues that the transaction was simply a pledge of "reciprocal toleration, a merely external concordat between Paul and the original Apostles."[47] The clasp of brotherly friendship was a sorry farce, if that were all it meant—if Paul and the Three just consented for the time to slur over irreconcilable differences; while Paul in turn has glossed over the affair for us in these artful verses! Baur, with characteristic *finesse*, says on the same point: "The κοινωνία was always a division; it could only be brought into effect by one party going εἰς τὰ ἔθνη, the other εἰς τὴν περιτομήν. As the Jewish Apostles could allege nothing against the principles on which Paul founded his evangelical mission, they were obliged to recognise them in a certain manner; but their recognition was a mere outward one. They left him to work on these principles still further in the cause of the gospel among the Gentiles; but for themselves they did not desire to know anything more about them."[48] So that, according to the Tübingen critics, we witness in ver. 9 not a union, but a divorce! The Jewish Apostles recognise Paul as a brother, only in order to get rid of him. Can misinterpretation be more unjust than this? Paul does not say, "They gave us the right hand of fellowship *on condition that,*" but, "*in order that* we should go this way, they that." As much as to say: The two parties came together and entered into a closer union, so that with the best mutual understanding each might go its own way and pursue its proper work in harmony with the other. For Paul it would have been a sacrilege to speak of the diplomatic compromise which Baur and Zeller describe as "giving the right hand of fellowship."

Never did the Church more deeply realise than at her first Council the truth, that "there is one body and one Spirit; one Lord, one faith, one baptism; one God and Father of all, who is above all, and through all, and in all" (Eph. iv. 4-6). Paul still seems to feel his hand in the warm grasp of Peter and of John when he writes to the Ephesians of "the foundation of the Apostles and prophets, with Christ Jesus Himself for chief corner-stone; in whom the whole building fitly framed together, groweth unto an holy temple in the Lord" (ch. ii. 20, 21). Alas for the criticism that is obliged to see in words like these the invention of second-century churchmanship, putting into the mouth of Paul catholic sentiments of which in reality he knew nothing! Such writers know nothing of the power of that fellowship of the Spirit which reigned in the glorious company of the Apostles.

"Only they would have us remember the poor"—a circumstance mentioned partly by way of reminder to the Galatians touching the collection for Jerusalem, which Paul had already set on foot amongst them (1 Cor. xvi. 1). The request was prompted by the affectionate confidence with which the Jewish chiefs embraced Paul and Barnabas. It awakened an eager response in the Apostle's breast. His love to his Jewish kindred made him welcome the suggestion. Moreover every deed of charity rendered by the wealthier Gentile Churches to "the poor saints in Jerusalem," was another tie helping to bind the two communities to each other. Of such liberality Antioch, under the direction of the Gentile missionaries, had already set the example (Acts xi. 29, 30).

James, Peter, John, and *Paul*—it was a memorable day when these four men met face to face. What a mighty quaternion! Amongst them they have virtually made the New Testament and the Christian Church. They represent the four sides of the one foundation of the City of God. Of the Evangelists, Matthew holds affinity with James; Mark with Peter; and Luke with Paul. James clings to the past and embodies the transition from Mosaism to Christianity. Peter is the man of the present, quick in thought and action, eager, buoyant, susceptible. Paul holds the future in his grasp, and schools the unborn nations. John gathers present, past, and future into one, lifting us into the region of eternal life and love.

With Peter and James Paul had met before, and was to meet again. But so far as we can learn, this was the only occasion on which his path crossed that of *John.* Nor is this Apostle mentioned again in Paul's letters. In the Acts he appears but once or twice, standing silent in Peter's shadow. A holy reserve surrounds John's person in the earlier Apostolic history. His hour was not yet come. But his name ranked in public estimation amongst the three foremost of the Jewish Church; and he exercised, doubtless, a powerful, though quiet, conciliatory influence in the settlement of the Gentile question. The personality of Paul excited, we may be sure, the profoundest interest in such a mind as that of John. He absorbed, and yet in a sense transcended, the Pauline theology. The Apocalypse, although the most Judaic book of the New Testament, is penetrated with the influence of Paulinism. The detection in it of a covert attack on the Gentile Apostle is simply one of the mare's nests of a super-subtle and suspicious criticism. John was to be the heir of Paul's labours at Ephesus and in Asia Minor. And John's long life, touching the verge of the second century, his catholic position, his serene and lofty spirit, blending in itself and resolving into a higher unity the tendencies of James and Peter and Paul, give us the best assurance that in the Apostolic age there was indeed "One, holy, catholic, Apostolic Church."

Paul's fellowship with Peter and with James was cordial and endeared. But to hold the hand of John, "the disciple whom Jesus loved," was a yet higher satisfaction. That clasp symbolized a union between men most opposite in temperament and training, and brought to the knowledge of Christ in very different ways, but whose communion in Him was deep as the life eternal. Paul and John are the two master minds of the New Testament. Of all men that ever lived, these two best understood Jesus Christ.

CHAPTER IX
PAUL AND PETER AT ANTIOCH

"But when Cephas came to Antioch, I resisted him to the face, because he stood condemned. For before that certain came from James, he did eat with the Gentiles; but when they came, he drew back and separated himself, fearing them that were of the circumcision. And the rest of the Jews dissembled likewise with him; insomuch that even Barnabas was carried away with their dissimulation. But when I saw that they walked not uprightly according to the truth of the gospel, I said unto Cephas before *them* all, If thou, being a Jew, livest as do the Gentiles, and not as do the Jews, how compellest thou the Gentiles to live as do the Jews? We being Jews by nature, and not sinners of the Gentiles, yet knowing that a man is not justified by works of law, but only through faith in Jesus Christ, even we believed on Christ Jesus, that we might be justified by faith in Christ, and not by the works of the law: because by the works of the law shall no flesh be justified. But if, while we sought to be justified in Christ, we ourselves also were found sinners, is Christ a minister of sin? God forbid. For if I build up again those things which I destroyed, I prove myself a transgressor."—Gal. ii. 11-18.

The conference at Jerusalem issued in the formal recognition by the Primitive Church of Gentile Christianity, and of Paul's plenary Apostleship. And it brought Paul into brotherly relations with the three great leaders of Jewish Christianity. But this fellowship was not to continue undisturbed. The same cause was still at work which had compelled the Apostle to go up to Jerusalem, taking Titus with him. The leaven of Pharisaic legalism remained in the Church. Indeed, as time went on and the national fanaticism grew more violent, this spirit of intolerance became increasingly bitter and active. The address of James to Paul on the occasion of his last visit to the Holy City, shows that the Church of Jerusalem was at this time in a state of the most sensitive jealousy in regard to the Law, and that the legalistic prejudices always existing in it had gained a strength with which it was difficult to cope (Acts xxi. 17-25).

But for the present the Judaizing faction had received a check. It does not appear that the party ever again insisted on circumcision as a thing essential to salvation for the Gentiles. The utterances of Peter and James at the Council, and the circular addressed therefrom to the Gentile Churches, rendered this impossible. The Legalists made a change of front; and adopted a subtler and seemingly more moderate policy. *They now preached circumcision as the prerogative of the Jew within the Church, and as a counsel of perfection for the Gentile believer in Christ* (ch. iii. 3). To quote the rescript of Acts xv. against this altered form of the circumcisionist doctrine, would have been wide of the mark.

It is against this newer type of Judaistic teaching that our Epistle is directed.[49] Circumcision, its advocates argued, was a Divine ordinance that must have its benefit. God has given to Israel an indefeasible pre-eminence in His kingdom.[50] Law-keeping children of Abraham enter the new Covenant on a higher footing than "sinners of the Gentiles:" they are still the elect race, the holy nation. If the Gentiles wish to share with them, they must add to their faith circumcision, they must complete their imperfect righteousness by legal sanctity. So they might hope to enter on the full heritage of the sons of Abraham; they would be brought into communion with the first Apostles and the Brother of the Lord; they would be admitted to the inner circle of the kingdom of God. The new Legalists sought, in fact, to superimpose Jewish on Gentile Christianity. They no longer refused all share in Christ to the uncircumcised; they offered them a larger share. So we construe the teaching which Paul had to combat in the second stage of his conflict with Judaism, to which his four major Epistles belong. And the signal for this renewed struggle was given by the collision with Peter at Antioch.

This encounter did not, we think, take place on the return of Paul and Barnabas from the Council. The compact of Jerusalem secured to the Church a few years of rest from the Judaistic agitation. The Thessalonian Epistles, written in 52 or 53 A.D., go to show, not only that the Churches of Macedonia were free from the legalist contention, but that it did not at this period occupy the Apostle's mind. Judas Barsabbas and Silas—not Peter—accompanied the Gentile missionaries in returning to Antioch; and Luke gives, in Acts xv., a tolerably full account of the circumstances which transpired there in the interval before the second missionary tour, without the slightest hint of any visit made at this time by the Apostle Peter. We can scarcely believe that the circumcision party had already recovered, and increased its influence, to the degree that it must have done when "even Barnabas was carried away"; still less that Peter on the very morrow of the settlement at Jerusalem and of his fraternal communion there with Paul would show himself so far estranged.

When, therefore, did "Cephas come down to Antioch?" The Galatians evidently knew. The Judaizers had given their account of the matter, to Paul's disadvantage. Perhaps he had referred to it himself on his last visit to Galatia, when we know he spoke explicitly and strongly against the Circumcisionists (ch. i. 9). Just before his arrival in Galatia on this occasion he had "spent some time" at Antioch (Acts xviii. 22, 23), in the interval between the second and third missionary journeys. Luke simply mentions the fact, without giving any details. This is the likeliest opportunity for the meeting of the two Apostles in the Gentile capital. M. Sabatier,[51] in the following sentences, appears to us to put the course of events in its true light:—"Evidently the Apostle had quitted Jerusalem and undertaken his second missionary journey full of satisfaction at the victory he had gained, and free from anxiety for the future. The decisive moment of the crisis therefore necessarily falls between the Thessalonian and Galatian Epistles. What had happened in the meantime? *The violent discussion with Peter at Antioch* (Gal. ii. 11-21), and all that this account reveals to us,—the arrival of the emissaries from James in the pagan-Christian circle, the counter-mission organized by the Judaizers to rectify the work of Paul. A new situation suddenly presents itself to the eyes of the Apostle on his return from his second missionary journey. He is compelled to throw himself into the struggle, and in doing so to formulate in all its rigour his principle of the abolishment of the Law."

The "troublers" in this instance were "certain from James." Like the "false brethren"[52] who appeared at Antioch three years before, they came from the mother Church, over which James presided. The Judaizing teachers at Corinth had their "commendatory letters" (2 Cor. iii. 1), derived assuredly from the same quarter. In all likelihood, their confederates in Galatia brought similar credentials. We have already seen that the authority of the Primitive Church was the chief weapon used by Paul's adversaries. These letters of commendation were part of the machinery of the anti-Pauline agitation. How the Judaizers obtained these credentials, and in what precise relation they stood to James, we can only conjecture. Had the Apostle held James responsible for their action, he would not have spared him any more than he has done Peter. James held a quasi-pastoral relation to Christian Jews of the Dispersion. And as he addressed his Epistle to them, so he would be likely on occasion to send delegates to visit them. Perhaps the Circumcisionists found opportunity to pass themselves off in this character; or they may have abused a commission really given them, by interfering with Gentile communities. That the Judaistic emissaries in some way or other adopted false colours, is plainly intimated in 2 Cor. xi. 13. James, living always at Jerusalem, being moreover a man of simple character, could have little suspected the crafty plot which was carried forward under his name.

These agents addressed themselves in the first instance to *the Jews*, as their commission from Jerusalem probably entitled them to do. They plead for the maintenance of the sacred customs. They insist that the Mosaic rites carry with them an indelible sanctity; that their observance constitutes a Church within the Church. If this separation is once established, and the Jewish believers in Christ can be induced to hold themselves aloof and to maintain the "advantage of circumcision," the rest will be easy. The way will then be open to "compel the Gentiles to Judaize." For unless they do this, they must be content to remain on a lower level, in a comparatively menial position, resembling that of uncircumcised proselytes in the Synagogue. The circular of the Jerusalem Council may have been interpreted by the Judaists in this sense, as though it laid down the terms, not of full communion between Jew and Gentile believers, but only of a permissive, secondary recognition. At Antioch the new campaign of the Legalists was opened, and apparently with signal success. In Galatia and Corinth we see it in full progress.

The withdrawal of Peter and the other Jews at Antioch from the table of the Gentiles virtually "compelled" the latter "to Judaize." Not that the Jewish Apostle had this intention in his mind. He was made the tool of designing men. By "separating himself" he virtually said to every uncircumcised brother, "Stand by thyself, I am holier than thou." Legal conformity on the part of the Gentiles was made the condition of their communion with Jewish Christians—a demand simply fatal to Christianity. It re-established the principle of salvation by works in a more invidious form. To supplement the righteousness of faith by that of law, meant to *supplant* it. To admit that the Israelite by virtue of his legal observances stood in a higher position than "sinners of the Gentiles," was to stultify the doctrine of the cross, to make Christ's death a gratuitous sacrifice. Peter's error, pushed to its logical consequences, involved the overthrow of the Gospel. This the Gentile Apostle saw at a glance. The situation was one of imminent danger. Paul needed all his wisdom, and all his courage and promptitude to meet it.

It had been Peter's previous rule, since the vision of Joppa, to lay aside Jewish scruples of diet and to live in free intercourse with Gentile brethren. He "was wont to eat with the Gentiles. Though a born Jew, he lived in Gentile fashion"—words unmistakably describing Peter's general habit in such circumstances. This Gentile conformity of Peter was a fact of no small moment for the Galatian readers. It contravenes the assertion of a radical divergence between Petrine and Pauline Christianity, whether made by Ebionites or Baurians.

The Jewish Apostle's present conduct was an act of "dissimulation." He was belying his known convictions, publicly expressed and acted on for years. Paul's challenge assumes that his fellow-Apostle is acting insincerely.

And this assumption is explained by the account furnished in the Acts of the Apostles respecting Peter's earlier relations with Gentile Christianity (ch. x. 1-xi. 18; xv. 6-11). The strength of Paul's case lay in the conscience of Peter himself. The conflict at Antioch, so often appealed to in proof of the rooted opposition between the two Apostles, in reality gives evidence to the contrary effect. Here the maxim strictly applies, *Exceptio probat regulam.*

Peter's lapse is quite intelligible. No man who figures in the New Testament is better known to us. Honest, impulsive, ready of speech, full of contagious enthusiasm, brave as a lion, firm as a rock against open enemies, he possessed in a high degree the qualities which mark out a leader of men. He was of the stuff of which Christ makes His missionary heroes. But there was a strain of weakness in Peter's nature. He was *pliable.* He was too much at the mercy of surroundings. His denial of Jesus set this native fault in a light terribly vivid and humiliating. It was an act of "dissimulation." In his soul there was a fervent love to Christ. His zeal had brought him to the place of danger. But for the moment he was alone. Public opinion was all against him. A panic fear seized his brave heart. He forgot himself; he denied the Master whom he loved more than life. His courage had failed; never his faith. "Turned back again" from his coward flight, Peter had indeed "strengthened his brethren" (Luke xxii. 31, 32). He proved a tower of strength to the infant Church, worthy of his cognomen of the *rock.* For more than twenty years he had stood unshaken. No name was so honoured in the Church as Peter's. For Paul to be compared to him was the highest possible distinction.

And yet, after all this lapse of time, and in the midst of so glorious a career, the old, miserable weakness betrays him once more. How admonitory is the lesson! The sore long since healed over, the infirmity of nature out of which we seemed to have been completely trained, may yet break out again, to our shame and undoing. Had Peter for a moment forgotten the sorrowful warning of Gethsemane? Be it ours to "watch and pray, lest we enter into temptation."

We have reason to believe that, if Peter rashly erred, he freely acknowledged his error, and honoured his reprover. Both the Epistles that bear his name, in different ways, testify to the high value which their author set upon the teaching of "our beloved brother Paul." Tradition places the two men at Rome side by side in their last days; as though even in their death these glorious Apostles should not be divided, despite the attempts of faction and mistrust to separate them.

Few incidents exhibit more strongly than this the grievous consequences that may ensue from a seemingly trivial moral error. It looked a little thing that Peter should prefer to take his meals away from Gentile company. And yet, as Paul tells him, his withdrawal was a virtual rejection of the Gospel, and imperilled the most vital interests of Christianity. By this act the Jewish Apostle gave a handle to the adversaries of the Church which they have used for generations and for ages afterwards. The dispute which it occassioned could never be forgotten. In the second century it still drew down on Paul the bitter reproaches of the Judaizing faction. And in our own day the rationalistic critics have been able to turn it to marvellous account. It supplies the corner-stone of their "scientific reconstruction" of Biblical theology. The entire theory of Baur is evolved out of Peter's blunder. Let it be granted that Peter in yielding to the "certain from James" followed his genuine convictions and the tradition of Jewish Christianity, and we see at once how deep a gulf lay between Paul and the Primitive Church. All that Paul argues in the subsequent discussion only tends, in this case, to make the breach more visible. This false step of Peter is the thing that chiefly lends a colour to the theory in question, with all the far-reaching consequences touching the origin and import of Christianity, which it involves. So long "the evil that men do lives after them"!

Paul's rebuke of his brother Apostle extends to the conclusion of the chapter. Some interpreters cut it short at the end of ver. 14; others at ver. 16; others again at ver. 18. But the address is consecutive and germane to the occasion throughout. Paul does not, to be sure, give a verbatim report, but the substance of what he said, and in a form suited to his readers. The narrative is an admirable prelude to the argument of chap. iii. It forms the transition from the historical to the polemical part of the Epistle, from the Apostle's personal to his doctrinal apology. The condensed form of the speech makes its interpretation difficult and much contested. We shall in the remainder of this Chapter trace the general course of Paul's reproof, proposing in the following Chapter to deal more fully with its doctrinal contents.

I. In the first place, *Paul taxes the Jewish Apostle with insincerity and unfaithfulness toward the gospel*. "I saw," he says, "that they were not holding a straight course, according to the truth of the gospel."

It is a *moral*, not a doctrinal aberration, that Paul lays at the door of Cephas and Barnabas. They did not hold a different creed from himself; they were disloyal to the common creed. They swerved from the path of rectitude in which they had walked hitherto. They had regard no longer to "the truth of the gospel" — the supreme consideration of the servant of Christ — but to the favour of men, to the public opinion of Jerusalem. "What will be said of us *there*?" they whispered to each other, "if these messengers of James report that we are discarding the sacred customs, and making no difference between Jew and Gentile? We shall alienate our Judean brethren. We shall bring a scandal on the Christian cause in the eyes of Judaism."

This withdrawal of the Jews from the common fellowship at Antioch was a public matter. It was an injury to the whole Gentile-Christian community. If the reproof was to be salutary, it must be equally public and explicit. The offence was notorious. Every one deplored it, except those who shared it, or profited by it. Cephas "stood condemned." And yet his influence and the reverence felt toward him were so great, that no one dared to put this condemnation into words. His sanction was of itself enough to give to this sudden recrudescence of Jewish bigotry the force of authoritative usage. "The truth of the gospel" was again in jeopardy. Once more Paul's intervention foiled the attempts of the Judaizers and saved Gentile liberties. And this time he stood quite alone. Even the faithful Barnabas deserted him. But what mattered that, if Christ and truth were on his side? *Amicus Cephas, amicus Barnabas; sed magis amicus Veritas.* Solitary amid the circle of opposing or dissembling Jews, Paul "withstood" the chief of the Apostles of Jesus "to the face." He rebuked him "before them all."

II. Peter's conduct is reproved by Paul *in the light of their common knowledge of salvation in Christ.*

Paul is not content with pointing out the inconsistency of his brother Apostle. He must probe the matter to the bottom. He will bring Peter's delinquency to the touchstone of the Gospel, in its fundamental principles. So he passes in ver. 15 from the outward to the inward, from the circumstances of Peter's conduct to the inner world of spiritual consciousness, in which his offence finds its deeper condemnation. "You and I," he goes on to say, "not Gentile sinners, but men of Jewish birth—yet for all that, knowing that there is no justification for man in works of law, only[53] through faith in Christ—we too put our faith in Christ, in order to be justified by faith in Him, not by works of law; for as Scripture taught us, in that way no flesh will be justified."

Paul makes no doubt that the Jewish Apostle's experience of salvation corresponded with his own. Doubtless, in their previous intercourse, and especially when he first "made acquaintance with Cephas" (ch. i. 18) in Jerusalem, the hearts of the two men had been opened to each other; and they had found that, although brought to the knowledge of the truth in different ways, yet in the essence of the matter—in respect of the personal conviction of sin, in the yielding up of self-righteousness and native pride, in the abandonment of every prop and trust but Jesus Christ—their history had run the same course, and face answered to face. Yes, Paul knew that he had an ally in the heart of his friend. He was not fighting as one that beateth the air, not making a rhetorical flourish, or a parade of some favourite doctrine of his own; he appealed from Peter dissembling to Peter faithful and consistent. Peter's dissimulation was a return to the Judaic ground of legal righteousness. By refusing to eat with uncircumcised men, he affirmed implicitly that, though believers in Christ, they were still to him "common and unclean," that the Mosaic rites imparted a higher sanctity than the righteousness of faith. Now the principles of evangelical and legal righteousness, of salvation by faith and by law-works, are diametrically opposed. It is logically impossible to maintain both. Peter had long ago accepted the former doctrine. He had sought salvation, just like any Gentile sinner, on the common ground of human guilt, and with a faith that renounced every consideration of Jewish privilege and legal performance. By what right can any Hebrew believer in Christ, after this, set himself above his Gentile brother, or presume to be by virtue of his circumcision and ritual law-keeping a holier man? Such we take to be the import of Paul's challenge in vv. 15, 16.

III. Paul is met at this point by the stock objection to the doctrine of salvation by faith—an objection brought forward in the dispute at Antioch not, we should imagine, by Peter himself, but by the Judaistic advocates. *To renounce legal righteousness was in effect*, they urged, *to promote sin—nay, to make Christ Himself a minister of sin* (ver. 17).

Paul retorts the charge on those who make it. *They promote sin*, he declares, *who set up legal righteousness again* (ver. 18). The objection is stated and met in the form of question and answer, as in Rom. iii. 5. We have in this sharp thrust and parry an example of the sort of fence which Paul must often have carried on in his discussions with Jewish opponents on these questions.

We must not overlook the close verbal connection of these verses with the two last. The phrase "seeking to be justified in Christ" carries us back to the time when the two Apostles, self-condemned sinners, severally sought and found a new ground of righteousness in Him. Now when Peter and Paul did this, they were "themselves also found[54] to be sinners,"— an experience how abasing to their Jewish pride! They made the great discovery that stripped them of legal merit, and brought them down in their own esteem to the level of common sinners. Peter's confession may stand for both, when he said, abashed by the glory of Christ, "Depart from me, for I am a sinful man, O Lord." Now this style of penitence, this profound self-abasement in the presence of Jesus Christ, revolted the Jewish moralist. To Pharisaic sentiment it was contemptible. If justification by faith requires this, if it brings the Jew to so abject a posture and makes no difference between lawless and law-keeping, between pious children of Abraham and heathen outcasts—if this be the doctrine of Christ, all moral distinctions are confounded, and Christ is "a minister of sin!" This teaching robs the Jew of the righteousness he before possessed; it takes from him the benefit and honour that God bestowed upon his race! So, we doubt not, many a Jew was heard angrily exclaiming against the Pauline doctrine, both at Antioch and elsewhere. This conclusion was, in the view of the Legalist, a *reductio ad absurdum* of Paulinism.

The Apostle repels this inference with the indignant μὴ γένοιτο, *Far be it!* His reply is indicated by the very form in which he puts the question: "If we were *found* sinners" (Christ did not *make* us such). "The complaint was this," as Calvin finely says: "Has Christ therefore come to take away from us the righteousness of the Law, to make us polluted who were holy? Nay, Paul says;—he repels the blasphemy with detestation. For Christ did not introduce sin, but revealed it. He did not rob them of righteousness, but of the false show thereof."[55] The reproach of the Judaizers was in reality the same that is urged against evangelical doctrine still—that it is *immoral,* placing the virtuous and vicious in the common category of "sinners."

Ver. 18 throws back the charge of promoting sin upon the Legalist. It is the counterpart, not of ver. 19, but rather of ver. 17. The "transgressor" is the sinner in a heightened and more specific sense, one who breaks known and admitted law.[56] This word bears, in Paul's vocabulary, a precise and strongly marked signification which is not satisfied by the common interpretation. It is not that Peter in setting up the Law which he had in principle overthrown, *puts himself in the wrong;* nor that Peter in re-establishing the Law, *contradicts the purpose of the Law itself* (Chrysostom, Lightfoot, Beet). This is to anticipate the next verse. In Paul's view and according to the experience common to Peter with himself, law and transgression are concomitant, every man "under law" is *ipso facto* a transgressor. He who sets up the first, constitutes himself the second. And this is what Peter is now doing; although Paul courteously veils the fact by putting it hypothetically, in the first person.[57] After dissolving, so far as in him lay, the validity of legal righteousness and breaking down the edifice of justification by works, Peter is now building it up again, and thereby constructing a prison-house for himself. *Returning to legal allegiance, he returns to legal condemnation;*[58] with his own hands he puts on his neck the burden of the Law's curse, which through faith in Christ he had cast off. By this act of timid conformity he seeks to commend himself to Jewish opinion; but it only serves, in the light of the Gospel, to "prove him a transgressor," to "commend"[59] him in that unhappy character. This is Paul's retort to the imputation of the Judaist. It carries the war into the enemies' camp. "No," says Paul, "*Christ* is no patron of sin, in bidding men renounce legal righteousness. But those promote sin—in themselves first of all—who after knowing His righteousness, turn back again to legalism."

IV. The conviction of Peter is now complete. From the sad bondage to which the Jewish Apostle, by his compliance with the Judaizers, was preparing to submit himself, *the Apostle turns to his own joyous sense of deliverance* (vv. 19-21). Those who resort to legalism, he has said, ensure their own condemnation. It is, on the other hand, by an entire surrender to Christ, by realizing the import of His death, that we learn to "live unto God." So Paul had proved it. At this moment he is conscious of a union with the crucified and living Saviour, which lifts him above the curse of the law, above the power of sin. To revert to the Judaistic state, to dream any more of earning righteousness by legal conformity, is a thing for him inconceivable. It would be to make void the cross of Christ!

And it was the Law itself that first impelled Paul along this path. "Through law" he "died to law." The Law drove him from itself to seek salvation in Jesus Christ. Its accusations allowed him no shelter, left him no secure spot on which to build the edifice of his self-righteousness. It said to him unceasingly, Thou art a transgressor.[60] He who seeks justification by its means contradicts the Law, while he frustrates the grace of God.

CHAPTER X
THE PRINCIPLES AT STAKE

"For I through law died unto law, that I might live unto God. I have been crucified with Christ; and it is no longer I that live, but Christ liveth in me: and that life which I now live in the flesh I live in faith, the faith which is in the Son of God, who loved me, and gave Himself up for me. I do not make void the grace of God: for if righteousness is through law, then Christ died for nought" — Gal. ii. 19-21.

Paul's personal apology is ended. He has proved his Apostolic independence, and made good his declaration, "My Gospel is not according to man." If he owed his commission to any man, it was to Peter; so his traducers persistently alleged. He has shown that, first *without* Peter, then *in equality with* Peter, and finally *in spite of* Peter, he had received and maintained it. Similarly in regard to James and the Jerusalem Church. Without their mediation Paul commenced his work; when that work was challenged, they could only approve it; and when afterwards men professing to act in their name disturbed his work, the Apostle had repelled them. He acted all along under the consciousness of a trust in the gospel committed to him directly by Jesus Christ, and an authority in its administration second to none upon earth. And events had justified this confidence.

Paul is compelled to say all this about himself. The vindication of his ministry is forced from him by the calumnies of false brethren. From the time of the conference at Jerusalem, and still more since he withstood Peter at Antioch, he had been a mark for the hatred of the Judaizing faction. He was the chief obstacle to their success. Twice he had foiled them, when they counted upon victory. They had now set on foot a systematic agitation against him, with its head-quarters at Jerusalem, carried on under some pretext of sanction from the authorities of the Church there. At Corinth and in Galatia the legalist emissaries had appeared simultaneously; they pursued in the main the same policy, adapting it to the character and disposition of the two Churches, and appealing with no little success to the Jewish predilections common even amongst Gentile believers in Christ.

In this controversy Paul and the gospel he preached were bound together. "I am set," he says, "for the defence of the gospel" (Ph. i. 16). He was the champion of the cross, the impersonation of the principle of salvation by faith. It is "the gospel of Christ," the "truth of the gospel," he reiterates, that is at stake. If he wards off blows falling upon him, it is because they are aimed through him at the truth for which he lives—nay, at Christ who lives in him. In his self-assertion there is no note of pride or personal anxiety. Never was there a man more completely lost in the greatness of a great cause, nor who felt himself in comparison with it more worthless. But that cause has lifted Paul with it to imperishable glory. Of all names named on earth, none stands nearer than his to that which is "above every name."

While Paul in ch. i. and ii. is busy with his own vindication, he is meantime behind the personal defence preparing the doctrinal argument. His address to Peter is an incisive outline of the gospel of grace. The three closing verses—the Χριστῷ συνεσταύρωμαιἤ in particular—are the heart of Paul's theology—*summa ac medulla Christianismi* (Bengel). Such a testimony was the Apostle's best defence before his audience at Antioch; it was the surest means of touching the heart of Peter and convincing him of his error. And its recital was admirably calculated to enlighten the Galatians as to the true bearing of this dispute which had been so much misrepresented. From ver. 15 onwards, Paul has been all the while addressing, under the person of Peter, the conscience of his readers,[61] and paving the way for the assault that he makes upon them with so much vigour in the first verses of ch. iii. Read in the light of the foregoing narrative, this passage is a compendium of the Pauline Gospel, invested with the peculiar interest that belongs to a confession of personal faith, made at a signal crisis in the author's life. Let us examine this momentous declaration.

I. At the foundation of Paul's theology lies his conception of *the grace of God*.

Grace is the Apostle's watchword. The word occurs twice as often in his Epistles as it does in the rest of the New Testament. Outside the Pauline Luke and Hebrews, and 1 Peter with its large infusion of Paulinism, it is exceedingly rare.[62] In this word the character, spirit, and aim of the revelation of Christ, as Paul understood it, are summed up. "The grace of God" is the touchstone to which Peter's dissimulation is finally brought. *Christ* is the embodiment of Divine grace—above all, in His death. So that it is one and the same thing to "bring to nought the grace of God," and "the death of Christ." Hence God's grace is called "the grace of Christ," —"of our Lord Jesus Christ." From Romans to Titus and Philemon, "grace reigns" in every Epistle. No one can counterfeit this mark of Paul, or speak of grace in his style and accent.

God's grace is not His love alone; it is *redeeming love*—love poured out upon the undeserving, love coming to seek and save the lost, "bringing salvation to all men" (Rom. v. 1-8; Tit. ii. 11). Grace decreed redemption, made the sacrifice, proclaims the reconciliation, provides and bestows the new sonship of the Spirit, and schools its children into all the habits of godliness and virtue that beseem their regenerate life, which it brings finally to its consummation in the life eternal.[63]

Grace in God is therefore the antithesis of *sin in man*, counterworking and finally triumphing over it. Grace belongs to the last Adam as eminently as sin to the first. The later thoughts of the Apostle on this theme are expressed in Tit. iii. 4-7, a passage singularly rich in its description of the working of Divine grace on human nature. "We were senseless," he says, "disobedient, wandering in error, in bondage to lusts and pleasures of many kinds, living in envy and malice, hateful, hating each other. But when the kindness and love to man of our Saviour God shone forth,"—then all was changed: "not by works wrought in our own righteousness, but according to His mercy He saved us, through the washing of regeneration and renewing of the Holy Spirit, that, justified by His grace, we might be made heirs in hope of life eternal." The vision of the grace of God drives stubbornness, lust, and hatred from the soul. It brings about, for man and for society, the *palingenesia*, the new birth of Creation, rolling back the tide of evil and restoring the golden age of peace and innocence; and crowns the joy of a renovated earth with the glories of a recovered heaven.

Being the antagonist of sin, grace comes of necessity into contrast with *the law.* Law is intrinsically the opposer of sin; sin is "lawlessness," with Paul as much as with John.[64] But law was powerless to cope with sin: it was "weak through the flesh." Instead of crushing sin, the interposition of law served to inflame and stimulate it, to bring into play its latent energy, reducing the man most loyally disposed to moral despair. "By the law therefore is the knowledge of sin; it worketh out wrath." Inevitably, it makes men transgressors; it brings upon them an inward condemnation, a crushing sense of the Divine anger and hostility.[65] That is all that law can do by itself. "Holy and just and good," notwithstanding, to our perverse nature it becomes *death* (Rom. vii. 13; 1 Cor. xv. 56). It is actually "the strength of sin," lending itself to extend and confirm its power. We find in it a "law of sin and death." So that to be "under law" and "under grace" are two opposite and mutually exclusive states. In the latter condition only is sin "no longer our lord" (Rom. vi. 14). Peter and the Jews of Antioch therefore, in building up the legal principle again, were in truth "abolishing the grace of God." If the Galatians follow their example, Paul warns them that they will "fall from grace." Accepting circumcision, they become "debtors to perform the whole law,"—and that means transgression and the curse (ch. v. 1-4; iii. 10-12; ii. 16-18).

While sin is the reply which man's nature makes to the demands of law, *faith* is the response elicited by grace; it is the door of the heart opening to grace.[66] Grace and Faith go hand in hand, as Law and Transgression. Limiting the domain of faith, Peter virtually denied the sovereignty of grace. He belied his confession made at the Council of Jerusalem: "By *the grace* of the Lord Jesus we *trust* to be saved, even as the Gentiles" (Acts xv. 11). With Law are joined such terms as Works, Debt, Reward, Glorying, proper to a "righteousness of one's own."[67] With Grace we associate Gift, Promise, Predestination, Call, Election, Adoption, Inheritance, belonging to the dialect of "the righteousness which is of God by faith."[68] Grace operates in the region of "the Spirit," making for freedom; but law, however spiritual in origin, has come to seek its accomplishment in the sphere of the flesh, where it "gendereth to bondage" (ch. iv. 23-v. 5; 2 Cor. iii. 6, 17).

Grace appears, however, in another class of passages in Paul's Epistles, of which ch. i. 15, ii. 9 are examples. To the Divine grace Paul ascribes *his personal salvation and Apostolic call*. The revelation which made him a Christian and an Apostle, was above all things a manifestation of grace. Wearing this aspect, "the glory of God" appeared to him "in the face of Jesus Christ." The splendour that blinded and overwhelmed Saul on his way to Damascus, was "the glory of His grace." The voice of Jesus that fell on the persecutor's ear spoke in the accents of grace. No scourge of the Law, no thunders of Sinai, could have smitten down the proud Pharisee, and beaten or scorched out of him his strong self-will, like the complaint of Jesus. All the circumstances tended to stamp upon his soul, fused into penitence in that hour, the ineffaceable impression of "the grace of God and of our Saviour Jesus Christ." Such confessions as those of 1 Cor. xv. 8-10, and Eph. ii. 7, iii. 7, 8, show how constantly this remembrance was present with the Apostle Paul and suffused his views of revelation, giving to his ministry its peculiar tenderness of humility and ardour of gratitude. This sentiment of boundless obligation to the grace of God, with its pervasive effect upon the Pauline doctrine, is strikingly expressed in the doxology of 1 Tim. i. 11-17,—words which it is almost a sacrilege to put into the mouth of a *falsarius*: "According to the gospel of the glory of the blessed God, wherewith *I* was intrusted, ... who was aforetime a blasphemer and persecutor.... But the grace of our Lord abounded even more exceedingly. Faithful is the saying, worthy to be received of all, 'Christ Jesus came into the world to save sinners'—of whom *I* am chief.... In me as chief Christ Jesus showed forth all His long-suffering.... Now to the King of the ages be honour and glory for ever. Amen." Who, reading the Apostle's story, does not echo that *Amen*? No wonder that Paul became the Apostle of *grace*; even as John, "the disciple whom Jesus loved," must perforce be the Apostle of *love*. First to him was God's grace revealed in its largest affluence, that through him it might be known to all men and to all ages.

II. Side by side with the grace of God, we find in ver. 21 *the death of Christ*. He sets aside the former, the Apostle argues, who by admitting legal righteousness nullifies the latter.

While grace embodies Paul's fundamental conception of the Divine character, the death of Christ is the fundamental fact in which that character manifests itself. So the cross becomes the centre of Paul's theology. But it was, in the first place, the basis of his personal life. "Faith in the Son of God, who loved me and gave Himself up for me," is the foundation of "the life he now lives in the flesh."

Here lay the stumbling-block of Judaism. Theocratic pride, Pharisaic tradition, could not, as we say, *get over* it. A crucified Messiah! How revolting the bare idea. But when, as in Paul's case, Judaistic pride did surmount this huge scandal and in spite of the offence of the cross arrive at faith in Jesus, it was at the cost of a severe fall. It was broken in pieces,—destroyed once and for ever. With the elder Apostles the change had been more gradual; they were never steeped in Judaism as Saul was. For him to accept the faith of Jesus was a revolution the most complete and drastic possible. As a Judaist, the preaching of the cross was an outrage on his faith and his Messianic hopes; now it was that which most of all subdued and entranced him. Its power was extreme, whether to attract or repel. The more he had loathed and mocked at it before, the more he is bound henceforth to exalt the cross of our Lord Jesus Christ. A proof of the Divine anger against the Nazarene he had once deemed it; now he sees in it the token of God's grace in Him to the whole world.

For Paul therefore the death of Christ imported the end of Judaism. "I died to law," he writes,—"I am crucified with Christ." Once understanding what this death meant, and realising his own relation to it, on every account it was impossible to go back to Legalism. The cross barred all return. The law that put Him, the sinless One, to death, could give no life to sinful men. The Judaism that pronounced His doom, doomed itself. Who would make peace with it over the Saviour's blood? From the moment that Paul knew the truth about the death of Jesus, he had done with Judaism for ever. Henceforth he knew nothing—cherished no belief or sentiment, acknowledged no maxim, no tradition, which did not conform itself to His death. The world to which he had belonged *died*, self-slain, when it slew Him. From Christ's grave a new world was rising, for which alone Paul lived.

But why should the grace of God take expression in a fact so appalling as Christ's death? What has *death* to do with grace? It is the legal penalty of sin. The conjunction of sin and death pervades the teaching of Scripture, and is a principle fixed in the conscience of mankind. Death, as man knows it, is the inevitable consequence and the universal witness of his transgression. He "carries about in his mortality the testimony that God is angry with the wicked every day" (Augustine). The death of Jesus Christ cannot be taken out of this category. He died a sinner's death. He bore the penalty of guilt. The prophetic antecedents of Calvary, the train of circumstances connected with it, His own explanations in chief—are all in keeping with this purpose. With amazement we behold the Sinless "made sin," the Just dying for the unjust. He was "born of a woman, born under law": under law He lived— and *died*. Grace is no law-breaker. God must above all things be "just Himself," if He is to justify others (Rom. iii. 26). The death of Jesus declares it. That sublime sacrifice is, as one might say, the *resultant* of grace and law. Grace "gives Him up for us all;" it meets the law's claims in Him, even to the extreme penalty, that from us the penalty may be lifted off. He puts Himself under law, in order "to *buy out* those under law" (ch. iv. 4, 5). In virtue of the death of Christ, therefore, men are dealt with on an extra-legal footing, on terms of grace; not because law is ignored or has broken down; but because it is satisfied beforehand. God has "set forth Christ Jesus a propitiation"; and in view of that accomplished fact, He proceeds "in the present time" to "justify him who is of faith in Jesus" (Rom. iii. 22-26). Legalism is at an end, for the Law has spent itself on our Redeemer. For those that are in Him "there is now no condemnation." This is to anticipate the fuller teaching of ch. iii.; but the vicarious sacrifice is already implied when Paul says, "He gave Himself up for me—gave Himself for our sins" (ch. i. 4).

The *resurrection of Christ* is, in Paul's thought, the other side of His death. They constitute one event, the obverse and reverse of the same reality. For Paul, as for the first Apostles, the resurrection of Jesus gave to His death an aspect wholly different from that it previously wore. But the transformation wrought in their minds during the "forty days," in his case came about in a single moment, and began from a different starting-point. Instead of being the merited punishment of a blasphemer and false Messiah, the death of Calvary became the glorious self-sacrifice of the Son of God. The dying and rising of Jesus were blended in the Apostle's mind; he always sees the one in the light of the other. The faith that saves, as he formulates it, is at once a faith that Christ died for our sins, and that God raised Him from the dead on the third day.[69] Whichever of the two one may first apprehend, it brings the other along with it. The resurrection is not an express topic of this Epistle. Nevertheless it meets us in its first sentence, where we discern that

Paul's knowledge of the gospel and his call to proclaim it, rested upon this fact. In the passage before us the resurrection is manifestly assumed. If the Apostle is "crucified with Christ,"—and yet "Christ *lives* in him," it is not simply the teaching, or the mission of Jesus that lives over again in Paul; the *life* of the risen Saviour has itself entered into his soul.

III. This brings us to the thought of *the union of the believer with Christ in death and life*, which is expressed in terms of peculiar emphasis and distinctness in ver. 20. "With Christ I have been crucified; and *I* live no longer; it is Christ that lives in me. My earthly life is governed by faith in Him who loved me and died for me." Christ and Paul are one. When Christ died, Paul's former self died with Him. Now it is the Spirit of Christ in heaven that lives within Paul's body here on earth.

This union is first of all *a communion with the dying Saviour*. Paul does not think of the sacrifice of Calvary as something merely accomplished *for* him, outside himself, by a legal arrangement in which one person takes the place of another and, as it were, *personates* him. The nexus between Christ and Paul is deeper than this. Christ is the centre and soul of the race, holding towards it a spiritual primacy of which Adam's natural headship was a type, mediating between men and God in all the relations which mankind holds to God.[70] The death of Jesus was more than substitutionary; it was representative. He had every right to act for us. He was the "One" who alone could "die for all;" in Him "all died" (2 Cor. v. 14, 15). He carried us with Him to the cross; His death was in effect the death of those who sins He bore. There was no legal fiction here; no federal compact extemporised for the occasion. "The second Man from heaven," if second in order of time, was first and fundamental in the spiritual order, the organic Head of mankind, "the root," as well as "the offspring" of humanity.[71] The judgement that fell upon the race was a summons to Him who held in His hands its interests and destinies. Paul's faith apprehends and endorses what Christ has done on his behalf,—"who loved me," he cries, "and gave Himself up *for me*." When the Apostle says, "I *have been* crucified with Christ," he goes back in thought to the scene of Calvary; there, potentially, all that was done of which he now realises in himself the issue. His present salvation is, so to speak, a *rehearsal* of the Saviour's death, a "likeness" (Rom. vi. 5) of the supreme act of atonement, which took place once for all when Christ died for our sins.

Faith is the link between the past, objective sacrifice, and the present, subjective apprehension of it, by which its virtue becomes our own. Without such faith, Christ would have "died in vain." His death must then have been a great sacrifice thrown away. Wilful unbelief repudiates what the Redeemer has done, provisionally, on our behalf. This repudiation, as individuals, we are perfectly free to make. "The objective reconciliation effected in Christ's death can after all benefit actually, in their own personal consciousness, only those who know and acknowledge it, and feel themselves in their solidarity with Christ to be so much one with Him as to be able to appropriate inwardly His death and celestial life, and to live over again His life and death; those only, in a word, who truly *believe* in Christ. Thus the idea of substitution in Paul receives its complement and realisation in the mysticism of his conception of faith. While Christ objectively represents the whole race, that relation becomes a subjective reality only in the case of those who connect themselves with Him in faith in such a way as to fuse together with Him into *one* spirit and *one* body, as to find in Him their Head, their soul, their life and self, and He in them His body, His members and His temple. Thereby the idea of 'one for all' receives the stricter meaning of 'all in and with one.'"[72]

Partaking the death of Christ, Paul has come to share in *His risen life*. On the cross he owned his Saviour—owned His wounds, His shame, His agony of death, and felt himself therein shamed, wounded, slain to death. Thus joined to his Redeemer, as by the nails that fastened Him to the tree, Paul is carried with Him down into the grave—into the grave, and out again! Christ is risen from the dead: so therefore is Paul. He "died to sin once," and now "liveth to God; death lords it over Him no more:" this Paul reckons equally true for himself (Rom. vi. 3-11). The *Ego*, the "old man" that Paul once was, lies buried in the grave of Jesus.

Jesus Christ alone, "the Lord of the Spirit" has risen from that sepulchre,—has risen in the spirit of Paul. "If any one should come to Paul's doors and ask, Who lives here? he would answer, Not Saul of Tarsus, but Jesus Christ lives in this body of mine." In this appropriation of the death and rising of the Lord Jesus, this interpenetration of the spirit of Paul and that of Christ, there are three stages corresponding to the Friday, Saturday, and Sunday of Eastertide. "Christ died for our sins; He was buried; He rose again the third day:" so, by consequence, "I am crucified with Christ; no longer do I live; Christ liveth in me."

This mystic union of the soul and its Saviour bears fruit in the activities of outward life. Faith is no mere abstract and contemplative affection; but a working energy, dominating and directing all our human faculties. It makes even the flesh its instrument, which defied the law of God, and betrayed the man to the bondage of sin and death. There is a note of triumph in the words,—"the life I now live *in the flesh*, I live in faith!" The impossible has been accomplished. "The body of death" is possessed by the Spirit of life in Christ Jesus (Rom. vi. 12; vii. 23-viii. 1). The flesh—the despair of the law— has become the sanctified vessel of grace.

Paul's entire theology of Redemption is contained in this mystery of union with Christ. The office of *the Holy Spirit*, whose communion holds together the glorified Lord and His members upon earth, is implied in the teaching of ver. 20. This is manifest, when in ch. iii. 2-5 we find the believer's union with Christ described as "receiving the Spirit, beginning in the Spirit;" and when a little later "the promise of the Spirit" embraces the essential blessings of the new life.[73] The doctrine of *the Church* is also here. For those in whom Christ dwells have therein a common life, which knows no "Jew and Greek; all are one man" in Him.[74] *Justification* and *sanctification* alike are here; the former being the realisation of our share in Christ's propitiation for sin, the latter our participation in His risen life, spent "to God." Finally, *the resurrection to eternal life* and *the heavenly glory* of the saints spring from their present fellowship with the Redeemer. "The Spirit that raised Jesus from the dead, dwelling in us, shall raise our mortal body" to share with the perfected spirit His celestial life. The resurrection of Christ is the earnest of that which all His members will attain,—nay, the material creation is to participate in the glory of the sons of God, made like to Him, the "firstborn of many brethren" (Rom. viii. 11, 16-23, 29, 30; Phil. iii. 20, 21).

In all these vital truths Paul's gospel was traversed by the Legalism countenanced by Peter at Antioch. *The Judaistic doctrine struck* directly, if not avowedly, *at the cross*, whose reproach its promoters sought to escape. This charge is the climax of the Apostle's contention against Peter, and the starting-point of his expostulation with the Galatians in the following chapter. "If righteousness could be obtained by way of law, then Christ died for nought!" What could one say worse of any doctrine or policy, than that it led to this? And if works of law actually justify men, and circumcision is allowed to make a difference between Jew and Greek before God, the principle of legalism is admitted, and the intolerable consequence ensues which Paul denounces. What did Christ die for, if men are able to redeem themselves after this fashion? How can any one dare to build up in face of the cross his paltry edifice of self-wrought goodness, and say by doing so that the expiation of Calvary was superfluous and that Jesus Christ might have spared Himself all that trouble!

And so, on the one hand, Legalism *impugns the grace of God*. It puts human relations to God on the footing of a debtor and creditor account; it claims for man a ground for boasting in himself (Rom. iv. 1-4), and takes from God the glory of His grace. In its devotion to statute and ordinance, it misses the soul of obedience—the love of God, only to be awakened by the knowledge of His love to us (ch. v. 14; 1 John iv. 7-11). It sacrifices the Father in God to the King. It forgets that trust is the first duty of a rational creature toward his Maker, that the law of faith lies at the basis of all law for man.

On the other hand, and by the same necessity, Legalism is *fatal to the spiritual life in man*. Whilst it clouds the Divine character, it dwarfs and petrifies the human. What becomes of the sublime mystery of the life hid with Christ in God, if its existence is made contingent on circumcision and ritual performance? To men who put "meat and drink" on a level with "righteousness and peace and joy in the Holy Ghost," or in their intercourse with fellow-Christians set points of ceremony above justice, mercy, and faith, the very idea of a spiritual kingdom of God is wanting. The religion of Jesus and of Paul regenerates the heart, and from that centre regulates and hallows the whole ongoing of life. Legalism guards the mouth, the hands, the senses, and imagines that through these it can drill the man into the Divine order. The latter theory makes religion a mechanical system; the former conceives it as an inward, organic life.

THE DOCTRINAL POLEMIC

CHAPTER XI
THE GALATIAN FOLLY

"O foolish Galatians, who did bewitch you, before whose
eyes Jesus Christ was openly set forth crucified? This only
would I learn from you, Received ye the Spirit by the works
of the law, or by the hearing of faith? Are ye so foolish?
having begun in the Spirit, are ye now perfected in the flesh?
Did ye suffer so many things in vain? if it be indeed in vain.
He therefore that supplieth to you the Spirit, and worketh
miracles among you, *doeth he it* by the works of the law, or
by the hearing of faith?" —Gal. iii. 1-5.

At the beginning of ch. iii. falls the most marked division of this Epistle.
So far, since the exordium, its course has been strictly narrative. The Apostle
has been "giving" his readers "to know" many things concerning himself
and his relations to the Judean Church of which they had been ignorant
or misinformed. Now this preliminary task is over. From explanation and
defence he passes suddenly to the attack. He turns sharply round upon the
Galatians, and begins to ply them with expostulation and argument. It is for
their sake that Paul has been telling this story of his past career. In the light
of the narration just concluded, they will be able to see their folly and to
understand how much they have been deceived.

Here also the indignation so powerfully expressed in the Introduction,
breaks forth again, directed this time, however, against the Galatians
themselves and breathing grief more than anger. And just as after that
former outburst the letter settled down into the sober flow of narrative, so
from these words of reproach Paul passes on to the measured course of
argument which he pursues through the next two chapters. In ch. iv. 8-20,
and again in ch. v. 1-12, doctrine gives way to appeal and warning. But these
paragraphs still belong to the polemical division of the Epistle, extending
from this point to the middle of ch. v. This section forms the central and

principal part of the letter, and is complete in itself. Its last words, in ch. v. 6-12, will bring us round to the position from which we are now setting out.

This chapter stands, nevertheless, in close connection of thought with the foregoing. The Apostle's doctrine is grounded in historical fact and personal experience. The theological argument has behind it the weight of his proved Apostleship. The Judaistic dispute at Antioch, in particular, bears immediately on the subject-matter of the third chapter. Peter's vacillation had its counterpart in the defection of the Galatians. The reproof and refutation which the elder Apostle brought upon himself, Paul's readers must have felt, touched them very nearly. In the crafty intriguers who made mischief at Antioch, they could see the image of the Judaists who had come into their midst. Above all, it was *the cross* which Cephas had dishonoured, whose efficacy he had virtually denied. His act of dissimulation, pushed to its issue, nullified the death of Christ. This is the gravamen of Paul's impeachment. And it is the foundation of all his complaints against the Galatians. Round this centre the conflict is waged. By its tendency to enhance or diminish the glory of the Saviour's cross, Paul judges of the truth of every teaching, the worth of every policy. Angel or Apostle, it matters not—whoever disparages the cross of Jesus Christ finds in Paul an unflinching enemy. The thought of Christ "dying in vain" rouses in him the strong emotion under which he indites the first verses of this chapter. What greater folly, what stranger bewitchment can there be, than for one who has seen "Jesus Christ crucified" to turn away to some other spectacle, to seek elsewhere a more potent and diviner charm! "O senseless Galatians!"

I. Here then was the beginning of their folly. *The Galatians forgot their Saviour's cross.*

This was the first step in their backsliding. Had their eyes continued to be fixed on Calvary, the Legalists would have argued and cajoled in vain. Let the cross of Christ once lose its spell for us, let its influence fail to hold and rule the soul, and we are at the mercy of every wind of doctrine. We are like sailors in a dark night on a perilous coast, who have lost sight of the lighthouse beacon. Our Christianity will go to pieces. If Christ crucified should cease to be its sovereign attraction, from that moment the Church is doomed.

This forgetfulness of the cross on the part of the Galatians is the more astonishing to Paul, because at first they had so vividly realised its power, and the scene of Calvary, as Paul depicted it,[75] had taken hold of their nature with extraordinary force. He was conscious at the time—so his words seem to intimate—that it was given him, amongst this susceptible people, to draw the picture with unwonted effect. The gaze of his hearers was rivetted upon the sight. It was as if the Lord Jesus hung there before their eyes. They beheld the Divine sufferer. They heard His cries of distress and of triumph. They felt the load which crushed Him. Nor was it their sympathies alone and their reverence, to which the spectacle appealed. It stirred their conscience to its depths. It awakened feelings of inward humiliation and contrition, of horror at the curse of sin, of anguish under the bitterness and blackness of its death. "It was *you*," Paul would say—"you and I, for whom He died. *Our* sins laid on Him that ignominy, those agonies of body and of spirit. He died the Just for the unjust, that He might bring us to God." They looked, they listened, till their hearts were broken, till all their sins cried out against them; and in a passion of repentance they cast themselves before the Crucified, and took Him for their Christ and King. From the foot of the cross they rose new men, with heaven's light upon their brow, with the cry *Abba, Father* rising from their lips, with the Spirit of God and of Jesus Christ, the consciousness of a Divine sonship, filling their breast.

Has all this passed away? Have the Galatians forgotten the shame, the glory of that hour—the tears of penitence, the cries of joy and gratitude which the vision of the cross drew from their souls, the new creation it had wrought within them, the ardour of spirit and high resolve with which they pledged themselves to Christ's service? Was the influence of that transforming experience to prove no more enduring than the morning cloud and early dew? Foolish Galatians! Had they not the wit to see that the teaching of the Legalists ran counter to all they had then experienced, that it "made the death of Christ of none effect," which had so mighty and saving an effect upon themselves? Were they "so senseless," so bereft of reason and recollection? The Apostle is amazed. He cannot understand how impressions so powerful should prove so transient, and that truths thus clearly perceived and realised should come to be forgotten. Some fatal spell has been cast over them. They are "bewitched" to act as they are doing. A deadly fascination, like that of the "evil eye," has paralyzed their minds.

The ancient belief alluded to in the word the Apostle uses here,[76] is not altogether a superstition. The malignity that darts out in the glance of the "evil eye" is a presage of mischief. Not without reason does it cause a shudder. It is the sign of a demonic jealousy and hate. "Satan has entered into" the soul which emits it, as once into Judas. Behind the spite of the Jewish false brethren Paul recognised a preternatural malice and cunning, like that with which "the Serpent beguiled Eve."[77] To this darker source of the fascination his question, "Who hath bewitched you?" appears to point.

II. Losing sight of the cross of Christ, the Galatians were furthermore *rejecting the Holy Spirit of God.*

This heavy reproach the Apostles urges upon his readers through the rest of the paragraph, pausing only for a moment in ver. 4 to recall their earlier sufferings for Christ's sake in further witness against them. "I have but one question to put to you," he says—"You received the Spirit: how did that come about? Was it through what you *did* according to law? or what you *heard* in faith? You know well that this great blessing was given to your *faith*. Can you expect to retain this gift of God on other terms than those on which you received it? Have you begun with the Spirit to be brought to perfection by the flesh? (ver. 3).... Nay, God still bestows on you His Spirit, with gifts of miraculous energy; and I ask again, whether these displays attend on the practice of law-works, or upon faith's hearing?" (ver. 5).

The Apostle wished the Galatians to test the competing doctrines by their effects. The Spirit of God had put His seal on the Apostle's teaching, and on the faith of his hearers. Did any such manifestation accompany the preaching of the Legalist? That is all he wants to know. His cause must stand or fall by "the demonstration of the Spirit." By "signs and wonders," and diverse gifts of the Holy Spirit, God was wont to "bear witness with" the ministers and witnesses of Jesus Christ (Heb. ii. 3, 4; 1 Cor. xii. 4-11): was this testimony on the side of Paul, or the Circumcisionists? Did it sustain the gospel of the grace of God, or the "other gospel" of Legalism?

"He, the Spirit of truth, shall testify of Me," Christ had said; and so John, at the end of the Apostolic age: "It is the Spirit that beareth witness, because the Spirit is truth." When the Galatians accepted the message of the cross proclaimed by Paul's lips, "the Holy Spirit fell" on them, as on the Jewish Church at the Pentecost, and the Gentile believers in the house of Cornelius (Acts x. 44); "the love of God was poured out in their hearts through the Holy Ghost that was given them" (Rom v. 5). As a mighty, rushing wind this supernatural influence swept through their souls. Like fire from heaven it kindled in their spirit, consuming their lusts and vanities, and fusing their nature into a new, holy passion of love to Christ and to God the Father. It broke from their lips in ecstatic cries, unknown to human speech; or moved them to unutterable groans and pangs of intercession (Rom. viii. 26).

There were men in the Galatian Churches on whom the baptism of the Spirit conferred besides miraculous *charismata*, superhuman powers of insight and of healing. These gifts God continued to "minister amongst" them (*God* is unquestionably the agent in ver. 5). Paul asks them to observe on what conditions, and to whom, these extraordinary gifts are distributed. For the "receiving of the Spirit" was an infallible sign of true Christian faith. This was the very proof which in the first instance had convinced Peter and the Judean Church that it was God's will to save the Gentiles, independently of the Mosaic law (Acts xi. 15-18).

Receiving the Spirit, the Galatian believers knew that they were the sons of God. "God sent forth the Spirit of His Son into their hearts, crying, *Abba, Father*" (ch. iv. 6, 7). When Paul speaks of "receiving the Spirit," it is this that he thinks of most of all. The miraculous phenomena attending His visitations were facts of vast importance; and their occurrence is one of the historical certainties of the Apostolic age. They were "signs," conspicuous, impressive, indispensable at the time—monuments set up for all time. But they were in their nature variable and temporary. There are powers greater and more enduring than these. The things that "abide" are "faith, hope, love;" love chiefest of the three. Hence when the Apostle in a later chapter enumerates the qualities that go to make up "the fruit of the Spirit," he says nothing of *tongues* or *prophecies*, or *gifts of healing*; he begins with *love*. Wonder-working powers had their times and seasons, their peculiar organs; but every believer in Christ—whether Jew or Greek, primitive or mediæval or modern Christian, the heir of sixty generations of faith or the latest convert from heathenism—joins in the testimony, "The love of God is shed abroad in our heart by the Holy Ghost given unto us." This mark of God's indwelling Spirit the Galatians had possessed. They were "sons of God through faith in Christ Jesus" (ch. iii. 26). And with the filial title they had received the filial nature. They were "taught of God to love one another." Being sons of God in Christ, they were also "heirs" (ch. iv. 7; Rom viii. 17). They possessed the earnest of the heavenly inheritance (Eph. i. 14), the pledge of their bodily redemption (Rom. viii. 10-23), and of eternal life in the fellowship of Christ. In their initial experience of "the salvation which is in Jesus Christ" they had the foretaste of its "eternal glory," of the "grace" belonging to "them that love our Lord Jesus Christ," which is "in incorruption."[78]

No legal condition was laid down at this beginning of their Christian life; no "work" of any kind interposed between the belief of the heart and the conscious reception of the new life in Christ. Even their baptism, significant and memorable as it was, had not been required as in itself a precondition of salvation. Sometimes after baptism, but often—as in the case of Cornelius' household—before the rite was administered, "the Holy Ghost fell" on believing souls (Acts x. 44-48; xi. 15, 16). They "confessed with their mouth the Lord Jesus;" they "believed in their hearts that God had raised Him from the dead,"—and they were saved. Baptism is, as Paul's teaching elsewhere shows,[79] the expression, not the medium—the symbol, and not the cause, of the new birth which it might precede or follow. The Catholic doctrine of the *opus operatum* in the sacraments is radically anti-Pauline; it is Judaism over again. The process by which the Galatians became Christians was essentially spiritual. They had begun *in the Spirit*.

And so they must continue. To begin in the Spirit, and then look for perfection to the flesh, to suppose that the work of faith and love was to be consummated by Pharisaic ordinances, that Moses could lead them higher than Christ, and circumcision effect for them what the power of the Holy Ghost failed to do—this was the height of unreason. "Are you so senseless?" the Apostle asks.

He dwells on this absurdity, pressing home his expostulation with an emphasis that shows he is touching the centre of the controversy between himself and the Judaizers. They admitted, as we have shown in Chapter IX., that Gentiles might *enter* the kingdom of God through faith and by the baptism of the Spirit. This was settled at the Council of Jerusalem. Without a formal acceptance of this evangelical principle, we do not see how the Legalists could again have found entrance into Gentile Christian Churches, much less have carried Peter and Barnabas and the liberal Jews of Antioch with them, as they did. They no longer attempted to deny salvation to the uncircumcised; but they claimed for the circumcised a more complete salvation, and a higher status in the Church. "Yes, Paul has laid the foundation," they would say; "now we have come to perfect his work, to give you the more advanced instruction, derived from the fountain-head of Christian knowledge, from the first Apostles in Jerusalem. *If you would be perfect, keep the commandments*; be circumcised, like Christ and His disciples, and observe the law of Moses. If you be circumcised, Christ will profit you much more than hitherto; and you will inherit all the blessings promised in Him to the children of Abraham."

Such was the style of "persuasion" employed by the Judaizers. It was well calculated to deceive Jewish believers, even those best affected to their Gentile brethren. It appeared to maintain the prescriptive rights of Judaism and to satisfy legitimate national pride, without excluding the Gentiles from the fold of Christ. Nor is it difficult to understand the spell which the circumcisionist doctrine exerted over susceptible Gentile minds, after some years of Christian training, of familiarity with the Old Testament and the early history of Israel. Who is there that does not feel the charm of ancient memories and illustrious names? Many a noble mind is at this present time "bewitched," many a gifted and pious spirit is "carried away" by influences precisely similar. *Apostolical succession, patristic usage, catholic tradition, the authority of the Church*—what words of power are these! How wilful and arbitrary it appears to rely upon any present experience of the grace of God, upon one's own reading of the gospel of Christ, in contradiction to claims advanced under the patronage of so many revered and time-honoured names. The man, or the community, must be deeply conscious of having "received the Spirit," that can feel the force of attractions of this nature, and yet withstand them. It requires a clear view of the cross of Jesus Christ, an absolute faith in the supremacy of spiritual principles to enable one to resist the fascinations of ceremonialism and tradition. They offer us a more "ornate worship," a more "refined" type of piety, "consecrated by antiquity;" they invite us to enter a selecter circle, and to place ourselves on a higher level than that of the vulgar religionism of faith and feeling. It is the Galatian "persuasion" over again. Ceremony, antiquity, ecclesiastical authority are after all poor substitutes for faith and love. If they come between us and the living Christ, if they limit and dishonour the work of His Spirit, we have a right to say, and we will say with the Apostle Paul, *Away with them!*

The men of tradition are well content that we should "begin in the Spirit," provided they may have the finishing of our faith. To prey upon the Pauline Churches is their ancient and natural habit. An evangelical beginning is too often followed by a ritualistic ending. And Paul is ever begetting spiritual children, to see himself robbed of them by these bewitching Judaizers. "O foolish Galatians," he seems still to be saying, What is it that charms you so much in all this ritual and externalism? Does it bring you nearer to the cross of Christ? Does it give you more of His Spirit? Is it a spiritual satisfaction that you find in these works of Church law, these priestly ordinances and performances? How can the sons of God return to such childish rudiments? Why should a religion which began so spiritually seek its perfection by means so formal and mechanical?

The conflict which this Epistle signalised is one that has never ceased. Its elements belong to human nature. It is the contest between the religion of the Spirit and that of the letter, between the spontaneity of personal faith and the rights of usage and prescription. The history of the Church is largely the record of this incessant struggle. In every Christian community, in every earnest and devout spirit, it is repeated in some new phase. When the Fathers of the Church in the second and third centuries began to write about "the new law" and to identify the Christian ministry with the Aaronic priesthood, it was evident that Legalism was regaining its ascendancy. Already the foundations were laid of the Catholic Church-system, which culminated in the Papacy of Rome. What Paul's opponents sought to do by means of circumcision and Jewish prerogatives, that the Catholic legalists have done, on a larger scale, through the claims of the priesthood and the sacramental offices. The spiritual functions of the private Christian, one after another, were usurped or carelessly abandoned. Step by step the hierarchy interposed itself between Christ and His people's souls, till its mediation became the sole channel and organ of the Holy Spirit's influence. So it has come to pass, by a strange irony of history, that under the forms of Pauline doctrine and in the name of the Apostle of the Gentiles joined with that of Peter, catholic Christendom, delivered by him from the Jewish yoke, has been entangled in a bondage in some respects even heavier and more repressive. If tradition and prescription are to regulate our Christian belief, they lead us infallibly to *Rome*, as they would have lead the Galatians to perishing Jerusalem.

III. Paul said he had but one question to ask his readers, that which we have already discussed. And yet he does put to them, by way of parenthesis, another (ver. 4), suggested by what he has already called to mind, touching the beginning of their Christian course: "Have ye suffered so many things in vain?" Their folly was the greater in that *it threatened to deprive them of the fruit of their past sufferings in the cause of Christ.*

The Apostle does not say this without a touch of softened feeling. Remembering the trials these Galatians had formerly endured, the sacrifices they had made in accepting the gospel, he cannot bear to think of their apostasy. Hope breaks through his fear, grief passes into tenderness as he adds, "If it be indeed in vain." The link of reminiscence connecting vv. 3 and 4 is the same as that we find in 1 Thess. i. 6: "Ye received the word in much affliction, with joy of the Holy Ghost."[80]

We need not seek for any peculiar cause of these sufferings; nor wonder that the Apostle does not mention them elsewhere. Every infant Church had its baptism of persecution. No one could come out of heathen society and espouse the cause of Jesus, without making himself a mark for ridicule and violence, without the rupture of family and public ties, and many painful sacrifices. The hatred of Paul's fellow-countrymen towards him was an additional cause of persecution to the Churches he had founded. They were followers of the crucified Nazarene, of the apostate Saul. And they had to suffer for it. With the joy of their new life in Christ, there had come sharp pangs of loss and grief, heart-wounds deep and lasting. This slight allusion sufficiently reminds the Apostle's readers of what they had passed through at the time of their conversion.

And now were they going to surrender the faith won by such a struggle? Would they let themselves be cheated of blessings which had cost them so dear? "*So many things,*" he asks, "did you suffer in vain?" He will not believe it. He cannot think that this brave beginning will have so mean an ending. If "God counts them worthy of His kingdom for which they suffered," let them not deem themselves unworthy. Surely they have not escaped from the tyranny of heathenism, in order to yield up their liberties to Jewish intrigue, to the cozenage of false brethren who seek to exalt themselves at their expense (ch. ii. 4; iv. 17; vi. 12, 13). Will flattery beguile from them the treasure to which persecution had made them cling the more closely?

Too often, alas, the Galatian defection is repeated. The generous devotion of youth is followed by the lethargy and formalism of a prosperous age; and the man who at twenty-five was a pattern of godly zeal, at fifty is a finished worldling. The Christ whom he adored, the cross at which he bowed in those early days—he seldom thinks of them now. "I remember thee, *the kindness of thy youth,* the love of thine espousals; how thou wentest after Me *in the wilderness.*" Success has spoiled him. The world's glamour has bewitched him. He bids fair to "end in the flesh."

In a broader sense, the Apostle's question addresses itself to Churches and communities untrue to the spiritual principles that gave them birth. The faith of the primitive Church, that endured three centuries of persecution, yielded its purity to Imperial blandishments. Our fathers, Puritan and Scottish, staked their lives for the crown-rights of Jesus Christ and the freedom of faith. Through generations they endured social and civil ostracism in the cause of religious liberty. And now that the battle is won, there are those amongst their children who scarcely care to know what the struggle was about. Out of indolence of mind or vanity of scepticism, they abandon at the bidding of priest or sophist the spiritual heritage bequeathed to them. Did *they* then suffer so many things in vain? Was it an illusion that sustained those heroic souls, and enabled them to "stop the mouths of lions and subdue kingdoms"? Was it for nought that so many of Christ's witnesses in these realms since the Reformation days have suffered the loss of all things rather than yield by subjection to a usurping and worldly priesthood? And can we, reaping the fruit of their faith and courage, afford in these altered times to dispense with the principles whose maintenance cost our forefathers so dear a price?

"O foolish Galatians," Paul in that case might well say to us again!

CHAPTER XII
ABRAHAM'S BLESSING AND THE LAW'S CURSE

"Even as Abraham believed God, and it was reckoned unto him for righteousness. Know therefore that they which be of faith, the same are sons of Abraham. And the scripture, foreseeing that God justifieth the Gentiles by faith, preached the gospel beforehand unto Abraham, *saying*, In thee shall all the nations be blessed. So then they which be of faith are blessed with the faithful Abraham. For as many as are of the works of the law are under a curse: for it is written, Cursed is every one which continueth not in all things that are written in the book of the law, to do them. Now that no man is justified in the law in the sight of God, is evident: for, The righteous shall live by faith; and the law is not of faith; but, He that doeth them shall live in them. Christ redeemed us from the curse of the law, having become a curse for us: for it is written, Cursed is every one that hangeth on a tree: that upon the Gentiles might come the blessing of Abraham in Christ Jesus; that we might receive the promise of the Spirit through faith." —Gal. iii. 6-14.

Faith then, we have learnt, not works of law, was the condition on which the Galatians received the Spirit of Christ. By this gate they entered the Church of God, and had come into possession of the spiritual blessings common to all Christian believers, and of those extraordinary gifts of grace which marked the Apostolic days.

In this mode of salvation, the Apostle goes on to show, there was after all nothing new. The righteousness of faith is more ancient than legalism. It is as old as *Abraham*. His religion rested on this ground. "The promise of the Spirit," held by him in trust for the world, was given to his faith. "You received the Spirit, God works in you His marvellous powers, by the hearing of faith—*even as Abraham believed God*, and it was reckoned to him for righteousness." In the hoary patriarchal days as now, in the time of promise as of fulfilment, faith is the root of religion; grace invites, righteousness waits upon the hearing of faith. So Paul declares in vv. 6-9, and re-affirms with emphasis in ver. 14. The intervening sentences set forth by contrast *the curse* that hangs over the man who seeks salvation by way of law and personal merit.

Thus the two standing types of religion, the two ways by which men seek salvation, are put in contrast with each other—faith with its blessing, law with its curse. The former is the path on which the Galatians had entered, under the guidance of Paul; the latter, that to which the Judaic teachers were leading them. So far the two principles stand only in antagonism. The antinomy will be resolved in the latter part of the chapter.

But why does Paul make so much of the faith of *Abraham*? Not only because it furnished him with a telling illustration, or because the words of Gen. xv. 6 supplied a decisive proof-text for his doctrine: he could not well have chosen any other ground. Abraham's case was the *instantia probans* in this debate. "We are Abraham's seed:"[81] this was the proud consciousness that swelled every Jewish breast. "Abraham's bosom" was the Israelite's heaven: even in Hades his guilty sons could claim pity from "Father Abraham" (Luke xvi. 19-31). In the use of this title was concentrated all the theocratic pride and national bigotry of the Jewish race. To the example of Abraham the Judaistic teacher would not fail to appeal. He would tell the Galatians how the patriarch was called, like themselves, out of the heathen world to the knowledge of the true God; how he was separated from his Gentile kindred, and received the mark of circumcision to be worn thenceforth by all who followed in his steps, and who sought the fulfilment of the promise granted to Abraham and his seed.

The Apostle holds, as strongly as any Judaist, that the promise belongs to the children of Abraham. *But what makes a son of Abraham?* "Birth, true Jewish blood, of course," replied the Judaist. The Gentile, in his view, could only come into a share of the heritage by receiving circumcision, the mark of legal adoption and incorporation. Paul answers this question by raising another. What was it that brought Abraham his blessing? To what did he owe his righteousness? It was *faith*: so Scripture declares—"Abraham believed God." Righteousness, covenant, promise, blessing—all turned upon this. And *the true sons of Abraham are those who are like him*: "Know then that the men of faith, these are Abraham's sons." This declaration is a blow, launched with studied effect full in the face of Jewish privilege. Only a Pharisee, only a Rabbi, knew how to wound in this fashion. Like the words of Stephen's defence, such sentences as these stung Judaic pride to the quick. No wonder that his fellow-countrymen, in their fierce fanaticism of race, pursued Paul with burning hate and set a mark upon his life.

But the identity of Abraham's blessing with that enjoyed by Gentile Christians is not left to rest on mere inference and analogy of principle. Another quotation clinches the argument: "In thee," God promised to the patriarch, "shall be blessed"—not the natural seed, not the circumcised alone—but "all the nations (Gentiles)"![82] And "the Scripture" said this, "foreseeing" what is now taking place, namely, "that God justifieth the Gentiles by faith." So that in giving this promise to Abraham it gave him his "gospel before the time (προευηγγελίσατο)." Good news indeed it was to the noble patriarch, that all the nations—of whom as a wide traveller he knew so much, and over whose condition he doubtless grieved—were finally to be blessed with the light of faith and the knowledge of the true God; and thus blessed through himself. In this prospect he "rejoiced to see Christ's day;" nay the Saviour tells us, like Moses and Elijah, "he saw it and was glad." Up to this point in Abraham's history, as Paul's readers would observe, there was no mention of circumcision or legal requirement (ver. 17; Rom. iv. 9-13). It was on purely evangelical principles, by a declaration of God's grace listened to in thankful faith, that he had received the promise which linked him to the universal Church and entitled every true believer to call him father. "So that the men of faith are blessed, along with faithful Abraham."

I. What then, we ask, was *the nature of Abraham's blessing*? In its essence, it was *righteousness*. The "blessing" of vv. 9 and 14 is synonymous with the "justification" of vv. 6 and 8, embracing with it all its fruits and consequences. No higher benediction could come to any man than that God should "count him righteous."

Paul and the Legalists agreed in designating righteousness before God man's chief good. But they and he intended different things by it. Nay, Paul's conception of righteousness, it is said, differed radically from that of the Old Testament, and even of his companion writers in the New Testament. Confessedly, his doctrine presents this idea under a peculiar aspect. But there is a spiritual identity, a common basis of truth, in all the Biblical teaching on this vital subject. Abraham's righteousness was the state of a man who trustfully accepts God's word of grace, and is thereby set right with God, and put in the way of being and doing right thenceforward. In virtue of his faith, God regarded and dealt with Abraham as a righteous man. Righteousness of character springs out of righteousness of standing. God makes a man righteous by counting him so! This is the Divine paradox of Justification by Faith. When the Hebrew author says, "God counted it to him for righteousness," he does not mean *in lieu of righteousness*, as though faith were a substitute for a righteousness not forthcoming and now rendered superfluous; but *so as to amount to righteousness, with a view to righteousness*. This "reckoning" is the sovereign act of the Creator, who gives what He demands, "who maketh alive the dead, and calleth the things that are not as though they were" (Rom. iv. 17-22). He sees the fruit in the germ.

There is nothing arbitrary, or merely forensic in this imputation. Faith is, for such a being as man, the spring of all righteousness before God, the one act of the soul which is primarily and supremely right. What is more just than that the creature should trust his Creator, the child his Father? Here is the root of all right understanding and right relations between men and God—that which gives God, so to speak, a moral hold upon us. And by this trust of the heart, yielding itself in the "obedience of faith" to its Lord and Redeemer, it comes into communion with all those energies and purposes in Him which make for righteousness. Hence from first to last, alike in the earlier and later stages of revelation, man's righteousness is "not his own;" it is "the righteousness that is of God, based upon faith" (Phil. iii. 9). Faith unites us to the source of righteousness, from which unbelief severs us. So that Paul's teaching leads us to the fountain-head, while other Biblical teachers for the most part guide us along the course of the same Divine righteousness for man. His doctrine is required by theirs; their doctrine is implied, and indeed more than once expressly stated, in his.[83]

The Old Testament deals with the materials of character, with the qualities and behaviour constituting a righteous man, more than with the cause or process that makes him righteous. All the more significant therefore are such pronouncements as that of Gen. xv. 6, and the saying of Hab. ii. 4, Paul's other leading quotation on this subject. This second reference, taken from the times of Israel's declension, a thousand years and more after Abraham, gives proof of the vitality of the righteousness of faith. The haughty, sensual Chaldean is master of the earth. Kingdom after kingdom he has trampled down. Judah lies at his mercy, and has no mercy to expect. But the prophet looks beyond the storm and ruin of the time. "Art Thou not from everlasting, my God, my Holy One? We shall not die" (Hab. i. 12). The faith of Abraham lives in his breast. The people in whom that faith is cannot die. While empires fall, and races are swept away in the flood of conquest, "The just shall live by his faith."[84] If faith is seen here at a different point from that given before, it is still the same faith of Abraham, the grasp of the soul upon the Divine word—*there* first evoked, *here* steadfastly maintained, there and here the one ground of righteousness, and therefore of life, for man or for people. Habakkuk and the "remnant" of his day were "blessed with faithful Abraham;" how blessed, his splendid prophecy shows. Righteousness is of faith; life of righteousness: this is the doctrine of Paul, witnessed to by law and prophets.

Into what a life of blessing the righteousness of faith introduced "faithful Abraham," these Galatian students of the Old Testament very well knew. Twice[85] is he designated "the friend of God." The Arabs still call him *el khalil,—the friend*. His image has impressed itself with singular force on the Oriental mind. He is the noblest figure of the Old Testament, surpassing Isaac in force, Jacob in purity, and both in dignity of character. The man to whom God said, "Fear not, Abraham: I am thy shield and thy exceeding great reward;" and again, "I am God Almighty; walk before me, and be thou perfect:" on how lofty a platform of spiritual eminence was he set! The scene of Gen. xviii. throws into striking relief the greatness of Abraham, the greatness of our human nature in him; when the Lord says, "Shall I hide from Abraham the thing that I do?" and allows him to make his bold intercession for the guilty cities of the Plain. Even the trial to which the patriarch was subjected in the sacrifice of Isaac, was a singular honour, done to one whose faith was "counted worthy to endure" this unexampled strain. His religion exhibits an heroic strength and firmness, but at the same time a large-hearted, genial humanity, an elevation and serenity of mind, to which the temper of those who boasted themselves his children was utterly opposed. Father of the Jewish race, Abraham was no Jew. He stands before us in the morning light of revelation a simple, noble, archaic type of *man*, true "father of many nations." And his faith was the secret of the greatness which has commanded for him the reverence of four thousand years. His trust in God made him worthy to receive so immense a trust for the future of mankind.

With Abraham's faith, the Gentiles inherit his blessing. They were not simply blessed *in* him, through his faith which received and handed down the blessing,—but blessed *with* him. Their righteousness rests on the same principle as his. Religion reverts to its earlier purer type. Just as in the Epistle to the Hebrews Melchizedek's priesthood is adduced as belonging to a more Christlike order, antecedent to and underlying the Aaronic; so we find here, beneath the cumbrous structure of legalism, the evidence of a primitive religious life, cast in a larger mould, with a happier style of experience, a piety broader, freer, at once more spiritual and more human. Reading the story of Abraham, we witness the bright dawn of faith, its spring-time of promise and of hope. These morning hours passed away; and the sacred history shuts us in to the hard school of Mosaism, with its isolation, its mechanical routine and ritual drapery, its yoke of legal exaction ever growing more burdensome. Of all this the Church of Christ was to know nothing. It was called to enter into the labours of the legal centuries, without the need of sharing their burdens. In the "Father of the faithful" and the "Friend of God" Gentile believers were to see their exemplar, to find the warrant for that sufficiency and freedom of faith of which the natural children of Abraham unjustly strove to rob them.

II. But if the Galatians are resolved to be under the Law, they must understand what this means. *The legal state*, Paul declares, instead of the blessing of Abraham, *brings with it a curse*: "As many as are of law-works, are under a curse."

This the Apostle, in other words, had told Peter at Antioch. He maintained that whoever sets up the law as a ground of salvation, "makes himself a transgressor" (ch. ii. 18); he brings upon himself the misery of having violated law. This is no doubtful contingency. The law in explicit terms pronounces its curse against every man who, binding himself to keep it, yet breaks it in any particular.

The Scripture which Paul quotes to this effect, forms the conclusion of the commination uttered by the people of Israel, according to the directions of Moses, from Mount Ebal, on their entrance into Canaan: "Cursed is every one that continueth not in all things written in the book of the law to do them."[86] How terribly had that imprecation been fulfilled! They had in truth pledged themselves to the impossible. The Law had not been kept—could not be kept on merely legal principles, by man or nation. The confessions of the Old Testament, already cited in ch. ii. 16, were proof of this. That no one had "continued in all things written in the law to do them," goes without saying. If Gentile Christians adopt the law of Moses, they must be prepared to render an obedience complete and unfaltering in every detail (ch. v. 3)—or have this curse hanging perpetually above their heads. They will bring on themselves the very condemnation which was lying so heavily upon the conscience of Israel after the flesh.

This sequence of law and transgression belonged to Paul's deepest convictions. "The law," he says, "worketh out wrath" (Rom. iv. 14, 15). This is an axiom of Paulinism. Human nature being what it is, law means transgression; and the law being what it is, transgression means Divine anger and the curse (see p. 143). The law is just; the penalty is necessary. The conscience of the ancient people of God compelled them to pronounce the imprecation dictated by Moses. The same thing occurs every day, and under the most varied moral conditions. Every man who knows what is right and will not do it, *execrates* himself. The consciousness of transgression is a clinging, inward curse, a witness of ill-desert, foreboding punishment. The law of conscience, like that of Ebal and Gerizim, admits of no exceptions, no intermission. In the majesty of its unbending sternness it can only be satisfied by our *continuing in all things* that it prescribes. Every instance of failure, attended with whatever excuse or condonation, leaves upon us its mark of self-reproach. And this inward condemnation, this consciousness of guilt latent in the human breast, is not self-condemnation alone, not a merely subjective state; but it proceeds from God's present judgement on the man. It is the shadow of His just displeasure.

What Paul here proves from Scripture, bitter experience had taught him. As the law unfolded itself to his youthful conscience, he approved it as "holy and just and good." He was pledged and resolved to observe it in every point. He must despise himself if he acted otherwise. He strove to be—in the sight of men indeed he was—"touching the righteousness which is in the law, blameless." If ever a man carried out to the letter the legal requirements, and fulfilled the moralist's ideal, it was Saul of Tarsus. Yet his failure was complete, desperate! While men accounted him a paragon of virtue, he loathed himself; he knew that before God his righteousness was worthless. The "law of sin in his members" defied "the law of his reason," and made its power the more sensible the more it was repressed. The curse thundered by the six tribes from Ebal resounded in his ears. And there was no escape. The grasp of the law was relentless, because it was just, like the grasp of death. Against all that was holiest in it the evil in himself stood up in stark, immitigable opposition. "O wretched man that I am," groans the proud Pharisee, "who shall deliver me!" From this curse Christ had redeemed him. And he would not, if he could help it, have the Galatians expose themselves to it again. On legal principles, there is no safety but in absolute, flawless obedience, such as no man ever has rendered, or ever will. Let them trust the experience of centuries of Jewish bondage.

Verses 11, 12 support the assertion that the Law issues in condemnation, by a further, negative proof. The argument is a syllogism, both whose premises are drawn from the Old Testament. It may be formally stated thus. *Major premise* (evangelical maxim): "The just man lives of faith"[87] (ver. 11). *Minor*: The man of law does not live of faith (for he lives by doing: legal maxim, ver. 12).[88] *Ergo*: The man of law is not just before God (ver. 11). While therefore the Scripture by its afore-cited commination closes the door of life against righteousness of works, that door is opened to the men of faith. The two principles are logical contradictories. To grant righteousness to faith is to deny it to legal works. This assumption furnishes our minor premise in ver. 12. The legal axiom is, "He that doeth them shall live in them:" that is to say, *The law gives life for doing*—not therefore *for believing*; we get no sort of legal credit for that. The two ways have different starting-points, as they lead to opposite goals. From faith one marches, through God's righteousness, to blessing; from works, through self-righteousness, to the curse.

The two paths now lie before us—the Pauline and the legal method of salvation, the Abrahamic and the Mosaic scheme of religion. According to the latter, one begins by keeping so many rules—ethical, ceremonial, or what not; and after doing this, one expects to be counted righteous by God. According to the former, the man begins by an act of self-surrendering trust in God's word of grace, and God already reckons him just on that account, without his pretending to anything in the way of merit for himself. In short, the Legalist *tries to make God believe in him*: Abraham and Paul are content *to believe in God*. They do not set themselves over against God, with a righteousness of their own which He is bound to recognise; they commit themselves to God, that He may work out His righteousness in them. Along this path lies blessing—peace of heart, fellowship with God, moral strength, *life* in its fulness, depth, and permanence. From this source Paul derives all that was noblest in the Church of the Old Covenant. And he puts the calm, grand image of Father Abraham before us for our pattern, in contrast with the narrow, painful, bitter spirit of Jewish legalism, inwardly self-condemned.

III. But how pass from this curse to that blessing? How escape from the nemesis of the broken law into the freedom of Abraham's faith? To this question ver. 13 makes answer: "Christ bought us out of the curse of the law, having become a curse for us." *Christ's redemption changes the curse into a blessing.*

We entered this Epistle under the shadow of the cross. It has been all along the centre of the writer's thought. He has found in it the solution of the terrible problem forced upon him by the law. Law had led him to Christ's cross; laid him in Christ's grave; and there left him, to rise with Christ a new, free man, living henceforth to God (ch. ii. 19-21). So we understand the purpose and the issue of the death of Jesus Christ; now we must look more narrowly at the fact itself.

"Christ became a curse!" Verily the Apostle was not "seeking to please or persuade men." This expression throws the scandal of the cross into the strongest relief. Far from veiling it or apologizing for it, Paul accentuates this offence. His experience taught him that Jewish pride must be compelled to reckon with it. No, he would not have "the offence of the cross abolished" (ch. v. 11).

And did not Christ *become a curse*? Could the fact be denied by any Jew? His death was that of the most abandoned criminals. By the combined verdict of Jew and Gentile, of civil and religious authority, endorsed by the voice of the populace, He was pronounced a malefactor and blasphemer. But this was not all. The hatred and injustice of men are hard to bear; yet many a sensitive man has borne them in a worthy cause without shrinking. It was a darker dread, an infliction far more crushing, that compelled the cry, "My God, why hast Thou forsaken Me!" Against the maledictions of men Jesus might surely at the worst have counted on the Father's good pleasure. But even that failed Him. There fell upon His soul the death of death, the very curse of sin—*abandonment by God!* Men "did esteem Him"—and for the moment He esteemed Himself—"smitten of God." He hung there abhorred of men, forsaken of His God; earth all hate, heaven all blackness to His view. Are the Apostle's words too strong? Delivering up His Son to pass through this baptism, God did in truth *make Him a curse* for us. By His "determinate counsel" the Almighty set Jesus Christ in the place of condemned sinners, and allowed the curse of this wicked world to claim Him for its victim.

The death that befell Him was chosen as if for the purpose of declaring Him accursed. The Jewish people have thus stigmatized Him. They made the Roman magistrate and the heathen soldiery their instrument in *gibbeting* their Messiah. "Shall I crucify your King?" said Pilate. "Yes," they answered, "crucify Him!" Their rulers thought to lay on the hated Nazarene an everlasting curse. Was it not written, "A curse of God is every one that hangeth on a tree?"[89] This saying attached in the Jewish mind a peculiar loathing to the person of the dead thus exposed. Once *crucified*, the name of Jesus would surely perish from the lips of men; no Jew would hereafter dare to profess faith in Him. His cause could never surmount this ignominy. In later times the bitterest epithet that Jewish scorn could fling against our Saviour (God forgive them!), was just this word of Deuteronomy, *hattalúy—the hangéd one.*

This sentence of execration, with its shame freshly smarting, Paul has seized and twined into a crown of glory. "Hanged on a tree, crushed with reproach—*accursed*, you say, He was, my Lord, my Saviour! It is true. But the curse He bore was *ours*. His death, unmerited by Him, was our ransom-price, endured to buy us out of our curse of sin and death." This is the doctrine of *the vicarious sacrifice*. In speaking of "ransom" and "redemption," using the terms of the market, Christ and His Apostles are applying human language to things in their essence unutterable, things which we define in their effects rather than in themselves. "We know, we prophesy, in part." We know that we were condemned by God's holy law; that Christ, Himself sinless, came under the law's curse, and taking the place of sinners, "became sin for us;" and that His interposition has brought us out of condemnation into blessing and peace. How can we conceive the matter otherwise than as it is put in His own words: He "gave Himself a ransom—The Good Shepherd giveth His life for the sheep?" He suffers in our room and stead; He bears inflictions incurred by our sins, and due to ourselves; He does this at the Divine Will, and under the Divine Law: what is this but to "buy us out," to pay the price which frees us from the prison-house of death?

"Christ redeemed *us*," says the Apostle, thinking questionless of himself and his Jewish kindred, on whom the law weighed so heavily. His redemption was offered "to the Jew first." But not to the Jew alone, nor as a Jew. The time of release had come for all men. "Abraham's blessing" long withheld, was now to be imparted, as it had been promised, to "all the tribes of the earth." In the removal of the legal curse, God comes near to men as in the ancient days. His love is shed abroad; His spirit of sonship dwells in human hearts. In Christ Jesus crucified, risen, reigning—a new world comes into being, which restores and surpasses the promise of the old.

CHAPTER XIII
THE COVENANT OF PROMISE

"Brethren, I speak after the manner of men: Though it be but a man's testament, yet when it hath been confirmed, no one maketh it void, or addeth thereto. Now to Abraham were the promises spoken, and to his seed. He saith not, And to seeds, as of many, but as of one, And to thy seed, which is Christ. Now this I say; A testament confirmed beforehand by God, the law, which came four hundred and thirty years after, doth not disannul, so as to make the promise of none effect. For if the inheritance is of the law, it is no more of promise: but God hath granted it to Abraham by promise." —Gal. iii. 15-18.

Gentile Christians, Paul has shown, are already sons of Abraham. Their faith proves their descent from the father of the faithful. The redemption of Christ has expiated the law's curse, and brought to its fulfilment the primeval promise. It has conferred on Jew and Gentile alike the gift of the Holy Spirit, sealing the Divine inheritance. "Abraham's blessing" has "come upon the Gentiles in Christ Jesus." What can Judaism do for them more? Except, in sooth, to bring them under its inevitable curse.

But here the Judaist might interpose: "Granting so much as this, allowing that God covenanted with Abraham on terms of faith, and that believing Gentiles are entitled to his blessing, did not God make *a second covenant with Moses*, promising further blessings upon terms of law? If the one covenant remains valid, why not the other? From the school of Abraham the Gentiles must pass on to the school of Moses." This inference might appear to follow, by parity of reasoning, from what the Apostle has just advanced. And it accords with the position which the legalistic opposition had now taken up. The people of the circumcision, they argued, retained within the Church of Christ their peculiar calling; and Gentiles, if they would be perfect Christians, must accept the covenant-token and the unchangeable ordinances of Israel. Faith is but the first step in the new life; the discipline of the law will bring it to completion. Release from the curse of the law, they might contend, leaves its obligations still binding, its ordinances unrepealed. Christ "came not to destroy, but to fulfil."

So we are brought to the question of *the relation of law and promise*, which is the theoretical, as that of Gentile to Jewish Christianity is the practical problem of the Epistle. The remainder of the chapter is occupied with its discussion. This section is the special contribution of the Epistle to Christian theology—a contribution weighty enough of itself to give to it a foremost place amongst the documents of Revelation. Paul has written nothing more masterly. The breadth and subtlety of his reason, his grasp of the spiritual realities underlying the facts of history, are conspicuously manifest in these paragraphs, despite the extreme difficulty and obscurity of certain sentences.

This part of the Epistle is in fact a piece of inspired *historical criticism*; it is a magnificent reconstruction of the course of sacred history. It is Paul's theory of doctrinal development, condensing into a few pregnant sentences the *rationale* of Judaism, explaining the method of God's dealings with mankind from Abraham down to Christ, and fitting the legal system into its place in this order with an exactness and consistency that supply an effectual verification of the hypothesis. To such a height has the Apostle been raised, so completely is he emancipated from the fetters of Jewish thought, that the whole Mosaic economy becomes to his mind no more than an interlude, a passing stage in the march of Revelation.

This passage finds its counterpart in Romans xi. Here the past, there the future fortunes of Israel are set forth. Together the two chapters form a Jewish theodicy, a vindication of God's treatment of the chosen people from first to last. Rom. v. 12-21 and 1 Cor. xv. 20-57 supply a wider exposition, on the same principles, of the fortunes of mankind at large. The human mind has conceived nothing more splendid and yet sober, more humbling and exalting, than the view of man's history and destiny thus sketched out.

The Apostle seeks to establish, in the first place, *the fixedness of the Abrahamic covenant*. This is the main purport of the passage. At the same time, in ver. 16, he brings into view *the Object of the covenant*, the person designated by it—*Christ*, its proper Heir. This consideration, though stated here parenthetically, lies at the basis of the settlement made with Abraham; its importance is made manifest by the after course of Paul's exposition.

At this point, where the discussion opens out into its larger proportions, we observe that the sharp tone of personal feeling with which the chapter commenced has disappeared. In ver. 15 the writer drops into a conciliatory key. He seems to forget the wounded Apostle in the theologian and instructor in Christ. "Brethren," he says, "I speak in human fashion—I put this matter in a way that every one will understand." He lifts himself above the Galatian quarrel, and from the height of his argument addresses himself to the common intelligence of mankind.

But is it *covenant*, or *testament*, that the Apostle intends here? "I speak after the manner of men," he continues; "if the case were that of a man's διαθήκη, once ratified, no one would set it aside, or add to it." The presumption is that the word is employed in its accepted, every-day significance. And that unquestionably was "testament." It would never occur to an ordinary Greek reader to interpret the expression otherwise. Philo and Josephus, the representatives of contemporary Hellenistic usage, read this term, in the Old Testament, with the connotation of διαθήκη in current Greek.[90] The context of this passage is in harmony with their usage. The "covenant" of ver. 15 corresponds to "the blessing of Abraham," and "the promise of the Spirit" in the two preceding verses. Again in ver. 17, "promise" and "covenant" are synonymous. Now a "covenant of promise" amounts to a "testament." It is the *prospective* nature of the covenant, the bond which it creates between Abraham and the Gentiles, which the Apostle has been insisting on ever since ver. 6. It belongs "to Abraham and to his seed"; it comes by way of "gift" and "grace" (vv. 18, 22); it invests those taking part in it with "sonship" and rights of "inheritance" (vv. 18, 26, 29, etc.) These ideas cluster round the thought of *a testament*; they are not inherent in *covenant*, strictly considered. Even in the Old Testament this latter designation fails to convey all that belongs to the Divine engagements there recorded. In a covenant the two parties are conceived as equals in point of law, binding themselves by a compact that bears on each alike. Here it is not so. The disposition of affairs is made by God, who in the sovereignty of His grace "hath granted it to Abraham." It was surely a reverent sense of this difference which dictated to the men of the Septuagint the use of διαθήκη rather than συνθήκη, the ordinary term for *covenant* or *compact*, in their rendering of the Hebrew *berith*.

This aspect of the covenants now becomes their commanding feature. Our Lord's employment of this word at the Last Supper gave it the affecting reference to His death which it has conveyed ever since to the Christian mind.[91] The Latin translators were guided by a true instinct when in the Scriptures of the New Covenant they wrote *testamentum* everywhere, not *fœdus* or *pactum*, for this word. The testament is a covenant—and something more. The testator designates his heir, and binds himself to grant to him at the predetermined time (ch. iv. 2) the specified boon, which it remains for the beneficiary simply to accept. Such a Divine *testament* has come down from Abraham to his Gentile sons.

I. Now when a man has made a testament, and it has been ratified — "proved," as we should say — *it stands good for ever*. No one has afterwards any power to set it aside, or to attach to it a new codicil, modifying its previous terms. There it stands — a document complete and unchangeable (ver. 15).

Such a testament God gave "to Abraham and his seed." It was "ratified" (or "confirmed") by the final attestation made to the patriarch after the supreme trial of his faith in the sacrifice of Isaac: "By myself have I sworn, saith the Lord, that in blessing I will bless thee, and in multiplying multiply thy seed as the stars of heaven; ... and in thy seed shall all the nations of the earth be blessed."[92] In human testaments the ratification takes place through another; but God "having no greater," yet "to show to the heirs of the promise the immutability of His counsel" confirmed it by His own oath. Nothing was wanting to mark the Abrahamic covenant with an indelible character, and to show that it expressed an unalterable purpose in the mind of God.

With such Divine asseveration "were the promises spoken to Abraham, and *his seed*." This last word diverts the Apostle's thoughts for a moment, and he gives a side-glance at the person thus designated in the terms of the promise. Then he returns to his former statement, urging it home against the Legalists: "Now this is what I mean: a testament previously ratified by God, the Law which dates four hundred and thirty years later cannot annul, so as to abrogate the Promise" (ver. 17). The bearing of Paul's argument is now perfectly clear. He is using the promise to Abraham to overthrow the supremacy of the Mosaic law. The Promise was, he says, the prior settlement. No subsequent transaction could invalidate it or disqualify those entitled under it to receive the inheritance. That testament lies at the foundation of the sacred history. The Jew least of all could deny this. How could such an instrument be set aside? Or what right has any one to limit it by stipulations of a later date?

When a man amongst ourselves bequeaths his property, and his will is publicly attested, its directions are scrupulously observed; to tamper with them is a crime. Shall we have less respect to this Divine settlement, this venerable charter of human salvation? You say, The Law of Moses has its rights: it must be taken into account as well as the Promise to Abraham. True; but it has no power to cancel or restrict the Promise, older by four centuries and a half. The later must be adjusted to the earlier dispensation, the Law interpreted by the Promise. God has not made *two* testaments — the one solemnly committed to the faith and hope of mankind, only to be retracted and substituted by something of a different stamp. He could not thus stultify Himself. And we must not apply the Mosaic enactments, addressed to a single people, in such a way as to neutralise the original provisions made for the race at large. Our human instincts of good faith, our reverence for public compacts and established rights, forbid our allowing the Law of Moses to trench upon the inheritance assured to mankind in the Covenant of Abraham.

This contradiction necessarily arises if the Law is put on a level with the Promise. To read the Law as a continuation of the older instrument is virtually to efface the latter, to "make the promise of none effect." The two institutes proceed on opposite principles. "If the inheritance is of law, it is no longer of promise" (ver. 18). Law prescribes certain things to be done, and guarantees a corresponding reward—so much pay for so much work. That, in its proper place, is an excellent principle. But the promise stands on another footing: "God hath *bestowed* it on Abraham *by way of grace*" (κεχάρισται, ver. 18). It holds out a blessing conferred by the Promiser's good will, to be conveyed at the right time without demanding anything more from the recipient than faith, which is just the will to receive. So God dealt with Abraham, centuries before any one had dreamed of the Mosaic system of law. God appeared to Abraham in His sovereign grace; Abraham met that grace with faith. So the Covenant was formed. And so it abides, clear of all legal conditions and claims of human merit, an "everlasting covenant" (Gen. xvii. 7; Heb. xiii. 20).

Its permanence is emphasized by the *tense* of the verb relating to it. The Greek *perfect* describes settled facts, actions or events that carry with them finality. Accordingly we read in vv. 15 and 17 of "a ratified covenant"—one that *stands* ratified. In ver. 18, "God hath granted it to Abraham"—a grace never to be recalled. Again (ver. 19), "the seed to whom the promise hath been made"—once for all. A perfect participle is used of the Law in ver. 17 (γεγονώς), for it is a fact of abiding significance that it was so much later than the Promise; and in ver. 24, "the Law hath been our tutor,"—its work in that respect is an enduring benefit. Otherwise, the verbs relating to Mosaism in this context are past in tense, describing what is now matter of history, a course of events that has come and gone. Meanwhile the Promise remains, an immovable certainty, a settlement never to be disturbed. The emphatic position of ὁ Θεός (ver. 18), at the very end of the paragraph, serves to heighten this effect. "It is *God* that hath bestowed this grace on Abraham." There is a challenge in the word, as though Paul asked, "Who shall make it void?"[93]

Paul's chronology in ver. 17 has been called in question. We are not much concerned to defend it. Whether Abraham preceded Moses by four hundred and thirty years, as the Septuagint and the Samaritan text of Exod. xii. 40, 41 affirm, and as Paul's contemporaries commonly supposed; or whether, as it stands in the Hebrew text of Exodus, this was the length of time covered by the sojourn in Egypt, so that the entire period would be about half as long again, is a problem that Old Testament historians must settle for themselves; it need not trouble the reader of Paul. The shorter period is amply sufficient for his purpose. If any one had said, "No, Paul; you are mistaken. It was six hundred and thirty, not four hundred and thirty years from Abraham to Moses;" he would have accepted the correction with the greatest goodwill. He might have replied, "So much the better for my argument."[94] It is possible to "strain out" the "gnats" of Biblical criticism, and yet to swallow huge "camels" of improbability.

II. Ver. 16 remains for our consideration. In proving the steadfastness of the covenant with Abraham, the Apostle at the same time directs our attention to *the Person designated by it*, to whom its fulfilment was guaranteed. "To Abraham were the promises spoken, and to his seed—'to thy seed,' which is Christ."

This identification the Judaist would not question. He made no doubt that the Messiah was the legatee of the testament, "the seed to whom it hath been promised." Whatever partial and germinant fulfilments the Promise had received, it is on Christ in chief that the inheritance of Israel devolves. In its true and full intent, this promise, like all predictions of the triumph of God's kingdom, was understood to be waiting for His advent.

The fact that this Promise looked to Christ, lends additional force to the Apostle's assertion of its indelibility. The words "unto Christ," which were inserted in the text of ver. 17 at an early time, are a correct gloss. The covenant did not lie between God and Abraham alone. It embraced Abraham's descendants in their unity, culminating in Christ. It looked down the stream of time to the last ages. Abraham was its starting-point; Christ its goal. "To thee—and to thy seed:" these words span the gulf of two thousand years, and overarch the Mosaic dispensation. So that the covenant vouchsafed to Abraham placed him, even at that distance of time, in close personal relationship with the Saviour of mankind. No wonder that it was so evangelical in its terms, and brought the patriarch an experience of religion which anticipated the privileges of Christian faith. God's covenant with Abraham, being in effect His covenant with mankind in Christ, stands both first and last. The Mosaic economy holds a second and subsidiary place in the scheme of Revelation.

The reason the Apostle gives for reading *Christ* into the promise is certainly peculiar. He has been taxed with false exegesis, with "rabbinical hair-splitting" and the like. Here, it is said, is a fine example of the art, familiar to theologians, of torturing out of a word a predetermined sense, foreign to its original meaning. "He doth not say, and to *seeds*, as referring to many; but as referring to one, and to thy *seed*, which is Christ." Paul appears to infer from the fact that the word "seed" is grammatically singular, and not plural, that it designates a single individual, who can be no other than Christ. On the surface this does, admittedly, look like a verbal quibble. The word "seed," in Hebrew and Greek as in English, is not used, and could not in ordinary speech be used in the plural to denote a number of descendants. It is a collective singular. The plural applies only to *different kinds* of seed. The Apostle, we may presume, was quite as well aware of this as his critics. It does not need philological research or grammatical acumen to establish a distinction obvious to common sense. This piece of word-play is in reality the vehicle of an historical argument, as unimpeachable as it is important. Abraham was taught, by a series of lessons,[95] to refer the promise to *the single line* of Isaac. Paul elsewhere lays great stress on this consideration; he brings Isaac into close analogy with Christ; for he was the child of faith, and represented in his birth a spiritual principle and the communication of a supernatural life.[96] The true seed of Abraham was in the first instance *one*, not many. In the primary realisation of the Promise, typical of its final accomplishment, it received a *singular* interpretation; it concentrated itself on the one, spiritual offspring, putting aside the many, natural and heterogeneous (Hagarite or Keturite) descendants. And this sifting principle, this law of election which singles out from the varieties of nature the Divine type, comes into play all along the line of descent, as in the case of Jacob, and of David. It finds its supreme expression in the person of Christ. The Abrahamic testament devolved under a law of spiritual selection. By its very nature it pointed ultimately to Jesus Christ. When Paul writes "Not to seeds, as of many," he virtually says that the word of inspiration was singular in *sense* as well as in form; in the mind of the Promiser, and in the interpretation given to it by events, it bore an individual reference, and was never intended to apply to Abraham's descendants at large, to the many and miscellaneous "children according to flesh."

Paul's interpretation of the Promise has abundant analogies. All great principles of human history tend to embody themselves in some "chosen seed." They find at last their true heir, the *one man* destined to be their fulfilment. Moses, David, Paul; Socrates and Alexander; Shakespere, Newton, are examples of this. The work that such men do belongs to themselves. Had any promise assured the world of the gifts to be bestowed through them, in each case one might have said beforehand, It will have to be, "Not as of many, but as of one." It is not multitudes, but men that rule the world. "By *one man* sin entered into the world: we shall reign in life through *the one* Jesus Christ." From the first words of hope given to the repentant pair banished from Eden, down to the latest predictions of the Coming One, the Promise became at every stage more determinate and individualising. The finger of prophecy pointed with increasing distinctness, now from this side, now from that, to the veiled form of the Chosen of God—"the seed of the woman," the "seed of Abraham," the "star out of Jacob," the "Son of David," the "King Messiah," the suffering "Servant of the Lord," the "smitten Shepherd," the "Son of man, coming in the clouds of heaven." In His person all the lines of promise and preparation meet; the scattered rays of Divine light are brought to a focus. And the desire of all nations, groping, half-articulate, unites with the inspired foresight of the seers of Israel to find its goal in Jesus Christ. There was but *One* who could meet the manifold conditions created by the world's previous history, and furnish the key to the mysteries and contradictions which had gathered round the path of Revelation.

Notwithstanding, the Promise had and has a *generic* application, attending its personal accomplishment. "Salvation is of the Jews." Christ belongs "to the Jew first." Israel was raised up and consecrated to be the trustee of the Promise given to the world through Abraham. The vocation of this gifted race, the secret of its indestructible vitality, lies in its relationship to Jesus Christ. They are "His own," though they "received Him not." Apart from Him, Israel is nothing to the world—nothing but a witness against itself. Premising its essential fulfilment in Christ, Paul still reserves for his own people their peculiar share in the Testament of Abraham—not a place of exclusive privilege, but of richer honour and larger influence. "Hath God cast away His people?" he asks: "Nay indeed. For I also am an Israelite, of *the seed of Abraham.*" So that, after all, it is something to be of Abraham's children by nature. Despite his hostility to Judaism, the Apostle claims for the Jewish race a special office in the dispensation of the Gospel, in the working out of God's ultimate designs for mankind.[97] Would they only accept their Messiah, how exalted a rank amongst the nations awaits them! The title "seed of Abraham" with Paul, like the "Servant of Jehovah" in Isaiah, has a double significance. The sufferings of the elect people made them in their national character a pathetic type of the great Sufferer and Servant of the Lord, His supreme Elect. In Jesus Christ the collective destiny of Israel is attained; its prophetic ideal, the spiritual conception of its calling, is realised, —"the seed to whom it hath been promised."

Paul is not alone in his insistence on the relation of Christ to Abraham. It is announced in the first sentence of the New Testament: "the book of the generation of Jesus Christ, *son of Abraham,* son of David." And it is set forth with singular beauty in the Gospel of the Infancy. Mary's song and Zacharias' prophecy recall the freedom and simplicity of an inspiration long silenced, as they tell how "the Lord hath visited and redeemed His people; He hath shown mercy to our fathers, in remembrance of His holy covenant, the oath which He sware *unto Abraham our father*." And again, "He hath helped Israel His servant in remembrance of His mercy, as He spake to our fathers, *to Abraham and to his seed* for ever."[98] These pious and tender souls who watched over the cradle of our Lord and stood in the dawning of His new day, instinctively cast their thoughts back to the Covenant of Abraham. In it they found matter for their songs and a warrant for their hopes, such as no ritual ordinances could furnish. Their utterances breathe a spontaneity of faith, a vernal freshness of joy and hope to which the Jewish people for ages had been strangers. The dull constraint and stiffness, the harsh fanaticism of the Hebrew nature, have fallen from them. They have put on the beautiful garments of Zion, her ancient robes of praise. For the time of the Promise draws near. Abraham's Seed is now to be born; and Abraham's faith revives to meet Him. It breaks forth anew out of the dry and long-barren soil of Judaism; it is raised up to a richer and an enduring life. Paul's doctrine of Grace does but translate into logic the poetry of Mary's and Zacharias' anthems. The Testament of Abraham supplies their common theme.

CHAPTER XIV
THE DESIGN OF THE LAW

"What then is the law? It was added because of transgressions, till the seed should come to whom the promise hath been made; *and it was* ordained through angels by the hand of a mediator. Now a mediator is not *a mediator* of one; but God is one. Is the law then against the promises of God? God forbid: for if there had been a law given which could make alive, verily righteousness would have been of the law. Howbeit the Scripture hath shut up all things under sin, that the promise by faith in Jesus Christ might be given to them that believe. But before faith came, we were kept in ward under the law, shut up unto the faith which should afterwards be revealed. So that the law hath been our tutor *to bring us* unto Christ, that we might be justified by faith." —Gal. iii. 19-24.

What then is the law? So the Jew might well exclaim. Paul has been doing nothing but disparage it. —"You say that the Law of Moses brings no righteousness or blessing, but only a curse; that the covenant made with Abraham ignores it, and does not admit of being in any way qualified by its provisions. What then do you make of it? Is it not God's voice that we hear in its commands? Have the sons of Abraham ever since Moses' day been wandering from the true path of faith?" Such inferences might be drawn, not unnaturally, from the Apostle's denunciation of Legalism. They were actually drawn by Marcion in the second century, in his extreme hostility to Judaism and the Old Testament.

This question must indeed have early forced itself upon Paul's mind. How could the doctrine of Salvation by Faith and the supremacy of the Abrahamic Covenant be reconciled with the Divine commission of Moses? How, on the other hand, could the displacement of the Law by the Gospel be justified, if the former too was authorised and inspired by God? Can the same God have given to men these two contrasted revelations of Himself? The answer, contained in the passage before us, is that the two revelations had different ends in view. They are complementary, not competing institutes. Of the two, the Covenant of Promise has the prior right; it points immediately to Christ. The Legal economy is ancillary thereto; it never professed to accomplish the work of grace, as the Judaists would have it do. Its office was external, but nevertheless accessory to that of the Promise. It guarded and schooled the infant heirs of Abraham's Testament, until the time of its falling due, when they should be prepared in the manhood of faith to enter on their inheritance. "The law hath been our tutor for Christ, with the intent we should be justified by faith" (ver. 24).

This aspect of the Law, under which, instead of being an obstacle to the life of faith, it is seen to subserve it, has been suggested already. "For I," the Apostle said, "*through law* died to law" (ch. ii. 19). The Law first impelled him to Christ. It constrained him to look beyond itself. Its discipline was a preparation for faith. Paul reverses the relation in which faith and Law were set by the Judaists. They brought in the Law to perfect the unfinished work of faith (ver. 3): he made it preliminary and propædeutic. What they gave out for more advanced doctrine, he treats as the "weak rudiments," belonging to the infancy of the sons of God (ch. iv. 1-11). Up to this point, however, the Mosaic law has been considered chiefly in a negative way, as a foil to the Covenant of grace. The Apostle has now to treat of its nature more positively and explicitly, first indeed *in contrast with the promise* (vv. 19, 20); and secondly, *in its co-operation with the promise* (vv. 22-24). Ver. 21 is the transition from the first to the second of these conceptions.

I. "For the sake of the transgressions (committed against it)[99] the law was added." The Promise, let us remember, was complete in itself. Its testament of grace was sealed and delivered ages before the Mosaic legislation, which could not therefore retract or modify it. The Law was "superadded," as something over and above, attached to the former revelation for a subsidiary purpose lying outside the proper scope of the Promise. What then was this purpose?

1. *For the sake of transgressions.* In other words, the object of the law of Moses was *to develope sin.* This is not the whole of the Apostle's answer; but it is the key to his explanation. This design of the Mosaic revelation determined its form and character. Here is the standpoint from which we are to estimate its working, and its relation to the kingdom of grace. The saying of Rom. v. 20 is Paul's commentary upon this sentence: "The law came in by the way, in order that the trespass (of Adam) might multiply." The same necessity is expressed in the paradox of 1 Cor. xv. 56: "The strength of sin is the law."

This enigma, as a psychological question, is resolved by the Apostle in Rom. vii. 13-24. The law acts as a spur and provocative, rousing the power of sin to conscious activity. However good in itself, coming into contact with man's evil flesh, its promulgation is followed inevitably by transgression. Its commands are so many occasions for sin to come into action, to exhibit and confirm its power. So that the Law practically assumes the same relation to sin as that in which the Promise stands to righteousness and life. In its union with the Law our sinful nature perpetually "brings forth fruit unto death." And this mournful result God certainly contemplated when He gave the Law of Moses.

But are we compelled to put so harsh a sense on the Apostle's words? May we not say that the Law was imposed in order to *restrain* sin, to keep it within bounds? Some excellent interpreters read the verse in this way. It is quite true that, in respect of public morals and the outward manifestations of evil, the Jewish law acted beneficially, as a bridle upon the sinful passions. But this is beside the mark. The Apostle is thinking only of inward righteousness, that which avails before God. The wording of the clause altogether excludes the milder interpretation. *For the sake of* (χάριν, Latin *gratia*) signifies *promotion*, not *prevention*. And the word *transgression*, by its Pauline and Jewish usage, compels us to this view.[100] Transgression presupposes law. It is the specific form which sin takes under law—the re-action of sin against law. What was before a latent tendency, a bias of disposition, now starts to light as a flagrant, guilty fact. By bringing about repeated transgressions the Law reveals the true nature of sin, so that it "becomes exceeding sinful." It does not make matters worse; but it shows how bad they really are. It aggravates the disease, in order to bring it to a crisis. And this is a necessary step towards the cure.

2. The Law of Moses was therefore *a provisional dispensation,*—"added until the seed should come to whom the promise hath been made." Its object was to make itself superfluous. It "is not made for a righteous man; but for the lawless and unruly" (1 Tim. i. 9). Like the discipline and drill of a strictly governed boyhood, it was calculated to produce a certain effect on the moral nature, after the attainment of which it was no longer needed and its continuance would be injurious. The essential part of this effect lay, however, not so much in the outward regularity it imposed, as in the inner repugnancy excited by it, the consciousness of sin unsubdued and defiant. By its operation on the conscience the Law taught man his need of redemption. It thus prepared the platform for the work of Grace. The Promise had been given. The coming of the Covenant-heir was assured. But its fulfilment was far off. "The Lord is not slack concerning His promise,"—and yet it was two thousand years before "Abraham's seed" came to birth. The degeneracy of the patriarch's children in the third and fourth generation showed how little the earlier heirs of the Promise were capable of receiving it. A thousand years later, when the Covenant was renewed with David, the ancient predictions

seemed at last nearing their fulfilment. But no; the times were still unripe; the human conscience but half-disciplined. The bright dawn of the Davidic monarchy was overclouded. The legal yoke is made more burdensome; sore chastisements fall on the chosen people, marked out for suffering as well as honour. Prophecy has many lessons yet to inculcate. The world's education for Christ has another millennium to run.

Nor when He came, did "the Son of man find faith in the earth"! The people of the Law had no sooner seen than they hated "Him to whom the law and the prophets gave witness." Yet, strangely enough, the very manner of their rejection showed how complete was the preparation for His coming. Two features, rarely united, marked the ethical condition of the Jewish people at this time—an intense moral consciousness, and a deep moral perversion; reverence for the Divine law, combined with an alienation from its spirit. The chapter of Paul's autobiography to which we have so often referred (Rom. vii. 7-24) is typical of the better mind of Judaism. It is the *ne plus ultra* of self-condemnation. The consciousness of sin in mankind has ripened.

3. And further, the Law of Moses revealed God's will *in a veiled and accommodated fashion*, while the Promise and the Gospel are its direct emanations. This is the inference which we draw from vv. 19, 20.

We are well aware of the extreme difficulty of this passage. Ver. 20 has received, it is computed, some four hundred and thirty distinct interpretations. Of all the "hard things our beloved brother Paul" has written, this is the very hardest. The words which make up the sentence are simple and familiar; and yet in their combination most enigmatic. And it stands in the midst of a paragraph among the most interesting and important that the Apostle ever wrote.

Let us look first at the latter clause of ver. 19: "ordained through angels, in the hand (*i.e.* by means) of a mediator." These circumstances, as the orthodox Jew supposed, *enhanced* the glory of the Law. The pomp and formality under which Mosaism was ushered in, the presence of the angelic host to whose agency the terrific manifestations attending the Law-giving were referred, impressed the popular mind with a sense of the incomparable sacredness of the Sinaitic revelation. It was this assumption which gave its force to the climax of Stephen's speech, of which we hear an echo in these words of Paul: "who received the law at the disposition of angels—and have not kept it!"[101] The simplicity and informality of the Divine communion with Abraham, and again of Christ's appearance in the world and His intercourse with men, afford a striking contrast to all this.

More is hinted than is expressly said in Scripture of the part taken by the angels in the Law-giving. Deut. xxxiii. 2[102] and Ps. lxviii. 17 give the most definite indications of the ancient faith of Israel on this point. But "the Angel of the Lord" is a familiar figure of Old Testament revelation. In Hebrew thought impressive physical phenomena were commonly associated with the presence of spiritual agents.[103] The language of Heb. i. 7 and ii. 2 endorses this belief, which in no way conflicts with natural science, and is in keeping with the Christian faith.

But while such intermediacy, from the Jewish standpoint, increased the splendour and authority of the Law, believers in Christ had learned to look at the matter otherwise.[104] A revelation "administered *through angels*," spoke to them of a God distant and obscured, of a people unfit for access to His presence. This is plainly intimated in the added clause, "by means of *a mediator*," —a title commonly given to Moses, and recalling the entreaty of Exod. xx. 19; Deut. v. 22-28: "The people said, Speak thou with us, and we will hear; but let not God speak with us, lest we die." These are the words of sinful men, receiving a law given, as the Apostle has just declared, on purpose to convict them of their sins. The form of the Mosaic revelation tended therefore in reality not to exalt the Law, but to exhibit its difference from the Promise and the distance at which it placed men from God.

The same thought is expressed, as Bishop Lightfoot aptly shows, by the figure of "the veil on Moses' face," which Paul employs with so much felicity in 2 Cor. iii. 13-18. In the external glory of the Sinaitic law-giving, as on the illuminated face of the Law-giver, there was a fading brightness, a visible lustre concealing its imperfect and transitory character. The theophanies of the Old Covenant were a magnificent veil, hiding while they revealed. Under the Law, *angels, Moses* came between God and man. It was God who in His own grace conveyed the promise to justified Abraham (ver. 18).[105]

The Law employed *a mediator*; the Promise did not (ver. 19.). With this contrast in our minds we approach ver. 20. On the other side of it (ver. 21), we find Law and Promise again in sharp antithesis. The same antithesis runs through the intervening sentence. The two clauses of ver. 20 belong to the Law and Promise respectively. "Now a mediator is not of one:" that is an axiom which holds good of *the Law*. "But God is one:" this glorious truth, the first article of Israel's creed, applies to *the Promise*. Where "a mediator" is necessary, unity is wanting,—not simply in a numerical, but in a moral sense, as matter of feeling and of aim. There are separate interests, discordant views to be consulted. This was true of Mosaism. Although in substance "holy and just and good," it was by no means purely Divine. It was not the absolute religion. Not only was it defective; it contained, in the judgement of Christ, positive elements of wrong, precepts given "for the hardness of men's hearts."[106] It largely consisted of "carnal ordinances, imposed till the time of rectification" (Heb. ix. 10). The theocratic legislation of the Pentateuch is lacking in the unity and consistency of a perfect revelation. Its disclosures of God were refracted in a manifest degree by the atmosphere through which they passed.

"But God is one." Here again the unity is moral and essential—of character and action, rather than of number. In the Promise God spoke immediately and for Himself. There was no screen to intercept the view of faith, no go-between like Moses, with God on the mountain-top shrouded in thunder-clouds and the people terrified or wantoning far below. Of all differences between the Abrahamic and Judaic types of piety this was the chief. The man of Abraham's faith sees God in His unity. The Legalist gets his religion at second-hand, mixed with undivine elements. He believes that there is one God; but his hold upon the truth is formal. There is no unity, no simplicity of faith in his conception of God. He projects on to the Divine image confusing shadows of human imperfection.

God is One: this great article of faith was the foundation of Israel's life. It forms the first sentence of the Shemá, the "Hear, O Israel" (Deut. vi. 4-9), which every pious Jew repeats twice a day, and which in literal obedience to the Law-giver's words he fixes above his house-door, and binds upon his arm and brow at the time of prayer. Three times besides has the Apostle quoted this sentence. The first of these passages, Rom. iii. 29, 30,[107] may help us to understand its application here. In that place he employs it as a weapon against Jewish exclusiveness. If there is but "*one* God," he argues, there can be only *one* way of justification, for Jew and Gentile alike. The inference drawn here is even more bold and singular. There is "one God," who appeared in His proper character in the Covenant with Abraham. If the Law of Moses gives us a conception of His nature in any wise different from this, it is because other and lower elements found a place in it. Through the whole course of revelation there is *one God*—manifest to Abraham, veiled in Mosaism, revealed again in His perfect image in "the face of Jesus Christ."

II. So far the Apostle has pursued the contrast between the systems of Law and Grace. When finally he has referred the latter rather than the former to the "one God," we naturally ask, "Is the Law then *against* the promises of God?" (ver. 21). Was the Legal dispensation a mere reaction, a retrogression from the Promise? This would be to push Paul's argument to an antinomian extreme. He hastens to protest.—"The law against the promises? Away with the thought." Not on the Apostle's premises, but on those of his opponents, did this consequence ensue. It is *they* who set the two at variance, by trying to make law do the work of grace. "For if a law had been given that could bring men to life, righteousness would verily in that case have been of law" (ver. 21). That righteousness, and therefore life, is not of law, the Apostle has abundantly shown (ch. ii. 16; iii. 10-13). Had the Law provided some efficient means of its own for winning righteousness, there would then indeed have been a conflict between the two principles. As matters stand, there is none. Law and Promise move on different planes. Their functions are distinct. Yet there is a connection between them. The design of the Law is to mediate between the Promise and its fulfilment. "The trespass" must be "multiplied," the knowledge of sin deepened, before Grace can do its office. The fever of sin has to come to its crisis, before the remedy can take effect. Law is therefore not the enemy, but the minister of Grace. It was charged with a purpose lying beyond itself. "Christ is the end of the law, for righteousness" (Rom. x. 4).

1. For, in the first place, *the law cuts men off from all other hope of salvation.*

On the Judaistic hypothesis, "righteousness would have been of law." But quite on the contrary, "the Scripture shuts up everything under sin, that the promise might be given in the way of faith in Jesus Christ, to them that believe" (ver. 22). Condemnation inevitable, universal, was pronounced by the Divine word under the Law, not in order that men might remain crushed beneath its weight, but that, abandoning vain hopes of self-justification, they might find in Christ their true deliverer.

The Apostle is referring here to the general purport of "the Scripture." His assertion embraces the whole teaching of the Old Testament concerning human sinfulness, embodied, for example, in the chain of citations drawn out in Rom. iii. 10-18. Wherever the man looking for legal justification turned, the Scripture met him with some new command which drove him back upon the sense of his moral helplessness. It fenced him in with prohibitions; it showered on him threatenings and reproaches; it besieged him in ever narrowing circles. And if he felt less the pressure of its outward burdens, all the more was he tormented by inward disharmony and self-accusation.

Now the judgement of Scripture is not uttered against this class of men or that, against this type of sin or that. Its impeachment sweeps the entire area of human life, sounding the depths of the heart, searching every avenue of thought and desire. It makes of the world one vast prison-house, with the Law for gaoler, and mankind held fast in chains of sin, waiting for death. In this position the Apostle had found himself (Rom. vii. 24-viii. 2); and in his own heart he saw a mirror of the world. "Every mouth was stopped, and all the world brought in guilty before God" (Rom. iii. 19). This condition he graphically describes in terms of his former experience, in ver. 23: "Before faith came, under law we were kept in ward, being shut up unto the faith that was to be revealed." The Law was all the while standing guard over its subjects, watching and checking every attempt to escape,[108] but intending to hand them over in due time to the charge of Faith. The Law posts its ordinances, like so many sentinels, round the prisoner's cell. The cordon is complete. He tries again and again to break out; the iron circle will not yield. But deliverance will yet be his. The day of Faith approaches. It dawned long ago in Abraham's Promise. Even now its light shines into his dungeon, and he hears the word of Jesus, "Thy sins are forgiven thee; go in peace." Law, the stern gaoler, has after all been a good friend, if it has reserved him for this. It prevents the sinner escaping to a futile and illusive freedom.

In this dramatic fashion Paul shows how the Mosaic law by its ethical discipline prepared men for a life which by itself it was incapable of giving. Where Law has done its work well, it produces, as in the Apostle's earlier experience, a profound sense of personal demerit, a tenderness of conscience, a contrition of heart which makes one ready thankfully to receive "the righteousness which is of God by faith." In every age and condition of life a like effect is wrought upon men who honestly strive to live up to an exacting moral standard. They confess their failure. They lose self-conceit. They grow "poor in spirit," willing to accept "the abundance of *the gift* of righteousness" in Jesus Christ.

Faith is trebly honoured here. It is the condition of the gift, the characteristic of its recipient (vv. 22, 24), and the end for which he was put under the charge of Law (ver. 23). "To them that believe" is "given," as it was in foretaste to Abraham (ver. 6), a righteousness unearned, and bestowed on Christ's account (ch. iii. 13; Rom. v. 17, 18); which brings with it the indwelling of the Holy Spirit, reserved in its conscious possession for Abraham's children in the faith of Christ (ch. iii. 14; iv. 4). These blessings form the commencement of that true life, whose root is a spiritual union with Christ, and which reaches on to eternity (ch. ii. 20; Rom. v. 21; vi. 23). Of such life the Law could impart nothing; but it taught men their need of it, and disposed them to accept it. This was the purpose of its institution. It was the forerunner, not the finisher, of Faith.

2. Paul makes use of a second figure to describe the office of the Law; under which he gives his final answer to the question of ver. 19. The metaphor of the gaoler is exchanged for that of *the tutor*. "The law hath been our παιδαγωγὸς for Christ." This Greek word (*boy-leader*) has no English equivalent; we have not the thing it represents. The "pedagogue" was a sort of nursery governor,—a confidential servant in the Greek household, commonly a slave, who had charge of the boy from his infancy, and was responsible for his oversight. In his food, his clothes, his home-lessons, his play, his walks—at every point the pedagogue was required to wait upon

his young charge, and to control his movements. Amongst other offices, his tutor might have to conduct the boy to school; and it has been supposed that Paul is thinking of this duty, as though he meant, "The Law has been our pedagogue, to take us to Christ, our true teacher." But he adds, "That we might be justified of faith." The "tutor" of ver. 24 is parallel to the "guard" of the last verse; he represents a distinctly disciplinary influence.

This figure implies not like the last the imprisoned condition of the subject—but *his childish, undeveloped state*. This is an advance of thought. The Law was something more than a system of restraint and condemnation. It contained an element of progress. Under the tutelage of his pedagogue the boy is growing up to manhood. At the end of its term the Law will hand over its charge mature in capacity and equal to the responsibilities of faith. "If then the Law is a παιδαγωγός, it is not hostile to Grace, but its fellow-worker; but should it continue to hold us fast when Grace has come, then it would be hostile" (Chrysostom).

Although the highest function, that of "giving life," is denied to the Law, a worthy part is still assigned to it by the Apostle. It was "a tutor to lead men to Christ." Judaism was an education for Christianity. It prepared the world for the Redeemer's coming. It drilled and moralised the religious youth of the human race. It broke up the fallow-ground of nature, and cleared a space in the weed-covered soil to receive the seed of the kingdom. Its moral regimen deepened the conviction of sin, while it multiplied its overt acts. Its ceremonial impressed on sensuous natures the idea of the Divine holiness; and its sacrificial rites gave definiteness and vividness to men's conceptions of the necessity of atonement, failing indeed to remove sin, but awakening the need and sustaining the hope of its removal (Heb. x. 1-18).

The Law of Moses has formed in the Jewish nation a type of humanity like no other in the world. "They dwell alone," said Balaam, "and shall not be reckoned amongst the nations." Disciplined for ages under their harsh "pedagogue," this wonderful people acquired a strength of moral fibre and a spiritual sensibility that prepared them to be the religious leaders of mankind. Israel has given us David and Isaiah, Paul and John. Christ above all was "born under law—of David's seed according to flesh." The influence of Jewish minds at this present time on the world's higher thought, whether for good or evil, is incalculable; and it penetrates everywhere. The Christian Church may with increased emphasis repeat Paul's anticipation, "What will the receiving of them be, but life from the dead!" They have a great service still to do for the Lord and for His Christ. It was well for them and for us that they have "borne the yoke in their youth."

CHAPTER XV
THE EMANCIPATED SONS OF GOD

"But now that faith is come, we are no longer under a tutor. For ye are all sons of God, through faith in Christ Jesus. For as many of you as were baptized into Christ did put on Christ. There can be neither Jew nor Greek, there can be neither bond nor free, there can be no male and female: for ye all are one *man* in Christ Jesus. And if ye are Christ's, then are ye Abraham's seed, heirs according to promise." —Gal. iii. 25-29.

"Faith has come!" At this announcement Law the tutor yields up his charge; Law the gaoler sets his prisoner at liberty. The age of servitude has passed. In truth it endured long enough. The iron of its bondage had entered into the soul. But at last Faith is come; and with it comes a new world. The clock of time cannot be put back. The soul of man will never return to the old tutelage, nor submit again to a religion of rabbinism and sacerdotalism. "We are no longer under a pedagogue;" we have ceased to be children in the nursery, schoolboys at our tasks—"ye are all sons of God." In such terms the newborn, free spirit of Christianity speaks in Paul. He had tasted the bitterness of the Judaic yoke; no man more deeply. He had felt the weight of its impossible exactions, its fatal condemnation. This sentence is a shout of deliverance. "Wretch that I am," he had cried, "who shall deliver me?—I give thanks to God through Jesus Christ our Lord; ... for the law of the Spirit of life in Him hath freed me from the law of sin and death" (Rom. vii. 24-viii. 2).

Faith is the true emancipator of the human mind. It comes to take its place as mistress of the soul, queen in the realm of the heart; to be henceforth its spring of life, the norm and guiding principle of its activity. "The life that I live in the flesh," Paul testifies, "I live in faith." The Mosaic law—a system of external, repressive ordinances—is no longer to be the basis of religion. Law itself, and for its proper purposes, Faith honours and magnifies (Rom. iii. 31). It is in the interests of Law that the Apostle insists on the abolishment of its Judaic form. Faith is an essentially just principle, the rightful, original ground of human fellowship with God. In the age of Abraham, and even under the Mosaic régime, in the religion of the Prophets and Psalmists, faith was the quickening element, the well-spring of piety and hope and moral vigour. Now it is brought to light. It assumes its sovereignty, and claims its inheritance. Faith is come—for Christ is come, its "author and finisher."

The efficacy of faith lies in *its object*. "Works" assume an intrinsic merit in the doer; faith has its virtue in Him it trusts. It is the soul's recumbency on Christ. "Through faith in Christ Jesus," Paul goes on to say, "ye are all sons of God." Christ evokes the faith which shakes off legal bondage, leaving the age of formalism and ritual behind, and beginning for the world an era of spiritual freedom. "*In* Christ Jesus" faith has its being; He constitutes for the soul a new atmosphere and habitat, in which faith awakens to full existence, bursts the confining shell of legalism, recognises itself and its destiny, and unfolds into the glorious consciousness of its Divine sonship.

We prefer, with Ellicott and Meyer, to attach the complement "in Christ Jesus"[109] to "faith" (so in A.V.), rather than to the predicate, "Ye are sons"—the construction endorsed by the *Revised* comma after "faith." The former connection, more obvious in itself, seems to us to fall in with the Apostle's line of thought. And it is sustained by the language of ver. 27. *Faith in Christ, baptism into Christ,* and *putting on Christ* are connected and correspondent expressions. The first is the spiritual principle, the ground or element of the new life; the second, its visible attestation; and the third indicates the character and habit proper thereto.

I. It is *faith in Christ* then which *constitutes us sons of God*. This principle is the foundation-stone of the Christian life.

In the Old Testament the sonship of believers lay in shadow. Jehovah was "the King, the Lord of Hosts," the "Shepherd of Israel." They are "His people, the sheep of His pasture"—"My servant Jacob," He says, "Israel whom I have chosen." If He is named *Father*, it is of the collective Israel, not the individual; otherwise the title occurs only in figure and apostrophe. The promise of this blessedness had never been explicitly given under the Covenant of Moses. The assurance quoted in 2 Cor. vi. 18 is pieced together from scattered hints of prophecy. Old-Testament faith hardly dared to dream of such a privilege as this. It is not ascribed even to Abraham. Only to the kingly "Son of David" is it said, "I will be a Father unto him; and he shall be to me for a son" (2 Sam. vii. 14).

But "beloved, now are we children of God" (1 John iii. 2). The filial consciousness is the distinction of the Church of Jesus Christ. The Apostolic writings are full of it. The unspeakable dignity of this relationship, the boundless hopes which it inspires, have left their fresh impress on the pages of the New Testament. The writers are men who have made a vast discovery. They have sailed out into a new ocean. They have come upon an infinite treasure. "Thou art no longer a slave, but a son!" What exultation filled the soul of Paul and of John as they penned such words! "The Spirit of glory and of God" rested upon them.

The Apostle is virtually repeating here what he said in vv. 2-5 touching the "receiving of the Spirit," which is, he declared, the distinctive mark of the Christian state, and raises its possessor *ipso facto* above the religion of externalism. The antithesis of *flesh and spirit* now becomes that of *sonship and pupilage*. Christ Himself, in the words of Luke xi. 13, marked out the gift of "the Holy Spirit" as the bond between the "heavenly Father" and His human children. Accordingly Paul writes immediately, in ch. iv. 6, 7, of "God sending forth the Spirit of His Son into our hearts" to show that we "are sons," where we find again the thought which follows here in ver. 27, viz. that *union with Christ* imparts this exalted status. This is after all the central conception of the Christian life. Paul has already stated it as the sum of his own experience: "Christ lives in me" (ch. ii. 20). "I have put on Christ" is the same thing in other words. In ch. ii. 20 he contemplates the union as an inner, vitalising force; here it is viewed as matter of status and condition. The believer is *invested with Christ*. He enters into the filial estate and endowments, since he is *in Christ Jesus*. "For if Christ is Son of God, and thou hast put on Him, having the Son in thyself and being made like to Him, thou wast brought into one kindred and one form of being with Him" (Chrysostom).

This was true of "so many as were baptized into Christ"—an expression employed not in order to limit the assertion, but to extend it coincidently with the "all" of ver. 26. There was no difference in this respect between the circumcised and uncircumcised. Every baptized Galatian was a son of God. Baptism manifestly presupposes faith. To imagine that the *opus operatum*, the mechanical performance of the rite apart from faith present or anticipated in the subject, "clothes us with Christ," is to hark back to Judaism. It is to substitute baptism for circumcision—a difference merely of form, so long as the doctrine of ritual regeneration remains the same. This passage is as clear a proof as could well be desired, that in the Pauline vocabulary "baptized" is synonymous with "believing." The baptism of these Galatians solemnised their spiritual union with Christ. It was the public acceptance, in trust and submission, of God's covenant of grace—for their children haply, as well as for themselves.

In the case of the infant, the household to which it belongs, the religious community which receives it to be nursed in its bosom, stand sponsors for its faith. On them will rest the blame of broken vows and responsibility disowned, if their baptized children are left to lapse into ignorance of

Christ's claims upon them. The Church which practises infant baptism assumes a very serious obligation. If it takes no sufficient care to have the rite made good, if children pass through its laver to remain unmarked and unshepherded, it is sinning against Christ. Such administration makes His ordinance an object of superstition, or of contempt.

The baptism of the Galatians signalised their entrance "into Christ," the union of their souls with the dying, risen Lord. They were "baptized," as Paul phrases it elsewhere, "into His death," to "walk" henceforth with Him "in newness of life." By its very form—the normal and most expressive form of primitive baptism, the descent into and rising from the symbolic waters—it pictured the soul's death with Christ, its burial and its resurrection in Him, its separation from the life of sin and entrance upon the new career of a regenerated child of God (Rom. vi. 3-14). This power attended the ordinance "through faith in the operation of God who raised Christ from the dead" (Col. ii. 11-13). Baptism had proved to them "the laver of regeneration" in virtue of "the renewing of the Holy Spirit," under those spiritual conditions of accepted mercy and "justification by grace through faith,"[110] without which it is a mere law-work, as useless as any other. It was the outward and visible sign of the inward transaction which made the Galatian believers sons of God and heirs of life eternal. It was therefore a "putting on of Christ," a veritable assumption of the Christian character, the filial relationship to God. Every such baptism announced to heaven and earth the passage of another soul from servitude to freedom, from death unto life, the birth of a brother into the family of God. From this day the new convert was a member incorporate of the Body of Christ, affianced to his Lord, not alone in the secret vows of his heart, but pledged to Him before his fellow-men. He had *put on Christ*—to be worn in his daily life, while He dwelt in the shrine of his spirit. And men would see Christ in him, as they see the robe upon its wearer, the armour glittering on the soldier's breast.

By receiving Christ, inwardly accepted in faith, visibly assumed in baptism, we are made sons of God. *He* makes us free of the house of God, where He rules as Son, and where no slave may longer stay. Those who called themselves "Abraham's seed" and yet were "slaves of sin," must be driven from the place in God's household which they dishonoured, and must forfeit their abused prerogatives. They were not Abraham's children, for they were utterly unlike him; the Devil surely was their father, whom by their lusts they featured. So Christ declared to the unbelieving Jews (John viii. 31-44). And so the Apostle identifies the children of Abraham with the sons of God, by faith united to "the Son." Alike in the historical sonship toward Abraham and the supernatural sonship toward God, Christ is the ground of filiation. Our sonship is grafted upon His. He is "the vine," we "branches" in Him. He is *the* seed of Abraham, *the* Son of God; we, sons of God and Abraham's seed—"if we are Christ's." Through Him we derive from God; through Him all that is best in the life of humanity comes down to us. Christ is the central stock, the spiritual root of the human race. His manifestation reveals God to man, and man also to himself. In Jesus Christ we regain the Divine image, stamped upon us in Him at our creation (Col. i. 15, 16; iii. 10, 11), the filial likeness to God which constitutes man's proper nature. Its attainment is the essential blessing, the promise which descended from Abraham along the succession of faith.

Now this dignity belongs universally to Christian faith. "Ye are *all*," the Apostle says, "sons of God through faith in Him." Sonship is a human, not a Jewish distinction. The discipline Israel had endured, it endured for the world. The Gentiles have no need to pass through it again. Abraham's blessing, when it came, was to embrace "all the families of the earth." The new life in Christ in which it is realised, is as large in scope as it is complete in nature. "Faith in Christ Jesus" is a condition that opens the door to every human being,—"Jew or Greek, bond or free, male or female." If then baptized, believing Gentiles are sons of God, they stand already on a level higher than any to which Mosaism raised its professors. "Putting on Christ," they are robed in a righteousness brighter and purer than that of the most blameless legalist. What can Judaism do for them more? How could they wish to cover their glorious dress with its faded, worn-out garments? To add circumcision to their faith would be not to rise, but to sink from the state of sons to that of serfs.

II. On this first principle of the new life there rests a second. The sons of God are brethren to each other. Christianity is the perfection of society, as well as of the individual. *The faith of Christ restores the broken unity of mankind.* "In Christ Jesus there is no Jew or Greek; there is no bondman or freeman; there is no male and female. You are all one in Him."

The Galatian believer at his baptism had entered a communion which gave him for the first time the sense of a common humanity. In Jesus Christ he found a bond of union with his fellows, an identity of interest and aim so commanding that in its presence secular differences appeared as nothing. From the height to which his Divine adoption raised him these things were invisible. Distinctions of race, of rank, even that of sex, which bulk so largely in our outward life and are sustained by all the force of pride and habit, are forgotten here. These dividing lines and party-walls have no power to sunder us from Christ, nor therefore from each other in Christ. The tide of Divine love and joy which through the gate of faith poured into the souls of these Gentiles of "many nations," submerged all barriers. They are one in the brotherhood of the eternal life. When one says "I am a child of God," one no longer thinks, "I am a Greek or Jew, rich or poor, noble or ignoble—man or woman." A son of God!—that sublime consciousness fills his being.

Paul, to be sure, does not mean that these differences have ceased to exist. He fully recognises them; and indeed insists strongly on the proprieties of sex, and on the duties of civil station. He values his own Jewish birth and Roman citizenship. But "in Christ Jesus" he "counts them refuse" (Phil. iii. 4-8). Our relations to God, our heritage in Abraham's Testament, depend on our faith in Christ Jesus and our possession of His Spirit. Neither birth nor office affects this relationship in the least degree. "As many as are led by the Spirit of God, they are the sons of God" (Rom. viii. 14). This is the Divine criterion of churchmanship, applied to prince or beggar, to archbishop or sexton, with perfect impartiality. "God is no respecter of persons."

This rule of the Apostle's was a new principle in religion, pregnant with immense consequences. The Stoic cosmopolitan philosophy made a considerable approach to it, teaching as it did the worth of the moral person and the independence of virtue upon outward conditions. Buddhism previously, and Mohammedanism subsequently, each in its own way, addressed themselves to man as man, declaring all believers equal and abolishing the privileges of race and caste. To their recognition of human brotherhood the marvellous victories won by these two creeds are largely due. These religious systems, with all their errors, were a signal advance upon Paganism with its "gods many and lords many," its local and national deities, whose worship belittled the idea of God and turned religion into an engine of hostility instead of a bond of union amongst men.

Greek culture, moreover, and Roman government, as it has often been observed, had greatly tended to unify mankind. They diffused a common atmosphere of thought and established one imperial law round the circuit of the Mediterranean shores. But these conquests of secular civilization, the victories of arms and arts, were achieved at the expense of religion. Polytheism is essentially barbarian. It flourishes in division and in ignorance. To bring together its innumerable gods and creeds was to bring them all into contempt. The *one law*, the *one learning* now prevailing in the world, created a void in the conscience of mankind, only to be filled by the *one faith*. Without a centre of spiritual unity, history shows that no other union will endure. But for Christianity, the Græco-Roman civilization would have perished, trampled out by the feet of Goths and Huns.

The Jewish faith failed to meet the world's demand for a universal religion. It could never have saved European society. Nor was it designed for such a purpose. True, its Jehovah was "the God of the whole earth." The teaching of the Old Testament, as Paul easily showed, had a universal import and brought all men within the scope of its promises. But in its actual shape and its positive institutions it was still tribal and exclusive. Mosaism planted round the family of Abraham a fence of ordinances, framed of set purpose to make them a separate people and preserve them from heathen contamination. This system, at first maintained with difficulty, in course of time gained control of the Israelitish nature, and its exclusiveness was aggravated by every device of Pharisaic ingenuity. Without an entire transformation, without in fact ceasing to be Judaism, the Jewish religion was doomed to isolation. Under the Roman Empire, in consequence of the ubiquitous dispersion of the Jews, it spread far and wide. It attracted numerous and influential converts. But these proselytes never were, and never could have been generally amalgamated with the sacred people. They remained in the outer court, worshipping the God of Israel "afar off" (Eph. ii. 11-22; iii. 4-6).

This particularism of the Mosaic system was, to Paul's mind, a proof of its temporary character. The abiding faith, the faith of "Abraham and his seed," must be broad as humanity. It could know nothing of Jew and Gentile, of master and slave, nor even of man and woman; it knows only *the soul and God*. The gospel of Christ allied itself thus with the nascent instinct of humanity, the fellow-feeling of the race. It adopted the sentiment of the Roman poet, himself an enfranchised slave, who wrote: *Homo sum, et humani a me nil alienum puto*. In our religion human kinship at last receives adequate expression. The Son of man lays the foundation of a world-wide fraternity. The one Father claims all men for His sons in Christ. A new, tenderer, holier humanity is formed around His cross. Men of the most distant climes and races, coming across their ancient battle-fields, clasp each other's hands and say, "Beloved, if God so loved us, we ought also to love one another."

The practice of the Church has fallen far below the doctrine of Christ and His Apostles. In this respect Mohammedans and Buddhists might teach Christian congregations a lesson of fraternity. The arrangements of our public worship seem often designed expressly to emphasize social distinctions, and to remind the poor man of his inequality. Our native *hauteur* and conventionality are nowhere more painfully conspicuous than in the house of God. English Christianity is seamed through and through with caste-feeling. This lies at the root of our sectarian jealousies. It is largely due to this cause that the social ideal of Jesus Christ has been so deplorably ignored, and that a frank brotherly fellowship amongst the Churches is at present impossible. Sacerdotalism first destroyed the Christian brotherhood by absorbing in the official ministry the functions of the individual believer. And the Protestant Reformation has but partially re-established these prerogatives. Its action has been so far too exclusively negative and *protéstant,* too little constructive and creative. It has allowed itself to be secularised and identified with existing national limitations and social distinctions. How greatly has the authority of our faith and the influence of the Church suffered from this error. The filial consciousness should produce *the fraternal consciousness.* With the former we may have a number of private Christians; with the latter only can we have a Church.

"Ye are all," says the Apostle, "one (man) in Christ Jesus." The numeral is masculine, not neuter—*one person* (no abstract unity),[111] as though possessing one mind and will, and that "the mind that was in Christ." Just so far as individual men are "in Christ" and He becomes the soul of their life, do they realise this unity. The Christ within them recognises the Christ without, as "face answereth to face in a glass." In this recognition social disparity vanishes. We think of it no more than we shall do before the judgement-seat of Christ. What matters it whether my brother wears velvet or fustian, if Christ be in him? The humbleness of his birth or occupation, the uncouthness of his speech, cannot separate him, nor can the absence of these peculiarities separate his neighbour, from the love of God in Christ Jesus our Lord. Why should these differences make them strangers to each other in the Church? If both are *in Christ,* why are they not *one in Christ*? A tide of patriotic emotion, a scene of pity or terror—a shipwreck, an earthquake— levels all classes and makes us feel and act as one man. Our faith in Christ should do no less. Or do we love God less than we fear death? Is our country more to us than Jesus Christ? In rare moments of exaltation we rise, it may be, to the height at which Paul sets our life. But until we can habitually and by settled principle in our Church-relations "know no man after the flesh," we come short of the purpose of Jesus Christ (comp. John xvii. 20-23).

The unity Paul desiderates would effectually counteract the Judaistic agitation. The force of the latter lay in antipathy. Paul's opponents contended that there must be "Jew and Greek." They fenced off the Jewish preserve from uncircumcised intruders. Gentile nonconformists must adopt their ritual; or they will remain a lower caste, outside the privileged circle of the covenant-heirs of Abraham. Compelled under this pressure to accept the Mosaic law, it was anticipated that they would add to the glory of Judaism and help to maintain its institutions unimpaired. But the Apostle has cut the ground from under their feet. It is *faith,* he affirms, which makes men sons of God. And faith is equally possible to Jew or Gentile. Then Judaism is doomed. No system of caste, no principle of social exclusion has, on this assumption, any foothold in the Church. Spiritual life, nearness and likeness to the common Saviour—in a word *character,* is the standard of worth in His kingdom. And the range of that kingdom is made wide as humanity; its charity, deep as the love of God.

And "if you—whether Jews or Greeks—are Christ's, then are you Abraham's seed, heirs in terms of the Promise." So the Apostle brings to a close this part of his argument, and links it to what he has said before touching the fatherhood of Abraham. Since ver. 18 we have lost sight of the patriarch; but he has not been forgotten. From that verse Paul has been conducting us onward through the legal centuries which parted Abraham from Christ. He has shown how the law of Moses interposed between promise and fulfilment, schooling the Jewish race and mankind in them for its accomplishment. Now the long discipline is over. The hour of release has struck. Faith resumes her ancient sway, in a larger realm. In Christ a new, universal humanity comes into existence, formed of men who by faith are grafted into Him. Partakers of Christ, Gentiles also are of the seed of Abraham; the wild scions of nature share "the root and fatness of the good olive-tree." All things are theirs; for they are Christ's (1 Cor. iii. 21-23).

Christ never stands alone. "In the midst of the Church—firstborn of many brethren" He presents Himself, standing "in the presence of God for us." He has secured for mankind and keeps in trust its glorious heritage. In Him we hold in fee the ages past and to come. The sons of God are heirs of the universe.

CHAPTER XVI
THE HEIR'S COMING OF AGE

"But I say that so long as the heir is a child, he differeth nothing from a bondservant, though he is lord of all; but is under guardians and stewards until the term appointed of the father. So we also, when we were children, were held in bondage under the rudiments of the world: but when the fulness of the time came, God sent forth His Son, born of a woman, born under the law, that He might redeem them which were under the law, that we might receive the adoption of sons. And because ye are sons, God sent forth the Spirit of His Son into our hearts, crying, Abba Father. So that thou art no longer a bondservant, but a son; and if a son, then an heir through God."—Gal. iv. 1-7.

The main thesis of the Epistle is now established. Gentile Christians, Paul has shown, are in the true Abrahamic succession of faith. And this devolution of the Promise discloses the real intent of the Mosaic law, as an intermediate and disciplinary system. Christ was the heir of Abraham's testament; He was therefore the end of Moses' law. And those who are Christ's inherit the blessings of the Promise, while they escape the curse and condemnation of the Law. The remainder of the Apostle's polemic, down to ch. v. 12, is devoted to the illustration and enforcement of this position.

In this, as in the previous chapter, the pre-Christian state is assigned to the Jew, who was the chief subject of Divine teaching in the former dispensation; it is set forth under the first person (ver. 3), in the language of recollection. Describing the opposite condition of sonship, the Apostle reverts from the first to the second person, identifying his readers with himself (comp. ch. iii. 25, 26). True, the Gentiles had been in bondage (vv. 7, 8). This goes without saying. Paul's object is to show that *Judaism* is a bondage. Upon this he insists with all the emphasis he can command. Moreover, the legal system contained worldly, unspiritual elements, crude and childish conceptions of truth, marking it, in comparison with Christianity, as an inferior religion. Let the Galatians be convinced of this, and they will understand what Paul is going to say directly; they will perceive that Judaic conformity is for them a backsliding in the direction of their former heathenism (vv. 8-10). But the force of this latter warning is discounted and its effect weakened when he is supposed, as by some interpreters, to include *Gentile* along with Jewish "rudiments" already in ver. 3. His readers could not have suspected this. The "So we also" and the "held in bondage" of this verse carry them back to ch. iii. 23. By calling the Mosaic ceremonies "rudiments of *the world*" he gives Jewish susceptibilities just such a shock as prepares for the declaration of ver. 9, which puts them on a level with heathen rites.

The difference between Judaism and Christianity, historically unfolded in ch. iii., is here restated in graphic summary. We see, first, *the heir of God in his minority*; and again, *the same heir in possession of his estate*.

I. One can fancy the Jew replying to Paul's previous argument in some such style as this. "You pour contempt," he would say, "on the religion of your fathers. You make them out to have been no better than slaves. Abraham's inheritance, you pretend, under the Mosaic dispensation lay dormant, and is revived in order to be taken from his children and conferred on aliens." No, Paul would answer: I admit that the saints of Israel were sons of God; I glory in the fact—"who are Israelites, whose is *the adoption of sons* and the glory and the covenants and the law-giving and the promises, whose are the fathers" (Rom. ix. 4, 5). *But they were sons in their minority.* "And I say that as long as the heir is (legally) an infant, he differs in nothing from a slave, though (by title) lord of all."

The man of the Old Covenant was a child of God *in posse*, not *in esse*, in right but not in fact. The "infant" is his father's trueborn son. In time he will be full owner. Meanwhile he is as subject as any slave on the estate. There is nothing he can command for his own. He is treated and provided for as a bondman might be; put "under stewards" who manage his property, "and guardians" in charge of his person, "until the day fore-appointed of the father." This situation does not exclude, it implies fatherly affection and care on the one side, and heirship on the other. But it forbids the recognition of the heir, his investment with filial rights. It precludes the access to the father and acquaintance with him, which the boy will gain in after years. He sees him at a distance and through others, under the aspect of authority rather than of love. In this position he does not yet possess the spirit of a son. Such was in truth the condition of Hebrew saints—heirs of God, but knowing it not.

This illustration raises in ver. 2 an interesting legal question, touching the latitude given by Roman or other current law to the father in dealing with his heirs. Paul's language is good evidence for the existence of the power he refers to. In Roman and in Jewish law the date of civil majority was fixed.

Local usage may have been more elastic. But the case supposed, we observe, is not that of a *dead* father, into whose place the son steps at the proper age. A grant is made by a father *still living*, who keeps his son in pupilage till he sees fit to put him in possession of the promised estate. There is nothing to show that paternal discretion was limited in these circumstances, any more than it is in English law. The father might fix eighteen, or twenty-one, or thirty years as the age at which he would give his son a settlement, just as he thought best.

This analogy, like that of the "testament" in ch. iii., is not complete at all points; nor could any human figure of these Divine things be made so. The essential particulars involved in it are first, *the childishness of the infant heir*; secondly, *the subordinate position in which he is placed for the time*; and thirdly, *the right of the father to determine the expiry of his infancy*.

1. "When we were children," says the Apostle. This implies, not a merely formal and legal bar, but an intrinsic disqualification. To treat the child as a man is preposterous. The responsibilities of property are beyond his strength and his understanding. Such powers in his hands could only be instruments of mischief, to himself most of all. In the Divine order, calling is suited to capacity, privilege to age. The coming of Christ was timed to the hour. The world of the Old Testament, at its wisest and highest, was unripe for His gospel. The revelation made to Paul could not have been received by Moses, or David, or Isaiah. His doctrine was only possible after and in consequence of theirs. There was a training of faculty, a deepening of conscience, a patient course of instruction and chastening to be carried out, before the heirs of the promise were fit for their heritage. Looking back to his own youthful days, the Apostle sees in them a reflex of the discipline which the people of God had required. The views he then held of Divine truth appear to him low and childish, in comparison with the manly freedom of spirit, the breadth of knowledge, the fulness of joy which he has attained as a son of God through Christ.

2. But what is meant by the "stewards and guardians" of this Jewish period of infancy? Ver. 3 tells us this, in language, however, somewhat obscure: "We were held in bondage under *the rudiments* (or *elements*) *of the world*" —a phrase synonymous with the foregoing "under law" (ch. iii. 23). The "guard" and "tutor" of the previous section re-appears, with these "rudiments of the world" in his hand. They form the system under which the young heir was schooled, up to the time of his majority. They belonged to "the world"[112] inasmuch as they were, in comparison with Christianity, unspiritual in their nature, uninformed by "the Spirit of God's Son" (ver. 6). The language of Heb. ix. 1, 10 explains this phrase: "The first covenant had a *worldly* sanctuary," with "ordinances of flesh, imposed till the time of

rectification." The sensuous factor that entered into the Jewish revelation formed the point of contact with Paganism which Paul brings into view in the next paragraph. Yet rude and earthly as the Mosaic system was in some of its features, it was Divinely ordained and served an essential purpose in the progress of revelation. It shielded the Church's infancy. It acted the part of a prudent steward, a watchful guardian. The heritage of Abraham came into possession of his heirs enriched by their long minority. Mosaism therefore, while spiritually inferior to the Covenant of grace in Christ, has rendered invaluable service to it (comp. ver. 24: Chapter XIV., p. 225).

3. *The will of the Father* determined the period of this guardianship. However it may be in human law, this right of fore-ordination resides in the Divine Fatherhood. In His unerring foresight He fixed the hour when His sons should step into their filial place. All such "times and seasons," Christ declared, "the Father hath appointed on His own authority" (Acts i. 7). He imposed the law of Moses, and annulled it, when He would. He kept the Jewish people, for their own and the world's benefit, tied to the legal "rudiments," held in the leading-strings of Judaism. It was His to say when this subjection should cease, when the Church might receive the Spirit of His Son. If this decree appeared to be arbitrary, if it was strange that the Jewish fathers—men so noble in faith and character—were kept in bondage and fear, we must remind ourselves that "so it seemed good in the Father's sight." Hebrew pride found this hard to brook. To think that God had denied this privilege in time past to His chosen people, to bestow it all at once and by mere grace on Gentile sinners, making them at "the eleventh hour" equal to those who had borne for so long the burden and heat of the day! that the children of Abraham had been, as Paul maintains, for centuries treated as *slaves*, and now these heathen aliens are made *sons* just as much as they! But this was God's plan; and it must be right. "Who art thou, O man, that repliest against God?"

II. However, the nonage of the Church has passed. God's sons are now to be owned for such. *It is Christ's mission to constitute men sons of God* (vv. 4, 5).

His advent was the turning-point of human affairs, "the fulness of time." Paul's glance in these verses takes in a vast horizon. He views Christ in His relation both to God and to humanity, both to law and redemption. The appearance of "the Son of God, woman-born," completes the previous course of time; it is the goal of antecedent revelation, unfolding "the mystery kept secret through times eternal," but now "made known to all the nations" (Rom. xvi. 25, 26). Promise and Law both looked forward to this hour. Sin had been "passed by" in prospect of it, receiving hitherto a partial and provisional forgiveness. The aspirations excited, the needs created by earlier religion demanded their satisfaction. The symbolism of type and ceremony, with their rude picture-writing, waited for their Interpreter. The prophetic soul of "the wide world, dreaming of things to come," watched for this day. They that looked for Israel's redemption, the Simeons and Annas of the time, the authentic heirs of the promise, knew by sure tokens that it was near. Their aged eyes in the sight of the infant Jesus descried its rising. The set time had come, to which all times looked since Adam's fall and the first promise. At the moment when Israel seemed farthest from help and hope, the "horn of salvation was raised up in the house of David,"— *God sent forth His Son.*

1. *The sending of the Son* brought the world's servitude to an end. "Henceforth," said Jesus, "I call you not servants" (John xv. 15). Till now "servant of God" had been the highest title men could wear. The heathen were enslaved to false gods (ver. 8). And Israel, knowing the true God, knew Him at a distance, serving too often in the spirit of the elder son of the parable, who said, "Lo these many years do I *slave* for thee" (Luke xv. 29). None could with free soul lift his eyes to heaven and say, "Abba, Father." Men had great thoughts about God, high speculations. They had learnt imperishable truths concerning His unity, His holiness, His majesty as Creator and Lawgiver. They named Him the "Lord," the "Almighty," the "I AM." But His *Fatherhood* as Christ revealed it, they had scarcely guessed. They thought of Him as humble bondmen of a revered and august master, as sheep might of a good shepherd. The idea of a personal *sonship* towards the Holy One of Israel was inconceivable, till Christ brought it with Him into the world, till *God sent forth His Son.*

He sent Him as "His Son." To speak of Christ, with the mystical Germans, as the *ideal Urmensch*—the ideal Son of man, the foretype of humanity—is to express a great truth. Mankind was created in Christ, who is "the image of God, firstborn of all creation." But this is not what Paul is saying here. The doubly compounded Greek verb at the head of this sentence (repeated with like emphasis in ver. 6) signifies "sent forth from" Himself: He came in the character of *God's* Son, bringing His sonship with Him. He was the Son of God before He was sent out. He did not become so in virtue of His mission to mankind. His relations with men, in Paul's conception, rested upon His pre-existing relationship to God. "The Word" who "became flesh, was with God, was God in the beginning." "He called God His own Father, making Himself equal with God" (John v. 18): so the Jews had gathered from His own declarations. Paul admitted the claim when "God revealed His Son" to him, and affirms it here unequivocally.

"The Son of God," arriving "in the fulness of time," enters human life. Like any other son of man, He is *born of a woman, born under law.* Here is the *kenosis*, the emptying of Divinity, of which the Apostle speaks in Phil. ii. 5-8. The phrase "born of woman," does not refer specifically to the *virgin-birth*; this term describes human origin on the side of its weakness and dependence (Job xiv. 1; Matt. xi. 11). Paul is thinking not of the difference, but of the identity of Christ's birth and our own. We are carried back to Bethlehem. We see Jesus a babe lying in His mother's arms—*God's Son a human infant*, drawing His life from a weak woman![113]

Nor is "born under law" a distinction intended to limit the previous term, as though it meant a *born Jew*, and not a mere woman's son. This expression, to the mind of the reader of ch. iii., conveys the idea of *subjection*, of humiliation rather than eminence. "Though He was (God's) Son," Christ must needs "learn His obedience" (Heb. v. 8). The Jewish people experienced above all others the power of the law to chasten and humble. Their law was to them more sensibly, what the moral law is in varying degree to the world everywhere, an instrument of condemnation. God's Son was now put under its power. As a man He was "under law;" as a Jew He came under its most stringent application. He declined none of the burdens of His birth. He submitted not only to the general moral demands of the Divine law for men, but to all the duties and proprieties incident to His position as a man, even to those ritual ordinances which His coming was to abolish. He set a perfect example of loyalty. "Thus it becometh us," He said, "to fulfil all righteousness."

The Son of God who was to end the legal bondage, was sent into it Himself. He wore the legal yoke that He might break it. He took "the form of a servant," to win our enfranchisement. "God sent forth His Son, human, law-bound—that He might *redeem those under law*."

Redemption was Christ's errand. We have learned already how "He redeemed us from the curse of the law," by the sacrifice of the cross (ch. iii. 13). This was the primary object of His mission: to ransom men from the guilt of past sin. Now we discern its further purpose—the positive and constructive side of the Divine counsel. Justification is the preface to *adoption*. The man "under law" is not only cursed by his failure to keep it; he lives in a servile state, debarred from filial rights. Christ "bought us out" of this condition. While the expiation rendered in His death clears off the entail of human guilt, His incarnate life and spiritual union with believing men sustain that action, making the redemption complete and permanent. As enemies, "we were reconciled to God by the death of His Son;" now "reconciled, we shall be saved by His life" (Rom. v. 10). Salvation is not through the death of Christ alone. The Babe of Bethlehem, the crowned Lord of glory is our Redeemer, as well as the Man of Calvary. The cross is indeed the centre of His redemption; but it has a vast circumference. All that Christ is, all that He has done and is doing as the Incarnate Son, the God-man, helps to make men sons of God. The purpose of His mission is therefore stated a second time and made complete in the words of ver. 5 b: "that we might *receive the adoption of sons*." The sonship carries everything else with it—"if children, then heirs" (ver. 7). There is no room for any supplementary office of Jewish ritual. That is left behind with our babyhood.

2. So much for the ground of sonship. Its proof lay in the *sending forth of the Spirit of the Son*.

The mission of the Son and that of the Spirit are spoken of in vv. 3-6 in parallel terms: "God *sent forth* His Son—*sent forth* the Spirit of His Son," the former into the world of men, the latter "into" their individual "hearts." The second act matches the first, and crowns it. Pentecost is the sequel of the Incarnation (John ii. 21; 1 Cor. vi. 19, 20). And Pentecost is repeated in the heart of every child of God. The Apostle addresses himself to his readers' experience ("because *ye* are sons") as in ch. iii. 3-6, and on the same point. They had "received the Spirit:" this marked them indubitably as heirs of Abraham (ch. iii. 14)—and what is more, sons of God. Had not the mystic cry, *Abba, Father*, sounded in their hearts? The filial consciousness was born within them, supernaturally inspired. When they believed in Christ, when they saw in Him the Son of God, their Redeemer, they were stirred with a new, ecstatic impulse; a Divine glow of love and joy kindled in their breasts; a voice not their own spoke to their spirit—their soul leaped forth upon their lips, crying to God, "Father, Father!" They were children of God, and knew it. "The Spirit Himself bore them witness" (Rom. viii. 15).

This sentiment was not due to their own reflection, not the mere opening of a buried spring of feeling in their nature. *God sent it* into their hearts. The outward miracles which attended the first bestowment of this gift, showed from what source it came (ch. iii. 5). Nor did Christ personally impart the assurance. He had gone, that the Paraclete might come. Here was another Witness, sent by a second mission from the Father (John xvi. 7). His advent is signalised in clear distinction from that of the Son. He comes in the joint name of Father and of Son. Jesus called Him "the Spirit of the Father;"[114] the Apostle, "the Spirit of God's Son."

To us He is "the Spirit of adoption," replacing the former "spirit of bondage unto fear." For by His indwelling we are "joined to the Lord" and made "one spirit" with Him, so that Christ lives in us (ch. ii. 20). And since Christ is above all things the Son, His Spirit is a spirit of sonship; those who receive Him are sons of God. Our sonship is through the Holy Spirit derived from His. Till Christ's redemption was effected, such adoption was in the nature of things impossible. This filial cry of Gentile hearts attested the entrance of a Divine life into the world. The Spirit of God's Son had become the new spirit of mankind.

Abba, the Syrian vocative for *father*, was a word familiar to the lips of Jesus. The instance of its use recorded in Mark xiv. 36, was but one of many such. No one had hitherto approached God as He did. His utterance of this word, expressing the attitude of His life of prayer and breathing the whole spirit of His religion, profoundly affected His disciples. So that the *Abba* of Jesus became a watchword of His Church, being the proper name of the God and Father of our Lord Jesus Christ. Gentile believers pronounced it, conscious that in doing so they were joined in spirit to the Lord who said, "My Father, and your Father!" Greek-speaking Christians supplemented it by their own equivalent, as we by the English *Father*. This precious vocable is carried down the ages and round the whole world in the mother-tongue of Jesus, a memorial of the hour when through Him men learned to call God Father.

"Because ye are sons, God sent forth the Spirit," with this cry. The witness of sonship follows on the adoption, and seals it. The child is born, then cries; the cry is the evidence of life. But this is not the first office of the Holy Spirit to the regenerate soul. Many a silent impulse has He given, frequent and long continued may have been His visitations, before His presence reveals itself audibly. From the first the new life of grace is implanted by His influence. "That which is *born of the Spirit*, is spirit." "He dwelleth with you, and *is in you*,"[115] said Jesus to His disciples, before the Pentecostal effusion. Important and decisive as the witness of the Holy Spirit to our sonship is, we must not limit His operation to this event. Deeply has He wrought already on the soul in which His work reaches this issue; and when it is reached, He has still much to bestow, much to accomplish in us. All truth, all holiness, all comfort are His; and into these He leads the children of God. Living by the Spirit, in Him we proceed to walk (ch. v. 25).

The interchange of person in the subject of vv. 5-8 is very noticeable. This agitated style betrays high-strung emotion. Writing first, in ver. 3, in the language of Jewish experience, in ver. 6 Paul turns upon his readers and claims them for witnesses to the same adoption which Jewish believers in Christ (ver. 5) had received. Instantly he falls back into the first person; it is his own joyous consciousness that breaks forth in the filial cry of ver. 6*b*. In the more calm concluding sentence the second person is resumed; and now in the individualising singular, as though he would lay hold of his readers one by one, and bid them look each into his own heart to find the proof of sonship, as he writes: "So that thou art no longer a slave, but a son; and if a son, also an heir through God."

An heir through God—this is the true reading, and is greatly to the point. It carries to a climax the emphatic repetition of "God" observed in vv. 4 and 6. "*God* sent His Son" into the world; "*God* sent" in turn "His Son's Spirit into your hearts." God then, and no other, has bestowed your inheritance. It is yours by His fiat. Who dares challenge it?[116] Words how suitable to reassure Gentile Christians, browbeaten by arrogant Judaism! Our reply is the same to those who at this day deny our Christian and churchly standing, because we reject their sacerdotal claims.

What this inheritance includes in its final attainment, "doth not yet appear." Enough to know that "now are we children of God." The redemption of the body, the deliverance of nature from its sentence of dissolution, the abolishment of death—these are amongst its certainties. Its supreme joy lies in the promise of being with Christ, to witness and share His glory.[117] "Heirs of God, joint-heirs with Christ"—a destiny like this overwhelms thought and makes hope a rapture. God's sons may be content to wait and see how their heritage will turn out. Only let us be sure that we are His sons. Doctrinal orthodoxy, ritual observance, moral propriety do not impart, and do not supersede "the earnest of the Spirit in our hearts." The religion of Jesus the Son of God is the religion of the filial consciousness.

CHAPTER XVII
THE RETURN TO BONDAGE

"Howbeit at that time, not knowing God, ye were in bondage to them which by nature are no gods: but now that ye have come to know God, or rather to be known of God, how turn ye back again to the weak and beggarly rudiments, whereunto ye desire to be in bondage over again? Ye observe days, and months, and seasons, and years. I am afraid of you, lest by any means I have bestowed labour upon you in vain"—Gal. iv. 8-11.

"Sons of God, whom He made His heirs in Christ, how are you turning back to legal bondage!" Such is the appeal with which the Apostle follows up his argument. "Foolish Galatians," we seem to hear him say again, "who has bewitched you into this?" They forget the call of the Divine grace; they turn away from the sight of Christ crucified; nay, they are renouncing their adoption into the family of God. Paul knew something of the fickleness of human nature; but he was not prepared for this. How can men who have tasted liberty prefer slavery, or fullgrown sons desire to return to the "rudiments" of childhood? After knowing God as He is in Christ, is it possible that these Galatians have begun to dote on ceremonial, to make a religion of "times and seasons;" that they are becoming devotees of Jewish ritual? What can be more frivolous, more irrational than this? On such people Paul's labours seem to be thrown away. "You make me fear," he says, "that I have toiled for you in vain."

In this expostulation two principles emerge with especial prominence.

I. First, that *knowledge of God, bringing spiritual freedom, lays upon us higher responsibilities.* "Then indeed," he says, "not knowing God, you were in bondage to false gods. Your heathen life was in a sense excusable. But now something very different is expected from you, since you have come to know God."

We are reminded of the Apostle's memorable words spoken at Athens: "The times of ignorance God overlooked" (Acts xvii. 30). "Ye say, We see," said Jesus; "your sin remaineth" (John ix. 41). Increased light brings stricter judgement. If this was true of men who had merely heard the message of Christ, how much more of those who had proved its saving power. Ritualism was well enough for Pagans, or even for Jews before Christ's coming and the outpouring of His Spirit—but for Christians! For those into whose hearts God had breathed the Spirit of His Son, who had learned to "worship God in the Spirit and to have no confidence in the flesh"—for Paul's Galatians to yield to the legalist "persuasion" was a fatal relapse. In principle, and in its probable issue, this course was a reverting toward their old heathenism.

The Apostle again recalls them, as he does so often his children in Christ, to the time of their conversion. They had been, he reminds them, idolaters; ignorant of the true God, they were "enslaved to things that by nature are no gods." Two definitions Paul has given of idolatry: "There is no idol in the world;" and again, "The things which the Gentiles sacrifice, they sacrifice to demons, and not to God" (1 Cor. viii. 4; x. 20). Half lies, half devilry: such was the popular heathenism of the day. "Gods many and lords many" the Galatian Pagans worshipped—a strange Pantheon. There were their old, weird Celtic deities, before whom our British forefathers trembled. On this ancestral faith had been superimposed the frantic rites of the Phrygian Mother, Cybele, with her mutilated priests; and the more genial and humanistic cultus of the Greek Olympian gods. But they were gone, the whole "damnéd crew," as Milton calls them; for those whose eyes had seen the glory in the face of Jesus Christ, their spell was broken; heaven was swept clear and earth pure of their foul presence. The old gods are dead. No renaissance of humanism, no witchcraft of poetry can re-animate them. To us after these eighteen centuries, as to the Galatian believers, "there is one God the Father, of whom are all things, and we for Him; and one Lord Jesus Christ, through whom are all things, and we through Him." A man who knew the Old Testament, to say nothing of the teaching of Christ, could never sacrifice to Jupiter and Mercurius any more, nor shout "Great is Diana of the Ephesians." They were painted idols, shams; he had seen through them. They might frighten children in the dark; but the sun was up. Christianity destroyed Paganism as light kills darkness. Paul did not fear that his readers would slide back into actual heathenism. That was intellectually impossible. There are warnings in his Epistles against the spirit of idolatry, and against conformity with its customs; but none against return to its beliefs.

The old heathen life was indeed a slavery, full of fear and degradation. The religious Pagan could never be sure that he had propitiated his gods sufficiently, or given to all their due. They were jealous and revengeful, envious of human prosperity, capable of infinite wrongdoing. In the worship of many of them acts were enjoined revolting to the conscience. And this is true of Polytheism all over the world. It is the most shameful bondage ever endured by the soul of man.

But Paul's readers had "come to know God." They had touched the great Reality. The phantoms had vanished; the Living One stood before them. His glory shone into their hearts "in the face of Jesus Christ." This, whenever it takes place, is for any man the crisis of his life—when he *comes to know God*, when *the God-consciousness* is born in him. Like the dawn of self-consciousness, it may be gradual. There are those, the happy few, who were "born again" so soon as they were born to thought and choice; they cannot remember a time when they did not love God, when they were not sensible of being "known of Him." But with others, as with Paul, the revelation is made at an instant, coming like a lightning-flash at midnight. But unlike the lightning it remained. Let the manifestation of God come how or when it may, it is decisive. The man into whose soul the Almighty has spoken His *I AM*, can never be the same afterwards. He may forget; he may deny it: but he has *known God*; he has seen the light of life. If he returns to darkness, his darkness is blacker and guiltier than before. On his brow there rests in all its sadness "Sorrow's crown of sorrow, remembering happier things."

Offences venial, excusable hitherto, from this time assume a graver hue. Things that in a lower stage of life were innocent, and even possessed religious value, may now be unlawful, and the practice of them a declension, the first step in apostasy. What is delightful in a child, becomes folly in a grown man. The knowledge of God in Christ has raised us in the things of the spirit to man's estate, and it requires that we should "put away childish things," and amongst them ritual display and sacerdotal officiations, Pagan, Jewish, or Romish. These things form no part of the knowledge of God, or of the "true worship of the Father."

The Jewish "rudiments" were designed for men who had not known God as Christ declares Him, who had never seen the Saviour's cross. Jewish saints could not worship God in the Spirit of adoption. They remained under the spirit of servitude and fear. Their conceptions were so far "weak and poor" that they supposed the Divine favour to depend on such matters as the "washing of cups and pots," and the precise number of feet that one walked on the Sabbath. These ideas belonged to a childish stage of the religious life. Pharisaism had developed to the utmost this lower element of the Mosaic system, at the expense of everything that was spiritual in it. Men who had been brought up in Judaism might indeed, after conversion to Christ, retain their old customs as matters of social usage or pious habit, without regarding them as vital to religion. With Gentiles it was otherwise. Adopting Jewish rites *de novo*, they must do so on grounds of distinct religious necessity. For this very reason the duty of circumcision was pressed upon them. It was a means, they were told, essential to their spiritual perfection, to the attainment of full Christian privileges. But to know God by the witness of the Holy Spirit of Christ, as the Galatians had done, was an experience sufficient to show that this "persuasion" was false. It did not "come of Him that called them." It introduced them to a path the opposite of that they had entered at their conversion, a way that led downwards and not upwards, from the spiritual to the sensuous, from the salvation of faith to that of self-wrought work of law.

"Known God," Paul says,—"or rather *were known of God.*" He hastens to correct himself. He will not let an expression pass that seems to ascribe anything simply to human acquisition. "Ye have not chosen Me," said Jesus; "I have chosen you." So the Apostle John: "Not that we loved God, but that He loved us." This is true through the entire range of the Christian life. "We apprehend that for which we were apprehended by Christ Jesus." Our love, our knowledge—what are they but the sense of the Divine love and knowledge in us? Religion is a bestowment, not an achievement. It is "God working in us to will and work for the sake of His good pleasure." In this light the gospel presented itself at first to the Galatians. The preaching of the Apostle, the vision of the cross of Christ, made them sensible of God's living presence. They felt the gaze of an Infinite purity and compassion, of an All-wise, All-pitiful Father, fixed upon them. He was calling them, slaves of idolatry and sin, "into the fellowship of His Son Jesus Christ." The illuminating glance of God pierced to their inmost being. In that light God and the soul met, and knew each other.

And now, after this profound, transforming revelation, this sublime communion with God, will they turn back to a life of puerile formalities, of slavish dependence and fear? Is the strength of their devotion to be spent, its fragrance exhaled in the drudgery of legal service? Surely they know God better than to think that He requires this. And He who knew them, as they have proved, and knows what was right and needful for them, has imposed no such burden. He granted them the rich gifts of His grace—the Divine sonship, the heavenly heirship—on terms of mere faith in Christ, and without legal stipulation of any kind. Is it not enough that God knows them, and counts them for His children!

So knowing, and so known, let them be content. Let them seek only to keep themselves in the love of God, and in the comfort of His Spirit. Raised to this high level, they must not decline to a lower. Their heathen "rudiments" were excusable before; but now even Jewish "rudiments" are things to be left behind.

II. It further appears that the Apostle saw *an element existing in Judaism common to it with the ethnic religions.* For he says that his readers, formerly "enslaved to idols," are "now *turning back* to the weak and beggarly rudiments, to which they would fain be in bondage *over again.*"

"The rudiments" of ver. 9 cannot, without exegetical violence, be detached from "the rudiments of the world" of ver. 3. And these latter plainly signify the Judaic rites (see Chapter XVI.). The Judaistic practices of the Galatians were, Paul declares, a *backsliding toward their old idolatries.* We can only escape this construction of the passage at the cost of making the Apostle's remonstrance inconsequent and pointless. The argument of the letter hitherto has been directed with concentrated purpose against Judaic conformity. To suppose that just at this point, in making its application, he turns aside without notice or explanation to an entirely different matter, is to stultify his reasoning. The only ground for referring the "days and seasons" of ver. 10 to any other than a Jewish origin, lies in the apprehension that such reference disparages the Christian Sabbath.

But how, we ask, was it possible for Paul to use language which identifies the revered law of God with rites of heathenism, which he accounted a "fellowship with demons"? Bishop Lightfoot has answered this question in words we cannot do better than quote: "The Apostle regards the higher element in heathen religion as corresponding, however imperfectly, to the lower in the Mosaic law. For we may consider both the one and the other as made up of two component parts, the *spiritual* and the *ritualistic.* Now viewed in their *spiritual* aspect, there is no comparison between the one and the other. In this respect the heathen religions, so far as they added anything of their own to that sense of dependence on God which is innate in man and which they could not entirely crush, were wholly bad. On the contrary, in the Mosaic law the spiritual element was most truly divine. But this does not enter into our reckoning here. For Christianity has appropriated all that was spiritual in its predecessor.... The *ritualistic* element alone remains to be considered, and here is the meeting-point of Judaism and Heathenism. In Judaism this was as much lower than its spiritual element, as in Heathenism it was higher. Hence the two systems approach within such a distance that they can, under certain limitations, be classed together. They have at least so much in common that a lapse into Judaism can be regarded as a relapse into the position of unconverted Heathenism. Judaism was a system of bondage like Heathenism. Heathenism had been a disciplinary training like Judaism" (Commentary *in loc.*).

This line of explanation may perhaps be carried a step further. Judaism was rudimentary throughout. A religion so largely ritualistic could not but be spiritually and morally defective. In its partial apprehension of the

Divine attributes, its limitation of God's grace to a single people, its dim perception of immortality, there were great deficiencies in the Jewish creed. Its ethical code, moreover, was faulty; it contained "precepts given for the hardness of men's hearts"—touching, for example, the laws of marriage, and the right of revenge. There was not a little in Judaism, especially in its Pharisaic form, that belonged to a half-awakened conscience, to a rude and sensuous religious faculty. Christ came to "fulfil the law;" but in that fulfilment He did not shrink from correcting it. He emended the letter of its teaching, that its true spirit might be elicited. For an enlightened Christian who had learned of Jesus the "royal law, the law of liberty," to conform to Judaism was unmistakably to "turn back." Moreover, it was just the weakest and least spiritual part of the system of Moses that the legalist teachers inculcated on Gentile Christians; while their own lives fell short of its moral requirements (ch. vi. 12).

Mosaism had been in the days of its inspiration and creative vigour the great opponent of idolatry. It was the Lord's witness throughout long centuries of heathen darkness and oppression, and by its testimony has rendered splendid service to God and man. But from the standpoint of Christianity a certain degree of resemblance begins to be seen underlying this antagonism. The faith of the Israelitish people combatted idolatry with weapons too much like its own. A worldly and servile element remained in it. To one who has advanced in front, positions at an earlier stage of his progress lying apart and paths widely divergent now assume the same general direction. To resort either to Jewish or heathen rites, meant *to turn back from Christ*. It was to adopt principles of religion obsolete and unfit for those who had known God through Him. What in its time and for its purpose was excellent, nay indispensable, in doctrine and in worship, in time also had "decayed and waxed old." To tie the living spirit of Christianity to dead forms is to tie it to corruption.

"Weak and beggarly rudiments"—it is a hard sentence; and yet what else were Jewish ceremonies and rules of diet, in comparison with "righteousness and peace and joy in the Holy Ghost"? What was circumcision, now that there was no longer "Jew and Greek?" What was there in Saturday more than in any other day of the week, if it ceased to be a sign between the Lord of the Sabbath and His people? These things were, as Paul saw them, the cast-clothes of religion. For Gentile Christians the history of the Jewish ordinances had much instruction; but their observance was no whit more binding than that of heathen ceremonies. Even in the ancient times God valued them only as they were the expression of a devout, believing spirit. "Your new moons and your appointed feasts," He had said to an ungodly generation, "My soul hateth" (Isa. i. 14). And was He likely to accept them now, when they were enforced by ambition and party-spirit, at the expense of His Church's peace; when their observance turned men's thoughts away from faith in His Son, and in the power of His life-giving Spirit? There is nothing too severe, too scornful for Paul to say of these venerable rites of Israel, now that they stand in the way of a living faith and trammel the freedom of the sons of God. He tosses them aside as the swaddling-bands of the Church's infancy—childish fetters, too weak to hold the limbs of grown men. "He brake in pieces the brazen serpent that Moses had made; for the children of Israel did burn incense to it; and he called it *Nehushtan*—*a piece of brass*" (2 Kings xviii. 4). Brave Hezekiah! Paul does the same with the whole ceremonial of Moses. "Beggarly rudiments," he says. What divine refreshment there is in a blast of wholesome scorn! It was their traditions, their ritual that the Judaists worshipped, not the Holy One of Israel. "They would compass sea and land to make one proselyte," and then "make him twofold more the child of hell than themselves." This was the only result that the success of the Judaistic agitation could have achieved.

In thus decrying Jewish ordinances, the Apostle by implication allows a certain value to the rites of Paganism. The Galatians were formerly in bondage to "them that are no gods." Now, he says, they are turning *again* to the like servitude by conforming to Mosaic legalism. They wish to come *again* under subjection to "the weak and poor rudiments." In Galatian heathenism Paul appears to recognise "rudiments" of truth and a certain preparation for Christianity. While Judaic rites amounted to no more than rudiments of a spiritual faith, there were influences at work in Paganism that come under the same category. Paul believed that "God had not left Himself without witness to any." He never treated heathen creeds with indiscriminate contempt, as though they were utterly corrupt and worthless. Witness his address to the "religious" Athenians, and to the wild people of Lycaonia (Acts xiv. 15-17; xvii. 22-31). He finds his text in "certain of your own (heathen) poets." He appeals to the sense of a Divine presence "not far from any one of us;" and declares that though God was "unknown" to the nations, they were under His guidance and were "feeling after Him." To this extent Paul admits a *Preparatio evangelica* in the Gentile world; he would have been prepared, with Clement of Alexandria and Origen, and with modern students of comparative religion, to trace in the poets and wise men of Greece, in the lawgivers of Rome, in the mystics of the East, presentiments of Christianity, ideas and aspirations that pointed to it as their fulfilment. The human race was not left in total darkness beyond the range of the light shining on Zion's hill. The old Pagans, "suckled in a creed outworn," were not altogether God-forsaken. They too, amid darkness like the shadow of death, had "glimpses that might make them less forlorn."

And so have the heathen still. We must not suppose either that revealed religion was perfect from the beginning; or that the natural religions were altogether without fragments and rudiments of saving truth.

"Days you are scrupulously keeping, and months, and seasons, and years,"—the weekly sabbath, the new moon, the annual festivals, the sacred seventh year, the round of the Jewish Kalendar. On these matters the Galatians had, as it seems, already fallen in with the directions of the Jewish teachers. The word by which the Apostle describes their practice, παρατηρεῖσθε, denotes, besides the fact, the manner and spirit of the observance—an *assiduous, anxious attention*, such as the spirit of legal exaction dictated. These prescriptions the Galatians would the more readily adopt, because in their heathen life they were accustomed to stated celebrations. The Pagan Kalendar was crowded with days sacred to gods and divine heroes. This resemblance justified Paul all the more in taxing them with relapsing towards heathenism.

The Church of later centuries, both in its Eastern and Western branch, went far in the same direction. It made the keeping of holy days a prominent and obligatory part of Christianity; it has multiplied them superstitiously and beyond all reason. Amongst the rest it incorporated heathen festivals, too little changed by their consecration.

Paul's remonstrance condemns in principle the enforcement of sacred seasons as things essential to salvation, in the sense in which the Jewish Sabbath was the bond of the ancient Covenant. We may not place even the Lord's Day upon this footing. Far different from this is the unforced and grateful celebration of the First Day of the week, which sprang up in the Apostolic Church, and is assumed by the Apostles Paul and John (1 Cor. xvi. 2; Rev. i. 10). The rule of the seventh day's rest has so much intrinsic fitness, and has brought with it so many benefits, that after it had been enforced by strict law in the Jewish Church for so long, its maintenance could now be left, without express re-enactment, as a matter of freedom to the good sense and right feeling of Christian believers, "sons of the resurrection." Its legislative sanction rests on grounds of public propriety and national well-being, which need not to be asserted here. Wherever the "Lord of the Sabbath" rules, His Day will be gladly kept for His sake.

The Apostle in protecting Gentile liberties is no enemy to order in worship and outward life. No one can justly quote his authority in opposition to such appointments as a Christian community may make, for reasons of expediency and decorum, in the regulation of its affairs. But he teaches that the essence of Christianity does not lie in things of this kind, not in questions of meat and drink, nor of time and place. To put these details, however important in their own order, on a level with righteousness, mercy, and faith, is to bring a snare upon the conscience; it is to introduce once more into the Church the leaven of justification by works of law.

"Weak and poor" the best forms of piety become, without inward knowledge of God. Liturgies, creeds and confessions, church music and architecture, Sundays, fasts, festivals, are beautiful things when they are the transcript of a living faith. When that is gone, their charm, their spiritual worth is gone. They no longer belong to *religion*; they have ceased to be a bond between the souls of men and God. "According to our faith"—our actual, not professional or "confessional" faith—"it shall be done unto us": such is the rule of Christ. To cling to formularies which have lost their meaning and to which the Spirit of truth gives no present witness, is a demoralising bondage.

But this is not the only, nor the commonest way in which the sons of God are tempted to return to bondage. "Whosoever *committeth sin*," Christ said, "is the servant of sin." And the Apostle will have to warn his readers that by their abuse of liberty, by their readiness to make it "an occasion to the flesh," they were likely to forfeit it. "They that are Christ's have crucified the flesh" (ch. v. 24). This warning must be balanced against the other. Our liberty from outward constraint should be still more a liberty from the dominion of self, from pride and desire and anger; or it is not the liberty of God's children. Inward servitude is after all the vilest and worst.

"You make me afraid," at last the Apostle is compelled to say, "that I have laboured in vain." His enemies had caused him no such fear. While his children in the faith were true to him, he was afraid of nothing. "Now we live," he says in one of his Epistles, "if ye stand fast in the Lord!" But if they should fall away? He trembles for his own work, for these wayward children who had already caused him so many pangs. It is in a tone of the deepest solicitude that he continues his expostulation in the following paragraph.

CHAPTER XVIII
PAUL'S ENTREATY

"I beseech you, brethren, be as I *am*, for I *am* as ye *are*. Ye did me no wrong: but ye know that because of an infirmity of the flesh I preached the gospel unto you the first time: and that which was a temptation to you in my flesh ye despised not, nor rejected; but ye received me as an angel of God, *even* as Christ Jesus. Where then is that gratulation of yourselves? for I bear you witness, that, if possible, ye would have plucked out your eyes and given them to me. So then am I become your enemy, because I tell you the truth? They zealously seek you in no good way; nay, they desire to shut you out, that ye may seek them. But it is good to be zealously sought in a good matter at all times, and not only when I am present with you,—my children, of whom I am again in travail until Christ be formed in you.[118] Yea, I could wish to be present with you now, and to change my voice; for I am perplexed about you."—Gal. iv. 12-20.

The reproof of the last paragraph ended in a sigh. To see Christ's freemen relapsing into bondage, and exchanging their Divine birthright for childish toys of ceremonial, what can be more saddening and disappointing than this? Their own experience of salvation, the Apostle's prayers and toils on their behalf, are, to all appearance, wasted on these foolish Galatians. One resource is still left him. He has refuted and anathematized the "other gospel." He has done what explanation and argument can do to set himself right with his readers, and to destroy the web of sophistry in which their minds had been entangled. He will now try to win them by a gentler persuasion. If reason and authority fail, "for love's sake he will rather beseech" them.

He had reminded them of their former idolatry; and this calls up to the Apostle's mind the circumstances of his first ministry in Galatia. He sees himself once more a stranger amongst this strange people, a traveller fallen sick and dependent on their hospitality, preaching a gospel with nothing to recommend it in the appearance of its advocate, and which the sickness delaying his journey had compelled him, contrary to his intention, to proclaim amongst them. Yet with what ready and generous hospitality they had received the infirm Apostle! Had he been an angel from heaven—nay, the Lord Jesus Himself, they could scarcely have shown him more attention than they did. His physical weakness, which would have moved the contempt of others, called forth their sympathies. However severely he may be compelled to censure them, however much their feelings toward him have changed, he will never forget the kindness he then received. Surely they cannot think him their enemy, or allow him to be supplanted by the unworthy rivals who are seeking their regard. So Paul pleads with his old friends, and seeks to win for his arguments a way to their hearts through the affection for himself which he fain hopes is still lingering there.

Hoc prudentis est pastoris, Calvin aptly says. But there is more in this entreaty than a calculated prudence. It is a cry of the heart. Paul's soul is in the pangs of travail (ver. 19). We have seen the sternness of his face relax while he pursues his mighty argument. As he surveys the working of God's counsel in past ages, the promise given to Abraham for all nations, the intervening legal discipline, the coming of Christ in the fulness of time, the bursting of the ancient bonds, the sending forth of the Spirit of adoption—and all this for the sake of these Galatian Gentiles, and then thinks how they are after all declining from grace and renouncing their Divine inheritance, the Apostle's heart aches with grief. Foolish, fickle as they have proved, they are his children. He will "travail over them in birth a second time," if "Christ may yet be formed in them." Perhaps he has written too harshly. He half repents of his severity.[119] Fain would he "change his voice." If he could only "be with them," and see them face to face, haply his tears, his entreaties, would win them back. A rush of tender emotion wells up in Paul's soul. All his relentings are stirred. He is no longer the master in Christ rebuking unfaithful disciples; he is the mother weeping over her misguided sons.

There are considerable difficulties in the exegesis of this passage. We note them in succession as they arise:—(1) In ver. 12 we prefer, with Meyer and Lightfoot, to read, "Be as I, for I *became* (rather than *am*) as you—brethren, I beseech you." The verses preceding and following both suggest the past tense in the ellipsis. Paul's memory is busy. He appeals to the "auld lang syne." He reminds the Galatians of what he "had been amongst them for their sake,"[120] how he then behaved in regard to the matters in dispute. He assumed no airs of Jewish superiority. He did not separate himself from his Gentile brethren by any practice in which they could not join. He "became as they," placing himself by their side on the ground of a common Christian faith. He asks for reciprocity, for "a recompense in like kind" (2 Cor. vi. 13).

Are they going to set themselves above their Apostle, to take their stand on that very ground of Mosaic privilege which he had abandoned for their sake? He implores them not to do this thing. The beseechment, in the proper order of the words, comes in at the close of the sentence, with a pathetic emphasis. He makes himself a suppliant. "I beg you," he says, "by our old affection, by our brotherhood in Christ, not to desert me thus."

(2) Suddenly Paul turns to another point, according to his wont in this emotional mood: "There is nothing in which you have wronged me." Is he contradicting some allegation which had helped to estrange the Galatians? Had some one been saying that Paul was affronted by their conduct, and was actuated by personal resentment? In that case we should have looked for a specific explanation and rebutment of the charge. Rather he is anticipating the thought that would naturally arise in the minds of his readers at this point. "Paul is asking us," they would say, "to let bygones be bygones, to give up this Judaistic attachment for his sake, and to meet him frankly on the old footing. But supposing we try to do so, he is very angry with us, as this letter shows; *he thinks we have treated him badly*; he will always have a grudge against us. Things can never be again as they were between ourselves and him."

Such feelings often arise upon the breach of an old friendship, to prevent the offending party from accepting the proffered hand of reconciliation. Paul's protest removes this hindrance. He replies, "I have no sense of injury, no personal grievance against *you*. It is impossible I should cherish ill-will towards you. You know how handsomely you treated me when I first came amongst you. Nothing can efface from my heart the recollection of that time. You must not think that I hate you, because I tell you the truth" (ver. 16).

(3) "Because of an infirmity of the flesh" (physical weakness), is the truer rendering of ver. 13; and "your temptation in my flesh" the genuine reading of ver. 14, restored by the Revisers. Sickness had arrested the Apostle's course during his second missionary tour, and detained him in the Galatic country. So that he had not only "been with" the Galatians "in weakness," as afterwards when during the same journey he preached at Corinth (1 Cor. ii. 3); but actually *"because of* weakness." His infirmities gave him occasion to minister there, when he had intended to pass them by.

Paul had no thought of evangelizing Galatia; another goal was in view. It was patent to them—indeed he confessed as much at the time—that if he had been able to proceed, he would not have lingered in their country. This was certainly an unpromising introduction. And the Apostle's state of health made it at that time a trial for any one to listen to him. There was something in the nature of his malady to excite contempt, even loathing for his person. "That which tried you in my flesh, ye did not *despise,* nor *spit out:*" such is Paul's vivid phrase. How few men would have humility enough to refer to a circumstance of this kind; or could do so without loss of dignity. He felt that the condition of the messenger might well have moved this Galatian people to derision, rather than to reverence for his message.

At the best Paul's appearance and address were none of the most prepossessing.[121] The "ugly little Jew" M. Renan calls him, repeating the taunts of his Corinthian contemners. His sickness in Galatia, connected, it would appear, with some constitutional weakness, from which he suffered greatly during his second and third missionary tours, assumed a humiliating as well as a painful form. Yet this "thorn in the flesh," a bitter trial assuredly to himself,[122] had proved at once a trial and a blessing to his unintended hearers in Galatia.

(4) So far from taking offence at Paul's unfortunate condition, they welcomed him with enthusiasm. They "blessed themselves" that he had come (ver. 15). They said one to another, "How fortunate we are in having this good man amongst us! What a happy thing for us that Paul's sickness obliged him to stay and give us the opportunity of hearing his good news!" Such was their former "gratulation." The regard they conceived for the sick Apostle was unbounded. "For I bear you witness," he says, "that, if possible, you would have *dug out your eyes* and given them me!"

Is this no more than a strong hyperbole, describing the almost extravagant devotion which the Galatians expressed to the Apostle? Or are we to read the terms more literally? So it has been sometimes supposed. In this expression some critics have discovered a clue to the nature of Paul's malady. The Galatians, as they read the sentence, wished they could have taken out their own eyes and given them to Paul, *in place of his disabled ones.* This hypothesis, it is argued, agrees with other circumstances of the case and gives shape to a number of scattered intimations touching the same subject. Infirmity of the eyes would explain the "large characters" of Paul's handwriting (ch. vi. 11), and his habit of using an amanuensis. It would account for his ignorance of the person of the High Priest at his trial in Jerusalem (Acts xxiii. 2-5). The blindness that struck him on the way to Damascus may have laid the foundation of a chronic affection of this kind, afterwards developed and aggravated by the hardships of his missionary life. And such an affliction would correspond to what is said respecting the "thorn" of 2 Cor. xii. 7, and the "temptation" of this passage. For it would be excessively painful, and at the same time disabling and disfiguring in its effects.

This conjecture has much to recommend it. But it finds a very precarious support in the text. Paul does not say, "You would have plucked out *your own* (A.V.) eyes and given them *me*," as though he were thinking of an exchange of eyes; but, "You would have plucked out your *eyes* and given them me" — as much as to say, "You would have done anything in the world for me then, — even taken out your eyes and given them to me."[123] In the phrase "dug out" we may detect a touch of irony. This was the genuine Galatian style. The Celtic temperament loves to launch itself out in vehemencies and flourishes of this sort. These ardent Gauls had been perfectly enraptured with Paul. They lavished upon him their most exuberant metaphors. They said these things in all sincerity; he "bears them record" to this. However cool they have become since, they were gushing enough and to spare in their affection towards him then. And now have they "so quickly" turned against him? Because he crosses their new fancies and tells them unwelcome truths, they rush to the opposite extreme and even think him their enemy!

(5) Suddenly the Apostle turns upon his opposers (ver. 17). The Judaizers had disturbed his happy relations with his Galatian flock; they had made them half believe that he was their enemy. The Galatians must choose between Paul and his traducers. Let them scrutinise the motives of these new teachers. Let them call to mind the claims of their father in Christ. "They are courting you," he says, — "these present suitors for your regard — dishonourably; they want to shut you out and have you to themselves, that you may pay court to them." They pretend to be zealous for your interests; but it is their own they seek (ch. vi. 12).

So far the Apostle's meaning is tolerably clear. But ver. 18 is obscure. It may be construed in either of two ways, as *Paul* or *the Galatians* are taken for the subject glanced at in the verb *to be courted* in its first clause: "But it is honourable to be courted always in an honourable way, and not only when I am present with you." Does Paul mean that he has no objection to the Galatians making other friends in his absence? or, that he thinks they ought not to forget him in his absence? The latter, as we think. The Apostle complains of their inconstancy towards himself. This is a text for friends and lovers. Where attachment is honourable, it should be lasting. "Set me as a seal upon thine heart," says the Bride of the Song of Songs. With the Galatians it seemed to be, "Out of sight, out of mind." They allowed Paul to be pushed out by scheming rivals. He was far away; they were on the spot. He told them the truth; the Judaizers flattered them. So their foolish heads were turned. They were positively "bewitched" by these new admirers; and preferred their sinister and designing compliments to Paul's sterling honour and proved fidelity.

The connection of vv. 17, 18 turns on the words *honourable* and *court*,[124] each of which is thrice repeated. There is a kind of play on the verb ζηλόω. In ver. 18 it implies a true, in ver. 17 a counterfeit affection (an affectation). Paul might have said, "It is good one should be *loved, followed with affection, always*," but for the sake of the verbal antithesis. In ver. 17 he taxes his opponents with unworthily courting the favour of the Galatians; in ver. 18 he intimates his grief that he himself in his absence is no longer courted by them.

(6) In the next verse this grief of wounded affection, checked at first by a certain reserve, breaks out uncontrollably: "My children, for whom again I am in travail, till Christ be formed in you!"[125] This outcry is a pathetic continuance of his expostulation. He cannot bear the thought of losing these children of his heart. He stretches out his arms to them. Tears stream from his eyes. He has been speaking in measured, almost playful terms, in comparing himself with his supplanters. But the possibility of their success, the thought of the mischief going on in Galatia and of the little power he has to prevent it, wrings his very soul. He feels a mother's pangs for his imperilled children, as he writes these distressful words.

There is nothing gained by substituting "little children" (John's phrase) for "children," everywhere else used by Paul, and attested here by the best witnesses. The sentiment is that of 1 Thess. ii. 7, 8; 1 Cor. iv. 14-16. The Apostle is not thinking of the littleness or feebleness of the Galatians, but simply of their relation to himself. His sorrow is the sorrow of bereavement. "You have not many *mothers*," he seems to say: "I have travailed over you in birth; and now a second time you bring on me a mother's pains, which I must endure until Christ is formed in you and His image is renewed in your souls."

Paul stands before us as an injured friend, a faithful minister of Christ robbed of his people's love. He is wounded in his tenderest affections. For the sake of the Gentile Churches he had given up everything in life that he prized (ver. 12; 1 Cor. ix. 21); he had exposed himself to the contempt and hatred of his fellow-countrymen—and this is his reward, "to be loved the less, the more abundantly he loves!" (2 Cor. xii. 15).

But if he is grieved at this defection, he is equally perplexed. He cannot tell what to make of the Galatians, or in what tone to address them. He has warned, denounced, argued, protested, pleaded as a mother with her children; still he doubts whether he will prevail. If he could only see them and meet them as in former days, laying aside the distance, the sternness of authority which he has been forced to assume, he might yet reach their hearts. At least he would know how matters really stand, and in what language he ought to speak. So his entreaty ends: "I wish I could only be present with you now, and speak in some different voice. For I am at a loss to know how to deal with you."

This picture of estrangement and reproach tells its own tale, when its lines have once been clearly marked. We may dwell, however, a little longer on some of the lessons which it teaches:—

I. In the first place, it is evident that *strong emotions and warm affections are no guarantee for the permanence of religious life.*

The Galatians resembled the "stony ground" hearers of our Lord's parable,—"such as hear the word, and immediately with joy receive it; but they have no root in themselves; they believe for a time." It was not "persecution" indeed that "offended" them; but flattery proved equally effectual. They were of the same fervid temper as Peter on the night of the Passion, when he said, "Though I should die with Thee, yet will I not deny Thee in anywise,"—within a few hours thrice denying his Master, with "oaths and curses." They lacked seriousness and depth. They had fine susceptibilities and a large fund of enthusiasm; they were full of eloquent protestations; and under excitement were capable of great efforts and sacrifices. But there was a flaw in their nature. They were creatures of impulse—soon hot, soon cold. One cannot help liking such people—but as for *trusting* them, that is a different matter.

Nothing could be more delightful or promising than the appearance these Churches presented in the early days of their conversion. They heard the Apostle's message with rapt attention; they felt its Divine power, so strangely contrasting with his physical feebleness. They were amazingly wrought upon. The new life in Christ kindled all the fervour of their passionate nature. How they triumphed in Christ! How they blessed the day when the gospel visited their land! They almost worshipped the Apostle. They could not do enough for him. Their hearts bled for his sufferings. Where are all these transports now? Paul is far away. Other teachers have come, with "another gospel." And the cross is already forgotten! They are contemplating circumcision; they are busy studying the Jewish ritual, making arrangements for feast-days and "functions", eagerly discussing points of ceremony. Their minds are poisoned with mistrust of their own Apostle, whose heart is ready to break over their folly and frivolity. All this for the want of a little reflection, for want of the steadiness of purpose without which the most genial disposition and the most ardent emotions inevitably run to waste. Their faith had been too much a matter of feeling, too little of principle.

II. Further, we observe *how prone are those who have put themselves in the wrong to fix the blame on others.*

The Apostle was compelled in fidelity to truth to say hard things to his Galatian disciples. He had previously, on his last visit, given them a solemn warning on account of their Judaic proclivities (ch. i. 9). In this Epistle he censures them roundly. He wonders at them; he calls them "senseless Galatians"; he tells them they are within a step of being cut off from Christ (ch. v. 4). And now they cry out, "Paul is our enemy. If he cared for us, how could he write so cruelly! We were excessively fond of him once, we could not do too much for him; but that is all over now. If we had inflicted on him some great injury, he could scarcely treat us more roughly." Thoughtless and excitable people commonly reason in this way. Personalities with them take the place of argument and principle. The severity of a holy zeal for truth is a thing they can never understand. If you disagree with them and oppose them, they put it down to some petty animosity. They credit you with a private grudge against them; and straightway enroll you in the number of their enemies, though you may be in reality their best friend. Flatter them, humour their vanity, and you have them at your bidding. Such men it is the hardest thing in the world honestly to serve. They will always prefer "the kisses of an enemy" to the faithful "wounds of a friend."

III. Men of the Galatian type are *the natural prey of self-seeking agitators*. However sound the principles in which they were trained, however true the friendships they have enjoyed, they must have change. The accustomed palls upon them. Giddy Athenians, they love nothing so much as "to hear and tell some new thing." They ostracize Aristides, simply because they are "tired of hearing him always called the Just." To hear "the same things," however "safe" it may be, even from an Apostle's lips is to them intolerably "grievous." They never think earnestly and patiently enough to find the deeper springs, the fresh delight and satisfaction lying hidden in the great unchanging truths. These are they who are "carried about with divers and strange doctrines," who run after the newest thing in ritualistic art, or sensational evangelism, or well-spiced heterodoxy. Truth and plain dealing, apostolic holiness and godly sincerity, are outmatched in dealing with them by the craft of worldly wisdom. A little judicious flattery, something to please the eye and catch the fancy—and they are persuaded to believe almost anything, or to deny what they have most earnestly believed.

What had the Legalists to offer compared with the gifts bestowed on these Churches through Paul? What was there that could make them rivals to him in character or spiritual power? And yet the Galatians flock round the Judaist teachers, and accept without inquiry their slanders and perversions of the gospel; while the Apostle, their true friend and father, too true to spare their faults, stands suspected, almost deserted. He must forsooth implore them to come down from the heights of their would-be legal superiority, and to meet him on the common ground of grace and saving faith. The sheep will not hear their shepherd's voice; they follow strangers, though they be thieves and hirelings. "O foolish Galatians!"

Whether the Apostle's entreaty prevailed to recall them or did not, we cannot tell. From the silence with which these Churches are passed over in the Acts of the Apostles, and the little that is heard of them afterwards, an unfavourable inference appears probable. The Judaistic leaven, it is to be feared, went far to leaven the whole lump. Paul's apprehensions were only too well-grounded. And these hopeful converts who had once "run well," were fatally "hindered" and fell far behind in the Christian race. Such, in all likelihood, was the result of the departure from the truth of the gospel into which the Galatians allowed themselves to be drawn.

Whatever was the sequel to this story, Paul's protest remains to witness to the sincerity and tenderness of the great Apostle's soul, and to the disastrous issues of the levity of character which distinguished his Galatian disciples.

CHAPTER XIX
THE STORY OF HAGAR

"Tell me, ye that desire to be under the law, do ye not hear the law? For it is written, that Abraham had two sons, one by the handmaid, and one by the freewoman. Howbeit the *son* by the handmaid is born after the flesh; but the *son* by the freewoman *is born* through promise. Which things contain an allegory: for these *women* are two covenants; one from mount Sinai, bearing children unto bondage, which is Hagar. For Sinai is a mountain in Arabia, and answereth to the Jerusalem that now is: for she is in bondage with her children. But the Jerusalem that is above is free, which is our mother. For it is written,

Rejoice, thou barren that bearest not;

Break forth and cry, thou that travailest not:

For more are the children of the desolate than of her which hath the husband.

Now we, brethren, as Isaac was, are children of promise. But as then he that was born after the flesh persecuted him *that was born* after the Spirit, even so it is now. Howbeit what saith the scripture? Cast out the handmaid and her son; for the son of the handmaid shall not inherit with the son of the freewoman. Wherefore, brethren, we are not children of a handmaid, but of the freewoman. For freedom did Christ set us free: stand fast therefore, and be not entangled again in a yoke of bondage." —Gal. iv. 21-v. 1.

The Apostle wished that he could "change his voice" (ver. 20). Indeed he has changed it more than once. "Any one who looks closely may see that there is much change and alteration of feeling in what the Apostle has previously written" (Theodorus). Now he will try another tone; he proceeds in fact to address his readers in a style which we find nowhere else in his Epistles. He will tell his "children" a story! Perhaps he may thus succeed better than by graver argument. Their quick fancy will readily apprehend the bearing of the illustration; it may bring home to them the force of his doctrinal contention, and the peril of their own position, as he fears they have not seen them yet. And so, after the pathetic appeal of the last paragraph, and before he delivers his decisive, official protest to the Galatians against their circumcision, he interjects this "allegory" of the two sons of Abraham.

Paul cites the history of *the sons of Abraham*. No other example would have served his purpose. The controversy between himself and the Judaizers turned on the question, Who are the true heirs of Abraham? (ch. iii. 7, 16, 29). He made faith in Christ, they circumcision and law-keeping, the ground of sonship. So the inheritance was claimed in a double sense. But now, if it should appear that this antithesis existed in principle in the bosom of the patriarchal family, if we should find that there was an elder son of Abraham's flesh opposed to the child of promise, how powerfully will this analogy sustain the Apostle's position. Judaism will then be seen to be playing over again the part of Ishmael; and "the Jerusalem that now is" takes the place of Hagar, the slave-mother. The moral situation created by the Judaic controversy had been rehearsed in the family life of Abraham.

"Tell me," the Apostle asks, "you that would fain be subject to the law, do you not know what it relates concerning Abraham? He had two sons, one of free, and the other of servile birth. Do you wish to belong to the line of Ishmael, or Isaac?" In this way Paul resumes the thread of his discourse dropped in ver. 7. Faith, he had told his readers, had made them sons of God. They were, in Christ, of Abraham's spiritual seed, heirs of his promise. God had sent His Son to redeem them, and the Spirit of His Son to attest their adoption. But they were not content. They were ambitious of Jewish privileges. The Legalists persuaded them that they must be circumcised and conform to Moses, in order to be Abraham's children in full title. "Very well," the Apostle says, "you may become Abraham's sons in this fashion. Only you must observe that Abraham had *two* sons. And the Law will make you his sons by Hagar, whose home is Sinai—not Israelites, but *Ishmaelites!*"

Paul's Galatian allegory has greatly exercised the minds of his critics. The word is one of ill repute in exegesis. *Allegory* was the instrument of Rabbinical and Alexandrine Scripturists, an infallible device for extracting the predetermined sense from the letter of the sacred text. The "spiritualising" of Christian interpreters has been carried, in many instances, to equal excess of riot. For the honest meaning of the word of God anything and everything has been substituted that lawless fancy and verbal ingenuity could read into it. The most arbitrary and grotesque distortions of the facts of Scripture have passed current under cover of the clause, "which things are an allegory." But Paul's allegory, and that of Philo and the Allegorical school, are very different things, as widely removed as the "words of truth and soberness" from the intoxications of a mystical idealism.

With Paul the spiritual sense of Scripture is based on the historical, is in fact the moral content and import thereof; for he sees in history a continuous manifestation of God's will. With the Allegorists the spiritual sense, arrived at by *à priori* means, replaces the historical, destroyed to make room for it. The Apostle points out in the story of Hagar a spiritual intent, such as exists in every scene of human life if we had eyes to see it, something other than the literal relation of the facts, but nowise alien from it. Here lies the difference between legitimate and illegitimate allegory. The utmost freedom may be given to this employment of the imagination, so long as it is true to the *moral* of the narrative which it applies. In principle the Pauline allegory does not differ from the type. In the type the correspondence of the sign and thing signified centres in a single figure or event; in such an allegory as this it is extended to a group of figures and a series of events. But the force of the application depends on the actuality of the original story, which in the illicit allegory is matter of indifference.

"Which things are allegorized"—so the Apostle literally writes in ver. 24—*made matters of allegory*. The phrase intimates, as Bishop Lightfoot suggests, that the Hagarene episode in Genesis (ch. xvi., xxi. 1-21) was commonly interpreted in a figurative way. The Galatians had heard from their Jewish teachers specimens of this popular mode of exposition. Paul will employ it too; and will give his own reading of the famous story of Ishmael and Isaac. Philo of Alexandria, the greatest allegorist of the day, has expounded the same history. These eminent interpreters both make Sarah the mother of the spiritual, Hagar of the worldly offspring; both point out how the barren is exalted over the fruitful wife. So far, we may imagine, Paul is moving on the accepted lines of Jewish exegesis. But Philo knows nothing of the correspondence between Isaac and *Christ*, which lies at the back of the Apostle's allegory. And there is this vital difference of method between the two divines, that whereas Paul's comparison is the illustration of a doctrine proved on other grounds—the painting which decorates the house already built (Luther)—with the Alexandrine idealist it forms the substance and staple of his teaching.

Under this allegorical dress the Apostle expounds once more his doctrine, already inculcated, of the difference between the Legal and Christian state. The former constitutes, as he now puts the matter, a bastard sonship like that of Ishmael, conferring only an external and provisional tenure in the Abrahamic inheritance. It is contrasted with the spiritual sonship of the true Israel in the following respects:—It is a state of *nature* as opposed to grace; of *bondage* as opposed to freedom; and further, it is *temporary* and soon to be ended by the Divine decree.

I. "He who is of the maid-servant is *after the flesh*; but he that is of the free-woman is through promise.... Just as then he that was *after the flesh* persecuted him that was after the Spirit, so now" (vv. 23, 29). The Apostle sees in the different parentage of Abraham's sons the ground of a radical divergence of character. One was the child of nature, the other was the son of a spiritual faith.

Ishmael was in truth the fruit of unbelief; his birth was due to a natural but impatient misreading of the promise. The patriarch's union with Hagar was ill-assorted and ill-advised. It brought its natural penalty by introducing an alien element into his family life. The low-bred insolence which the serving-woman, in the prospect of becoming a mother, showed toward the mistress to whom she owed her preferment, gave a foretaste of the unhappy consequences. The promise of posterity made to Abraham with a childless wife, was expressly designed to try his faith; and he had allowed it to be overborne by the reasonings of nature. It was no wonder that the son of the Egyptian slave, born under such conditions, proved to be of a lower type, and had to be finally excluded from the house.

In Ishmael's relation to his father there was nothing but the ordinary play of human motives. "The son of the handmaid was born after the flesh." He was a *natural* son. But Ishmael was not on that account cut off from the Divine mercies. Nor did his father's prayer, "O that Ishmael might live before Thee" (Gen. xvii. 18), remain unanswered. A great career was reserved by Divine Providence for his race. The Arabs, the fiery sons of the desert, through him claim descent from Abraham. They have carved their name deeply upon the history and the faith of the world. But sensuousness and lawlessness are everywhere the stamp of the Ishmaelite. With high gifts and some generous qualities, such as attracted to his eldest boy the love of Abraham, their fierce animal passion has been the curse of the sons of Hagar. Mohammedanism is a bastard Judaism; it is the religion of Abraham sensualised. Ishmael stands forth as the type of the carnal man. On outward grounds of flesh and blood he seeks inheritance in the kingdom of God; and with fleshly weapons passionately fights its battles.

To a similar position Judaism, in the Apostle's view, had now reduced itself. And to this footing the Galatian Churches would be brought if they yielded to the Judaistic solicitations. To be circumcised would be for them to be born again after the flesh, to link themselves to Abraham in the unspiritual fashion of Hagar's son. Ishmael was the first to be circumcised (Gen. xvii. 23-26). It was to renounce salvation by faith and the renewing of the Holy Spirit. This course could only have one result. The Judaic ritualism they were adopting would bear fruit after its kind, in a worldly, sensuous life.

Like Ishmael they would claim kinship with the Church of God on fleshly grounds; and their claim must prove as futile as did his.

The persecution of the Church by Judaism gave proof of the Ishmaelite spirit, the carnal animus by which it was possessed. A religion of externalism naturally becomes repressive. It knows not "the demonstration of the Spirit"; it has "confidence in the flesh." It relies on outward means for the propagation of its faith; and naturally resorts to the secular arm. The Inquisition and the Auto-da-fé are a not unfitting accompaniment of the gorgeous ceremonial of the Mass. Ritualism and priestly autocracy go hand in hand. "So now," says Paul, pointing to Ishmael's "persecution" of the infant Isaac, hinted at in Gen. xxi. 8-10.

The laughter of Hagar's boy at Sarah's weaning-feast seems but a slight offence to be visited with the punishment of expulsion; and the incident one beneath the dignity of theological argument. But the principle for which Paul contends is there; and it is the more easily apprehended when exhibited on this homely scale. The family is the germ and the mirror of society. In it are first called into play the motives which determine the course of history, the rise and fall of empires or churches. The gravamen of the charge against Ishmael lies in the last word of Gen. xxi. 9, rendered in the Authorized Version *mocking*, and by the Revisers *playing*, after the Septuagint and the Vulgate. This word in the Hebrew is evidently a play on the name *Isaac*, *i.e.*, *laughter*, given by Sarah to her boy with genial motherly delight (vv. 6, 7). Ishmael, now a youth of fourteen, takes up the child's name and turns it, on this public and festive occasion, into ridicule. Such an act was not only an insult to the mistress of the house and the young heir at a most untimely moment, it betrayed a jealousy and contempt on the part of Hagar's son towards his half-brother which gravely compromised Isaac's future. "The wild, ungovernable and pugnacious character ascribed to his descendants began to display itself in Ishmael, and to appear in language of provoking insolence; offended at the comparative indifference with which he was treated, he indulged in mockery, especially against Isaac, whose very name furnished him with satirical sneers."[126] Ishmael's jest cost him dear. The indignation of Sarah was reasonable; and Abraham was compelled to recognise in her demand the voice of God (vv. 10-12). The two boys, like Esau and Jacob in the next generation, represented opposite principles and ways of life, whose counterworking was to run through the course of future history. Their incompatibility was already manifest.

The Apostle's comparison must have been mortifying in the extreme to the Judaists. They are told in plain terms that they are in the position of outcast Ishmael; while uncircumcised Gentiles, without a drop of Abraham's blood in their veins, have received the promise forfeited by their unbelief. Paul could not have put his conclusion in a form more unwelcome to Jewish pride. But without this radical exposure of the legalist position it was impossible for him adequately to vindicate his gospel and defend his Gentile children in the faith.

II. From this contrast of birth "according to flesh" and "through promise" is deduced the opposition between *the slave-born and free-born sons*. "For these (the slave-mother and the free-woman) are two covenants, one indeed bearing children unto bondage—which is Hagar" (ver. 24). The other side of the antithesis is not formally expressed; it is obvious. Sarah the princess, Abraham's true wife, has her counterpart in the original covenant of promise renewed in Christ, and in "the Jerusalem above, which is our mother" (ver. 26). Sarah is the typical mother,[127] as Abraham is the father of the children of faith. In the *systoichia*, or tabular comparison, which the Apostle draws up after the manner of the schools, *Hagar* and *the Mosaic covenant, Sinai* and *the Jerusalem that now is* stand in one file and "answer to" each other; *Sarah* and *the Abrahamic covenant, Zion* and *the heavenly Jerusalem* succeed in the same order, opposite to them. "Zion" is wanting in the second file; but "Sinai and Zion" form a standing antithesis (Heb. xii. 18-22); the second is implied in the first. It was to *Zion* that the words of Isaiah cited in ver. 27, were addressed.

The first clause of ver. 25 is best understood in the shorter, marginal reading of the R. V., also preferred by Bishop Lightfoot (τὸ γὰρ Σινᾶ ὄρος ἐστίν κ.τ.λ.). It is a parenthesis—"for mount Sinai[128] is in Arabia"—*covenant* running on in the mind from ver. 24 as the continued subject of ver. 25 *b*: "and it answereth to the present Jerusalem." This is the simplest and most consistent construction of the passage. The interjected geographical reference serves to support the identification of the Sinaitic covenant with Hagar, *Arabia* being the well-known abode of the Hagarenes. Paul had met them in his wanderings there. Some scholars have attempted to establish a verbal agreement between the name of the slave-mother and that locally given to the Sinaitic range; but this explanation is precarious, and after all unnecessary. There was a real correspondence between place and people on the one hand, as between place and covenant on the other. Sinai formed a visible and imposing link between the race of Ishmael and the Mosaic law-giving. That awful, desolate mountain, whose aspect, as we can imagine, had vividly impressed itself on Paul's memory (ch. i. 17), spoke to him of bondage and terror. It was a true symbol of the working of the law of Moses, exhibited in the present condition of Judaism. And round the base of Sinai Hagar's wild sons had found their dwelling.

Jerusalem was no longer the mother of freemen. The boast, "we are Abraham's sons; we were never in bondage" (John viii. 33), was an unconscious irony. Her sons chafed under the Roman yoke. They were loaded with self-inflicted legal burdens. Above all, they were, notwithstanding their professed law-keeping, enslaved to sin, in servitude to their pride and evil lusts. The spirit of the nation was that of rebellious, discontented slaves. They were Ishmaelite sons of Abraham, with none of the nobleness, the reverence, the calm and elevated faith of their father. In the Judaism of the Apostle's day the Sinaitic dispensation, uncontrolled by the higher patriarchal and prophetic faith, had worked out its natural result. It "gendered to bondage." A system of repression and routine, it had produced men punctual in tithes of mint and anise, but without justice, mercy, or faith; vaunting their liberty while they were "servants of corruption." The law of Moses could not form a "new creature." It left the Ishmael of nature unchanged at heart, a child of the flesh, with whatever robes of outward decorum his nakedness was covered. The Pharisee was the typical product of law apart from grace. Under the garb of a freeman he carried the soul of a slave.

But ver. 26 sounds the note of deliverance: "The Jerusalem above is free; and she is our mother!" Paul has escaped from the prison of Legalism, from the confines of Sinai; he has left behind the perishing earthly Jerusalem, and with it the bitterness and gloom of his Pharisaic days. He is a citizen of the heavenly Zion, breathing the air of a Divine freedom. The yoke is broken from the neck of the Church of God; the desolation is gone from her heart. There come to the Apostle's lips the words of the great prophet of the Exile, depicting the deliverance of the spiritual Zion, despised and counted barren, but now to be the mother of a numberless offspring. In Isaiah's song, "Rejoice, thou barren that bearest not" (ch. liv.), the laughter of the childless Sarah bursts forth again, to be gloriously renewed in the persecuted Church of Jesus. Robbed of all outward means, mocked and thrust out as she is by Israel after the flesh, her rejection is a release, an emancipation. Conscious of the Spirit of sonship and freedom, looking out on the boundless conquests lying before her in the Gentile world, the Church of the New Covenant glories in her tribulations. In Paul is fulfilled the joy of prophet and psalmist, who sang in former days of gloom concerning Israel's enlargement and world-wide victories. No legalist could understand words like these. "The veil" was upon his heart "in the reading of the Old Testament." But with "the Spirit of the Lord" comes "liberty." The prophetic inspiration has returned. The voice of rejoicing is heard again in the dwellings of Israel. "If the Son make you free," said Jesus, "ye shall be free indeed." This Epistle proves it.

III. "And the bondman *abideth not in the house for ever*; the Son abideth for ever" (John viii. 35). This also the Lord had testified: the Apostle repeats His warning in the terms of this allegory.

Sooner or later the slave-boy was bound to go. He has no proper birthright, no permanent footing in the house. One day he exceeds his licence, he makes himself intolerable; he must begone. "What saith the Scripture? Cast out the maidservant and her son; for the son of the maidservant shall not inherit with the son of the freewoman" (ver. 30). Paul has pronounced the doom of Judaism. His words echo those of Christ: "Behold your house is left unto you desolate" (Matt. xxiii. 38); they are taken up again in the language of Heb. xiii. 13, 14, uttered on the eve of the fall of Jerusalem: "Let us go forth unto Jesus without the camp, bearing His reproach. We have here no continuing city, but we seek that which is to come." On the walls of Jerusalem *ichabod* was plainly written. Since it "crucified our Lord" it was no longer the Holy City; it was "spiritually Sodom and Egypt" (Rev. xi. 8),— *Egypt*, the country of Hagar. Condemning Him, the Jewish nation passed sentence on itself. They were slaves who in blind rage slew their Master when He came to free them.

The Israelitish people showed more than Ishmael's jealousy towards the infant Church of the Spirit. No weapon of violence or calumny was too base to be used against it. The cup of their iniquity was filling fast. They were ripening for the judgement which Christ predicted (1 Thess. ii. 16). Year by year they became more hardened against spiritual truth, more malignant towards Christianity, and more furious and fanatical in their hatred towards their civil rulers. The cause of Judaism was hopelessly lost. In Rom. ix.-xi., written shortly after this Epistle, Paul assumes this as a settled thing, which he has to account for and to reconcile with Scripture. In the demand of Sarah for the expulsion of her rival, complied with by Abraham against his will, the Apostle reads the secret judgement of the Almighty on the proud city which he himself so ardently loved, but which had crucified his Lord and repented not. "Cut it down," Jesus cried; "why cumbereth it the ground?" (Luke xiii. 7). The voice of Scripture speaks again: "Cast her out; she and her sons are slaves. They have no place amongst the sons of God." Ishmael was in the way of Isaac's safety and prosperity. And the Judaic ascendency was no less a danger to the Church. The blow which shattered Judaism, at once cleared the ground for the outward progress of the gospel and arrested the legalistic reaction which hindered its internal development. The two systems were irreconcilable. It was Paul's merit to have first apprehended this contradiction in its full import. The time had come to apply in all its rigour Christ's principle of combat, "He that is not with Me, is against Me." It is the same rule of exclusion which Paul announces: "If any man hath not the Spirit of Christ, he is none of His" (Rom. viii. 9). Out of Christ is no salvation. When the day of judgement comes, whether for men or nations, this is the touchstone: Have we, or have we not "the Spirit of God's Son?" Is our character that of sons of God, or slaves of sin? On the latter falls inevitably the sentence of expulsion, "He will gather out of His kingdom all things that offend, and them that do iniquity" (Matt. xiii. 41).

This passage signalises the definite breach of Christianity with Judaism. The elder Apostles lingered in the porch of the Temple; the primitive Church clung to the ancient worship. Paul does not blame them for doing so. In their case this was but the survival of a past order, in principle acknowledged to be obsolete. But the Church of the future, the spiritual seed of Abraham gathered out of all nations, had no part in Legalism. The Apostle bends all his efforts to convince his readers of this, to make them sensible of the impassable gulf lying between them and outworn Mosaism. Again he repeats, "We are not children of a maidservant, but of her that is free" (ver. 31). The Church of Christ can no more hold fellowship with Judaism than could Isaac with the spiteful, mocking Ishmael. Paul leads the Church across the Rubicon. There is no turning back.

Ver. 1 of ch. v. is the application of the allegory. It is a triumphant assertion of liberty, a ringing summons to its defence. Its separation from ch. iv. is ill-judged, and runs counter to the ancient divisions of the Epistle. "Christ set us free," Paul declares; "and it was *for freedom* [129] — not that we might fall under a new servitude. *Stand fast* therefore; do not let yourselves be made bondmen over again." Bondmen the Galatians had been before (ch. iv. 8), bowing down to false and vile gods. Bondmen they will be again, if they are beguiled by the Legalists to accept the yoke of circumcision, if they take "the Jerusalem that now is" for their mother. They have tasted the joys of freedom; they know what it is to be sons of God, heirs of His kingdom and partakers of His Spirit; why do they stoop from their high estate? Why should Christ's freemen put a yoke upon their own neck? Let them only know their happiness and security in Christ, and refuse to be cheated out of the substance of their spiritual blessings by the illusive shadows which the Judaists offer them. Freedom once gained is a prize never to be lost. No care, no vigilance in its preservation can be too great. Such liberty inspires courage and good hope in its defence. "Stand fast therefore. Quit yourselves like men."

How the Galatians responded to the Apostle's challenge, we do not know. But it has found an echo in many a heart since. The Lutheran Reformation was an answer to it; so was the Scottish Covenant. The spirit of Christian liberty is eternal. Jerusalem or Rome may strive to imprison it. They might as well seek to bind the winds of heaven. Its home is with God. Its seat is the throne of Christ. It lives by the breath of His Spirit. The earthly powers mock at it, and drive it into the wilderness. They do but assure their own ruin. It leaves the house of the oppressor desolate. Whosoever he be — Judaist or Papist, priest, or king, or demagogue — that makes himself lord of God's heritage and would despoil His children of the liberties of faith, let him beware lest of him also it be spoken, "Cast out the bondwoman and her son."

CHAPTER XX
SHALL THE GALATIANS BE CIRCUMCISED

"Behold, I Paul say unto you, that, if ye receive circumcision, Christ will profit you nothing. Yea, I testify again to every man that receiveth circumcision, that he is a debtor to do the whole law. Ye are severed from Christ, ye who would be justified by the law; ye are fallen away from grace. For we through the Spirit by faith wait for the hope of righteousness. For in Christ Jesus neither circumcision availeth anything, nor uncircumcision; but faith working through love."—Gal. v. 2-6.

Shall the Galatians be circumcised, or shall they not? This is the decisive question. The denunciation with which Paul begins his letter, the narrative which follows, the profound argumentation, the tender entreaty of the last two chapters, all converge toward this crucial point. So far the Galatian Churches had been only dallying with Judaism. They have been tempted to the verge of apostasy; but they are not yet over the edge. Till they consent to be circumcised, they have not finally committed themselves; their freedom is not absolutely lost. The Apostle still hopes, despite his fears, that they will stand fast (ver. 10; ch. iv. 11; iii. 4). The fatal step is eagerly pressed on them by the Judaizers (ch. vi. 12, 13), whose persuasion the Galatians had so far entertained, that they had begun to keep the Hebrew sabbath and feast-days (ch. iv. 10). If they yield to this further demand, the battle is lost; and this powerful Epistle, with all the Apostle's previous labour spent upon them, has been in vain. To sever this section from the polemical in order to attach it to the practical part of the Epistle, as many commentators do, is to cut the nerve of the Apostle's argument and reduce it to an abstract theological discussion.

This momentous question is brought forward with the greater emphasis and effect, because it has hitherto been kept out of sight. The allusion to Titus in ch. ii. 1-5 has already indicated the supreme importance of the matter of circumcision. But the Apostle has delayed dealing with it formally and directly, until he is able to do so with the weight of the foregoing chapters to support his interdict. He has shattered the enemies' position with his artillery of logic, he has assailed the hearts of his readers with all the force of his burning indignation and subduing pathos. Now he gathers up his strength for the final charge home, which must decide the battle.

I. Lo, I Paul tell you! When he begins thus, we feel that the decisive moment is at hand. Everything depends on the next few words. Paul stands like an archer with his bow drawn at full stretch and the arrow pointed to the mark. "Let others say what they may; this is what *I* tell you. If my word has any weight with you, give heed to this:—if you be circumcised, Christ will profit you nothing."

Now his bolt is shot; we see what the Apostle has had in his mind all this time. Language cannot be more explicit. Some of his readers will have failed to catch the subtler points of his argument, or the finer tones of his voice of entreaty; but every one will understand this. The most "senseless" and volatile amongst the Galatians will surely be sobered by the terms of this warning. There is no escaping the dilemma. Legalism and Paulinism, the true and the false gospel, stand front to front, reduced to their barest form, and weighed each in the balance of its practical result. *Christ—or Circumcision*: which shall it be?

This declaration is no less authoritative and judicially threatening than the anathema of ch. i. That former denouncement declared the false teachers severed from Christ. Those who yield to their persuasion, will be also "severed from Christ." They will fall into the same ditch as their blind leaders. The Judaizers have forfeited their part in Christ; they are false brethren, tares among the wheat, troublers and hinderers to the Church of God. And Gentile Christians who choose to be led astray by them must take the consequences. If they obey the "other gospel," Christ's gospel is theirs no longer. If they rest their faith on circumcision, they have withdrawn it from His cross. Adopting the Mosaic regimen, they forego the benefits of Christ's redemption. "Christ will profit you nothing." The sentence is negative, but no less fearful on that account. It is as though Christ should say, "Thou hast no part with Me."

Circumcision will cost the Galatian Christians all they possess in Jesus Christ. But is not this, some one will ask, an over-strained assertion? Is it consistent with Paul's professions and his policy in other instances? In ver. 6, and again in the last chapter, he declares that "Circumcision is nothing, and uncircumcision nothing"; and yet here he makes it *everything!* The Apostle's position is this. In itself the rite is valueless. It was the sacrament of the Old Covenant, which was brought to an end by the death of Christ. For the new Church of the Spirit, it is a matter of perfect indifference whether a man is circumcised or not. Paul had therefore circumcised Timothy, whose mother was a Jewess (Acts xvi. 1-3), though neither he nor his young disciple supposed that it was a religious necessity. It was done as a social convenience; "uncircumcision was nothing," and could in such a case be surrendered without prejudice. On the other hand, he refused to submit Titus to the same rite; for he was a pure Greek, and on him it could only have been imposed on religious grounds and as a passport to salvation. For this, and for no other reason, it was demanded by the Judaistic party. In this instance it was needful to show that "circumcision is nothing." The Galatians stood in the same position as Titus. Circumcision, if performed on them, must have denoted, not as in Timothy's case, the fact of Jewish birth, but *subjection to the Mosaic law*. Regarded in this light, the question was one of life or death for the Pauline Churches. To yield to the Judaizers would be to surrender the principle of salvation by faith. The attempt of the legalist party was in effect to force Christianity into the grooves of Mosaism, to reduce the world-wide Church of the Spirit to a sect of moribund Judaism.

With what views, with what aim were the Galatians entertaining this Judaic "persuasion"? Was it to make them sons of God and heirs of His kingdom? This was the object with which "God sent forth His Son;" and the Spirit of sonship assured them that it was realised (ch. iv. 4-7). To adopt the former means to this end was to renounce the latter. In turning their eyes to this new bewitchment, they must be conscious that their attention was diverted from the Redeemer's cross and their confidence in it weakened (ch. iii. 1). To be circumcised would be to rest their salvation formally and definitely on works of law, in place of the grace of God. The consequences of this Paul has shown in relating his discussion with Peter, in ch. ii. 15-21. They would "make" themselves "transgressors;" they would "make Christ's death of none effect." In the soul's salvation Christ will be all, or nothing. If we trust Him, we must trust Him altogether. The Galatians had already admitted a suspicion of the power of His grace, which if cherished and acted on in the way proposed, must sever all communion between their souls and Him. Their circumcision would be "the sacrament of their excision from Christ" (Huxtable).

The tense of the verb is *present*. Paul's readers may be in the act of making this disastrous compliance. He bids them look for a moment at the depth of the gulf on whose brink they stand. "Stop!" he cries, "another step in that direction, and you have lost Christ."

And what will they get in exchange? They will saddle themselves with all the obligations of the Mosaic law (ver. 3). This probably was more than they bargained for. They wished to find a *via media*, some compromise between the new faith and the old, which would secure to them the benefits of Christ without His reproach, and the privileges of Judaism without its burdens. This at least was the policy of the Judaic teachers (ch. vi. 12, 13). But it was a false and untenable position. "Circumcision verily profiteth, *if thou art a doer of the law*" (Rom. ii. 25); otherwise it brings only condemnation. He who receives the sacrament of Mosaism, by doing so pledges himself to "keep and do" every one of its "ordinances, statutes, and judgements"—a yoke which, honest Peter said, "Neither we nor our fathers were able to bear" (Acts xv. 10). Let the Galatians read the law, and consider what they are going to undertake. He who goes with the Judaists a mile, will be compelled to go twain. They will not find themselves at liberty to pick and choose amongst the legal requirements. Their legalist teachers will not raise a finger to lighten the yoke (Luke xi. 46), when it is once fastened on their necks; nor will their own consciences acquit them of its responsibilities. This obligation Paul, himself a master in Jewish law, solemnly affirms: "I protest (I declare before God) to every man that is circumcised, that he is a debtor to perform the whole law."

Now this is a proved impossibility. Whoever "sets up the law," he had avouched to Cephas, "makes himself a transgressor" (ch. ii. 18). Nay, it was established of set purpose to "multiply transgressions," to deepen and sharpen the consciousness of sin (ch. iii. 19; Rom. iii. 20; iv. 15; v. 20). Jewish believers in Christ, placed under its power by their birth, had thankfully found in the faith of Christ a refuge from its accusations (ch. ii. 16; Rom. vii. 24-viii. 4). Surely the Galatians, knowing all this, will not be so foolish as to put themselves gratuitously under its power. To do this would be an insult to Christ, and an act of moral suicide. This further warning reinforces the first, and is uttered with equal solemnity. "I tell you, Christ will profit you nothing; and again I testify, the law will lay its full weight upon you." They will be left, without the help of Christ, to bear this tremendous burden.

This double threatening is blended into one in ver. 4. The pregnant force of Paul's Greek is untranslatable. Literally his words run, "You were nullified from Christ (κατηργήθητε ἀπὸ Χριστοῦ)—brought to nought (being severed) from Him, you that in law are seeking justification." He puts his assertion in the past (*aorist*) tense, stating that which ensues so soon as the principle of legal justification is endorsed. From that moment the Galatians cease to be Christians. In this sense they "are abolished," just as "the cross is" virtually "abolished" if the Apostle "preaches circumcision" (ver. 11), and "death is being abolished" under the reign of Christ (1 Cor. xv. 26). He has said in ver. 2 that Christ will be made of none effect to them; now he adds that they "are made of none effect" in relation to Christ. Their Christian standing is destroyed. The joyous experiences of their conversion, their share in Abraham's blessing, their Divine sonship witnessed to by the Holy Spirit—all this is nullified, cancelled at a stroke, if they are circumcised.

The detachment of their faith "from Christ" is involved in the process of attaching it to Jewish ordinances, and brings spiritual destruction upon them. The root of the Christian life is faith in Him. Let that root be severed, let the branch no longer "abide in the vine"—it is dead already.[130]

Cut off from Christ, they "have fallen from grace." Paul has already twice identified *Christ* and *grace*, in ch. i. 6 and ii. 21. The Divine mercies centre in Jesus Christ; and he who separates himself from Him, shuts these out of his soul. The verb here used by the Apostle (ἐξεϱέσατε) is commonly applied (four times *e.g.* in Acts xxvii.) to a ship driven out of her course. Some such image seems to be in the writer's mind in this passage. These racers made an excellent start, but they have stumbled (ver. 7; ch. iii. 3); the vessel set out from harbour in gallant style, but she is drifting fast upon the rocks. This sentence "is the exact opposite of 'stand in the grace,' Rom. v. 2" (Beet).[131]

That he who "seeks justification in *law* has fallen from *grace*," needs no proof after the powerful demonstration of ch. ii. 14-21. The moralist claims quittance on the ground of his deservings. He pleads the quality of his "works," his punctual discharge of every stipulated duty, from circumcision onwards. "I fast twice a week," he tells his Divine Judge; "I tithe all my gains. I have kept all the commandments from my youth up." What can God expect more than this? But with these performances Grace has nothing to do. The man is not in its order. If he invokes its aid, it is as a make-weight, a supplement to the possible shortcomings in a virtue for the most part competent for itself. Now the grace of God is not to be set aside in this way; it refuses to be treated as a mere *succedaneum* of human virtue. Grace, like Christ, insists on being "all in all." "If salvation is by grace, it is no longer of works;" and "if of works, it is no more grace" (Rom. xi. 6). These two methods of justification imply different moral tempers, an opposite set and direction of the current of life. This question of circumcision brings the Galatians to the parting of the ways. *Grace* or *Law*—which of the two roads will they follow? Both they cannot. They may become Jewish proselytes; but they will cease to be Christians. Leaving behind them the light and joy of the heavenly Zion, they will find themselves wandering in the gloomy desolations of Sinai.

II. From this prospect the Apostle bids his readers turn to that which he himself beholds, and which they erewhile shared with him. Again he seems to say, "Be ye as I am, brethren" (ch. iv. 12); not in outward condition alone, but still more in inward experience and aspiration. "For *we* by the Spirit, on the ground of faith, are awaiting the hope of righteousness" (ver. 5).

Look on this picture, and on that. Yonder are the Galatians, all in tumult about the legalistic proposals, debating which of the Hebrew feasts they shall celebrate and with what rites, absorbed in the details of Mosaic ceremony, all but persuaded to be circumcised and to settle their scruples out of hand by a blind submission to the Law. And here, on the other side, is Paul with the Church of the Spirit, walking in the righteousness of faith and the communion of the Holy Spirit, joyfully awaiting the Saviour's final coming and the hope that is laid up in heaven. How vexed, how burdened, how narrow and puerile is the one condition of life; how large and lofty and secure the other. "We," says the Apostle, "are looking *forwards* not backwards, to Christ and not to Moses."

Every word in this sentence is full of meaning. *Faith* carries an emphasis similar to that it has in ch. ii. 16; iii. 22; and in Rom. iv. 16. Paul supports by contrast what he has just said: "Your share in the kingdom of grace is lost who seek a legal righteousness (ver. 4); it is *by faith* that we look for our heritage." *Hope* is clearly *matter of hope*, the future glory of the redeemed, described in Rom. viii. 18-25, Phil. iii. 20, 21, in both of which places there appears the remarkably compounded verb ($\dot{\alpha}\pi$-εκ-δεχόμεθα) that concludes this verse. It implies an intent expectancy, sure of its object and satisfied with it. The hope is "righteousness' hope"—the hope of the righteous—for it has in righteousness its warrant. The saying of Psalm xvi., verified in Christ's rising from the dead, contains its principle: "Thou wilt not leave my soul to death; nor suffer Thine holy one to see the pit." This was the secret "hope of Israel,"[132] that grew up in the hearts of the men of faith, whose accomplishment is the crowning glory of the redemption of Christ. It is the goal of faith. Righteousness is the path that leads to it. The Galatians had been persuaded of this hope and embraced it; if they accept the "other gospel," with its phantom of a legal righteousness, their hope will perish.

The Apostle is always true to the order of thought here indicated. Faith saves from first to last. The present righteousness and future glory of the sons of God alike have their source in faith. The act of reliance by which the initial justification of the sinner was attained, now becomes the habit of the soul, the channel by which its life is fed, rooting itself ever more deeply into Christ and absorbing more completely the virtue of His death and heavenly life. Faith has its great ventures; it has also its seasons of endurance, its moods of quiet expectancy, its unweariable patience. It can wait as well as work. It rests upon the past, seeing in Christ crucified its "author;" then it looks on to the future, and claims Christ glorified for its "finisher." So faith prompts her sister Hope and points her to "the glory that shall be revealed."

If faith fails, hope quickly dies. Unbelief is the mother of despair. "Of faith," the Apostle says, "we look out!"

A second condition, inseparable from the first, marks the hope proper to the Christian righteousness. It is sustained "by the Spirit." The connection of faith and hope respectively with the gift of the Holy Spirit is marked very clearly by Paul in Eph. i. 13, 14: "Having believed, you were sealed with the Holy Spirit, who is *the earnest of our inheritance*." The Holy Spirit seals the sons of God—"sons, then heirs" (ch. iv. 6, 7; Rom. viii. 15-17). This stamps on Christian hope a *spiritual* character. The conception which we form of it, the means by which it is pursued, the temper and attitude in which it is expected, are determined by the Holy Spirit who inspires it. This pure and celestial hope is therefore utterly removed from the selfish ambitions and the sensuous methods that distinguished the Judaistic movement (ch. iv. 3, 9; vi. 12-14). "Men of worldly, low design" like Paul's opponents in Galatia, had no right to entertain "the hope of righteousness." These matters are spiritually discerned; they are "the things of the Spirit, the things which God hath prepared for them that love Him" (1 Cor. ii. 9-14).

If faith and hope are in sight, *love* cannot be far off. In the next verse it comes to claim its place beside the other two: "faith working through love." And so the blessed trio is complete, *Fides, amor, spes: summa Christianismi* (Bengel). Faith waits, but it also *works*;[133] and love is its working energy. Love gives faith hands and feet; hope lends it wings. Love is the fire at its heart, the life-blood coursing in its veins; hope the light that gleams and dances in its eyes. Looking back to the Christ that hath been manifested, faith kindles into a boundless love; looking onward to the Christ that shall be revealed, it rises into an exultant hope.

These closing words are of no little theological importance. "They bridge over the gulf which seems to separate the language of Paul and James. Both assert a principle of practical energy, as opposed to a barren, inactive theory" (Lightfoot). Had the faith of Paul's readers been more practical, had they been of a diligent, enterprising spirit, "ready for every good word and work," they would not have felt, to the same degree, the spell of the Judaistic fascination. Idle hands, vain and restless minds, court temptation. A manly, energetic faith will never play at ritualism or turn religion into a round of ceremonial, an æsthetic exhibition. Loving and self-devoting faith in Christ is the one thing Paul covets to see in the Galatians. This is the working power of the gospel, the force that will lift and regenerate mankind. In comparison with this, questions of Church-order and forms of worship are "nothing." "The body is more than the raiment." Church organization is a means to a certain end; and that end consists in the life of faith and love in Christian souls. Each man is worth to Christ and to His Church just so much as he possesses of this energy of the Spirit, just so much as he has of love to Christ and to men in Him. Other gifts and qualities, offices and orders of ministry, are but instruments for love to employ, machinery for love to energize.

The Apostle wishes it to be understood that he does not condemn circumcision on its own account, as though the opposite condition were in itself superior. If "circumcision does not avail anything, *neither does uncircumcision.*" The Jew is no better or worse a Christian because he is circumcised; the Gentile no worse or better, because he is not. This difference in no way affects the man's spiritual standing or efficiency. Let the Galatians dismiss the whole question from their minds. "One thing is needful," to be filled with the Spirit of love. "God's kingdom is not meat and drink;" it is not "days and seasons and years;" it is not circumcision, nor rubrics and vestments and priestly functions; it is "righteousness and peace and joy in the Holy Spirit." These are the true *notes* of the Church; "by love," said Christ, "all men will know that you are My disciples."

In these two sentences (vv. 5 and 6) the religion of Christ is summed up. Ver. 5 gives us its *statics*; ver. 6 its *dynamics*. It is a condition, and an occupation; a grand outlook, and an intent pursuit; a Divine hope for the future, and a sovereign power for the present, with an infinite spring of energy in the love of Christ. The active and passive elements of the Christian life need to be justly balanced. Many of the errors of the Church have arisen from one-sidedness in this respect. Some do nothing but sit with folded hands till the Lord comes; others are too busy to think of His coming at all. So waiting degenerates into indolence; and serving into feverish hurry and anxiety, or mechanical routine. Let hope give calmness and dignity, buoyancy and brightness to our work; let work make our hope sober, reasonable, practical.

"These three abide—faith, hope, and love." They cannot change while God is God and man is man. Forms of dogma and of worship have changed and must change. There is a perpetual "removing of the things that are shaken, as of things that are made;" but through all revolutions there "remain the things which are not shaken." To these let us rally. On these let us build. New questions thrust themselves to the front, touching matters as little essential to the Church's life as that of circumcision in the Apostolic age. The evil is that we make so much of them. In the din of controversy we grow bewildered; our eyes are blinded with its dust; our souls chafed with its fretting. We lose the sense of proportion; we fail to see who are our true friends, and who our foes. We need to return to the simplicity that is in Christ. Let us "consider Him"—Christ incarnate, dying, risen, reigning—till we are changed into the same image, till His life has wrought itself into ours. Then these questions of dispute will fall into their proper place. They will resolve themselves; or wait patiently for their solution. Loyalty to Jesus Christ is the only solvent of our controversies.

Will the Galatians be true to Christ? Or will they renounce their righteousness in Him for a legal status, morally worthless, and which will end in taking from them the hope of eternal life? They have nothing to gain, they have everything to lose in submitting to circumcision.

CHAPTER XXI
THE HINDERERS AND TROUBLERS

"Ye were running well; who did hinder you that ye should not obey the truth? This persuasion *came* not of him that calleth you. A little leaven leaveneth the whole lump. I have confidence to you-ward, in the Lord, that ye will be none otherwise minded: but he that troubleth you shall bear his judgement, whosoever he be. But I, brethren, if I still preach circumcision, why am I still persecuted? then hath the stumblingblock of the cross been done away. I would that they which unsettle you would even mutilate themselves."—Gal. v. 7-12.

The Apostle's controversy with the Legalists is all but concluded. He has pronounced on the question of circumcision. He has shown his readers, with an emphasis and clearness that leave nothing more to be said, how fearful is the cost at which they will accept the "other gospel," and how heavy the yoke which it will impose upon them. A few further observations remain to be made—of regret, of remonstrance, blended with expressions of confidence more distinct than any the Apostle has hitherto employed. Then with a last contemptuous thrust, a sort of *coup de grace* for the Circumcisionists, Paul passes to the practical and ethical part of his letter.

This section is made up of short, disconnected sentences, shot off in various directions; as though the writer wished to have done with the Judaistic debate, and would discharge at a single volley the arrows remaining in his quiver. Its prevailing tone is that of conciliation towards the Galatians (comp. Chapter xviii.), with increasing severity towards the legalist teachers. "See how bitter he is against the deceivers. For indeed at the beginning he directed his censures against the deceived, calling them 'senseless' both once and again. But now that he has sufficiently chastened and corrected them, for the rest he turns against their deceivers. And we should observe his wisdom in both these things, in that he admonishes the one party and brings them to a better mind, being his own children and capable of amendment; but the deceivers, who are a foreign element and incurably diseased, he cuts off" (Chrysostom).

There lie before us therefore in this paragraph the following considerations:—*Paul's hope concerning the Galatian Churches, his protest on his own behalf,* and finally, *his judgement respecting the troublers.*

I. The more hopeful strain of the letter at this point appears to be due to the effect of his argument upon the writer's own mind. As the breadth and grandeur of the Christian faith open out before him, and he contrasts its spiritual glory with the ignoble aims of the Circumcisionists, Paul cannot think that the readers will any longer doubt which is the true gospel. Surely they will be disenchanted. His irrefragable reasonings, his pleading entreaties and solemn warnings are bound to call forth a response from a people so intelligent and so affectionate. "For my part," he says, "*I am confident in the Lord that you will be no otherwise minded* (ver. 10), that you will be faithful to your Divine calling, despite the hindrances thrown in your way." They will, he is persuaded, come to see the proposals of the Judaizers in their proper light. They will think about the Christian life—its objects and principles—as he himself does; and will perceive how fatal would be the step they are urged to take. They will be true to themselves and to the Spirit of sonship they have received. They will pursue more earnestly the hope set before them and give themselves with renewed energy to the work of faith and love (vv. 5, 6), and forget as soon as possible this distracting and unprofitable controversy.

"In the Lord" Paul cherishes this confidence. "In Christ's grace" the Galatians were called to enter the kingdom of God (ver. 8; ch. i. 6); and He was concerned that the work begun in them should be completed (Phil. i. 6). It may be the Apostle at this moment was conscious of some assurance from his Master that his testimony in this Epistle would not prove in vain. The recent[134] submission of the Corinthians would tend to increase Paul's confidence in his authority over the Gentile Churches.

Another remembrance quickens the feeling of hope with which the Apostle draws the conflict to a close. He reminds himself of the good confession the Galatians had aforetime witnessed,[135] the zeal with which they pursued the Christian course, until this deplorable hindrance arose: "You were running well—*finely.* You had fixed your eyes on the heavenly prize. Filled with an ardent faith, you were zealously pursuing the great spiritual ends of the Christian life (comp. vv. 5, 6). Your progress has been arrested. You have yielded to influences which are not of God who called you, and admitted amongst you a leaven that, if not cast out, will corrupt you utterly (vv. 8, 9). But I trust that this result will be averted. You will return to better thoughts. You will resume the interrupted race, and by God's mercy will be enabled to bring it to a glorious issue" (ver. 10).

There is kindness and true wisdom in this encouragement. The Apostle has "told them the truth;" he has "reproved with all authority;" now that this is done, their remains nothing in his heart but good-will and good wishes for his Galatian children. If his chiding has wrought the effect it was intended to produce, then these words of softened admonition will be grateful and healing. They have "stumbled, but not that they might fall." The Apostle holds out the hand of restoration; his confidence animates them to hope better things for themselves. He turns his anger away from them, and directs it altogether upon their injurers.

II. The Judaizers had troubled the Churches of Galatia; *they had also maligned the Apostle Paul.* From them undoubtedly the imputation proceeded which he repudiates so warmly in ver. 11: "And I, brethren, if I am still preaching circumcision, why am I still persecuted?" This supposition a moment's reflection would suffice to refute. The contradiction was manifest. The persecution which everywhere followed the Apostle marked him out in all men's eyes as the adversary of Legalism.

There were circumstances, however, that lent a certain colour to this calumny. The circumcision of Timothy, for instance, might be thought to look in this direction (Acts xvi. 1-3). And Paul valued his Hebrew birth. He loved his Jewish brethren more than his own salvation (Rom. ix. 1-5; xi. 1). There was nothing of the revolutionary or the iconoclast about him. Personally he preferred to conform to the ancient usages, when doing so did not compromise the honour of Christ (Acts xviii. 18; xxi. 17-26). It was false that he "taught the Jews not to circumcise their children, nor to walk by the customs" (Acts xxi. 20-26). He did teach them that these things were "of no avail in Christ Jesus;" that they were in no sense necessary to salvation; and that it was contrary to the will of Christ to impose them upon Gentiles. But it was no part of his business to alter the social customs of his people, or to bid them renounce the glories of their past. While he insists that "there is no difference" between Jew and Gentile in their need of the gospel and their rights in it, he still claims for the Jew the first place in the order of its manifestation.

This was an entirely different thing from "preaching circumcision" in the legalist sense, from heralding (κηρύσσω: ver. 11) and crying up the Jewish ordinance, and making it a religious duty. This difference the Circumcisionists affected not to understand. Some of Paul's critics will not understand it even now. They argue that the Apostle's hostility to Judaism in this Epistle discredits the narrative of the Acts of the Apostles, inasmuch as the latter relates several instances of Jewish conformity on his part. What pragmatical narrowness is this! Paul's adversaries said, "He derides Judaism amongst you Gentiles, who know nothing of his antecedents, or of his practice in other places. But when he pleases, this liberal Paul will be as zealous for circumcision as any of us. Indeed he boasts of his skill in 'becoming all things to all men;' he trims his sail to every breeze. In *Galatia* he is all breadth and tolerance; he talks about our 'liberty which we have in Christ Jesus;' he is ready to 'become as you are;' no one would imagine he had ever been a Jew. In *Judea* he makes a point of being strictly orthodox, and is indignant if any one questions his devotion to the Law."

Paul's position was a delicate one, and open to misrepresentation. Men of party insist on this or that external custom as the badge of their own side; they have their party-colours and their uniform. Men of principle adopt or lay aside such usages with a freedom which scandalizes the partisan. What right, he says, has any one to wear our colours, to pronounce our shibboleth, if he is not one of ourselves? If the man will not be with us, let him be against us. Had Paul renounced his circumcision and declared himself a Gentile out and out, the Judaists might have understood him. Had he said, *Circumcision is evil*, they could have endured it better; but to preach that *Circumcision is nothing*, to reduce this all-important rite to insignificance, vexed them beyond measure. It was in their eyes plain proof of dishonesty. They tell the Galatians that Paul is playing a double part, that his resistance to their circumcision is interested and insincere.

The charge is identical with that of "man-pleasing" which the Apostle repelled in ch. i. 10 (see Chapter III). The emphatic "still" of that passage recurs twice in this, bearing the same meaning as it does there. Its force is not *temporal*, as though the Apostle were thinking of a former time when he did "preach circumcision:" no such reference appears in the context, and these terms are inappropriate to his pre-Christian career. The particle points a *logical* contrast, as *e.g.* in Rom. iii. 7; ix. 19: "If I still (notwithstanding my professions as a Gentile apostle) preach circumcision, why am I still (notwithstanding my so preaching) persecuted?" Had Paul been known by the Jews to be in other places a promoter of circumcision, they would have treated him very differently. He could not then have been, as the Galatians knew him everywhere to be, "in perils from his fellow-countrymen."

The rancour of the Legalists was sufficient proof of Paul's sincerity. They were themselves guilty of the baseness with which they taxed him. It was in order to escape the reproach of the cross (ver. 11), to atone for their belief in the Nazarene, that they persuaded Gentile Christians to be circumcised (ch. vi. 11, 12). *They* were the man-pleasers. The Judaizers knew perfectly well that the Apostle's observance of Jewish usage was no endorsement of their principles. The print of the Jewish scourge upon his back attested his loyalty to Gentile Christendom (ch. vi. 17; 2 Cor. xi. 24). A further consequence would have ensued from the duplicity imputed to Paul, which he resents even more warmly: "Then," he says, "if I preach circumcision, the offence of the cross is done away!" He is charged with treason against the cross of Christ. He has betrayed the one thing in which he glories (ch. vi. 14), to which the service of his life was consecrated! For the doctrine of the cross was at an end if the legal ritual were re-established and men were taught to trust in the saving efficacy of circumcision—above all, if the Apostle of the Gentiles had preached this doctrine! The Legalists imputed to him the very last thing of which he was capable. This was in fact the error into which Peter had weakly fallen at Antioch. The Jewish Apostle had then acted as though "Christ died in vain" (ch. ii. 21). For himself Paul indignantly denies that his conduct bore any such construction.

But he says, "*the scandal* of the cross"—that scandalous, offensive cross, the stumbling-block of Jewish pride (1 Cor. i. 23). The death of Christ was not only revolting in its form to Jewish sentiment;[136] it was a fatal event for Judaism itself. It imported the end of the Mosaic economy. The Church at Jerusalem had not yet fully grasped this fact; they sought, as far as possible, to live on good terms with their non-Christian Jewish brethren, and admitted perhaps too easily into their fellowship men who cared more for Judaism than for Christ and His cross. For them also the final rupture was approaching, when they had to "go forth unto Jesus without the camp." Paul had seen from the first that the breach was irreparable. He determined to keep his Gentile Churches free from Judaic entanglements. In his view, Calvary was the terminus of Mosaism.

This was true *historically*. The crime of national Judaism in slaying its Messiah was capital. Its spiritual blindness and its moral failure had received the most signal proof. The congregation of Israel had become a synagogue of Satan. And these were "the chosen people," the world's *élite*, who "crucified the Lord of glory!" *Mankind* had done this thing. The world has "both seen and hated both Him and the Father." Now to set up circumcision again, or any kind of human effort or performance, as a ground of justification before God, is to ignore this judgement; it is to make void the sentence which the cross of Christ has passed upon all "works of righteousness which we have done." This teaching sorely offends moralists and ceremonialists, of whatever age or school; it is "the offence of the cross."

And further, as matter of *Divine appointment* the sacrifice of Calvary put an end to Jewish ordinances. Their significance was gone. The Epistle to the Hebrews developes this consequence at length in other directions. For himself the Apostle views it from a single and very definite standpoint. The Law, he says, had brought on men a curse; it stimulated sin to its worst developments (ch. iii. 10, 19). Christ's death under this curse has expiated and removed it for us (ch. iii. 13). His atonement met man's guilt in its culmination. The Law had not prevented—nay, it gave occasion to the crime; it necessitated, but could not provide expiation, which was supplied "outside the law" (Rom. iii. 21: ὧρις νόμου). The "offence" of the doctrine of the cross lay just here. It reconciled man with God on an extra-legal footing. It provided a new ground of justification and pronounced the old worthless. It fixed the mark of moral impotence and rejection upon the system to which the Jewish nature clung with passionate pride. To preach the cross was to declare legalism abolished: to preach circumcision was to declare the cross and its offence abolished.

This dilemma the Circumcisionists would fain escape. They fought shy of Calvary. Like some later moralists, they did not see why the cross should be always pushed to the front, and its offence forced upon the world. Surely there was in the wide range of Christian truth abundance of other profitable topics to discuss, without wounding Jewish susceptibilities in this way. But this endeavour of theirs is just what Paul is determined to frustrate. He confronts Judaism at every turn with that dreadful cross. He insists that it shall be realised in its horror and its shame, that men shall feel the tremendous shock which it gives to the moral conceit, the self-justifying spirit of human nature, which in the Jew of this period had reached its extreme point. "If law could save, if the world were not guilty before God," he reiterates, "why that death of the cross? God hath set Him forth *a propitiation*." And whoso accepts Jesus Christ must accept Him *crucified*, with all the offence and humiliation that the fact involves.

In later days the death of Christ has been made void in other ways. It is veiled in the steam of our incense. It is invested with the halo of a sensuous glorification. The cross has been for many turned into an artistic symbol, a beautiful idol, festooned with garlands, draped in poetry, but robbed of its spiritual meaning, its power to humble and to save. Let men see it "openly set forth," in its naked terror and majesty, that they may know what they are and what their sins have done.

We rely on birth and good breeding, on art and education as instruments of moral progress. Improved social arrangements, a higher environment, these, we think, will elevate the race. Within their limits these forces are invaluable; they are ordained of God. But they are only *law* at the best. When they have done their utmost, they leave man still unsaved—proud, selfish, unclean, miserable. To rest human salvation on self-improvement and social reform, is legalism over again. To civilise is not to regenerate. These methods were tried in Mosaism, under circumstances in many respects highly favourable. "The scandal of the cross" was the result. Education and social discipline may produce a Pharisee, nothing higher. Legislation and environment work from the outside. They cannot touch the essential human heart. Nothing has ever done this like the cross of Jesus Christ. He who "makes it of none effect," whether in the name of Jewish tradition or of modern progress, takes away the one practicable hope of the moral regeneration of mankind.

III. We are now in a position to estimate more precisely the character and motives of the Judaistic party, *the hinderers and troublers* of this Epistle.

In the first place, it appears that they had entered the Galatian communities from without. The fact that they are called *troublers (disturbers)* of itself suggests this (ver. 10; ch. i. 7). They came with a professed "gospel," as messengers bringing new tidings; the Apostle compares them to himself, the first Galatian evangelist, "or an angel from heaven" (ch. i. 8, 9). He glances at them in his reference to "false brethren" at an earlier time "brought into (the Gentile Church) unawares" (ch. ii. 4). These men are "courting" the favour of Paul's Galatian disciples, endeavouring to gain them over in his absence (ch. iv. 17, 18). They have made misleading statements respecting his early career and relations to the Church, which he is at pains to correct. They professed to represent the views of the Pillars at Jerusalem, and quoted their authority against the Apostle Paul.

From these considerations we infer that "the troublers" were *Judaistic emissaries from Palestine.* The second Epistle to Corinth, contemporaneous with this letter, reveals the existence of a similar propaganda in the Greek capital at the same period. Paul had given the Galatians warning on the subject at his last visit (ch. i. 9). There were already, we should suppose, in the Galatian societies, before the arrival of the Judaizers, Jewish believers in Christ of legalistic tendencies, prepared to welcome and support the new teachers. But it was the coming of these agitators from without that threw the Churches of Galatia into such a ferment, and brought about the situation disclosed in this Epistle.

The allusion made in chap. ii. 12 to "certain from James,"[137] taken in connection with other circumstances, points, as we think, to the outbreak of a systematic agitation against the Apostle Paul, which was carried on during his third missionary tour, and drew from him the great evangelical Epistles of this epoch. This anti-Pauline movement emanated from Jerusalem and pretended to official sanction. Set on foot at the time of the collision with Peter at Antioch, the conflict is now in full progress. The Apostle's denunciation of his opponents is unsparing. They "hinder" the Galatians "from obeying truth" (ver. 7); they entice them from the path in which they had bravely set out, and are robbing them of their heritage in Christ. It was a false, a perverted gospel that they taught (ch. i. 7). They cast on their hearers an envious spell which drew them away from the cross and its salvation (ch.

ii. 21; iii. 1). Not truth, but self-interest and party-ends were the objects they pursued (ch. iv. 17; vi. 12, 13). Their "persuasion" was assuredly not of God, "who had called" the Galatians through the Apostle's voice. If God had sent Paul amongst them, as the Galatians had good reason to know, clearly He had not sent these men, with their "other gospel."

The vitiating "leaven" at work in the spiritual life of the Galatians, if not arrested, would soon "leaven the whole lump." The Apostle applies to the Judaistic doctrine the same figure under which he described the taint of immorality found in the Church of Corinth (1 Cor. v. 6-8). So zealous and unscrupulous, so deadly in its effect on evangelical faith and life was the spirit of Jewish legalism. The Apostle trusts that his Galatians will after all escape from this fatal infection, that they will leave "the troublers" alone to "bear the judgement" which must fall upon them (ver. 10). The Lord is the Keeper, and the Avenger of His Church. No one, "whosoever he be," will injure it with impunity. Let the man that makes mischief in the Church of Jesus Christ take care what he is about. The tempted may escape; sins of ignorance and weakness can be forgiven. But woe unto the tempter!

Against the wilful perverters of the gospel the Apostle at the outset delivered his anathema. For these Circumcisionists in particular he has one further wish to express. It is a grim sort of suggestion, to be read rather by way of sarcasm than in the strict letter of fulfilment. The devotees of circumcision, he means to say, might as well go a step farther. If the physical mark of Judaism, the mere surgical act, is so salutary, why not "cut off" the member altogether, like the emasculated priests of Cybelé? (ver. 12). [138] This mutilation belonged to the worship of the great heathen goddess of Asia Minor, and was associated with her debasing cultus. Moreover it excluded its victim from a place in the congregation of Israel (Deut. xxiii. 1).

This mockery, though not to be judged by modern sentiment, in any case went to the verge of what charity and decency permit. It breathes a burning contempt for the Judaizing policy. It shows how utterly circumcision had lost its sacredness for the Apostle. Its spiritual import being gone, it was now a mere "concision" (Phil. iii. 2), a cutting of the body—nothing more.

Such language was well calculated to disgust Gentile Christians with the rite of circumcision. It helps to account for the implacable hatred with which Paul was regarded by orthodox Jews. It accords with what he intimated in ch. iv. 9, to the effect that Jewish conformity was for the Gentiles in effect *heathenish*. Apart from its relation to the obsolete Mosaic covenant, circumcision was in itself no holier than the deformities inflicted by Paganism on its votaries.

The Judaizers are finally described, not merely as "troublers" and "hinderers," but as "those that *unsettle* you"—or more strongly still, "*overthrow* you." The Greek word (ἀναστατέω) occurs in Acts xvii. 6, xxi. 38, where it is rendered, *turn upside down, stir to sedition*. These men were carrying on a treasonable agitation. False themselves to the gospel of Christ, they incited the Galatians to belie their Christian professions, to betray the cause of Gentile liberty, and to desert their own Apostle. They deserved to suffer some degrading punishment. "Full" as they were "of subtlety and mischief, perverting the right ways of the Lord," Paul did well to denounce them and to turn their zeal for circumcision to derisive scorn.

THE ETHICAL APPLICATION

CHAPTER XXII
THE PERILS OF LIBERTY

"For ye, brethren, were called for freedom; only *use* not your freedom for an occasion to the flesh, but through love be servants one to another. For the whole law is fulfilled in one word, *even* in this; Thou shalt love thy neighbour as thyself. But if ye bite and devour one another, take heed that ye be not consumed one of another." —Gal. v. 13-15.

Our analysis has drawn a strong line across the middle of this chapter. At ver. 13 the Apostle turns his mind in the ethical direction. He has dismissed "the troublers" with contempt in ver. 12; and until the close of the Epistle does not mention them again; he addresses his readers on topics in which they are left out of view. But this third, ethical section of the letter is still continuous with its polemical and doctrinal argument.

It applies the maxim of ver. 6, "Faith works through love"; it reminds the Galatians how they had "received the Spirit of God" (ch. iii. 2, 3; iv. 6). The rancours and jealousies opposed to love, the carnal mind that resists the Spirit—these are the objects of Paul's dehortations. The moral disorders which the Apostle seeks to correct arose largely out of the mischief caused by the Judaizers. And his exhortations to love and good works are themselves indirectly polemical. They vindicate Paul's gospel from the charge of antinomianism, while they guard Christians from giving occasion to the charge. They protect from exaggeration and abuse the liberty already defended from legalistic encroachments. The more precious and sacred is the freedom of Gentile believers, the more on the one hand do those deserve punishment who would defraud them of it; and the more earnestly must they on their part guard this treasure from misuse and dishonour. In this sense ver. 13a stands between the sentence against the Circumcisionists in ver. 12 and the appeal to the Galatians that follows. It repeats the proclamation of freedom made in ver. 1, making it the ground at once of the judgement pronounced against the foes of freedom and the admonition addressed to its possessors. *"For you were called* (summoned by God to enter the kingdom of His Son) *with a view to liberty*—not to legal bondage; nor, on the other hand, that you might run into licence and give the reins to self-will and appetite—not *liberty for an occasion to the flesh."*

I. Here lies *the danger of liberty,* especially when conferred on a young, untrained nature, and in a newly emancipated community.

Freedom is a priceless boon; but it is a grave responsibility. It has its temptations, as well as its joys and dignities. The Apostle has spoken at length of the latter: it is the former that he has now to urge. Keep your liberties, he seems to say; for Christ's sake and for truth's sake hold them fast, guard them well. You are God's regenerated sons. Never forego your high calling. God is on your side; and those who assail you shall feel the weight of His displeasure. Yes, "stand fast" in the liberty wherewith "Christ made you free." But take care how you employ your freedom; "only use not liberty for an occasion to the flesh." This significant *only* turns the other side of the medal, and bids us read the legend on its reverse front. On the obverse we have found it written, "The Lord knoweth them that are His" (2 Tim. ii. 19; comp. Gal. iv. 6, 9). This is the side of *privilege* and of grace, the spiritual side of the Christian life. On the reverse it bears the motto, "Let every one that nameth the name of the Lord depart from iniquity." This is the second, the ethical side of our calling, the side of *duty,* to which we have now to turn.

The man, or the nation that has won its freedom, has won but half the battle. It has conquered external foes; it has still to prevail over itself. And this is the harder task. Men clamour for liberty, when they mean licence; what they seek is the liberty of the flesh, not of the Spirit, freedom to indulge their lusts and to trample on the rights of others, the freedom of outlaws and brigands. The natural man defines freedom as the power to do as he likes; not the right of self-regulation, but the absence of regulation is what he desires. And this is just what the Spirit of God will never allow (ver. 17). When such a man has thrown off outward constraint and the dread of punishment, there is no inward law to take its place. It is his greed, his passion, his pride and ambition that call for freedom; not his conscience. And to all such libertarians our Saviour says, "He that committeth sin is *the slave of sin."* No tyrant is so vile, so insatiable as our own self-indulged sin. A pitiable triumph, for a man to have secured his religious liberty only to become the thrall of his vices!

It is possible that some men accepted the gospel under the delusion that it afforded a shelter for sin. The sensualist, deterred from his indulgences by fear of the Law, joined in Paul's campaign against it, imagining that Grace would give him larger freedom. If "where sin abounded grace did superabound," he would say in his heart, Why not sin the more, so that grace might have a greater victory? This is no fanciful inference. Hypocrisy has learned to wear the garb of evangelical zeal; and teachers of the gospel have not always guarded sufficiently against this shocking perversion. Even the man whose heart has been truly touched and changed by Divine grace, when the freshness of his first love to Christ has passed away and temptation renews its assaults, is liable to this deception. He may begin to think that sin is less perilous, since forgiveness was so easily obtained. He may presume that as a son of God, sealed by the Spirit of adoption, he will not be allowed to fall, even though he stumble. He is one of "God's elect"; what "shall separate him" from the Divine love in Christ? In this assurance he holds a talisman that secures his safety. What need to "watch and pray lest he enter into temptation," when the Lord is his keeper? He is God's enfranchised son; "all things are lawful" to him; "things present" as well as "things to come" are his in Christ. By such reasonings his liberty is turned into an *occasion to the flesh*. And men who before they boasted themselves sons of God were restrained by the spirit of bondage and fear, have found in this assurance the occasion, the "starting-point" (ἀφορμή) for a more shameless course of evil.

In the view of Legalism, this is the natural outcome of Pauline teaching. From the first it has been charged with fostering lawlessness. In the Lutheran Reformation Rome pointed to the Antinomians, and moralists of our own day speak of "canting Evangelicals," just as the Judaists alleged the existence of immoral Paulinists, whose conduct, they declared, was the proper fruit of the preaching of emancipation from the Law. These, they would say to the Apostle, are your spiritual children; they do but carry your doctrine to its legitimate issue. This reproach the gospel has always had to bear; there have been those, alas, amongst its professors whose behaviour has given it plausibility. Sensualists will "turn the grace of our God into lasciviousness;" swine will trample under their feet the pure pearls of the gospel. But they are pure and precious none the less.

This possibility is, however, a reason for the utmost watchfulness in those who are stewards in the administration of the gospel. They must be careful, like Paul, to make it abundantly clear that they "establish" and do not "make void law through faith" (Rom. iii. 31). There is an evangelical Ethics, as well as an evangelical Dogmatics. The ethics of the Gospel have been too little studied and applied. Hence much of the confessed failure of evangelical Churches in preserving and building up the converts that they win.

II. Faith in Christ gives in truth a new efficacy to the moral law. For it works through love; and love fulfils all laws in one (vv. 13b, 14). Where faith has this operation, liberty is safe; not otherwise. *Love's slaves are the true freemen.*

The legalist practically takes the same view of human nature as the sensualist. He knows nothing of "the desire of the Spirit" arrayed against that of the flesh (ver. 17), nothing of the mastery over the heart that belongs to the love of Christ. In his analysis the soul consists of so many desires, each blindly seeking its own gratification, which must be drilled into order under external pressure, by an intelligent application of law. Modern Utilitarians agree with the ancient Judaists in their ethical philosophy. Fear of punishment, hope of reward, the influence of the social environment— these are, as they hold, the factors which create character and shape our moral being. "Pain and pleasure," they tell us, "are the masters of human life." Without the faith that man is the child of God, formed in His image, we are practically shut up to this suicidal theory of morals. *Suicidal* we say, for it robs our spiritual being of everything distinctive in it, of all that raises the moral above the natural; it makes duty and personality illusions.

Judaism is a proof that this scheme of life is impracticable. For the Pharisaic system which produced such deplorable moral results, was an experiment in external ethics. It was in fact the application of a highly developed and elaborate traditional code of law, enforced by the strongest outward sanctions, *without personal loyalty to the Divine Lawgiver.* In the national conscience of the Jews this was wanting. Their faith in God, as the Epistle of James declares, was a "dead" faith, a bundle of abstract notions. Loyalty is true law-keeping. And loyalty springs from the personal relationship of the subject and the law-making power. This nexus Christian sonship supplies, in its purest and most exalted form. When I see in the Lawgiver my Almighty Father, when the law has become incarnate in the person of my Saviour, my heart's King and Lord, it wears a changed aspect. "*His commandments* are not grievous." Duty, required by Him, is honour and delight. No abstract law, no "stream of tendency" can command the homage or awaken the moral energy that is inspired by "the love of God in Christ Jesus our Lord."

Here the Apostle traverses antinomian deductions from his doctrine of liberty. In the Epistle to the Romans (ch. vi.) he deals at length with the theoretical objection to his teaching on this subject. He shows there that salvation by faith, rightly understood and experienced, renders continuance in sin impossible. For faith in Christ is in effect the union of the soul with Christ, first in His death, and then consequently in His risen life, wherein He lives only "to God." Nay, Christ Himself lives in the believing man (Gal.

ii. 20). Instead of our sinning "because we are not under the law, but under grace," this is precisely the reason why we need not and must not sin. Faith joins us to the risen Christ, whose life we share—so Paul argues—and we should not sin any more than He. Here, from the practical standpoint, he lays it down that *faith works by love; and love casts out sin, for it unites all laws in itself.* Faith links us to Christ in heaven (Romans); faith fills us with His love on earth (Galatians). So love, marked out in ver. 6 as the energy of faith, now serves as the guard of liberty. Neither legalist nor law-breaker understands the meaning of faith in Christ.

At this point Paul throws in one of his bold paradoxes. He has been contending all through the Epistle for freedom, bidding his readers scorn the legal yoke, breathing into them his own contempt for the pettiness of Judaistic ceremonial. But now he turns round suddenly and bids them *be slaves*: "but let love," he says, "make you bondmen to each other" (ver. 13). Instead of breaking bonds, he seeks to create stronger bonds, stronger because dearer. Paul preaches no gospel of individualism, of egotistic salvation-seeking. The self-sacrifice of Christ becomes in turn a principle of sacrifice in those who receive it. Paul's own ideal is, to be "conformed to His death" (Phil. iii. 10). There is nothing anarchic or self-asserting in his plea for freedom. He opposes the law of Pharisaic externalism in the interests of the law of Christian love. The yoke of Judaism must be broken, its bonds cast aside, in order to give free play to "the law of the Spirit of life in Christ Jesus." Faith transfers authority from flesh to spirit, giving it a surer seat, a more effective, and in reality more lawful command over man's nature. It restores the normal equipoise of the soul. Now the Divine law is written on "the tablets of the heart"; and this makes it far more sovereign than when engraved on the stone slabs of Sinai. Love and law for the believer in Christ are fused into one. In this union law loses nothing of its holy severity; and love nothing of its tenderness. United they constitute the Christian sense of *duty*, whose sternest exactions are enforced by gratitude and devotion.

And love is ever conqueror. To it toil and endurance that mock the achievement of other powers, are a light thing. Needing neither bribe nor threat, love labours, waits, braves a thousand dangers, keeps the hands busy, the eye keen and watchful, the feet running to and fro untired through the longest day. There is no industry, no ingenuity like that of love. Love makes the mother the slave of the babe at her breast, and wins from the friend for his friend service that no compulsion could exact, rendered in pure gladness and free-will. Its power alone calls forth what is best and strongest in us all. Love is mightier than death. In Jesus Christ, love has "laid down life for its friends"; the fulness of life has encountered and overcome the uttermost of death. Love esteems it bondage to be prevented, liberty only to be allowed to serve.

Without love, freedom is an empty boon. It brings no ease, no joy of heart. It is objectless and listless. Bereft of faith and love, though possessing the most perfect independence, the soul drifts along like a ship rudderless and masterless, with neither haven nor horizon. Wordsworth, in his Ode to Duty, has finely expressed the weariness that comes of such liberty, unguided by an inward law and a Divine ideal:

"Me this unchartered freedom tires;

I feel the weight of chance desires:

My hopes no more must change their name;

I long for a repose that ever is the same."

But on the other hand,

"Serene will be our days and bright,

And happy will our nature be,

When love is an unerring light,

And joy its own security."

This "royal law" (Jam. ii. 8) blends with its sovereignty of power the charm of simplicity. "The whole law," says the Apostle, "hath been fulfilled in one word—Love" (ver. 14). The Master said, "I came not to destroy the law, but to fulfil." The key to His fulfilment was given in the declaration of the twofold command of love to God and to our neighbour. "On these two hang all the law and the prophets." Hence the Apostle's phrase, *hath been fulfilled*. This unification of the moral code is accomplished. Christ's life and death have given to this truth full expression and universal currency. Love's fulfilment of law stands before us a positive attainment, an incontestable fact. Paul does not speak here, as in Rom. xiii. 9, of the comprehending, the "summing up" of all laws in one; but of the bringing of law to its completion, its realisation and consummation in the love of Christ. "O how I love Thy law," said the purer spirit of the Old Testament. "Thy love is my law," says the true spirit of the New.

It is remarkable that this supreme principle of Christian ethics is first enunciated in the most legal part of the Old Testament. Leviticus is the Book of the Priestly Legislation. It is chiefly occupied with ceremonial and civil regulations. Yet in the midst of the legal minutiæ is set this sublime and simple rule, than which Jesus Christ could prescribe nothing more Divine: *Thou shalt love thy neighbour as thyself* (Levit. xix. 18). This sentence is the conclusion of a series of directions (vv. 9-18) forbidding unneighbourly conduct, each of them sealed with the declaration, "I am Jehovah." This brief code of brotherly love breathes a truly Christian spirit; it is a beautiful expression of "the law of kindness" that is on the lips and in the heart of the child of God. We find in the law-book of Mosaism, side by side with elaborate rules of sacrificial ritual and the homeliest details touching the life of a rude agricultural people, conceptions of God and of duty of surpassing loftiness and purity, such as meet us in the religion of no other ancient nation.

The law, therefore, opposed and cast out in the name of faith, is brought in again under the shield of love. "If ye love Me," said Jesus, "*keep my commandments.*" Love reconciles law and faith. Law by itself can but prohibit this and that injury to one's neighbour, when they are likely to arise. Love excludes the doing of any injury; it "worketh no ill to its neighbour, therefore love is the fulfilling of the law" (Rom. xiii. 10). That which law restrains or condemns after the fact, love renders impossible beforehand. It is not content with the negative prevention of wrong; it "overcomes" and displaces "evil with good."

"What law could not do," with all its multiplied enactments and redoubled threats, faith "working by love" has accomplished at a stroke. "The righteousness of the law is fulfilled in those who walk not after the flesh, but after the Spirit" (Rom. viii. 3, 4). Gentile Christians have been raised to the level of a righteousness "exceeding that of scribes and pharisees" (Matt. v. 20). The flesh which defied law's terrors and evaded its control, is subdued by the love of Christ. Law created the need of salvation; it defined its conditions and the direction which it must take. But there its power ceased. It could not change the sinful heart. It supplied no motive adequate to secure obedience. The moralist errs in substituting duty for love, works for faith. He would make the rule furnish the motive, the path supply strength to walk in it. The distinction of the gospel is that it is "*the power* of God unto salvation," while the law is "*weak* through the flesh."

Paul does not therefore override the law in the interest of faith. Quite the contrary, he establishes, he magnifies it. His theology rests on the idea of Righteousness, which is strictly a legal conception. But he puts the law in its proper place. He secures for it the alliance of love. The legalist, desiring to exalt law, in reality stultifies it. Striving to make it omnipotent, he makes it impotent. In the Apostle's teaching, law is the rule, faith the spring of action. Law marks the path, love gives the will and power to follow it. Who then are the truest friends of law—Legalists or Paulinists, moralists or evangelicals?

III. Alas, the Galatians at the present moment afford a spectacle far different from the ideal which Paul has drawn. Instead of "serving each other in love," they are "biting and devouring one another." The Church is in danger of being "consumed" by their jealousies and quarrels (ver. 15).

These Asiatic Gauls were men of a warm temperament, quick to resent wrong and prone to imagine it. The dissensions excited by the Judaic controversy had excited their combative temper to an unusual degree. "Biting" describes the wounding and exasperating effect of the manner in which their contentions were carried on; "devour" warns them of its destructiveness. Taunts were hurled across the field of debate; vituperation supplied the lack of argument. Differences of opinion engendered private feuds and rankling injuries. In Corinth the spirit of discord had taken a factious form. It arrayed men in conflicting parties, with their distinctive watchwords and badges and sectional platforms. In these Churches it bore fruit in personal affronts and quarrels, in an angry, vindictive temper, which spread through the Galatian societies and broke out in every possible form of contention (v. 20). If this state of things continued, the Churches of Galatia would cease to exist. Their liberty would end in complete disintegration.

Like some other communities, the Galatian Christians were oscillating between despotism and anarchy; they had not attained the equilibrium of a sober, ordered liberty, the freedom of a manly self-control. They had not sufficient respect either for their own or for each other's rights. Some men must be bridled or they will "bite;" they must wear the yoke or they run wild. They are incapable of being a law unto themselves. They have not faith enough to make them steadfast, nor love enough to be an inward guide, nor the Spirit of God in measure sufficient to overcome the vanity and self-indulgence of the flesh. But the Apostle still hopes to see his Galatian disciples worthy of their calling as sons of God. He points out to them the narrow but sure path that leads between the desert of legalism on the one hand, and the gulf of anarchy and licence on the other.

The problem of the nature and conditions of Christian liberty occupies the Apostle's mind in different ways in all the letters of this period. The young Churches of the Gentiles were in the gravest peril. They had come out of Egypt to enter the Promised Land, the heritage of the sons of God. The Judaists sought to turn them aside into the Sinaitic wilderness of Mosaism; while their old habits and associations powerfully tended to draw them back into heathen immorality. Legalism and licence were the Scylla and Charybdis on either hand, between which it needed the most firm and skilful pilotage to steer the bark of the Church. The helm of the vessel is in Paul's hands. And, through the grace of God, he did not fail in his task. It is in *the love of Christ* that the Apostle found his guiding light. "Love," he has written, "never faileth."

Love is the handmaid of faith, and the firstborn fruit of the Spirit of Christ (vv. 6, 22). Blending with the law, love refashions it, changing it into its own image. Thus moulded and transfigured, law is no longer an exterior yoke, a system of restraint and penalty; it becomes an inner, sweet constraint. Upon the child of God it acts as an organic and formative energy, the principle of his regenerated being, which charges with its renovating influence all the springs of life. Evil is met no longer by a merely outward opposition, but by a repugnance proceeding from within. "The Spirit lusteth against the flesh" (v. 17). The law of the Spirit of life in Christ Jesus becomes the law of the man's new nature. God known and loved in Christ is the central object of his life. Within the Divine kingdom so created, the realm of love and of the Spirit, the soul henceforth dwells; and under that kingdom it places for itself all other souls, loved like itself in Christ.

CHAPTER XXIII
CHRIST'S SPIRIT AND HUMAN FLESH

[*He showeth the battell of the flesh and the Spirit; and the fruits of them both.* Heading in Genevan Bible.]

"But I say, Walk by the Spirit, and ye shall not fulfil the lust of the flesh. For the flesh lusteth against the Spirit, and the Spirit against the flesh; for these are contrary the one to the other; that ye may not do the things that ye would. But if ye are led by the Spirit, ye are not under the law.... And they that are of Christ Jesus have crucified the flesh with the passions and the lusts thereof. If we live by the Spirit, by the Spirit let us also walk. Let us not be vainglorious, provoking one another, envying one another." —Gal. v. 16-26.

Love is the guard of Christian freedom. The Holy Spirit is its guide. These principles accomplish what the law could never do. It withheld liberty, and yet did not give purity. The Spirit of love and of sonship bestows both, establishing a happy, ordered freedom, the liberty of the sons of God.

From the first of these two factors of Christian ethics the Apostle passes in ver. 16 to the second. He conducts us from the consequence to the cause, from the human aspect of spiritual freedom to the Divine. Love, he has said, fulfils all laws in one. It casts out evil from the heart; it stays the injurious hand and tongue; and makes it impossible for liberty to give the rein to any wanton or selfish impulse. But the law of love is no natural, automatic impulse. It is a Divine inspiration. "Love is of God." It is the characteristic "fruit of the Spirit" of adoption (ver. 22), implanted and nourished from above. When I bid you "by love serve each other," the Apostle says, I do not expect you to keep this law of yourselves, by force of native goodness: I know how contrary it is to your Galatic nature; "but I say, walk in the Spirit," and this will be an easy yoke; to "fulfil the desire of the flesh" will then be for you a thing impossible.

The word *Spirit* (πνεύματι) is written indefinitely; but the Galatians knew well what Spirit the Apostle meant. It is "the Spirit" of whom he has spoken so often in this letter, the Holy Spirit of God, who had entered their hearts when they first believed in Christ and taught them to call God Father. He gave them their freedom: He will teach them how to use it. The absence of the definite article in *Pneuma* does not destroy its personal force, but allows it at the same time a broad, qualitative import, corresponding to that of the opposed "desire of the flesh." The walk governed "by the Spirit" is a *spiritual* walk. As for the interpretation of the *dative* case (rendered variously *by*, or *in*, or even *for the Spirit*), that is determined by the meaning of the noun itself. "The Spirit" is not the path "in" which one walks; rather He supplies *the motive principle, the directing influence* of the new life.[139] Ver. 16 is interpreted by vv. 18 and 25. To "walk in the Spirit" is to be "led by the Spirit"; it is so to "live in the Spirit" that one habitually "moves" (*marches*: ver. 25) under His direction.

This conception of the indwelling Spirit of God as the actuating power of the Christian's moral life predominates in the rest of this chapter. We shall pursue the general line of the Apostle's teaching on the subject in the present Chapter, leaving for future exposition the detailed enumeration of the "fruit of the Spirit" and "works of the flesh" contained in vv. 19-23. This antithesis of Flesh and Spirit presents the following considerations: — (1) *the diametrical opposition of the two forces*; (2) *the effect of the predominance of one or the other*; (3) *the mastery over the flesh which belongs to those who are Christ's.* In a word, Christ's Spirit is the absolute antagonist and the sure vanquisher of our sinful human flesh.

I. "I say, Walk by the Spirit, and you will verily not fulfil the lust of the flesh." On what ground does this bold assurance rest? Because, the Apostle replies, *the Spirit and the flesh are opposites* (ver. 17). Each is bent on destroying the ascendency of the other. Their cravings and tendencies stand opposed at every point. Where the former rules, the latter must succumb. "For the flesh lusteth against the Spirit, and the Spirit against the flesh."

The verb *lust* in Greek, as in English, bears commonly an evil sense; but not necessarily so, nor by derivation. It is a sad proof of human corruption that in all languages words denoting strong desire tend to an impure significance. Paul extends to "the desire of the Spirit" the term which has just been used of "the lust of the flesh," in this way sharpening the antithesis. [140] Words appropriated to the vocabulary of the flesh and degraded by its use, may be turned sometimes to good account and employed in the service of the Holy Spirit, whose influence redeems our speech and purges the uncleanness of our lips.

The opposition here affirmed exists on the widest scale. All history is a battlefield for the struggle between God's Spirit and man's rebellious flesh. In the soul of a half-sanctified Christian, and in Churches like those of Corinth and Galatia whose members are "yet carnal and walk as men," the conflict is patent. The Spirit of Christ has established His rule in the heart; but His supremacy is challenged by the insurrection of the carnal powers. The contest thus revived in the soul of the Christian is internecine; it is that of the kingdoms of light and darkness, of the opposite poles of good and evil. It is an incident in the war of human sin against the Holy Spirit of God, which extends over all time and all human life. Every lust, every act or thought of evil is directed, knowingly or unknowingly, against the authority of the Holy Spirit, against the presence and the rights of God immanent in the creature. Nor is there any restraint upon evil, any influence counteracting it in man or nation or race, which does not proceed from the Spirit of the Lord. The spirit of man has never been without a Divine Paraclete. "God hath not left Himself without witness" to any; and "it is the Spirit that beareth witness, because the Spirit is truth." The Spirit of truth, the Holy Spirit, is the Spirit of all truth and holiness. In the "truth as it is in Jesus" He possesses His highest instrument. But from the beginning it was His office to be God's Advocate, to uphold law, to convict the conscience, to inspire the hope of mercy, to impart moral strength and freedom. We "believe in the Holy Ghost, the Lord and Giver of life."

This war of Spirit and Flesh is first ostensibly declared in the words of Gen. vi. 3. This passage indicates the moral reaction of God's Spirit against the world's corruption, and the protest which in the darkest periods of human depravity He has maintained. God had allowed men to do despite to His good Spirit. But it cannot always be so. A time comes when, outraged and defied, He withdraws His influence from men and from communities; and the Flesh bears them along to swift destruction. So it was in the world before the Flood. So largely amongst later heathen peoples, when God "suffered all nations to walk in their own ways." Even the Mosaic law had proved rather a substitute than a medium for the free action of the Spirit of God on men. "The law was spiritual," but "weak through the flesh." It denounced the guilt which it was powerless to avert.

With the advent of Christ all this is changed. The Spirit of God is now, for the first time, sent forth in His proper character and His full energy. At last His victory draws near. He comes as the Spirit of Christ and the Father, "*poured out* upon all flesh." "A new heart will I give you, and a new spirit will I put within you. I will put My Spirit within you" (Ezek. xxxvi. 25-27): this was the great hope of prophecy; and it is realised. The Spirit of God's Son regenerates the human heart, subdues the flesh, and establishes the communion of God with men. The reign of the Spirit on earth was the immediate purpose of the manifestation of Jesus Christ.

But what does Paul really mean by "the flesh?" It includes everything that is not "of the Spirit." It signifies the entire potency of sin. It is the contra-spiritual, the undivine in man. Its "works," as we find in vv. 20, 21, are not bodily vices only, but include every form of moral debasement and aberration. *Flesh* in the Apostle's vocabulary follows the term *spirit*, and deepens and enlarges its meaning precisely as the latter does. Where *spirit* denotes the supersensible in man, *flesh* is the sensible, the bodily nature as such. When *spirit* rises into the supernatural and superhuman, *flesh* becomes the natural, the human by consequence. When *spirit* receives its highest signification, denoting the holy Effluence of God, His personal presence in the world, *flesh* sinks to its lowest and represents unrenewed nature, the evil principle oppugnant and alien to God. It is identical with *sin*. But in this profound moral significance the term is more than a figure. Under its use *the body* is marked out, not indeed as the cause, but as the instrument, the vehicle of sin. Sin has incorporated itself with our organic life, and extends its empire over the material world. When the Apostle speaks of "the body of sin" and "of death," and bids us "mortify the deeds of the body" and "the members which are upon the earth,"[141] his expressions are not to be resolved into metaphors.

On this definition of the terms, it is manifest that the antagonism of the Flesh and Spirit is fundamental. They can never come to terms with each other, nor dwell permanently in the same being. Sin must be extirpated, or the Holy Spirit will finally depart. The struggle must come to a definitive issue. Human character tends every day to a more determinate form; and an hour comes in each case when the victory of flesh or spirit is irrevocably fixed, when "the filthy" will henceforth "be filthy still," and "the holy, holy still" (Rev. xxii. 11).

The last clause of ver. 17, "that ye may not do the things that ye would," has been variously interpreted. The rendering of the Authorized Version ("so that ye *cannot*") is perilously misleading. Is it that the flesh prevents the Galatians doing the good they would? Or is the Spirit to prevent them doing the evil they otherwise would? Or are both these oppositions in existence at once, so that they waver between good and evil, leading a partly spiritual, partly carnal life, consistent neither in right nor wrong? The last is the actual state of the case. Paul is perplexed about them (ch. iv. 20); they are in doubt about themselves. They did not "walk in the Spirit," they were not true to their Christian principles; the flesh was too strong for that. Nor would they break away from Christ and follow the bent of their lower nature; the Holy Spirit held them back from doing this. So they have two wills,—or practically none. This state of things was designed by God,—"*in order that* ye may not do the things ye haply would;*"* it accords with the methods of His government. Irresolution is the necessary effect of the course the Galatians had pursued. So far they stopped short of apostasy; and this restraint witnessed to the power of the Holy Spirit still at work in their midst (ch. iii. 5; vi. 1). Let this Divine hand cease to check them, and the flesh would carry them, with the full momentum of their will, to spiritual ruin. Their condition is just now one of suspense. They are poised in a kind of moral equilibrium, which cannot continue long, but in which, while it lasts, the action of the conflicting forces of Flesh and Spirit is strikingly manifest.

II. These two principles in their development lead to entirely opposite results.

(1) *The works of the flesh*—"manifest" alas, both then and now—*exclude from the kingdom of God.* "I tell you beforehand," the Apostle writes, "as I have already told you: they who practise such things will not inherit God's kingdom" (v. 21).

This warning is essential to Paul's gospel (Rom. ii. 16); it is good news for a world where wrong so often and so insultingly triumphs, that there is a judgement to come. Whatever may be our own lot in the great award, we rejoice to believe that there will be a righteous settlement of human affairs, complete and final; and that this settlement is in the hands of Jesus Christ. In view of His tribunal the Apostle goes about "*warning* and teaching every man." And this is his constant note, amongst profligate heathen, or hypocritical Jews, or backsliding and antinomian Christians,—"The unrighteous shall not inherit the kingdom of God." For that kingdom is, above all, *righteousness.* Men of fleshly minds, in the nature of things, have no place in it. They are blind to its light, dead to its influence, at war with its aims and principles. "If we say that we have fellowship with Him—the Father of our Lord Jesus Christ—and walk in darkness, *we lie*" (1 John i. 6). "Those who do such things" forfeit by doing them the character of sons of God. His children seek to be "perfect as their heavenly Father is perfect." They are "blameless and harmless, imitators of God, walking in love as Christ loved us" (Phil. ii. 15; Eph. v. 1, 2). The Spirit of God's Son is a spirit of love and peace, of temperance and gentleness (v. 22). If these fruits are wanting, the Spirit of Christ is not in us and we are none of His. We are without the one thing by which He said all men would know His disciples (John xiii. 35). When the Galatians "bite and devour one another," they resemble Ishmael the persecutor (ch. iv. 29), rather than the gentle Isaac, heir of the Covenant.

"If children, *then heirs.*" Future destiny turns upon present character. The Spirit of God's Son, with His fruit of love and peace, is "the earnest of our inheritance, sealing us against the day of redemption" (Eph. i. 14;

iv. 30). By selfish tempers and fleshly indulgences He is driven from the soul; and Losing Him, it is shut out from the kingdom of grace on earth, and from the glory of the redeemed. "There shall in no wise enter into it anything unclean;" such is the excommunication written above the gate of the Heavenly City (Rev. xxi. 27). This sentence of the Apocalypse puts a final seal upon the teaching of Scripture. The God of revelation is the Holy One; His Spirit is the Holy Spirit; His kingdom is the kingdom of the saints, whose atmosphere burns like fire against all impurity. Concerning the men of the flesh the Apostle can only say, "Whose end is perdition" (Phil. iii. 19).

Writing to the Corinthians, Paul entreats his readers not to be deceived upon this point (1 Cor. vi. 9, 10; Eph. v. 5). It seems so obvious, so necessary a principle, that one wonders how it should be mistaken, why he is compelled to reiterate it as he does in this place. And yet this has been a common delusion. No form of religion has escaped being touched by Antinomianism. It is the divorce of piety from morality. It is the disposition to think that ceremonial works on the one hand, or faith on the other, supersede the ethical conditions of harmony with God. Foisting itself on evangelical doctrine this error leads men to assume that salvation is the mere pardon of sin. The sinner appears to imagine he is saved in order to remain a sinner. He treats God's mercy as a kind of bank, on which he may draw as often as his offences past or future may require. He does not understand that sanctification is the sequel of justification, that the evidence of a true pardon lies in a changed heart that loathes sin.

(2) Of the opposite principle the Apostle states not the ultimate, but the more immediate consequences. "Led by the Spirit, *ye are not under the law*" (ver. 18); and "Against such things—love, peace, goodness, and the like—*there is no law*" (ver. 23).

The declaration of ver. 18 is made with a certain abruptness. Paul has just said, in ver. 17, that the Spirit is the appointed antagonist *of the flesh*. And now he adds, that if we yield ourselves to His influence we shall be no longer *under the law*. This identification of sin and the law was established in ch. ii. 16-18; iii. 10-22. The law by itself, the Apostle showed, does not overcome sin, but aggravates it; it shuts men up the hopeless prisoners of their own past mis-doing. To be "under law" is to be in the position of Ishmael, the slave-born and finally outcast son, whose nature and temper are of the flesh (ch. iv. 21-31). After all this we can understand his writing *law* for *sin* in this passage, just as in 1 Cor. xv. 56 he calls "the law the *power* of sin." To be under law was, in Paul's view, to be held consciously in the grasp of sin. This was the condition to which Legalism would reduce the Galatians. From this calamity the Spirit of Christ would keep them free.

The phrase "under law" reminds us once more of the imperilled liberty of the Galatians. Their spiritual freedom and their moral safety were assailed in common. In ver. 16 he had said, "Let the Holy Spirit guide you, and you will vanquish sin"; and now, "By the same guidance you will escape the oppressive yoke of the law." Freedom from sin, freedom from the Jewish law—these two liberties were virtually one. "Sin shall not lord it over you, because ye are not under law, but under grace" (Rom. vi. 14). Ver. 23 explains this double freedom. Those who possess the Spirit of Christ bear His moral fruits. Their life fulfils the demands of the law, *without being due to its compulsion.* Law can say nothing against them. It did not produce this fruit; but it is bound to approve it. It has no hold on the men of the Spirit, no charge to bring against them. Its requirements are satisfied; its constraints and threatenings are laid aside.

Law therefore, in its Judaistic sense and application, has been abolished since "faith has come." No longer does it rule the soul by fear and compulsion. This office, necessary once for the infant heirs of the Covenant, it has no right to exercise over spiritual men. Law cannot give life (ch. iii. 21). This is the prerogative of the Spirit of God. Law says, "Thou shalt love the Lord thy God;" but it never inspired such love in any man's breast. If he does so love, the law approves him, without claiming credit to itself for the fact. If he does not love his God, law condemns him and brands him a transgressor. But "the love of God is shed abroad in our hearts *by the Holy Ghost.*" The teaching of this paragraph on the relation of the believer in Christ to God's law is summed up in the words of Rom. viii. 2: "The law of the Spirit of life in Christ Jesus made me free from the law of sin and death." Law has become my friend, instead of my enemy and accuser. For God's Spirit fills my soul with the love in which its fulfilment is contained. And now eternal life is the goal that stands in my view, in place of the death with the prospect of which, as a man of the flesh, the law appalled me.

III. We see then that *deliverance from sin belongs* not to the subjects of the law, but *to the freemen of the Spirit.* This deliverance, promised in ver. 16, is declared in ver. 24 as an accomplished fact. "Walk by the Spirit, and ye shall not fulfil the lust of the flesh.... They that are of Christ Jesus have crucified the flesh with its passions and its lusts." The tyranny of the flesh is ended for those who are "in Christ Jesus." His cross has slain their sins. The entrance of His Spirit imports the death of all carnal affections.

"They who are Christ's did crucify the flesh." This is the moral application of Paul's mystical doctrine, central to all his theology, of the believer's union with the Redeemer (see Chapter X, pp. 156-160). "Christ in me—I in Him:" there is Paul's secret. He was "one spirit" with Jesus Christ—dying, risen, ascended, reigning, returning in glory. His old self, his old world was dead and gone—slain by Christ's cross, buried in His grave (ch. ii. 20; vi. 14). And the flesh, common to the evil world and the evil self—that above all was crucified. The death of shame and legal penalty, the curse of God had overtaken it in the death of Jesus Christ. Christ has risen, the "Lord of the Spirit" (2 Cor. iii. 18), who "could not be holden" by the death which fell on "the body of His flesh." They who are Christ's rose with Him; while "the flesh of sin" stays in His grave. Faith sees it there, and leaves it there. We "reckon ourselves dead unto sin, and living unto God, in Christ Jesus." For such men, the flesh that was once—imperious, importunate, law-defying— is no more. It has received its death-stroke. "God, sending His own Son in the likeness of sinful flesh and a sacrifice for sin, *condemned sin in the flesh*" (Rom. viii. 3). Sin is smitten with the lightning of His anger. Doom has taken hold of it. Destroyed already in principle, it only waits for men to know this and to understand what has been done, till it shall perish everywhere. The destruction of the sinful flesh—more strictly of "sin in the flesh"—occurred, as Paul understood the matter, virtually and potentially in the moment of Christ's death. It was our human flesh that was crucified in Him—slain on the cross because, though in Him not personally sinful, yet in us with whom He had made Himself one, it was steeped in sin. Our sinful flesh hung upon His cross; it has risen, cleansed and sanctified, from His grave.

What was then accomplished in principle when "One died for all," is realised in point of fact when we are "baptized into His death"—when, that is to say, faith makes His death ours and its virtue passes into the soul. The scene of the cross is inwardly rehearsed. The wounds which pierced the Redeemer's flesh and spirit now pierce our consciences. It is a veritable crucifixion through which the soul enters into communion with its risen Saviour, and learns to live His life. Nor is its sanctification complete till it is "conformed unto His death" (Phil. iii. 10). So with all his train of "passions and of lusts," the "old man" is fastened and nailed down upon the new, interior Calvary, set up in each penitent and believing heart. The flesh may still, as in these Galatians, give mournful evidence of life. But it has no right to exist a single hour. *De jure* it is dead—dead in the reckoning of faith. It may die a lingering, protracted death, and make convulsive struggles; but die it must in all who are of Christ Jesus.

Let the Galatians consider what their calling of God signified. Let them recall the prospects which opened before them in the days of their first faith in Christ, the love that glowed in their hearts, the energy with which the Holy Spirit wrought upon their nature. Let them know how truly they were called to liberty, and in good earnest were made sons of God. They have only to continue as heretofore to be led by the Spirit of Christ and to march forward along the path on which they had entered, and neither Jewish law nor their own lawless flesh will be able to bring them into bondage. "Where the Spirit of the Lord is, there is liberty." Where He is not, there is legalism, or licence; or, it may be, both at once.

CHAPTER XXIV
THE WORKS OF THE FLESH

"Now the works of the flesh are manifest, which are *these*, fornication, uncleanness, lasciviousness, idolatry, sorcery, enmities, strife, jealousies, wraths, factions, divisions, parties, envyings, drunkenness, revellings, and such like: of the which I forewarn you, even as I did forewarn you, that they which practise such things shall not inherit the kingdom of God."—Gal. v. 19-21.

The tree is known by its fruits: the flesh by its "works." And these works are "manifest." The field of the world—"this present evil world" (ch. i. 4)— exhibits them in rank abundance. Perhaps at no time was the civilised world so depraved and godless as in the first century of the Christian era, when Tiberius, Caligula, Nero, Domitian, wore the imperial purple and posed as masters of the earth. It was the cruelty and vileness of the times which culminated in these deified monsters. By no accident was mankind cursed at this epoch with such a race of rulers. The world that worshipped them was worthy of them. Vice appeared in its most revolting and abandoned forms. Wickedness was rampant and triumphant. The age of the early Roman Empire has left a foul mark in human history and literature. Let Tacitus and Juvenal speak for it.

Paul's enumeration of the current vices in this passage has however a character of its own. It differs from the descriptions drawn by the same hand in other Epistles; and this difference is due doubtless to the character of his readers. Their temperament was sanguine; their disposition frank and impulsive. Sins of lying and injustice, conspicuous in other lists, are not found in this. From these vices the Galatic nature was comparatively free. Sensual sins and sins of passion—*unchastity, vindictiveness, intemperance*— occupy the field. To these must be added *idolatry*, common to the Pagan world. Gentile idolatry was allied with the practice of impurity on the one side; and on the other, through the evil of "sorcery," with "enmities" and "jealousies." So that these works of the flesh belong to four distinct types of depravity; three of which come under the head of immorality, while the fourth is the universal principle of Pagan irreligion, being in turn both cause and effect of the moral debasement connected with it.

I. "The works of the flesh are these—*fornication, uncleanness, lasciviousness*." A dark beginning! Sins of impurity find a place in every picture of Gentile morals given by the Apostle. In whatever direction he writes—to Romans or Corinthians, Galatians, Ephesians, or Thessalonians—it is always necessary to warn against these evils. They are equally "manifest" in heathen literature. The extent to which they stain the pages of the Greek and Roman classics sets a heavy discount against their value as instruments of Christian education. Civilised society in Paul's day was steeped in sexual corruption.

Fornication was practically universal. Few were found, even among severe moralists, to condemn it. The overthrow of the splendid classical civilisation, due to the extinction of manly virtues in the dominant race, may be traced largely to this cause. Brave men are the sons of pure women. John in the Apocalypse has written on the brow of Rome, "the great city which reigneth over the kings of the earth," this legend: "*Babylon the great, mother of harlots*" (Rev. xvii. 5). Whatever symbolic meaning the saying has, in its literal sense it was terribly true. Our modern Babylons, unless they purge themselves, may earn the same title and the same doom.

In writing to Corinth, the metropolis of Greek licentiousness, Paul deals very solemnly and explicitly with this vice. He teaches that this sin, above others, is committed "against the man's own body." It is a prostitution of the physical nature which Jesus Christ wore and still wears, which He claims for the temple of His Spirit, and will raise from the dead to share His immortality. Impurity degrades the body, and it affronts in an especial degree "the Holy Spirit which we have from God." Therefore it stands first amongst these "works of the flesh" in which it shows itself hostile and repugnant to the Spirit of our Divine sonship. "Joined to the harlot" in "one body," the vile offender gives himself over in compact and communion to the dominion of the flesh, as truly as he who is "joined to the Lord" is "one spirit with Him" (1 Cor. vi. 13-20).

On this subject it is difficult to speak faithfully and yet directly. There are many happily in our sheltered Christian homes who scarcely know of the existence of this heathenish vice, except as it is named in Scripture. To them it is an evil of the past, a nameless thing of darkness. And it is well it should be so. Knowledge of its horrors may be suitable for seasoned social reformers, and necessary to the publicist who must understand the worst as well as the best of the world he has to serve; but common decency forbids its being put within the reach of boys and innocent maidens. Newspapers and novels which reek of the divorce-court and trade in the garbage of human life, in "things of which it is a shame even to speak," are no more fit for ordinary consumption than the air of the pest-house is for breathing.

They are sheer poison to the young imagination, which should be fed on whatsoever things are honourable and pure and lovely. But bodily self-respect must be learned in good time. Modesty of feeling and chastity of speech must adorn our youth. "Let marriage be honourable in the eyes of all," let the old chivalrous sentiments of reverence and gentleness towards women be renewed in our sons, and our country's future is safe. Perhaps in our revolt from Mariolatry we Protestants have too much forgotten the honour paid by Jesus to the Virgin Mother, and the sacredness which His birth has conferred on motherhood. "Blessed," said the heavenly voice, "art thou among women." All our sisters are blessed and dignified in her, the holy "mother of our Lord" (Luke i. 42, 43).[142]

Wherever, and in whatever form, the offence exists which violates this relationship, Paul's fiery interdict is ready to be launched upon it. The anger of Jesus burned against this sin. In the wanton look He discerns the crime of adultery, which in the Mosaic law was punished with death by stoning. "The Lord is an avenger in all these things"—in everything that touches the honour of the human person and the sanctity of wedded life (1 Thess. iv. 1-8). The interests that abet whoredom should find in the Church of Jesus Christ an organization pledged to relentless war against them. The man known to practise this wickedness is an enemy of Christ and of his race. He should be shunned as we would shun a notorious liar—or a fallen woman. Paul's rule is explicit, and binding on all Christians, concerning "the fornicator, the drunkard, the extortioner—with such a one no, not to eat" (1 Cor. v. 9-11). That Church little deserves the name of a Church of Christ, which has not means of discipline sufficient to fence its communion from the polluting presence of "such a one."

Uncleanness and *lasciviousness* are companions of the more specific impurity. The former is the general quality of this class of evils, and includes whatever is contaminating in word or look, in gesture or in dress, in thought or sentiment. "Lasciviousness" is uncleanness open and shameless. The filthy jest, the ogling glance, the debauched and sensual face, these tell their own tale; they speak of a soul that has rolled in corruption till respect for virtue has died out of it. In this direction "the works of the flesh" can go no further. A lascivious human creature is loathsomeness itself. To see it is like looking through a door into hell.

A leading critic of our own times has, under this word of Paul's, put his finger upon the plague-spot in the national life of our Gallic neighbours—*Aselgeia*, or Wantonness. There may be a certain truth in this charge. Their disposition in several respects resembles that of Paul's Galatians. But we can scarcely afford to reproach others on this score. English society is none too clean. *Home* is for our people everywhere, thank God, the nursery of innocence. But outside its shelter, and beyond the reach of the mother's voice, how many perils await the weak and unwary. In the night-streets of the city the "strange woman" spreads her net, "whose feet go down to death." In workshops and business-offices too often coarse and vile language goes on unchecked, and one unchaste mind will infect a whole circle. Schools, wanting in moral discipline, may become seminaries of impurity. There are crowded quarters in large towns, and wretched tenements in many a country village, where the conditions of life are such that decency is impossible; and a soil is prepared in which sexual sin grows rankly. To cleanse these channels of social life is indeed a task of Hercules; but the Church of Christ is loudly called to it. Her vocation is in itself a purity crusade, a war declared against "all filthiness of flesh and spirit."

II. Next to *lust* in this procession of the Vices comes *idolatry*. In Paganism they were associated by many ties. Some of the most renowned and popular cults of the day were open purveyors of sensuality and lent to it the sanctions of religion. Idolatry is found here in fit company (comp. 1 Cor. x. 6-8). Peter's First Epistle, addressed to the Galatian with other Asiatic Churches, speaks of "the desire of the Gentiles" as consisting in "lasciviousness, lusts, winebibbings, revellings, carousings, and *abominable idolatries*" (ch. iv. 3).

Idolatry forms the centre of the awful picture of Gentile depravity drawn by our Apostle in his letter to Rome (ch. i.). It is, as he there shows, the outcome of man's native antipathy to the knowledge of God. Willingly men "took lies in the place of truth, and served the creature rather than the Creator." They merged God in nature, debasing the spiritual conception of the Deity with fleshly attributes. This blending of God with the world gave rise, amongst the mass of mankind, to Polytheism; while in the minds of the more reflective it assumed a Pantheistic shape. The manifold of nature, absorbing the Divine, broke it up into "gods many and lords many" — gods of the earth and sky and ocean, gods and goddesses of war, of tillage, of love, of art, of statecraft and handicraft, patrons of human vices and follies as well as of excellencies, changing with every climate and with the varying moods and conditions of their worshippers. No longer did it appear that God made man in His image; now men made gods in "the likeness of the image of corruptible man, and of winged and four-footed and creeping things."

When at last under the Roman Empire the different Pagan races blended their customs and faiths, and "the Orontes flowed into the Tiber," there came about a perfect chaos of religions. Gods Greek and Roman, Phrygian, Syrian, Egyptian jostled each other in the great cities—a *colluvies deorum* more bewildering even than the *colluvies gentium*,—each cultus striving to outdo the rest in extravagance and licence. The system of classic Paganism was reduced to impotence. The false gods destroyed each other. The mixture of heathen religions, none of them pure, produced complete demoralisation.

The Jewish monotheism remained, the one rock of human faith in the midst of this dissolution of the old nature-creeds. Its conception of the Godhead was not so much metaphysical as ethical. "Hear O Israel," says every Jew to his fellows, "the Lord our God is one Lord." But that "one Lord" was also *the Holy One* of Israel." Let his holiness be sullied, let the thought of the Divine ethical transcendence suffer eclipse, and He sinks back again into the manifold of nature. Till God was manifest in the flesh through the sinless Christ, it was impossible to conceive of a perfect purity allied to the natural. To the mind of the Israelite, God's holiness was one with the *aloneness* in which he held Himself sublimely aloof from all material forms, one with the pure spirituality of His being. "There is none holy save the Lord; neither is there any rock like our God:" such was his lofty creed. On this ground prophecy carried on its inspired struggle against the tremendous forces of naturalism. When at length the victory of spiritual religion was gained in Israel, unbelief assumed another form; the knowledge of the Divine unity hardened into a sterile and fanatic legalism, into the idolatry of dogma and tradition; and Scribe and Pharisee took the place of Prophet and of Psalmist.

The idolatry and immorality of the Gentile world had a common root. God's anger, the Apostle declared, blazed forth equally against both (Rom. i. 18). The monstrous forms of uncleanness then prevalent were a fitting punishment, an inevitable consequence of heathen impiety. They marked the lowest level to which human nature can fall in its apostasy from God. Self-respect in man is ultimately based on reverence for the Divine. Disowning his Maker, he degrades himself. Bent on evil, he must banish from his soul that warning, protesting image of the Supreme Holiness in which he was created.

"He tempts his reason to deny

God whom his passions dare defy."

"They did not like to retain God in their knowledge." "They loved darkness rather than light, because their deeds were evil." These are terrible accusations. But the history of natural religion confirms their truth.

Sorcery is the attendant of idolatry. A low, naturalistic conception of the Divine lends itself to immoral purposes. Men try to operate upon it by material causes, and to make it a partner in evil. Such is the origin of magic. Natural objects deemed to possess supernatural attributes, as the stars and the flight of birds, have divine omens ascribed to them. Drugs of occult power, and things grotesque or curious made mysterious by the fancy, are credited with influence over the Nature-gods. From the use of drugs in incantations and exorcisms the word *pharmakeia*, here denoting *sorcery*, took its meaning. The science of chemistry has destroyed a world of magic connected with the virtues of herbs. These superstitions formed a chief branch of sorcery and witchcraft, and have flourished under many forms of idolatry. And the magical arts were common instruments of malice. The sorcerer's charms were in requisition, as in the case of Balaam, to curse one's enemies, to weave some spell that should involve them in destruction. Accordingly *sorcery* finds its place there between *idolatry* and *enmities*.

III. On this latter head the Apostle enlarges with edifying amplitude. *Enmities, strife, jealousies, ragings, factions, divisions, parties, envyings*—what a list! Eight out of fifteen of "the works of the flesh manifest" to Paul in writing to Galatia belong to this one category. The Celt all over the world is known for a hot-tempered fellow. He has high capabilities; he is generous, enthusiastic, and impressionable. Meanness and treachery are foreign to his nature. But he is *irritable*. And it is in a vain and irritable disposition that these vices are engendered. Strife and division have been proverbial in the history of the Gallic nations. Their jealous temper has too often neutralised their engaging qualities; and their quickness and cleverness have for this reason availed them but little in competition with more phlegmatic races. In Highland clans, in Irish septs, in French wars and Revolutions the same moral features reappear which are found in this delineation of Galatic life. This persistence of character in the races of mankind is one of the most impressive facts of history.

"Enmities" are private hatreds or family feuds, which break out openly in "strife." This is seen in Church affairs, when men take opposite sides not so much from any decided difference of judgement, as from personal dislike and the disposition to thwart an opponent. "Jealousies" and "wraths" (or "rages") are passions attending enmity and strife. There is *jealousy* where one's antagonist is a rival, whose success is felt as a wrong to oneself. This may be a silent passion, repressed by pride but consuming the mind inwardly. *Rage* is the open eruption of anger which, when powerless to inflict injury, will find vent in furious language and menacing gestures. There are natures in which these tempests of rage take a perfectly demonic form. The face grows livid, the limbs move convulsively, the nervous organism is seized by a storm of frenzy; and until it has passed, the man is literally beside himself. Such exhibitions are truly appalling. They are "works of the flesh" in which, yielding to its own ungoverned impulse, it gives itself up to be possessed by Satan and is "set on fire of hell."

Factions, divisions, parties are words synonymous. "Divisions" is the more neutral term, and represents the state into which a community is thrown by the working of the spirit of strife. "Factions" imply more of self-interest and policy in those concerned; "parties" are due rather to self-will and opinionativeness. The Greek word employed in this last instance, as in 1 Cor. xi. 19, has become our *heresies*. It does not imply of necessity any doctrinal difference as the ground of the party distinctions in question. At the same time, this expression is an advance on those foregoing, pointing to such divisions as have grown, or threaten to grow into "distinct and organized parties" (Lightfoot).

Envyings (or *grudges*) complete this bitter series. This term might have found a place beside "enmities" and "strife." Standing where it does, it seems to denote the rankling anger, the persistent ill-will caused by party-feuds. The Galatian quarrels left behind them grudges and resentments which became inveterate. These "envyings," the fruit of old contentions, were in turn the seed of new strife. Settled rancour is the last and worst form of contentiousness. It is so much more culpable than "jealousy" or "rage," as it has not the excuse of personal conflict; and it does not subside, as the fiercest outburst of passion may, leaving room for forgiveness. It nurses its revenge, waiting, like Shylock, for the time when it shall "feed fat its ancient grudge."

"Where jealousy and faction are, there," says James, "is confusion and every vile deed." This was the state of things to which the Galatian societies were tending. The Judaizers had sown the seeds of discord, and it had fallen on congenial soil. Paul has already invoked Christ's law of love to exorcise this spirit of destruction (vv. 13-15). He tells the Galatians that their vainglorious and provoking attitude towards each other and their envious disposition are entirely contrary to the life in the Spirit which they professed to lead (vv. 25, 26), and fatal to the existence of the Church. These were the "passions of the flesh" which most of all they needed to crucify.

IV. Finally, we come to sins of intemperance—*drunkenness, revellings, and the like.*

These are the vices of a barbarous people. Our Teutonic and Celtic forefathers were alike prone to this kind of excess. Peter warns the Galatians against "wine-bibbings, revellings, carousings." The passion for strong drink, along with "lasciviousness" and "lusts" on the one hand, and "abominable idolatries" on the other, had in Asia Minor swelled into a "cataclysm of riot," overwhelming the Gentile world (1 Pet. iv. 3, 4). The Greeks were a comparatively sober people. The Romans were more notorious for gluttony than for hard drinking. The practice of seeking pleasure in intoxication is a remnant of savagery, which exists to a shameful extent in our own country. It appears to have been prevalent with the Galatians, whose ancestors a few generations back were northern barbarians.

A strong and raw animal nature is in itself a temptation to this vice. For men exposed to cold and hardship, the intoxicating cup has a potent fascination. The flesh, buffeted by the fatigues of a rough day's work, finds a strange zest in its treacherous delights. The man "drinks and forgets his poverty, and remembers his misery no more." For the hour, while the spell is upon him, he is a king; he lives under another sun; the world's wealth is his. He wakes up to find himself a sot! With racked head and unstrung frame he returns to the toil and squalor of his life, adding new wretchedness to that he had striven to forget. Anon he says, "I will seek it yet again!" When the craving has once mastered him, its indulgence becomes his only pleasure. Such men deserve our deepest pity. They need for their salvation all the safeguards that Christian sympathy and wisdom can throw around them.

There are others "given to much wine," for whom one feels less compassion. Their convivial indulgences are a part of their general habits of luxury and sensuality, an open, flagrant triumph of the flesh over the Spirit. These sinners require stern rebuke and warning. They must understand that "those who practise such things shall not inherit the kingdom of God," that "he who soweth to his own flesh, shall of the flesh reap corruption." Of these and their like it was that Jesus said, "Woe unto you that laugh now; for ye shall mourn and weep."

Our British Churches at the present time are more alive to this than perhaps to any other social evil. They are setting themselves sternly against drunkenness, and none too soon. Of all the works of the flesh this has been, if not the most potent, certainly the most conspicuous in the havoc it has wrought amongst us. Its ruinous effects are "manifest" in every prison and asylum, and in the private history of innumerable families in every station of life. Who is there that has not lost a kinsman, a friend, or at least a neighbour or acquaintance, whose life was wrecked by this accursed passion? Much has been done, and is doing, to check its ravages. But more remains to be accomplished before civil law and public opinion shall furnish all the protection against this evil necessary for a people so tempted by climate and by constitution as our own.

With *fornication* at the beginning and *drunkenness* at the end, Paul's description of "the works of the flesh" is, alas! far indeed from being out of date. The dread procession of the Vices marches on before our eyes. Races and temperaments vary; science has transformed the visible aspect of life; but the ruling appetites of human nature are unchanged, its primitive vices are with us to-day. The complicated problems of modern life, the gigantic evils which confront our social reformers, are simply the primeval corruptions of mankind in a new guise—the old lust and greed and hate. Under his veneer of manners, the civilized European, untouched by the grace of the Holy Spirit of God, is still apt to be found a selfish, cunning, unchaste, revengeful, superstitious creature, distinguished from his barbarian progenitor chiefly by his better dress and more cultivated brain, and his inferior agility. Witness the great Napoleon, a very "god of this world," but in all that gives worth to character no better than a savage!

With Europe turned into one vast camp and its nations groaning audibly under the weight of their armaments, with hordes of degraded women infesting the streets of its cities, with discontent and social hatred smouldering throughout its industrial populations, we have small reason to boast of the triumphs of modern civilisation. Better circumstances do not make better men. James' old question has for our day a terrible pertinence: "Whence come wars and fightings among you? Come they not hence, even of your pleasures that war in your members? Ye lust, and have not: ye kill, and covet, and cannot obtain. Ye ask and receive not, because ye ask amiss, that ye may spend it on your pleasures."

CHAPTER XXV
THE FRUIT OF THE SPIRIT

"But the fruit of the Spirit is love, joy, peace, longsuffering, kindness, goodness, faith, meekness, temperance: against such there is no law." —Gal. v. 22, 23.

"The tree is known by its fruits." Such was the criterion of religious profession laid down by the Founder of Christianity. This test His religion applies in the first instance to itself. It proclaims a final judgement for all men; it submits itself to the present judgement of all men—a judgement resting in each case on the same ground, namely that of *fruit*, of moral issue and effects. For character is the true *summum bonum*; it is the thing which in our secret hearts and in our better moments we all admire and covet. The creed which produces the best and purest character, in the greatest abundance and under the most varied conditions, is that which the world will believe.

These verses contain the ideal of character furnished by the gospel of Christ. Here is the religion of Jesus put in practice. These are the sentiments and habits, the views of duty, the temper of mind, which faith in Jesus Christ tends to form. Paul's conception of the ideal human life at once "commends itself to every man's conscience." And he owed it to the gospel of Christ. His ethics are the fruit of his dogmatic faith. What other system of belief has produced a like result, or has formed in men's minds ideas of duty so reasonable and gracious, so just, so balanced and perfect, and above all so practicable, as those inculcated in the Apostle's teaching?

"Men do not gather grapes of thorns, or figs of thistles." Thoughts of this kind, lives of this kind, are not the product of imposture or delusion. The "works" of systems of error are "manifest" in the moral wrecks they leave behind them, strewing the track of history. But the virtues here enumerated are the fruits which the Spirit of Christ has brought forth, and brings forth at this day more abundantly than ever. As a theory of morals, a representation of what is best in conduct, Christian teaching has held for 1800 years an unrivalled place. Christ and His Apostles are still the masters of morality. Few have been bold enough to offer any improvements on the ethics of Jesus; and smaller still has been the acceptance which their proposals have obtained. The new idea of virtue which Christianity has given to the world, the energy it has imparted to the moral will, the immense and beneficial revolutions it has brought about in human society, supply a powerful argument for its divinity. Making every deduction for unfaithful Christians, who dishonour "the worthy name" they bear, still "the fruit of the Spirit" gathered in these eighteen centuries is a glorious witness to the virtue of the tree of life from which it grew.

This picture of the Christian life takes its place side by side with others found in Paul's Epistles. It recalls the figure of Charity in 1 Cor. xiii., acknowledged by moralists of every school to be a master-piece of characterization. It stands in line also with the oft-quoted enumeration of Phil. iv. 8: "Whatsoever things are true, whatsoever things are reverend, whatsoever things are just, whatsoever things are chaste, whatsoever things are lovely, whatsoever things are kindly spoken, if there be any virtue, and if there be any praise, think on these things." These representations do not pretend to theoretical completeness. It would be easy to specify important virtues not mentioned in the Apostle's categories. His descriptions have a practical aim, and press on the attention of his readers the special forms and qualities of virtue demanded from them, under the given circumstances, by their faith in Christ.

It is interesting to compare the Apostle's definitions with Plato's celebrated scheme of the four cardinal virtues. They are *wisdom, courage, temperance*, with *righteousness* as the union and co-ordination of the other three. The difference between the cast of the Platonic and Pauline ethics is most instructive. In the Apostle's catalogue the first two of the philosophical virtues are wanting; unless "courage" be included, as it properly may, under the name of "virtue" in the Philippian list. With the Greek thinker, *wisdom* is the fundamental excellence of the soul. Knowledge is in his view the supreme desideratum, the guarantee for moral health and social well-being. The philosopher is the perfect man, the proper ruler of the commonwealth. Intellectual culture brings in its train ethical improvement. For "no man is knowingly vicious:" such was the dictum of Socrates, the father of Philosophy. In the ethics of the gospel, *love* becomes the chief of virtues, parent of the rest.

Love and *humility* are the two features whose predominance distinguishes the Christian from the purest classical conceptions of moral worth. The ethics of Naturalism know love as a passion, a sensuous instinct (ἔρως); or again, as the personal affection which binds friend to friend through common interest or resemblance of taste and disposition (φιλία). Love in its highest sense (ἀγάπη) Christianity has re-discovered, finding in it a universal law for the reason and spirit. It assigns to this principle a like place to that which gravitation holds in the material universe, as the attraction which binds each man to his Maker and to his fellows. Its obligations neutralise self-interest and create a spiritual solidarity of mankind, centring in Christ, the God-man. Pre-Christian philosophy exalted the intellect, but left the heart cold and vacant, and the deeper springs of will untouched. It was reserved for Jesus Christ to teach men how to love, and in love to find the law of freedom.

If love was wanting in natural ethics, *humility* was positively excluded. The pride of philosophy regarded it as a vice rather than a virtue. "Lowliness" is ranked with "pettiness" and "repining" and "despondency" as the product of "littleness of soul." On the contrary, the man of lofty soul is held up to admiration, who is "worthy of great things and deems himself so," —who is "not given to wonder, for nothing seems great to him," —who is "ashamed to receive benefits," and "has the appearance indeed of being supercilious" (Aristotle). How far removed is this model from our Example who has said, "Learn of Me, for I am meek and lowly in heart." The classical idea of virtue is based on the greatness of man; the Christian, on the goodness of God. Before the Divine glory in Jesus Christ the soul of the believer bows in adoration. It is humbled at the throne of grace, chastened into self-forgetting. It gazes on this Image of love and holiness, till it repeats itself within the heart.

Nine virtues are woven together in this golden chain of the Holy Spirit's fruit. They fall into three groups of three, four, and two respectively— according as they refer primarily to God, *love, joy, peace*; to one's fellow-men, *longsuffering, kindness, goodness, faith*; and to oneself, *meekness, temperance*. But the successive qualities are so closely linked and pass into one another with so little distance, that it is undesirable to emphasize the analysis; and while bearing the above distinctions in mind, we shall seek to give to each of the nine graces its separate place in the catalogue.

1. *The fruit of the Spirit is love.* That fitliest first. Love is the Alpha and Omega of the Apostle's thoughts concerning the new life in Christ. This queen of graces is already enthroned within this chapter. In ver. 6 Love came forward to be the minister of Faith; in ver. 14 it reappeared as the ruling principle of Divine law. These two offices of love are united here, where it becomes the prime fruit of the Holy Spirit of God, to whom the heart is opened by the act of faith, and who enables us to keep God's law. Love is "the fulfilling of the law;" for it is the essence of the gospel; it is the spirit of sonship; without this Divine affection, no profession of faith, no practice of good works has any value in the sight of God or intrinsic moral worth. Though I have all other gifts and merits—wanting this, "I am nothing" (1 Cor. xiii. 1-3). The cold heart is dead. Whatever appears to be Christian that

has not the love of Christ, is an unreality—a matter of orthodox opinion or mechanical performance—dead as the body without the spirit. In all true goodness there is an element of love. Here then is the fountain-head of Christian virtue, the "well of water springing up into eternal life" which Christ opens in the believing soul, from which flow so many bounteous streams of mercy and good fruits.

This love is, in the first instance and above all, *love to God*. It springs from the knowledge of His love to man. "God is love," and "love is of God" (1 John iv. 7, 8). All love flows from one fountain, from the One Father. And the Father's love is revealed in the Son. Love has the cross for its measure and standard. "He sent the Only-begotten into the world, that we might live through Him. Herein is love: hereby know we love" (1 John iii. 16; iv. 9, 10). The man who knows this love, whose heart responds to the manifestation of God in Christ, is "born of God." His soul is ready to become the abode of all pure affections, his life the exhibition of all Christ-like virtues. For the love of the Father is revealed to him; and the love of a son is enkindled in his soul by the Spirit of the Son.

In Paul's teaching, love forms the antithesis to *knowledge*. By this opposition the wisdom of God is distinguished from "the wisdom of this world and of its princes, which come to nought" (1 Cor. i. 23; ii. 8; viii. 1, 3). Not that love despises knowledge, or seeks to dispense with it. It requires knowledge beforehand in order to discern its object, and afterwards to understand its work. So the Apostle prays for the Philippians "that their love may abound yet more and more in knowledge and all discernment" (ch. i. 9, 10). It is not *love without knowledge*, heat without light, the warmth of an ignorant, untempered zeal that the Apostle desiderates. But he deplores the existence of *knowledge without love*, a clear head with a cold heart, an intellect whose growth has left the affections starved and stunted, with enlightened apprehensions of truth that awaken no corresponding emotions. Hence comes the pride of reason, the "knowledge that puffeth up." Love alone knows the art of building up.

Loveless knowledge is not wisdom. For wisdom is lowly in her own eyes, mild and gracious. What the man of cold intellect sees, he sees clearly; he reasons on it well. But his data are defective. He discerns but the half, the poorer half of life. There is a whole heaven of facts of which he takes no account. He has an acute and sensitive perception of phenomena coming within the range of his five senses, and of everything that logic can elicit from such phenomena. But he "cannot see afar off." Above all, "he that loveth not, *knoweth not God*." He leaves out the Supreme Factor in human life; and all his calculations are vitiated. "Hath not *God* made foolish the wisdom of the world?"

If knowledge then is the enlightened eye, love is the throbbing, living heart of Christian goodness.

2. *The fruit of the Spirit is joy.* Joy dwells in the house of Love; nor elsewhere will she tarry.

Love is the mistress both of joy and sorrow. Wronged, frustrated, hers is the bitterest of griefs. Love makes us capable of pain and shame; but equally of triumph and delight. Therefore the Lover of mankind was the "Man of sorrows," whose love bared its breast to the arrows of scorn and hate; and yet "for the joy that was set before Him, He endured the cross, despising the shame." There was no sorrow like that of Christ rejected and crucified; no joy like the joy of Christ risen and reigning. This joy, the delight of love satisfied in those it loves, is that whose fulfilment He has promised to His disciples (John xv. 8-11).

Such joy the selfish heart never knows. Life's choicest blessings, heaven's highest favours fail to bring it happiness. Sensuous gratification, and even intellectual pleasure by itself wants the true note of gladness. There is nothing that thrills the whole nature, that stirs the pulses of life and sets them dancing, like the touch of a pure love. It is the pearl of great price, for which "if a man would give all the substance of his house, he would be utterly contemned." But of all the joys love gives to life, that is the deepest which is ours when "the love of God is shed abroad in our heart." Then the full tide of blessedness pours into the human spirit. Then we know of what happiness our nature was made capable, when we know the love that God hath toward us.

This joy in the Lord quickens and elevates, while it cleanses, all other emotions. It raises the whole temperature of the heart. It gives a new glow to life. It lends a warmer and a purer tone to our natural affections. It sheds a diviner meaning, a brighter aspect over the common face of earth and sky. It throws a radiance of hope upon the toils and weariness of mortality. It "glories in tribulation." It triumphs in death. He who "lives in the Spirit" cannot be a dull, or peevish, or melancholy man. One with Christ his heavenly Lord, he begins already to taste His joy,—a joy which none taketh away and which many sorrows cannot quench.

Joy is the beaming countenance, the elastic step, the singing voice of Christian goodness.

3. But joy is a thing of seasons. It has its ebb and flow, and would not be itself if it were constant. It is crossed, varied, shadowed unceasingly. On earth sorrow ever follows in its track, as night chases day. No one knew this better than Paul. "Sorrowful," he says of himself (2 Cor. vi. 10), "yet always rejoicing:" a continual alternation, sorrow threatening every moment to

extinguish, but serving to enhance his joy. Joy leans upon her graver sister *Peace*.

There is nothing fitful or febrile in the quality of Peace. It is a settled quiet of the heart, a deep, brooding mystery that "passeth all understanding," the stillness of eternity entering the spirit, the *Sabbath of God* (Heb. iv. 9). It is theirs who are "justified by faith" (Rom. v. 1, 2). It is the bequest of Jesus Christ (John xiv. 27). He "made peace for us through the blood of His cross." He has reconciled us with the eternal law, with the Will that rules all things without effort or disturbance. We pass from the region of misrule and mad rebellion into the kingdom of the Son of God's love, with its ordered freedom, its clear and tranquil light, its "central peace, subsisting at the heart of endless agitation."

After the war of the passions, after the tempests of doubt and fear, Christ has spoken, "Peace, be still!" A great calm spreads over the troubled waters; wind and wave lie down hushed at His feet. The demonic powers that lashed the soul into tumult, vanish before His holy presence. The Spirit of Jesus takes possession of mind and heart and will. And His fruit is peace—always peace. This one virtue takes the place of the manifold forms of contention which make life a chaos and a misery. While He rules, "the peace of God guards the heart and thoughts" and holds them safe from inward mutiny or outward assault; and the dissolute, turbulent train of the works of the flesh find the gates of the soul barred against them.

Peace is the calm, unruffled brow, the poised and even temper which Christian goodness wears.

4. The heart at peace with God has patience with men. "Charity *suffereth long*." She is not provoked by opposition; nor soured by injustice; no, nor crushed by men's contempt. She can afford to wait; for truth and love will conquer in the end. She knows in whose hand her cause is, and remembers how long *He* has suffered the unbelief and rebellion of an insensate world; she "considers Him that endured such contradiction of sinners against Himself." Mercy and longsuffering are qualities that we share with God Himself, in which God was, and is, "manifest in the flesh." In this ripe fruit of the Spirit there are joined "the love of God, and the patience of Christ" (2 Thess. iii. 5).

Longsuffering is the patient magnanimity of Christian goodness, the broad shoulders on which it "beareth all things" (1 Cor. xiii. 7).

5. "Charity suffereth long and *is kind*."

Gentleness (or *kindness*, as the word is more frequently and better rendered,) resembles "longsuffering" in finding its chief objects in the evil and unthankful. But while the latter is passive and self-contained, kindness is an active, busy virtue. She is moreover of a humble and tender spirit, stooping to the lowest need, thinking nothing too small in which she may help, ready to give back blessing for cursing, benefit for harm and wrong.

Kindness is the thoughtful insight, the delicate tact, the gentle ministering hand of Charity.

6. Linked with *kindness* comes *goodness*, which is its other self, differing from it only as twin sisters may, each fairer for the beauty of the other. Goodness is perhaps more affluent, more catholic in its bounty; kindness more delicate and discriminating. The former looks to the benefit conferred, seeking to make it as large and full as possible; the latter has respect to the recipients, and studies to suit their necessity. While kindness makes its opportunities, and seeks out the most needy and miserable, goodness throws its doors open to all comers. Goodness is the more masculine and large-hearted form of charity; and if it errs, errs through blundering and want of tact. Kindness is the more feminine; and may err through exclusiveness and narrowness of view. United, they are perfect.

Goodness is the honest, generous face, the open hand of Charity.

7. This procession of the Virtues has conducted us, in the order of Divine grace, from the thought of a loving, forgiving God, the Object of our *love*, our *joy* and *peace*, to that of an evil-doing, unhappy world, with its need of *longsuffering* and *kindness*; and we now come to the inner, sacred circle of brethren beloved in Christ, where, with goodness, *faith*—that is, *trustfulness, confidence*—is called into exercise.

The Authorised rendering "faith" seems to us in this instance preferable to the "faithfulness" of the Revisers. "Possibly," says Bishop Lightfoot:, "πίστις may here signify 'trustfulness, reliance,' in one's dealings with others; comp. 1 Cor. xiii. 7:" we should prefer to say "probably," or even "unmistakably," to this. The use of *pistis* in any other sense is rare and doubtful in Paul's Epistles. It is true that "God" or "Christ" is elsewhere implied as the object of faith; but where the word stands, as it does here, in a series of qualities belonging to human relationships, it finds, in agreement with its current meaning, another application. As a link between *goodness* and *meekness, trustfulness,* and nothing else, appears to be in place. The parallel expression of 1 Cor. xiii., of which chapter we find so many echoes in the text, we take to be decisive: "Charity *believeth* all things."

The faith that unites man to God, in turn joins man to his fellows. Faith in the Divine Fatherhood becomes trust in the human brotherhood. In this generous attribute the Galatians were sadly deficient. "Honour all men," wrote Peter to them; "love the brotherhood" (1 Pet. ii. 17). Their factiousness and jealousies were the exact opposite of this fruit of the Spirit. Little was there to be found in them of the love that "envieth and vaunteth not," which "imputeth not evil, nor rejoiceth in unrighteousness," which "beareth, believeth, hopeth, endureth all things." They needed more faith in *man*, as well as in God.

The true heart knows how to *trust*. He who doubts every one is even more deceived than the man who blindly confides in every one. There is no more miserable vice than cynicism; no man more ill-conditioned than he who counts all the world knaves or fools except himself. This poison of mistrust, this biting acid of scepticism is a fruit of irreligion. It is one of the surest signs of social and national decay.

The Christian man knows not only how to stand alone and to "bear all things," but also how to lean on others, strengthening himself by their strength and supporting them in weakness. He delights to "think others better" than himself; and here "meekness" is one with "faith." His own goodness gives him an eye for everything that is best in those around him.

Trustfulness is the warm, firm clasp of friendship, the generous and loyal homage which goodness ever pays to goodness.

8. *Meekness*, as we have seen, is the other side of *faith*. It is not tameness and want of spirit, as those who "judge after the flesh" are apt to think. Nor is meekness the mere quietness of a retiring disposition. "The man Moses was very meek, above all the men which were upon the face of the earth." It comports with the highest courage and activity; and is a qualification for public leadership. Jesus Christ stands before us as the perfect pattern of meekness. "I intreat you," pleads the Apostle with the self-asserting Corinthians, "by the meekness and gentleness of Christ!" Meekness is self-repression in view of the claims and needs of others; it is the "charity" which "seeketh not her own, looketh not to her own things, but to the things of others." For her, self is of no account in comparison with Christ and His kingdom, and the honour of His brethren.

Meekness is the content and quiet mien, the willing self-effacement that is the mark of Christlike goodness.

9. Finally *temperance*, or *self-control*, — third of Plato's cardinal virtues.

By this last link the chain of the virtues, at its higher end attached to the throne of the Divine love and mercy, is fastened firmly down into the actualities of daily habit and bodily regimen. *Temperance*, to change the figure, closes the array of the graces, holding the post of the rear-guard which checks all straggling and protects the march from surprise and treacherous overthrow.

If *meekness* is the virtue of the whole man as he stands before his God and in the midst of his fellows, *temperance* is that of his body, the tenement and instrument of the regenerate spirit. It is the antithesis of "drunkenness and revellings," which closed the list of "works of the flesh," just as the preceding graces, from "peace" to "meekness," are opposed to the multiplied forms of "enmity" and "strife." Amongst ourselves very commonly the same limited contrast is implied. But to make "temperance" signify only or chiefly the avoidance of strong drink is miserably to narrow its significance. It covers the whole range of moral discipline, and concerns every sense and passion of our nature. Temperance is a practised mastery of self. It holds the reins of the chariot of life. It is the steady and prompt control of the outlooking sensibilities and appetencies, and inwardly moving desires. The tongue, the hand and foot, the eye, the temper, the tastes and affections, all require in turn to feel its curb. He is a temperate man, in the Apostle's meaning, who *holds himself well in hand*, who meets temptation as a disciplined army meets the shock of battle, by skill and alertness and tempered courage baffling the forces that outnumber it.

This also is a "fruit of the Spirit"—though we may count it the lowest and least, yet as indispensable to our salvation as the love of God itself. For the lack of this safeguard how many a saint has stumbled into folly and shame! It is no small thing for the Holy Spirit to accomplish in us, no mean prize for which we strive in seeking the crown of a perfect self-control. This mastery over the flesh is in truth the rightful prerogative of the human spirit, the dignity from which it fell through sin, and which the gift of the Spirit of Christ restores.

And this virtue in a Christian man is exercised for the behoof of others, as well as for his own. "I keep my body under," cries the Apostle, "I make it my slave and not my master; lest, having preached to others, I myself should be a castaway"—that is self-regard, mere common prudence; but again, "It is good not to eat flesh, nor drink wine, nor to do anything whereby a brother is made to stumble or made weak" (1 Cor. ix. 27; Rom. xiv. 21).

Temperance is the guarded step, the sober, measured walk in which Christian goodness keeps the way of life, and makes straight paths for stumbling and straying feet.

CHAPTER XXVI
OUR BROTHER'S BURDEN AND OUR OWN

"Brethren, even if a man be overtaken in any trespass, ye which are spiritual, restore such a one in a spirit of meekness; looking to thyself, lest thou also be tempted. Bear ye one another's burdens, and so fulfil the law of Christ. For if a man thinketh himself to be something, when he is nothing, he deceiveth himself. But let each man prove his own work, and then shall he have his glorying in regard of himself alone, and not of his neighbour. For each man shall bear his own burden." —Gal. vi. 1-5.

The division of the chapters at this point is almost as unfortunate as that between chaps. iv. and v. The introductory "Brethren" is not a form of transition to a new topic; it calls in the brotherly love of the Galatians to put an end to the bickerings and recriminations which the Apostle has censured in the preceding verses. How unseemly for *brethren* to be "vainglorious" towards each other, to be "provoking and envying one another!" If they are spiritual men, they should look more considerately on the faults of their neighbours, more seriously on their own responsibilities.

The Galatic temperament, as we have seen, was prone to the mischievous vanity which the Apostle here reproves. Those who had, or fancied they had, some superiority over others in talent or in character, prided themselves upon it. Even spiritual gifts were made matter of ostentation; and display on the part of the more gifted excited the jealousy of inferior brethren. The same disposition which manifests itself in arrogance on the one side, on the other takes the form of discontent and envy. The heart-burnings and the social tension which this state of things creates, make every chance collision a danger; and the slightest wound is inflamed into a rankling sore. The stumbling brother is pushed on into a fall; and the fallen man, who might have been helped to his feet, is left to lie there, the object of unpitying reproach. Indeed, the lapse of his neighbour is to the vainglorious man a cause of satisfaction rather than of sorrow. The other's weakness serves for a foil to his strength. Instead of stooping down to "restore such a one," he holds stiffly aloof in the eminence of conscious virtue; and bears himself more proudly in the lustre added to his piety by his fellow's disgrace. "God, I thank Thee," he seems to say, "that I am not as other men,—nor even as this wretched backslider!" The compellation "Brethren" is itself a rebuke to such heartless pride.

There are two reflections which should instantly correct the spirit of vain-glory. The Apostle appeals in the first place to *brotherly love*, to the claims that an erring fellow-Christian has upon our sympathy, to the meekness and forbearance which the Spirit of grace inspires, in fine to Christ's law which makes compassion our duty. At the same time he points out to us *our own infirmity* and exposure to temptation. He reminds us of the weight of our individual responsibility and the final account awaiting us. A proper sense at once of the rights of others and of our own obligations will make this shallow vanity impossible.

This double-edged exhortation takes shape in two leading sentences, sharply clashing with each other in the style of paradox in which the Apostle loves to contrast the opposite sides of truth: "Bear ye one another's burdens" (ver. 2); and yet "Every man shall bear his own burden" (ver. 5).

I. What then are the considerations that commend *the burdens of others* for our bearing?

The burden the Apostle has in view is that of *a brother's trespass*: "Brethren, if a man be overtaken in some trespass."

Here the question arises as to whether Paul means *overtaken by the temptation*, or *by the discovery of his sin*—surprised *into* committing, or *in* committing the trespass. Winer, Lightfoot, and some other interpreters, read the words in the latter sense: "*surprised, detected* in the act of committing any sin, so that his guilt is placed beyond a doubt" (Lightfoot). We are persuaded, notwithstanding, that the common view of the text is the correct one. The manner of the offender's detection has little to do with the way in which he should be treated; but the circumstances of his fall have everything to do with it. The suddenness, the surprise of his temptation is both a reason for more lenient judgment, and a ground for hope of his restoration. The preposition "in" (ἐν), it is urged, stands in the way of this interpretation. We might have expected to read "(surprised) *by*," or perhaps "*into* (any sin)." But the word is "trespass," not "sin." It points not to the cause of the man's fall, but to *the condition in which it has placed him*. The Greek preposition (according to a well known idiom of verbs of *motion*)[143] indicates the result of the unexpected assault to which the man has been subject. A gust of temptation has caught him unawares; and we now see him lying overthrown and prostrate, involved "in some trespass."

The Apostle is supposing an instance—possibly an actual case—in which the sin committed was due to weakness and surprise, rather than deliberate intention; like that of Eve, when "the woman being beguiled fell into transgression."[144] Such a fall deserves commiseration. The attack was unlooked for; the man was off his guard. The Gallic nature is heedless and impulsive. Men of this temperament should make allowance for each other. An offence committed in a rash moment, under provocation, must not be visited with implacable severity, nor magnified until it become a fatal barrier between the evil-doer and society. And Paul says expressly, "If *a man* be overtaken"—a delicate reminder of our human infirmity and common danger (comp. 1 Cor. x. 13). Let us remember that it is a man who has erred, of like passions with ourselves; and his trespass will excite pity for him, and apprehension for ourselves.

Such an effect the occurrence should have upon "the spiritual," on the men of love and peace, who "walk in the Spirit." The Apostle's appeal is qualified by this definition. Vain and self-seeking men, the irritable, the resentful, are otherwise affected by a neighbour's trespass. They will be angry with him, lavish in virtuous scorn; but it is not in them to "restore such a one." They are more likely to aggravate than heal the wound, to push the weak man down when he tries to rise, than to help him to his feet. The work of restoration needs a knowledge of the human heart, a self-restraint and patient skill, quite beyond their capability.

The *restoration* here signified, denotes not only, or not so much, the man's inward, spiritual renewal, as his recovery for the Church, the mending of the rent caused by his removal. In 1 Cor. i. 10; 2 Cor. xiii. 11; 1 Thess. iii. 10, where, as in other places, the English verb "perfect" enters into the rendering of παταρτίζω, it gives the idea of re-adjustment, the right fitting of part to part, member to member, in some larger whole. Writing to the Corinthian Church at this time respecting a flagrant trespass committed there, for which the transgressor was now penitent, the Apostle bids its members "confirm their love" to him (2 Cor. ii. 5-11). So here "the spiritual" amongst the Galatians are urged to make it their business to *set right* the lapsed brother, to bring him back as soon and safely as might be to the fold of Christ.

Of all the fruits of the Spirit, *meekness* is most required for this office of restoration, the meekness of Christ the Good Shepherd—of Paul who was "gentle as a nurse" amongst his children, and even against the worst offenders preferred to "come in love and a spirit of meekness," rather than "with a rod" (1 Thess. ii. 7; 1 Cor. iv. 21). To reprove without pride or acrimony, to stoop to the fallen without the air of condescension, requires the "spirit of meekness" in a singular degree. Such a bearing lends peculiar grace to compassion. This "gentleness of Christ" is one of the finest and rarest marks of the spiritual man. The moroseness sometimes associated with religious zeal, the disposition to judge hardly the failings of weaker men is anything but according to Christ. It is written of Him, "A bruised reed shall He not break, and the smoking flax shall He not quench" (Isa. xlii. 3; Matt xii. 20).

Meekness becomes sinful men dealing with fellow-sinners. "Considering *thyself*," says the Apostle, "lest thou also be tempted." It is a noticeable thing that men morally weak in any given direction are apt to be the severest judges of those who err in the same respect, just as people who have risen out of poverty are often the harshest towards the poor. They wish to forget their own past, and hate to be reminded of a condition from which they have suffered. Or is the judge, in sentencing a kindred offender, seeking to reinforce his own conscience and to give a warning to himself? One is inclined sometimes to think so. But reflection on our own infirmities should counteract, instead of fostering censoriousness. Every man knows enough of himself to make him chary of denouncing others. "Look to *thyself*," cries the Apostle. "Thou hast considered thy brother's faults. Now turn thine eye inward, and contemplate thine own. Hast thou never aforetime committed the offence with which he stands charged; or haply yielded to the like temptation in a less degree? Or if not even that, it may be thou art guilty of sins of another kind, though hidden from human sight, in the eyes of God no less heinous." "Judge not," said the Judge of all the earth, "lest ye be judged. With what measure ye mete, it shall be measured unto you" (Matt. vii. 1-5).

This exhortation begins in general terms; but in the latter clause of ver. 1 it passes into the individualising singular—"looking to *thyself*, lest even *thou* be tempted." The disaster befalling one reveals the common peril; it is a signal for every member of the Church to take heed to himself. The scrutiny which it calls for belongs to each man's private conscience. And the faithfulness and integrity required in those who approach the wrongdoer with a view to his recovery, must be chastened by personal solicitude. The fall of a Christian brother should be in any case the occasion of heart-searching, and profound humiliation. Feelings of indifference towards him, much more of contempt, will prove the prelude of a worse overthrow for ourselves.

The burden of a brother's trespass is the most painful that can devolve upon a Christian man. But this is not the only burden we bring upon each other. There are burdens of anxiety and sorrow, of personal infirmity, of family difficulty, of business embarrassment, infinite varieties and complications of trial in which the resources of brotherly sympathy are taxed. The injunction of the Apostle has an unlimited range. That which burdens my friend and brother cannot be otherwise than a solicitude to me. Whatever it be that cripples him and hinders his running the race set before him, I am bound, according to the best of my judgement and ability, to assist him to overcome it. If I leave him to stagger on alone, to sink under his load when my shoulder might have eased it for him, the reproach will be mine.

This is no work of supererogation, no matter of mere liking and choice. I am not at liberty to refuse to share the burdens of the brotherhood. "Bear ye one another's burdens," Paul says, "and so fulfil *the law of Christ*." This law the Apostle has already cited and enforced against the contentions and jealousies rife in Galatia (ch. v. 14, 15). But it has a further application. Christ's law of love not only says, "Thou shalt not bite and devour; thou shalt not provoke and envy thy brother;" but also, "Thou shalt help and comfort him, and regard his burden as thine own."

This law makes of the Church one body, with a solidarity of interests and obligations. It finds employment and discipline for the energy of Christian freedom, in yoking it to the service of the over-burdened. It reveals the dignity and privilege of moral strength, which consist not in the enjoyment of its own superiority, but in its power to bear "the infirmities of the weak." This was the glory of Christ, who "pleased not Himself" (Rom. xv. 1-4). The Giver of the law is its great Example. "Being in the form of God," He "took the form of a servant," that in love He might serve mankind; He "became obedient, unto the death of the cross" (Phil. ii. 1-8). Justly is the inference drawn, "We also ought to lay down our lives for the brethren" (1 John iii. 16). There is no limit to the service which the redeemed brotherhood of Christ may expect from its members.

Only this law must not be abused by the indolent and the overreaching, by the men who are ready to throw their burdens on others and make every generous neighbour the victim of their dishonesty. It is the need not the demand of our brother which claims our help. We are bound to take care that it is his necessity to which we minister, not his imposture or his slothfulness. The warning that "each man shall bear his own burden" is addressed to those who *receive*, as well as to those who render aid in the common burden-bearing of the Church.

II. The adjustment of social and individual duty is often far from easy, and requires the nicest discernment and moral tact. Both are brought into view in this paragraph, in its latter as well as in its former section. But in vv. 1, 2 the need of others, in vv. 3-5 our personal responsibility forms the leading consideration. We see on the one hand, that a true self-regard teaches us to identify ourselves with the moral interests of others: while, on the other hand, a false regard to others is excluded (ver. 4) which disturbs the judgement to be formed respecting ourselves. The thought of *his own burden* to be borne by each man now comes to the front of the exhortation.

Ver. 3 stands between the two counterpoised estimates. It is another shaft directed against Galatian vain-glory, and pointed with Paul's keenest irony. "For if a man thinketh he is something, being nothing he deceiveth himself."

This truth is very evident. But what is its bearing on the matter in hand? The maxim is advanced to support the foregoing admonition. It was their self-conceit that led some of the Apostle's readers to treat with contempt the brother who had trespassed; he tells them that this opinion of theirs is a *delusion*, a kind of mental hallucination (φρεναπατᾷ ἑαυτόν). It betrays a melancholy ignorance. The "spiritual" man who "thinks himself to be something," says to you, "I am quite above these weak brethren, as you see. Their habits of life, their temptations are not mine. Their sympathy would be useless to me. And I shall not burden myself with their feebleness, nor vex myself with their ignorance and rudeness." If any man separates himself from the Christian commonalty and breaks the ties of religious fellowship on grounds of this sort, and yet imagines he is following Christ, he "deceives himself." Others will see how little his affected eminence is worth. Some will humour his vanity; many will ridicule or pity it; few will be deceived by it.

The fact of a man's "thinking himself to be something" goes far to prove that he "is nothing." "Woe unto them that are wise in their own eyes, and prudent in their own sight." Real knowledge is humble; it knows its nothingness. Socrates, when the oracle pronounced him the wisest man in Greece, at last discovered that the response was right, inasmuch as he alone was aware that he knew nothing, while other men were confident of their knowledge. And a greater than Socrates, our All-wise, All-holy Saviour, says to us, "Learn of Me, for I am meek and lowly in heart." It is in humility and dependence, in self-forgetting that true wisdom begins. Who are we, although the most refined or highest in place, that we should despise plain, uncultured members of the Church, those who bear life's heavier burdens and amongst whom our Saviour spent His days on earth, and treat them as unfit for our company, unworthy of fellowship with us in Christ?

They are themselves the greatest losers who neglect to fulfil Christ's law. Such men might learn from their humbler brethren, accustomed to the trials and temptations of a working life and a rough world, how to bear more worthily their own burdens. How foolish of "the eye to say to the hand" or "foot, I have no need of thee!" "God hath chosen the poor of this world rich in faith." There are truths of which they are our best teachers—priceless lessons of the power of Divine grace and the deep things of Christian experience. This isolation robs the poorer members of the Church in their turn of the manifold help due to them from communion with those more happily circumstanced. How many of the evils around us would be ameliorated, how many of our difficulties would vanish, if we could bring about a truer Christian fraternisation, if caste-feeling in our English Church-life were once destroyed, if men would lay aside their stiffness and social *hauteur*, and cease to think that they "are something" on grounds of worldly distinction and wealth which in Christ are absolutely nothing.

The vain conceit of their superiority indulged in by some of his readers, the Apostle further corrects by reminding the self-deceivers of *their own responsibility*. The irony of ver. 3 passes into a sterner tone of warning in vv. 4 and 5. "Let each man try his own work," he cries. "Judge yourselves, instead of judging one another. Mind your own duty, rather than your neighbours' faults. Do not think of your worth or talents in comparison with theirs; but see to it that your *work* is right." The question for each of us is not, What do others fail to do? but, What am I myself really doing? What will my life's work amount to, when measured by that which God expects from me?

This question shuts each man up within his own conscience. It anticipates the final judgement-day. "Every one of us must give account of *himself* to God" (Rom. xiv. 12). Reference to the conduct of others is here out of place. The petty comparisons which feed our vanity and our class-prejudices are of no avail at the bar of God. I may be able for every fault of my own to find some one else more faulty. But this makes *me* no whit better. It is the intrinsic, not the comparative worth of character and daily work of which God takes account. If we study our brother's work, it should be with a view to enable him to do it better, or to learn to improve our own by his example; not in order to find excuses for ourselves in his shortcomings.

"And then"—if our work abide the test—"we shall have our glorying in ourselves alone, not in regard to our neighbour." Not his flaws and failures, but my own honest work will be the ground of my satisfaction. This was Paul's "glorying" in face of the slanders by which he was incessantly pursued. It lay in the testimony of his conscience. He lived under the severest self-scrutiny. He knew himself as the man only can who "knows the fear of the Lord," who places himself every day before the dread tribunal of Christ Jesus. He is "made manifest unto God;" and in the light of that searching Presence he can affirm that he "knows nothing against himself."[145] But this boast makes him humble. "*By the grace of God*" he is enabled to "have his conversation in the world in holiness and sincerity coming of God." If he had seemed to claim any credit for himself, he at once corrects the thought:

"Yet not I," he says, "but God's grace that was with me. I have my glorying in Christ Jesus in the things pertaining to God, in that which Christ hath wrought in me" (1 Cor. xv. 10; Rom. xv. 16-19).

So that this boast of the Apostle, in which he invites the vainglorious Galatians to secure a share, resolves itself after all into his one boast, "in the cross of our Lord Jesus Christ" (ver. 14). If his work on trial should prove to be gold, "abiding" amongst the world's imperishable treasures and fixed foundations of truth (1 Cor. iii. 10-15), Christ only was to be praised for this. Paul's glorying is the opposite of the Legalist's, who presumes on his "works" as his own achievements, commending him for righteous before God. "Justified by works," such a man hath "whereof to glory, but not toward God" (Rom. iv. 2). His boasting redounds to himself. Whatever glory belongs to the work of the Christian must be referred to God. Such work furnishes no ground for magnifying the man at the expense of his fellows. If we praise the stream, it is to commend the fountain. If we admire the lives of the saints and celebrate the deeds of the heroes of faith, it is *ad majorem Dei gloriam*—"that in all things God may be glorified through Jesus Christ" (1 Pet. iv. 11).

"For each will bear his own load." Here is the ultimate reason for the self-examination to which the Apostle has been urging his readers, in order to restrain their vanity. The emphatic repetition of the words *each man* in vv. 4 and 5 brings out impressively the personal character of the account to be rendered. At the same time, the deeper sense of our own burdens thus awakened will help to stir in us sympathy for the loads under which our fellows labour. So that this warning indirectly furthers the appeal for sympathy with which the chapter began.

Faithful scrutiny of our work may give us reasons for satisfaction and gratitude towards God. But it will yield matter of another kind. It will call to remembrance old sins and follies, lost opportunities, wasted powers, with their burden of regret and humiliation. It will set before us the array of our obligations, the manifold tasks committed to us by our heavenly Master, compelling us to say, "Who is sufficient for these things?" And beside the reproofs of the past and the stern demands of the present, there sounds in the soul's ear the message of the future, the summons to our final reckoning. Each of us has his own life-load, made up of this triple burden. A thousand varying circumstances and individual experiences go to constitute the ever-growing load which we bear with us from youth to age, like the wayfarer his bundle, like the soldier his knapsack and accoutrements—the individual lot, the peculiar untransferable vocation and responsibility fastened by the hand of God upon our shoulders. This burden we shall have to carry up to Christ's judgement-seat. He is our Master; He alone can give us our discharge. His lips must pronounce the final "Well done"—or, "Thou wicked and slothful servant!"

In this sentence the Apostle employs a different word from that used in ver. 2. There he was thinking of the weight, the *burdensomeness* of our brother's troubles, which we haply may lighten for him, and which is so far common property. But the second word, φορτίον (applied for instance to *a ship's lading*), indicates *that which is proper to each* in the burdens of life. There are duties that we have no power to devolve, cares and griefs that we must bear in secret, problems that we must work out severally and for ourselves. To consider them aright, to weigh well the sum of our duty will dash our self-complacency; it will surely make us serious and humble. Let us wake up from dreams of self-pleasing to an earnest, manly apprehension of life's demands—"while," like the Apostle, "we look not at the things which are seen, but at the things which are not seen and eternal" (2 Cor. iv. 18).

After all, it is the men who have the highest standard for themselves that as a rule are most considerate in their estimate of others. The holiest are the most pitiful. They know best how to enter into the struggles of a weaker brother. They can appreciate his unsuccessful resistance to temptation; they can discern where and how he has failed, and how much of genuine sorrow there is in his remorse. From the fulness of their own experience they can interpret a possibility of better things in what excites contempt in those who judge by appearance and by conventional rules. He who has learned faithfully to "consider himself" and meekly to "bear his own burden," is most fit to do the work of Christ, and to shepherd His tempted and straying sheep. Strict with ourselves, we shall grow wise and gentle in our care for others.

In the Christian conscience the sense of personal and that of social responsibility serve each to stimulate and guard the other. Duty and sympathy, love and law are fused into one. For Christ is all in all; and these two hemispheres of life unite in Him.

CHAPTER XXVII
SOWING AND REAPING

"But let him that is taught in the word communicate unto him that teacheth in all good things. Be not deceived; God is not mocked: for whatsoever a man soweth, that shall he also reap. For he that soweth unto his own flesh shall of the flesh reap corruption; but he that soweth unto the Spirit shall of the Spirit reap eternal life. And let us not be weary in well-doing: for in due season we shall reap, if we faint not. So then, as we have opportunity, let us work that which is good toward all men, and especially toward them that are of the household of the faith"—Gal. vi. 6-10.

Each shall bear his own burden (ver. 5)—*but let there be communion of disciple with teacher in all that is good.* The latter sentence is clearly intended to balance the former. The transition turns upon the same antithesis between social and individual responsibility that occupied us in the foregoing Chapter. But it is now presented on another side. In the previous passage it concerned the conduct of "the spiritual" toward erring brethren whom they were tempted to despise; here, their behaviour toward teachers whom they were disposed to neglect. There it is inferiors, here superiors that are in view. The Galatian "vain-glory" manifested itself alike in provocation toward the former, and in envy toward the latter (ch. v. 26). In both ways it bred disaffection, and threatened to break up the Church's unity. The two effects are perfectly consistent. Those who are harsh in their dealings with the weak, are commonly rude and insubordinate toward their betters, where they dare to be so. Self-conceit and self-sufficiency engender in the one direction a cold contempt, in the other a jealous independence. The former error is corrected by a due sense of our own infirmities; the latter by the consideration of our responsibility to God. We are compelled to feel for the burdens of others when we realise the weight of our own. We learn to respect the claims of those placed over us, when we remember what we owe to God through them. Personal responsibility is the last word of the former paragraph; social responsibility is the first word of this. Such is the contrast marked by the transitional *But*.

From this point of view ver. 6 gains a very comprehensive sense. "All good things" cannot surely be limited to the "carnal things" of 1 Cor. ix. 11. As Meyer and Beet amongst recent commentators clearly show, the context gives to this phrase a larger scope. At the same time, there is no necessity to exclude the thought of temporal good. The Apostle designedly makes his appeal as wide as possible. The reasoning of the corresponding passage in the Corinthian letter is a deduction from the general principle laid down here.

But it is *spiritual fellowship* that the Apostle chiefly desiderates. The true minister of Christ counts this vastly more sacred, and has this interest far more at heart than his own temporalities. He labours for the unity of the Church; he strives to secure the mutual sympathy and co-operation of all orders and ranks— teachers and taught, officers and private members—"in every good word and work." He must have the heart of his people with him in his work, or his joy will be faint and his success scant indeed. Christian teaching is designed to awaken this sympathetic response. And it will take expression in the rendering of whatever kind of help the gifts and means of the hearer and the needs of the occasion call for. Paul requires every member of the Body of Christ to make her wants and toils his own. We have no right to leave the burdens of the Church's work to her leaders, to expect her battles to be fought and won by the officers alone. This neglect has been the parent of innumerable mischiefs. Indolence in the laity fosters sacerdotalism in the clergy. But when, on the contrary, an active, sympathetic union is maintained between "him that is taught" and "him that teacheth," that other matter of the temporal support of the Christian ministry, to which this text is so often exclusively referred, comes in as a necessary detail, to be generously and prudently arranged, but which will not be felt on either side as a burden or a difficulty. Everything depends on the fellowship of spirit, on the strength of the bond of love that knits together the members of the Body of Christ. Here, in Galatia, that bond had been grievously weakened. In a Church so disturbed, the fellowship of teachers and taught was inevitably strained.

Such communion the Apostle craves from his children in the faith with an intense yearning. This is the one fruit of God's grace in them which he covets to reap for himself, and feels he has a right to expect. "Be ye as I am," he cries—"do not desert me, my children, for whom I travail in birth. Let me not have to toil for you in vain" (ch. iv. 12-19). So again, writing to the Corinthians: "It was *I* that begat you in Christ Jesus; I beseech you then, be followers of me. Let me remind you of my ways in the Lord.... O ye Corinthians, to you our mouth is open, our heart enlarged. Pay me back in kind (you are my children), and be ye too enlarged" (1 Cor. iv. 14-17; 2 Cor. vi. 11-13). He "thanks God" for the Philippians "on every remembrance of them," and "makes his supplication" for them "with joy, because of their fellowship in regard to the gospel from the first day until now" (Phil. i. 3-7). Such is the fellowship which Paul wished to see restored in the Galatian Churches.

In ver. 10 he extends his appeal to embrace in it all the kindly offices of life. For the love inspired by the Church, the service rendered to her, should quicken all our human sympathies and make us readier to meet every claim of pity or affection. While our sympathies, like those of a loving family, will be concerned "especially" with "the household of faith," and within that circle more especially with our pastors and teachers in Christ, they have no limit but that of "opportunity;" they should "work that which is good toward all men." True zeal for the Church widens instead of narrowing, our charities. Household affection is the nursery, not the rival, of love to our fatherland and to humanity.

Now the Apostle is extremely urgent in this matter of communion between teachers and taught. It concerns the very life of the Christian community. The welfare of the Church and the progress of the kingdom of God depend on the degree to which its individual members accept their responsibility in its affairs. Ill-will towards Christian teachers is paralyzing in its effects on the Church's life. Greatly are *they* to blame, if their conduct gives rise to discontent. Only less severe is the condemnation of those in lower place who harbour in themselves and foster in the minds of others sentiments of disloyalty. To cherish this mistrust, to withhold our sympathy from him who serves us in spiritual things, this, the Apostle declares, is not merely a wrong done to the man, it is an affront to God Himself. If it be God's Word that His servant teaches, then God expects some fitting return to be made for the gift He has bestowed. Of that return the pecuniary contribution, the meed of "carnal things" with which so many seem to think their debt discharged, is often the least and easiest part. How far have men a right to be hearers—profited and believing hearers—in the Christian congregation, and yet decline the duties of Church fellowship? They eat the Church's bread, but will not do her work. They expect like children to be fed and nursed and waited on; they think that if they *pay* their minister tolerably well, they have "communicated with" him quite sufficiently. This apathy has much the same effect as the Galatian bickerings and jealousies. It robs the Church of the help of the children whom she has nourished and brought up. Those who act thus are trying in reality to "mock God." They expect *Him* to sow his bounties upon them, but will not let Him reap. They refuse Him the return that He most requires for His choicest benefits.

Now, the Apostle says, God is not to be defrauded in this way. Men may wrong each other; they may grieve and affront His ministers. But no man is clever enough to cheat God. It is not Him, it is *themselves* they will prove to have deceived. Vain and selfish men who take the best that God and man can do for them as though it were a tribute to their greatness, envious and restless men who break the Church's fellowship of peace, will reap at last even as they sow. The mischief and the loss may fall on others now; but in its full ripeness it will come in the end upon themselves. The final reckoning awaits us in another world. And as we act by God and by His Church now, in our day, so He will act hereafter by us in His day.

Thus the Apostle, in vv. 6 and 7, places this matter in the searching light of eternity. He brings to bear upon it one of the great spiritual maxims characteristic of his teaching. Paul's unique influence as a religious teacher lies in his mastery of principles of this kind, in the keenness of insight and the incomparable vigour with which he applies eternal truths to commonplace occurrences. The paltriness and vulgarity of these local broils and disaffections lend to his warning a more severe impressiveness. With what a startling and sobering force, one thinks, the rebuke of these verses must have fallen on the ears of the wrangling Galatians! How unspeakably mean their quarrels appear in the light of the solemn issues opening out before them! It was *God* whom their folly had presumed to mock. It was the harvest of eternal life of which their factiousness threatened to defraud them.

The principle on which this warning rests is stated in terms that give it universal application: *Whatsoever a man soweth, that shall he also reap.* This is in fact the postulate of all moral responsibility. It asserts the continuity of personal existence, the connection of cause and effect in human character. It makes man the master of his own destiny. It declares that his future doom hangs upon his present choice, and is in truth its evolution and consummation. The twofold lot of "corruption" or "life eternal" is in every case no more, and no less, than the proper harvest of the kind of sowing practised here and now. The use made of our seed-time determines exactly, and with a moral certainty greater even than that which rules in the natural field, what kind of fruitage our immortality will render.

This great axiom deserves to be looked at in its broadest aspect. It involves the following considerations:—

I. *Our present life is the seed-time of an eternal harvest.*

Each recurring year presents a mirror of human existence. The analogy is a commonplace of the world's poetry. The spring is in every land a picture of youth—its morning freshness and innocence, its laughing sunshine, its opening blossoms, its bright and buoyant energy; and, alas, oftentimes its cold winds and nipping frosts and early, sudden blight! Summer images a vigorous manhood, with all the powers in action and the pulses of life beating at full swing; when the dreams of youth are worked out in sober, waking earnest; when manly strength is tested and matured under the heat of mid-day toil, and character is disciplined, and success or failure in life's battle must be determined. Then follows mellow autumn, season of shortening days and slackening steps and gathering snows; season too of ripe experience, of chastened thought and feeling, of widened influence and clustering honours. And the story ends in the silence and winter of the grave! *Ends?* Nay, that is a new beginning! This whole round of earthly vicissitude is but a single spring-time. It is the mere childhood of man's existence, the threshold of the vast house of life.

The oldest and wisest man amongst us is only a little child in the reckoning of eternity. The Apostle Paul counted himself no more. "We know in part," he says; "we prophesy in part—talking, reasoning like children. We shall become *men*, seeing face to face, knowing as we are known" (1 Cor. xiii. 8, 11, 12). Do we not ourselves feel this in our higher moods? There is an instinct of immortality, a forecasting of some ampler existence, "a stirring of blind life" within the soul; there are visionary gleams of an unearthly Paradise haunting at times the busiest and most unimaginative men. We are intelligences in the germ, lying folded up in the chrysalis stage of our existence. Eyes, wings are still to come. "It doth not yet appear what we shall be," no more than he who had seen but the seed-sowing of early spring and the bare wintry furrows, could imagine what the golden, waving harvest would be like. There is a glorious, everlasting kingdom of heaven, a world which in its duration, its range of action and experience, its style of equipment and occupation, will be worthy of the elect children of God. Worship, music, the purest passages of human affection and of moral elevation, may give us some foretaste of its joys. But what it will be really like, "Eye hath not seen, nor ear heard; nor heart of man conceived."

Think of that, struggling heart, worn with labour, broken by sorrow, cramped and thwarted by the pressure of an unkindly world. "The earnest expectancy of the creation" waits for your revealing (Rom. viii. 19). You will have your enfranchisement; your soul will take wing at last. Only have faith in God, and in righteousness; only "be not weary in well-doing." Those crippled powers will get their full play. Those baffled purposes and frustrated affections will unfold and blossom into a completeness undreamed of now, in the sunshine of heaven, in "the liberty of the glory of the sons of God." Why look for your harvest here! It is *March*, not August yet. "*In due season* we shall reap, if we faint not." See to it that you "sow to the Spirit," that your life be of the true seed of the kingdom; and for the rest, have no care nor fear. What should we think of the farmer who in winter, when his fields were frost-bound, should go about wringing his hands and crying that his labour was all lost! Are we wiser in our despondent moods? However dreary and unpromising, however poor and paltry in its outward seeming the earthly seed-time, your life's work will have its resurrection. Heaven lies hidden in those daily acts of humble, difficult duty, even as the giant oak with its centuries of growth and all its summer glory sleeps in the acorn-cup. No eye may see it now; but "the Day will declare it!"

II. In the second place, *the quality of the future harvest depends entirely on the present sowing.*

In *quantity*, as we have seen, in outward state and circumstance, there is a complete contrast. The harvest surpasses the seed from which it sprang, by thirty, sixty or a hundred-fold. But in *quality* we find a strict agreement. In degree they may differ infinitely; in kind they are one. The harvest multiplies the effect of the sower's labour; but it multiplies exactly that effect, and nothing else. This law runs through all life. If we could not count upon it, labour would be purposeless and useless; we should have to yield ourselves passively to nature's caprice. The farmer sows wheat in his cornfield, the gardener plants and trains his fig-tree; and he gets wheat, or figs, for his reward—nothing else. Or is he a "sluggard" that "will not plow by reason of the cold?" Does he let weeds and thistledown have the run of his garden-plot? Then it yields him a plentiful harvest of thistles and of weeds! What could he expect? "Men do not gather grapes of thorns, or figs of thistles." From the highest to the lowest order of living things, each grows and fructifies "after its kind." This is the rule of nature, the law which constituted *Nature* at the beginning. The good tree brings forth good fruit; and the good seed makes the good tree.

All this has its moral counterpart. The law of reproduction in kind holds equally true of the relation of this life to the next. Eternity for us will be the multiplied, consummated outcome of the good or evil of the present life. Hell is just sin ripe—rotten ripe. Heaven is the fruitage of righteousness. There will be two kinds of reaping, the Apostle tells us, because there are two different kinds of sowing. "He that soweth to his flesh, shall of the flesh reap corruption:" there is nothing arbitrary or surprising in that. "Corruption"—the moral decay and dissolution of the man's being—is the natural retributive effect of his carnality. And "he that soweth to the Spirit, shall of the Spirit reap life everlasting." Here, too, the sequence is inevitable. Like breeds its like. Life springs of life; and death eternal is the culmination of the soul's present death to God and goodness. The future glory of the saints is at once a Divine reward, and a necessary development of their present faithfulness. And eternal life lies germinally contained in faith's earliest beginning, when it is but as "a grain of mustard seed." We may expect in our final state the outcome of our present conduct, as certainly as the farmer who puts wheat into his furrows in November will count on getting wheat out of them again next August.

Under this law of the harvest we are living at this moment, and sowing every day the seed of an immortality of honour or of shame. Life is the seed-plot of eternity; and *youth is above all the seed-time of life*. What are our children doing with these precious, vernal years? What is going into their minds? What ideas, what desires are rooting themselves in these young souls? If it be pure thoughts and true affections, love to God, self-denial, patience and humility, courage to do what is right—if these be the things that are sown in their hearts, there will be for them, and for us, a glorious harvest of wisdom and love and honour in the years to come, and in the day of eternity. But if sloth and deceit be there, and unholy thoughts, vanity and envy and self-indulgence, theirs will be a bitter harvesting. Men talk of "sowing their wild oats," as though that were an end of it; as though a wild and prodigal youth might none the less be followed by a sober manhood and an honoured old age. But it is not so. If wild oats have been sown, there will be wild oats to reap, as certainly as autumn follows spring. For every time the youth deceives parent or teacher, let him know that he will be deceived by the Father of lies a hundred times. For every impure thought or dishonourable word, shame will come upon him sixty-fold. If his mind be filled with trash and refuse, then trash and refuse are all it will be able to produce. If the good seed be not timely sown in his heart, thorns and nettles will sow themselves there fast enough; and his soul will become like the sluggard's garden, rank with base weeds and poison-plants, a place where all vile things will have their resort,—"rejected and nigh unto a curse."

Who is "he that soweth to his own flesh?" It is, in a word, the *selfish* man. He makes his personal interest, and as a rule his bodily pleasure, directly or ultimately, the object of life. The sense of responsibility to God, the thought of life as a stewardship of which one must give account, have no place in his mind. He is a "lover of pleasure rather than a lover of God." His desires, unfixed on God, steadily tend downwards. Idolatry of self becomes slavery to the flesh. Every act of selfish pleasure-seeking, untouched by nobler aims, weakens and worsens the soul's life. The selfish man gravitates downward into the sensual man; the sensual man downward into the bottomless pit.

This is the "minding of the flesh" which "is death" (Rom. viii. 5-8, 13). For it is "enmity against God" and defiance of His law. It overthrows the course of nature, the balance of our human constitution; it brings disease into the frame of our being. The flesh, unsubdued and uncleansed by the virtue of the Spirit, breeds "corruption." Its predominance is the sure presage of death. The process of decay begins already, this side the grave;

and it is often made visible by appalling signs. The bloated face, the sensual leer, the restless, vicious eye, the sullen brow tell us what is going on within. The man's soul is rotting in his body. Lust and greed are eating out of him the capacity for good. And if he passes on to the eternal harvest as he is, if that fatal corruption is not arrested, what doom can possibly await such a man but that of which our merciful Saviour spoke so plainly that we might tremble and escape—"the worm that dieth not, and the fire that is not quenched!"

III. And finally, *God Himself is the Lord of the moral harvest.* The rule of retribution, the nexus that binds together our sowing and our reaping, is not something automatic and that comes about of itself; it is directed by the will of God, who "worketh all in all."

Even in the natural harvest we look upwards to Him. The order and regularity of nature, the fair procession of the seasons waiting on the silent and majestic march of the heavens, have in all ages directed thinking and grateful men to the Supreme Giver, to the creative Mind and sustaining Will that sits above the worlds. As Paul reminded the untutored Lycaonians, "He hath not left Himself without witness, in that He gave us rains from heaven and fruitful seasons, filling our hearts with food and gladness." It is "God" that "gives the increase" of the husbandman's toil, of the merchant's forethought, of the artist's genius and skill. We do not sing our harvest songs, with our Pagan forefathers, to sun and rain and west wind, to mother Earth and the mystic powers of Nature. In these poetic idolatries were yet blended higher thoughts and a sense of Divine beneficence. But "to us there is one God, the Father, of whom are all things, and we for Him; and one Lord, Jesus Christ, through whom are all things, and we through Him." In the harvest of the earth man is a worker together with God. The farmer does his part, fulfilling the conditions God has laid down in nature; "he putteth in the wheat in rows, and the barley in its appointed place; for his God doth instruct him aright, and doth teach him." He tills the ground, he sows the seed—and there he leaves it *to God.* "He sleeps and rises night and day; and the seed springs and grows up, he knows not how." And the wisest man of science cannot tell him how. "God giveth it a body, as it hath pleased Him." But *how*—that is His own secret, which He seems likely to keep. All life in its growth, as in its inception, is a mystery, hid with Christ in God. Every seed sown in field or garden is a deposit committed to the faithfulness of God; which He honours by raising it up again, thirty, sixty, or a hundred-fold, in the increase of the harvest.

In the moral world this Divine co-operation is the more immediate, as the field of action lies nearer, if one may so say, to the nature of God Himself. The earthly harvest may, and does often fail. Storms waste it; blights canker it; drought withers, or fire consumes it. Industry and skill, spent in years of patient labour, are doomed not unfrequently to see their reward snatched from them. The very abundance of other lands deprives our produce of its value. The natural creation "was made subject to vanity." Its frustration and disappointment are over-ruled for higher ends. But in the spiritual sphere there are no casualties, no room for accident or failure. Here life comes directly into contact with the Living God, its fountain; and its laws partake of His absoluteness.

Each act of faith, of worship, of duty and integrity, is a compact between the soul and God. We "*commit our souls* in well-doing unto a faithful Creator" (1 Pet. iv. 19). By every such volition the heart is yielding itself to the direction of the Divine Spirit. It "sows unto the Spirit," whenever in thought or deed His prompting is obeyed and His will made the law of life. And as in the soil, by the Divine chemistry of nature, the tiny germ is nursed and fostered out of sight, till it lifts itself from the sod a lovely flower, a perfect fruit, so in the order of grace it will prove that from the smallest seeds of goodness in human hearts, from the feeblest beginnings of the life of faith, from the lowliest acts of love and service, God in due season will raise up a glorious harvest for which heaven itself will be the richer.

THE EPILOGUE

CHAPTER XXVIII
THE FALSE AND THE TRUE GLORYING

"See with how large letters I write unto you with mine own hand. As many as desire to make a fair show in the flesh, they compel you to be circumcised; only that they may not be persecuted for the cross of Christ. For not even they who receive circumcision do themselves keep the law; but they desire to have you circumcised, that they may glory in your flesh. But far be it from me to glory, save in the cross of our Lord Jesus Christ, through which the world hath been crucified unto me, and I unto the world."—Gal. vi. 11-14.

The rendering of ver. 11 in the Authorised Version is clearly erroneous (*see how large a letter*). Wickliff, guided by the Latin Vulgate—*with what maner lettris*—escaped this error. It is a *plural* term the Apostle uses, which occasionally in Greek writers denotes an epistle (as in Acts xxviii. 21), but nowhere else in Paul. Moreover the noun is in the *dative* (instrumental) case, and cannot be made the object of the verb.

Paul draws attention at this point to his penmanship, to the size of the letters he is using and their autographic form. "See," he says, "I write this in large characters, and under my own hand." But does this remark apply to *the whole Epistle*, or to *its concluding paragraph* from this verse onwards? To the latter only, as we think. The word "look" is a kind of *nota bene*. It marks something new, designed by its form and appearance in the manuscript to arrest the eye. It was Paul's practice to write through an amanuensis, adding with his own hand a few final words of greeting or blessing, by way of authentication.[146] Here this usage is varied. The Apostle wishes to give these closing sentences the utmost possible emphasis and solemnity. He would print them on the very heart and soul of his readers. This intention explains the language of ver. 11; and it is borne out by the contents of the verses that follow. They are a postscript, or *Epilogue,* to the Epistle, rehearsing with incisive brevity the burden of all that it was in the Apostle's heart to say to these troubled and shaken Galatians.

The past tense of the verb (literally, *I have written*: ἔγραψα) is in accordance with Greek epistolary idiom. The writer associates himself with his readers. When the letter comes to them, Paul *has written* what they now peruse. On the assumption that the whole Epistle is autographic it is hard to see what object the large characters would serve, or why they should be referred to just at this point.

Ver. 11 is in fact a sensational heading. The last paragraph of the Epistle is penned in larger type and in the Apostle's characteristic hand, in order to fasten the attention of these impressionable Galatians upon his final deliverance. This device Paul employs but once. It is a kind of practice easily vulgarised and that loses its force by repetition, as in the case of "loud" printing and declamatory speech.

In this emphatic finalé the interest of the Epistle, so powerfully sustained and carried through so many stages, is raised to a yet higher pitch. Its pregnant sentences give us—*first,* another and still severer denunciation of "the troublers" (vv. 12, 13); *secondly,* a renewed protestation of the Apostle's devotion to the cross of Christ (vv. 14, 15); *thirdly,* a repetition in animated style of the practical doctrine of Christianity, and a blessing pronounced upon those who are faithful to it (vv. 15, 16). A pathetic reference to the writer's personal sufferings, followed by the customary benediction, brings the letter to a close. The first two topics of the Epilogue stand in immediate contrast with each other.

I. *The glorying of the Apostle's adversaries.* "They would have you circumcised, that they may glory in your flesh" (ver. 12).

This is the climax of his reproach against them. It gives us the key to their character. The boast measures the man. The aim of the Legalists was to get so many Gentiles circumcised, to win proselytes through Christianity to Judaism. Every Christian brother persuaded to submit himself to this rite was another trophy for them. His circumcision, apart from any moral or spiritual considerations involved in the matter, was of itself enough to fill these proselytizers with joy. They counted up their "cases;" they rivalled each other in the competition for Jewish favour on this ground. To "glory in your flesh—to be able to point to your bodily condition as the proof of their influence and their devotion to the Law—this," Paul says, "is the object for which they ply you with so many flatteries and sophistries."

Their aim was intrinsically low and unworthy. They "want to make a fair show (to present a good face) in the flesh." *Flesh* in this place (ver. 12) recalls the contrast between *Flesh* and *Spirit* expounded in the last chapter. Paul does not mean that the Judaizers wish to "make a good appearance *in outward respects, in human opinion:*" this would be little more than tautology. The expression stamps the Circumcisionists as "carnal" men. They are "not in the Spirit," but "in the flesh;" and "after the flesh" they walk. It is on worldly principles that they seek to commend themselves, and to unspiritual men. What the Apostle says of himself in Phil. iii. 3, 4, illustrates by contrast his estimate of the Judaizers of Galatia: "We are the circumcision, who worship by the Spirit of God, and glory in Christ Jesus, and *have no confidence in the flesh.*" He explains "having confidence in the flesh" by enumerating his own advantages and distinctions as a Jew, the circumstances which commended him in the eyes of his fellow-countrymen—"which were gain to me," he says, "but I counted them loss for Christ" (ver. 7). In that realm of fleshly motive and estimate which Paul had abandoned, his opponents still remained. They had exchanged Christian fidelity for worldly favour. And their religion took the colour of their moral disposition. To *make a fair show,* an imposing, plausible appearance in ceremonial and legal observance, was the mark they set themselves. And they sought to draw the Church with them in this direction, and to impress upon it their own ritualistic type of piety.

This was a worldly, and in their case a *cowardly* policy. "They constrain you to be circumcised, only that for the cross of Christ they may not suffer persecution" (ver. 12). This they were determined by all means to avoid. Christ had sent His servants forth "as sheep in the midst of wolves." The man that would serve Him, He said, must "follow Him, taking up his cross." But the Judaists thought they knew better than this. They had a plan by which they could be the friends of Jesus Christ, and yet keep on good terms with the world that crucified Him. They would make their faith in Jesus a means for winning over proselytes to Judaism. If they succeeded in this design, their apostasy might be condoned. The circumcised Gentiles would propitiate the anger of their Israelite kindred, and would incline them to look more favourably upon the new doctrine. These men, Paul says to the Galatians, are sacrificing you to their cowardice. They rob you of your liberties in Christ in order to make a shield for themselves against the enmity of their kinsmen. They pretend great zeal on your behalf; they are eager to introduce you into the blessings of the heirs of Abraham: the truth is, they are victims of a miserable fear of persecution.

The cross of Christ, as the Apostle has repeatedly declared (comp. Chapters XII and XXI), carried with it in Jewish eyes a flagrant reproach; and its acceptance placed a gulf between the Christian and the orthodox Jew. The depth of that gulf became increasingly apparent the more widely the gospel spread, and the more radically its principles came to be applied. To Paul it was now sorrowfully evident that the Jewish nation had rejected Christianity. They would not hear the Apostles of Jesus any more than the Master. For the preaching of the cross they had only loathing and contempt. Judaism recognised in the Church of the Crucified its most dangerous enemy, and was opening the fire of persecution against it all along the line. In this state of affairs, for the party of men to compromise and make private terms for themselves with the enemies of Christ was treachery. They were surrendering, as this Epistle shows, all that was most vital to Christianity. They gave up the honour of the gospel, the rights of faith, the salvation of the world, rather than face the persecution in store for those "who will live godly in Christ Jesus."

Not that they cared so much for the law in itself. Their glorying was *insincere,* as well as selfish: "For neither do the circumcised themselves keep the law.—These men who profess such enthusiasm for the law of Moses and insist so zealously on your submission to it, dishonour it by their own behaviour." The Apostle is denouncing the same party throughout. Some interpreters make the first clause of ver. 13 a parenthesis, supposing that "the circumcised" (participle present: *those being circumcised*) are *Gentile perverts* now being gained over to Judaism, while the foregoing and following sentences relate to the Jewish teachers. But the context does not intimate, nor indeed allow such a change of subject. It is "the circumcised" of ver. 13 *a* who in ver. 13 *b* wish to see the Galatians circumcised, "in order to boast over their flesh,"—the same who, in ver. 12, "desire to make a fair show in the flesh" and to escape Jewish persecution. Reading this in the light of the previous chapters, there seems to us no manner of doubt as to the persons thus designated. They are the Circumcisionists, Jewish Christians who sought to persuade the Pauline Gentile Churches to adopt circumcision and to receive their own legalistic perversion of the gospel of Christ. The present tense of the Greek participle, used as it is here with the definite article,[147] has the power of becoming a *substantive,* dropping its reference to time; for the act denoted passes into an abiding characteristic, so that the expression acquires the form of a title. "The circumcised" are *the men of the circumcision,* those known to the Galatians in this character.

The phrase is susceptible, however, of a wider application. When Paul writes thus, he is thinking of others besides the handful of troublers in Galatia. In Rom. ii. 17-29 he levels this identical charge of hypocritical law-breaking against the Jewish people at large: "Thou who gloriest in the law," he exclaims, "through thy transgression of the law dishonourest thou God?" This shocking inconsistency, notorious in contemporary Judaism, was to be observed in the conduct of the legalist zealots in Galatia. They broke themselves the very law which they tried to force on others. Their pretended jealousy for the ordinances of Moses was itself their condemnation. It was not the glory of the law they were concerned about, but their own.

The policy of the Judaizers was dishonourable both in spirit and in aim. They were false to Christ in whom they professed to believe; and to the law which they pretended to keep. They were facing both ways, studying the safest, not the truest course, anxious in truth to be friends at once with the world and Christ. Their conduct has found many imitators, in men who "make godliness a way of gain," whose religious course is dictated by considerations of worldly self-interest. A little persecution, or social pressure, is enough to "turn them out of the way." They cast off their Church obligations as they change their clothes, to suit the fashion. Business patronage, professional advancement, a tempting family alliance, the *entrée* into some select and envied circle—such are the things for which creeds are bartered, for which men put their souls and the souls of their children knowingly in peril. *Will it pay?*—this is the question which comes in with a decisive weight in their estimate of matters of religious profession and the things pertaining to God. But "what shall it profit?" is the question of Christ.

Nor are they less culpable who bring these motives into play, and put this kind of pressure on the weak and dependent. There are forms of social and pecuniary influence, bribes and threats quietly applied and well understood, which are hardly to be distinguished morally from persecution. Let wealthy and dominant Churches see to it that they be clear of these offences, that they make themselves the protectors, not the oppressors of spiritual liberty. The adherents that a Church secures by its worldly prestige do not in truth belong to the "kingdom that is not of this world." Such successes are no triumphs of the cross. Christ repudiates them. The glorying that attends proselytism of this kind is, like that of Paul's Judaistic adversaries, a "glorying in the flesh."

II. "But as for me," cries the Apostle, "far be it to glory, save in the cross of our Lord Jesus Christ" (ver. 14). Paul knows but one ground of exultation, one object of pride and confidence—*his Saviour's cross.*

Before he had received his gospel and seen the cross in the light of revelation, like other Jews he regarded it with horror. Its existence covered the cause of Jesus with ignominy. It marked Him out as the object of Divine abhorrence. To the Judaistic Christian the cross was still an embarrassment. He was secretly ashamed of a crucified Messiah, anxious by some means to excuse the scandal and make amends for it in the face of Jewish public opinion. But now this disgraceful cross in the Apostle's eyes is the most glorious thing in the universe. Its message is the good news of God to all mankind. It is the centre of faith and religion, of all that man knows of God or can receive from Him. Let it be removed, and the entire structure of revelation falls to pieces, like an arch without its keystone. The shame of the cross was turned into honour and majesty. Its foolishness and weakness proved to be the wisdom and the power of God. Out of the gloom in which Calvary was shrouded there now shone forth the clearest light of holiness and love.

Paul gloried in the cross of Christ because it manifested to him *the character of God*. The Divine love and righteousness, the entire range of those moral excellences which in their sovereign perfection belong to the holiness of God, were there displayed with a vividness and splendour hitherto inconceivable. "God so loved the world," and yet so honoured the law of right, that "He spared not His own Son, but delivered Him up for us all." How stupendous is this sacrifice, which baffles the mind and overwhelms the heart! Nowhere in the works of creation, nor in any other dispensation of justice or mercy touching human affairs, is there a spectacle that appeals to us with an effect to be compared with that of the Sufferer of Calvary.

Let me look, let me think again. Who is He that bleeds on that tree of shame? Why does the Holy One of God submit to these indignities? Why those cruel wounds, those heart-breaking cries that speak of a soul pierced by sorrows deeper than all that bodily anguish can inflict? Has the Almighty indeed forsaken Him? Has the Evil One sealed his triumph in the blood of the Son of God? Is it God's mercy to the world, or is it not rather Satan's hate and man's utter wickedness that stand here revealed? The issue shows with whom victory lay in the dread conflict fought out in the Redeemer's soul and flesh. "*God* was in Christ"—living, dying, rising. And what was He doing in Christ?—"reconciling the world unto Himself."

Now we know what the Maker of the worlds is like. "He that hath seen Me," said Jesus on Passion Eve, "hath seen the Father. From henceforth ye know Him, and have seen Him." What the world knew before of the Divine character and intentions towards man was but "poor, weak rudiments." Now the believer has come to *Peniel*; like Jacob, he has "seen the face of God." He has touched the centre of things. He has found the secret of love.

Moreover, the Apostle gloried in the cross because it was *the salvation of men*. His love for men made him boast of it, no less than his zeal for God. The gospel burning in his heart and on his lips, was "God's power unto salvation, both to Jew and Greek." He says this not by way of speculation or theological inference, but as the testimony of his constant experience. It was bringing men by thousands from darkness into light, raising them from the slough of hideous vices and guilty despair, taming the fiercest passions, breaking the strongest chains of evil, driving out of human hearts the demons of lust and hate. This message, wherever it went, was *saving* men, as nothing had done before, as nothing else has done since. What lover of his kind would not rejoice in this?

We are members of a weak and suffering race, groaning each in his own fashion under "the law of sin and death," crying out ever and anon with Paul, "O wretched man that I am!" If the misery of our bondage was acute its darkness extreme, how great is the joy with which we hail our Redeemer! It is the gladness of an immense relief, the joy of salvation. And our triumph is redoubled when we perceive that His grace brings us not deliverance for ourselves alone, but commissions us to impart it to our fellow-men. "Thanks be to God," cries the Apostle, "who always leadeth us in triumph, and maketh known the savour of His knowledge by us in every place" (2 Cor. ii. 14).

The essence of the gospel revealed to Paul, as we have observed more than once, lay in its conception of the office of the cross of Christ. Not the Incarnation—the basis of the manifestation of the Father in the Son; not the sinless life and superhuman teaching of Jesus, which have moulded the spiritual ideal of faith and supplied its contents; not the Resurrection and Ascension of the Redeemer, crowning the Divine edifice with the glory of life eternal; but *the sacrifice of the cross* is the focus of the Christian revelation. This gives to the gospel its *saving* virtue. Round this centre all other acts and offices of the Saviour revolve, and from it receive their healing grace. From the hour of the Fall of man the manifestations of the Divine grace to him ever looked forward to Calvary; and to Calvary the testimony of that grace has looked backward ever since. "By this sign" the Church has conquered; the innumerable benefits with which her teaching has enriched mankind must all be laid in tribute at the foot of the cross.

The atonement of Jesus Christ demands from us a faith like Paul's, a faith of *exultation*, a boundless enthusiasm of gratitude and confidence. If it is worth believing in at all, it is worth believing in heroically. Let us so boast of it, so exhibit in our lives its power, so spend ourselves in serving it, that we may justly claim from all men homage toward the Crucified. Let us lift up the cross of Christ till its glory shines world-wide, till, as He said, it "draws all men unto Him." If we triumph in the cross, we shall triumph by it. It will carry the Church to victory.

And the cross of Jesus Christ is the salvation of men, just because it is the revelation of God. It is "life eternal," said Jesus to the Father, "*to know Thee.*" The gospel does not save by mere pathos, but by knowledge—by bringing about a right understanding between man and his Maker, a reconciliation.

It brings God and man together in the light of truth. In this revelation we see *Him*, the Judge and the Father, the Lord of the conscience and the Lover of His children; and we see *ourselves*—what our sins mean, what they have done. God is face to face with the world. Holiness and sin meet in the shock of Calvary, and flash into light, each illuminated by contrast with the other. And the view of what God is in Christ—how He judges, how He pities us— once fairly seen, breaks the heart, kills the love of sin. "The glory of God in the face of Jesus Christ," sitting on that thorn-crowned brow, clothing that bleeding Form rent with the anguish of Mercy's conflict with Righteousness on our behalf—it is this which "shines in our hearts" as in Paul's, and cleanses the soul by its pity and its terror. But this is no dramatic scene, it is Divine, eternal fact. "We have beheld and do testify that the Father sent the Son to be the Saviour of the world. We *know* and have believed the love that God hath to us" (1 John iv. 14, 16).

Such is the relation to God which the cross has established for the Apostle. In what position does it place him toward *the world*? To it, he tells us, he has bidden farewell. Paul and the world are dead to each other. The cross stands between them. In ch. ii. 20 he had said, "*I* am crucified with Christ;" in ch. v. 24, that his "*flesh* with its passions and lusts" had undergone this fate; and now he writes, "Through the cross of our Lord Jesus Christ *the world* is crucified to me, and I to the world."

Literally, *a world*—a whole world was crucified for Paul when his Lord died upon the cross. The world that slew Him put an end to itself, so far as he is concerned. He can never believe in it, never take pride in it, nor do homage to it any more. It is stripped of its glory, robbed of its power to charm or govern him. The death of shame that old "evil world" inflicted upon Jesus has, in Paul's eyes, reverted to itself; while for the Saviour it is changed into a life of heavenly glory and dominion. The Apostle's life is withdrawn from it, to be "hid with Christ in God."

This "crucifixion" is therefore mutual. The Apostle also "is crucified to the world." Saul the Pharisee was a reputable, religious man of the world, recognised by it, alive to it, taking his place in its affairs. But that "old man" has been "crucified with Christ." The present Paul is in the world's regard another person altogether—"the filth of the world, the offscouring of all things," no better than his crucified Master and worthy to share His punishment. He is dead—"crucified" to it. Faith in Jesus Christ placed a gulf, wide as that which parts the dead and living, between the Church of the Apostles and men around them. The cross parted two worlds wholly different. He who would go back into that other world, the world of godless self-pleasing and fleshly idolatry, must step over the cross of Christ to do it.

"*To me,*" testifies Paul, "the world is crucified." And the Church of Christ has still to witness this confession. We read in it a prophecy. Evil must die. The world that crucified the Son of God, has written its own doom. With its Satanic Prince it "has been judged" (John xii. 31; xvi. 11). Morally, it is dead already. The sentence has passed the Judge's lips. The weakest child of God may safely defy it, and scorn its boasting. Its visible force is still immense; its subjects multitudinous; its empire to appearance hardly shaken. It towers like Goliath confronting "the armies of the living God." But the foundation of its strength is gone. Decay saps its frame. Despair creeps over its heart. The consciousness of its impotence and misery grows upon it.

Worldliness has lost its old serenity irrecoverably. The cross incessantly disturbs it, and haunts its very dreams. Antichristian thought at the present time is one wide fever of discontent. It is sinking into the vortex of pessimism. Its mockery is louder and more brilliant than ever; but there is something strangely convulsive in it all; it is the laughter of despair, the dance of death.

Christ the Son of God *has* come down from the cross, as they challenged Him. But coming down, He has fastened there in His place the world that taunted Him. Struggle as it may, it cannot unloose itself from its condemnation, from the fact that it has killed its Prince of Life. The cross of Jesus Christ must save—or destroy. The world must be reconciled to God, or it will perish. On the foundation laid of God in Zion men will either build or break themselves for ever. The world that hated Christ and the Father, the world that Paul cast from him as a dead thing, cannot endure. It "passeth away, and the lust thereof."

CHAPTER XXIX
RITUAL NOTHING: CHARACTER EVERYTHING

"For neither is circumcision anything, nor uncircumcision, but a new creation. And as many as shall walk by this rule, peace *be* upon them, and mercy, and upon the Israel of God." —Gal. vi. 15, 16.

Verse 14 comprehends the whole theology of the Epistle, and ver. 15 brings to a head its practical and ethical teaching. This apophthegm is one of the landmarks of religious history. It ranks in importance with Christ's great saying: "God is a Spirit; and they that worship Him, must worship in spirit and truth" (John iv. 21-24). These sentences of Jesus and of Paul taken together mark the dividing line between the Old and the New Economy. They declare the nature of the absolute religion, from the Divine and human side respectively. God's pure spiritual being is affirmed by Jesus Christ to be henceforth the norm of religious worship. The exclusive sacredness of Jerusalem, or of Gerizim, had therefore passed away. On the other hand, and regarding religion from its psychological side, as matter of experience and attainment, it is set forth by our Apostle as an inward life, a spiritual condition, dependent on no outward form or performance whatsoever. Paul's principle is a consequence of that declared by his Master. If "God is a Spirit," to be known and approached as such, ceremonial at once loses its predominance; it sinks into the accidental, the merely provisional and perishing element of religion. Faith is no longer bound to material conditions; it passes inward to its proper seat in the spirit of man. And the dictum that "Circumcision is nothing, and uncircumcision nothing" (comp. ch. v. 6; 1 Cor. vii. 19), becomes a watchword of Christian theology.

This Pauline axiom is advanced to justify the confession of the Apostle made in ver. 14; it supports the protest of vv. 12-14 against the devotees of circumcision, who professed faith in Christ but were ashamed of His cross. "That Judaic rite in which you glory," he says, "is nothing. Ritual qualifications and disqualifications are abolished. Life in the Spirit, the new creation that begins with faith in Christ crucified—that is everything." The boasts of the Judaizers were therefore folly: they rested on "nothing."

The Apostle's glorying alone was valid: the new world of "the kingdom of God," with its "righteousness and peace and joy in the Holy Ghost," was there to justify it.

I. *For neither is circumcision anything.*—Judaism is abolished at a stroke! With it circumcision was *everything*. "The circumcision" and "the people of God" were in Israelitish phrase terms synonymous. "Uncircumcision" embraced all that was heathenish, outcast and unclean.

The Mosaic polity made the status of its subjects, their relation to the Divine covenant, to depend on this initiatory rite. "Circumcised the eighth day," the child came under the rule and guardianship of the sacred Law. In virtue of this mark stamped upon his body, he was *ipso facto* a member of the congregation of the Lord, bound to all its duties, so far as his age permitted, and partner in all its privileges. The constitution of Mosaism—its ordinances of worship, its ethical discipline, its methods of administration, and the type of character which it formed in the Jewish nation—rested on this fundamental sacrament, and took their complexion therefrom.

The Judaists necessarily therefore made it their first object to enforce circumcision. If they secured this, they could carry everything; and the complete Judaizing of Gentile Christianity was only a question of time. This foundation laid, the entire system of legal obligation could be reared upon it (ch. v. 3). To resist the imposition of this yoke was for the Pauline Churches a matter of life and death. They could not afford to "yield by subjection—no, not for an hour." The Apostle stands forth as the champion of their freedom, and casts all Jewish pretensions to the winds when he says, "Neither is *circumcision* anything."

This absolute way of putting the matter must have provoked the orthodox Jew to the last degree. The privileges and ancestral glories of his birth, the truth of God in His covenants and revelations to the fathers, were to his mind wrapped up in this ordinance, and belonged of right to "the Circumcision." To say that circumcision is nothing seemed to him as good as saying that the Law and the Prophets were nothing, that Israel had no pre-eminence over the Gentiles, no right to claim "the God of Abraham" as her God. Hence the bitterness with which the Apostle was persecuted by his fellow-countrymen, and the credence given, even by orthodox Jewish Christians, to the charge that he "taught to the Jews apostasy from Moses" (Acts xxi. 21). In truth Paul did nothing of the kind, as James of Jerusalem very well knew. But a sentence like this, torn from its context, and repeated amongst Jewish communities, naturally gave rise to such imputations.

In his subsequent Epistle to the Romans the Apostle is at pains to correct erroneous inferences drawn from this and similar sayings of his concerning the Law. He shows that circumcision, in its historical import, was of the highest value. "What is the advantage of the Jew? What the benefit of circumcision? Much every way," he acknowledges. "Chiefly in that to them were entrusted the oracles of God" (Rom. iii. 1, 2). And again: "Who are Israelites; whose is the adoption, and the glory, and the covenants, and the lawgiving, and the service of God, and the promises; whose are the fathers,—and of whom is the Christ as concerning the flesh, who is over all, God blessed for ever" (Rom. ix. 4, 5). Eloquently has Paul vindicated himself from the reproach of indifference to the ancient faith. Never did he love his Jewish kindred more fervently, nor entertain a stronger confidence in their Divine calling, than at the moment when in that Epistle he pronounced the reprobation that ensued on their rejecting the gospel of Christ. He repeats in the fullest terms the claim which Jesus Himself was careful to assert, in declaring the extinction of Judaism as a local and tribal religion, that "Salvation is of the Jews" (John iv. 21-24). In the Divine order of history it is still "to the Jew first." But natural relationship to the stock of Abraham has in itself no spiritual virtue; "circumcision of the flesh" is worthless, except as the symbol of a cleansed and consecrated heart. The possession of this outward token of God's covenant with Israel, and the hereditary blessings it conferred, brought with them a higher responsibility, involving heavier punishment in case of unfaithfulness (Rom. ii. 17-iii. 8). This teaching is pertinent to the case of children of Christian families, to those formally attached to the Church by their baptism in infancy and by attendance on her public rites. These things certainly have "much advantage every way." And yet in themselves, without a corresponding inner regeneration, without a true death unto sin and life unto righteousness, these also are nothing. The limiting phrase "in Christ Jesus" is no doubt a copyist's addition to the text, supplied from ch. v. 6; but the qualification is in the Apostle's mind, and is virtually given by the context. No ceremony is of the essence of Christianity. No outward rite by itself makes a Christian. We are "joined to the Lord" in "one Spirit." This is the vital tie.

Nor is uncircumcision anything. This is the counter-balancing assertion, and it makes still clearer the bearing of the former saying. Paul is not contending against Judaism in any anti-Judaic spirit. He is not for setting up Gentile in the place of Jewish customs in the Church; he excludes both impartially. Neither, he declares, have any place "in Christ Jesus," and amongst the things that accompany salvation. Paul has no desire to humiliate the Jewish section of the Church; but only to protect the Gentiles from its aggressions. He lays his hand on both parties and by this evenly balanced declaration restrains each of them from encroaching on the other. "Was any one called circumcised"? he writes to Corinth: "let him not renounce his circumcision. Hath any one been called in uncircumcision? Let him not be circumcised." The two states alike are "nothing" from the Christian standpoint. The essential thing is "keeping the commandments of God" (1 Cor. vii. 18, 19).

Christian Gentiles retained in some instances, doubtless, their former antipathy to Jewish practices. And while many of the Galatians were inclined to Legalism, others cherished an extreme repugnance to its usages. The pretensions of the Legalists were calculated to excite in the minds of enlightened Gentile believers a feeling of contempt, which led them to retort on Jewish pride with language of ridicule. Anti-Judaists would be found arguing that circumcision was a degradation, the brand of a servile condition; and that its possessor must not presume to rank with the free sons of God. In their opinion, *uncircumcision* was to be preferred and had "much advantage every way." Amongst Paul's immediate followers there may have been some who, like Marcion in the second century, would fain be more Pauline than the Apostle himself, and replied to Jewish intolerance with an anti-legal intolerance of their own. To this party it was needful to say, "Neither is uncircumcision anything."

The pagan in his turn has nothing for which to boast over the man of Israel. This is the caution which the Apostle urges on his Gentile readers so earnestly in Rom. xi. 13-24. He reminds them that they owe an immense debt of gratitude to the ancient people of God. Wild branches grafted into the stock of Abraham, they were "partaking of the root and fatness" of the old "olive-tree." If the "natural branches" had been "broken off through unbelief," much more might they. It became them "not to be high-minded but to fear." So Paul seeks to protect Israel after the flesh, in its rejection and sorrowful exile from the fold of Christ, against Gentile insolence. Alas! that his protection has been so little availing. The Christian persecutions of the Jews are a dark blot on the Church's record.

The enemies of bigotry and narrowness too oft imbibe the same spirit. When others treat us with contempt, we are apt to pay them back in their own coin. They unchurch us, because we cannot pronounce their shibboleths; they refuse to see in our communion the signs of Christ's indwelling. It requires our best charity in that case to appreciate their excellencies and the fruit of the Spirit manifest in them. "I am of Cephas," say they; and we answer with the challenge "I of Paul." Sectarianism is denounced in a sectarian spirit. The enemies of form and ceremony make a religion of their Anti-ritualism. Church controversies are proverbially bitter; the love which "hopeth and believeth all things," under their influence suffers a sad eclipse. On both sides let us be on our guard. The spirit of partisanship is not confined to the assertors of Church prerogative. An obstinate and uncharitable pride has been known to spring up in the breasts of the defenders of liberty, in those who deem themselves the exponents of pure spiritual religion. "Thus I trample on the pride of Plato," said the Cynic, as he trod on the philosopher's sumptuous carpets; and Plato justly retorted, "You do it with greater pride."

The Apostle would fain lift his readers above the level of this legalist contention. He bids them dismiss their profitless debates respecting the import of circumcision, the observance of Jewish feasts and sabbaths. These debates were a mischief in themselves, destroying the Church's peace and distracting men's minds from the spiritual aims of the Gospel; they were fatal to the dignity and elevation of the Christian life. When men allow themselves to be absorbed by questions of this kind, and become Circumcisionist or Uncircumcisionist partisans, eager Ritualists or Anti-ritualists, they lose the sense of proportion in matters of faith and the poise of a conscientious and charitable judgement. These controversies pre-eminently "minister questions" to no profit but to the subverting of the hearers, instead of furthering "the dispensation of God, which is in faith" (1 Tim. i. 4). They disturb the City of God with intestine strife, while the enemy thunders at the gates. Could we only let such disputes alone, and leave them to perish by inanition! So Paul would have the Galatians do; he tells them that the great Mosaic rite is no longer worth defending or attacking. The best thing is to forget it.

II. What then has the Apostle to put in the place of ritual, as the matter of cardinal importance and chief study in the Church of Christ? He presents to view *a new creation*.

It is something *new* that he desiderates. Mosaism was effete. The questions arising out of it were dying, or dead. The old method of revelation which dealt with Jew and Gentile as different religious species, and conserved Divine truth by a process of exclusion and prohibition, had served its purpose. "The middle wall of partition was broken down." The age of faith and freedom had come, the dispensation of grace and of the Spirit. The Legalists minimised, they practically ignored the significance of Calvary. Race-distinctions and caste-privileges were out of keeping with such a religion as Christianity. The new creed set up a new order of life, which left behind it the discussions of rabbinism and the formularies of the legal schools as survivals of bygone centuries.

The novelty of the religion of the gospel was most conspicuous in *the new type of character* that it created. The faith of the cross claims to have produced not a new style of ritual, a new system of government, but new men. By this product it must be judged. *The Christian* is the "new creature" which it begets.

Whatever Christianity has accomplished in the outer world—the various forms of worship and social life in which it is embodied, the changed order of thought and of civilisation which it is building up—is the result of its influence over the hearts of individual men. Christ, above all other teachers, addressed Himself directly to the heart, whence proceed the issues of life. There His gospel establishes its seat. The Christian is the man with a "new heart." The prophets of the Old Testament looked forward to this as the essential blessing of religion, promised for the Messianic times (Heb. viii. 8-13). Through them the Holy Spirit uttered His protest against the mechanical legalism to which the religion of the temple and the priesthood was already tending. But this witness had fallen on deaf ears; and when Christ proclaimed, "It is the Spirit that quickeneth, the flesh profiteth nothing," when He said, "The things that defile a man come out of his heart," He preached revolutionary doctrine. It is the same principle that the Apostle vindicates. The religion of Christ has to do in the first place with the individual man, and in man with his heart.

What then, we further ask, is the character of this hidden man of the heart, "created anew in Christ Jesus"? Our Epistle has given us the answer. In him "faith working by love" takes the place of circumcision and uncircumcision—that is, of Jewish and Gentile ceremonies and moralities, powerless alike to save (ch. v. 6). Love comes forward to guarantee the "fulfilling of the law," whose fulfilment legal sanctions failed to secure (ch. v. 14). And the Spirit of Christ assumes His sovereignty in this work of new creation, calling into being His array of inward graces to supersede the works of the condemned flesh that no longer rules in the nature of God's redeemed sons (ch. v. 16-24).

The Legalists, notwithstanding their idolatry of the law, did not *keep* it. So the Apostle has said, without fear of contradiction (ver. 13). But the men of the Spirit, actuated by a power above law, in point of fact do keep it, and "law's righteousness is fulfilled" in them (Rom. viii. 3, 4). This was a new thing in the earth. Never had the law of God been so fulfilled, in its essentials, as it was by the Church of the Crucified. Here were men who truly "loved God with all their soul and strength, and their neighbour as themselves." From Love the highest down to Temperance the humblest, all "the fruit of the Spirit" in its clustered perfection flourished in their lives. Jewish discipline and Pagan culture were both put to shame by this "new creation" of moral virtue. These graces were produced not in select instances of individuals favoured by nature, in souls disposed to goodness, or after generations of Christian discipline; but in multitudes of men of every grade of life—Jews and Greeks, slaves and freemen, wise and unwise—in those who had been steeped in infamous vices, but were now "washed, sanctified, justified in the name of the Lord Jesus and by the Spirit of our God."

Such regenerated men were the credentials of Paul's gospel. As he looked on his Corinthian converts, drawn out of the very sink of heathen corruption, he could say, "The seal of my apostleship are ye in the Lord." The like answer Christianity has still to give to its questioners. If it ever ceases to render this answer, its day is over; and all the strength of its historical and philosophical evidences will not avail it. The Gospel is "God's power unto salvation"—or it is nothing!

Such is Paul's *canon*, as he calls it in ver. 16—the rule which applies to the faith and practice of every Christian man, to the pretensions of all theological and ecclesiastical systems. The true Christianity, the true churchmanship, is that which turns bad men into good, which transforms the slaves of sin into sons of God. A true faith is a *saving* faith. The "new creation" is the sign of the Creator's presence. It is God "who quickeneth the dead" (Rom. iv. 17).

When the Apostle exalts character at the expense of ceremonial, he does this in a spirit the very opposite of religious indifference. His maxim is far removed from that expressed in the famous couplet of Pope:

"For modes of faith let graceless zealots fight;

His can't be wrong whose life is in the right."

The gospel of Christ is above all things a *mode of faith*. The "new creature" is a son of God, seeking to be like God. His conception of the Divine character and of his own relationship thereto governs his whole life. His "life is in the right," because his heart is right with God. All attempts to divorce morality from religion, to build up society on a secular and non-religious basis, are indeed foredoomed to failure. The experience of mankind is against them. As a nation's religion has been, so its morals. The ethical standard in its rise or fall, if at some interval of time, yet invariably, follows the advance or decline of spiritual faith. For practical purposes, and for society at large, religion supplies the mainspring of ethics. Creed is in the long run the determinant of character. The question with the Apostle is not in the least whether religion is vital to morals; but whether this or that formality is vital to religion.

One cannot help wondering how Paul would have applied his canon to the Church questions of our own day. Would he perchance have said, "Episcopacy is nothing, and Presbyterianism is nothing;—but keeping the commandments of God"? Or might he have interposed in another direction, to testify that "Church Establishments are nothing, and Disestablishment is nothing; charity is the one thing needful?" Nay, can we even be bold enough to imagine the Apostle declaring, "Neither Baptism availeth anything, nor the Lord's Supper availeth anything,—apart from the faith that works by love"? His rule at any rate conveys an admonition to us when we magnify questions of Church ordinance and push them to the front, at the cost of the weightier matters of our common faith. Are there not multitudes of Romanists on the one hand who have, as we believe, perverted sacraments, and Quakers on the other hand who have no sacraments, but who have, notwithstanding, a penitent, humble, loving faith in Jesus Christ? And their faith saves them: who will doubt it? Although faith must ordinarily suffer, and does in our judgement manifestly suffer, when deprived of these appointed and most precious means of its expression and nourishment. But what authority have we to forbid to such believers a place in the Body of Christ, in the brotherhood of redeemed souls, and to refuse them the right hand of fellowship, "who have received the Holy Ghost as well as we"? "It is the Spirit that beareth witness:" who is he that gainsayeth? Grace is more than the means of grace.

"And as many as shall walk by this rule, peace be on them and mercy, and upon the Israel of God." Here is an Apostolic benediction for every loyal Church. The "walk" that the Apostle approves is the measured, even pace, the steady *march* [148] of the redeemed host of Israel. On all who are thus minded, who are prepared to make spiritual perfection the goal of their endeavours for themselves and for the Church, Paul invokes God's peace and mercy.

Peace is followed by the *mercy* which guards and restores it. Mercy heals backslidings and multiplies pardons. She loves to bind up a broken heart, or a rent and distracted Church. Like the pillar of fire and cloud in the wilderness, this twofold blessing rests day and night upon the tents of Israel. Through all their pilgrimage it attends the children of Abraham, who follow in the steps of their father's faith.

With this tender supplication Paul brings his warnings and dissuasives to an end. For the betrayers of the cross he has stern indignation and alarms of judgement. Towards his children in the faith nothing but peace and mercy remains in his heart. As an evening calm shuts in a tempestuous day, so this blessing concludes the Epistle so full of strife and agitation. We catch in it once more the chime of the old benediction, which through all storm and peril ever rings in ears attuned to its note: *Peace shall be upon Israel* (Ps. cxxv. 5).

CHAPTER XXX
THE BRAND OF JESUS

"From henceforth let no man trouble me: for I bear branded
on my body the marks of Jesus. The grace of our Lord Jesus
Christ be with your spirit, brethren. Amen." —Gal. vi. 17, 18.

The Apostle's pen lingers over the last words of this Epistle. His
historical self-defence, his theological argument, his practical admonitions,
with the blended strain of expostulation and entreaty that runs through
the whole—now rising into an awful severity, now sinking into mother-
like tenderness—have reached their conclusion. The stream of deep and
fervent thought pouring itself out in these pages has spent its force. This
prince of the Apostles in word and doctrine has left the Church no more
powerful or characteristic utterance of his mind. And Paul has marked the
special urgency of his purpose by his closing message contained in the last
six verses, an Epistle within the Epistle, penned in large, bold strokes from
his own hand, in which his very soul transcribes itself before our eyes.

It only remains for him to append his signature. We should expect him
to do this in some striking and special way. His first sentence (ch. i. 1-10)
revealed the profound excitement of spirit under which he is labouring; not
otherwise does he conclude. Ver. 17 sharply contrasts with the words of
peace that hushed our thoughts at the close of the last paragraph. Perhaps
the peace he wishes these troubled Churches reminds him of his own
troubles. Or is it that in breathing his devout wishes for "the Israel of God,"
he cannot but think of those who were "of Israel," but no sons of peace, in
whose hearts was hatred and mischief toward himself? Some such thought
stirs anew the grief with which he has been shaken; and a pathetic cry breaks
from him like the sough of the departing tempest.

Yet the words have the sound of triumph more than of sorrow. Paul
stands a conscious victor, though wounded and with scars upon him that he
will carry to his grave. Whether this letter will serve its immediate purpose,
whether the defection in Galatia will be stayed by it, or not, the cause of the
cross is sure of its triumph; his contention against its enemies has not been
in vain. The force of inspiration that uplifted him in writing the Epistle, the
sense of insight and authority that pervades it, are themselves an earnest of

victory. The vindication of his authority in Corinth, which, as we read the order of events, had very recently occurred, gave token that his hold on the obedience of the Gentile Churches was not likely to be destroyed, and that in the conflict with legalism the gospel of liberty was certain to prevail. His courage rises with the danger. He writes as though he could already say, "I have fought the good fight. Thanks be to God, which always leadeth us in triumph" (2 Tim. iv. 7; 2 Cor. ii. 14).

The warning of ver. 17 has the ring of *Apostolic dignity*. "From henceforth let no man give me trouble!" Paul speaks of himself as a sacred person. God's mark is upon him. Let men beware how they meddle with him. "He that toucheth you," the Lord said to His people after the sorrows of the Exile, "toucheth the apple of Mine eye" (Zech. ii. 8). The Apostle seems to have had a similar feeling respecting himself. He announces that whosoever from this time lays an injurious hand upon him does so at his peril. *Henceforth*—for the struggle with Legalism was the crisis of Paul's ministry. It called forth all his powers, natural and supernatural, into exercise. It led him to his largest thoughts respecting God and man, sin and salvation; and brought him his heaviest sorrows. The conclusion of this letter signalises the culmination of the Judaistic controversy, and the full establishment of Paul's influence and doctrinal authority. The attempt of Judaism to strangle the infant Church is foiled. In return it has received at Paul's hands its death-blow. The position won in this Epistle will never be lost; the doctrine of the cross, as the Apostle taught it, cannot be overthrown. Looking back from this point to "prove his own work," he can in all humility claim this "glorying in regard to himself" (ver. 4). He stands attested in the light of God's approval as a good soldier of Christ Jesus. He has done the cause of truth an imperishable service. He takes his place henceforth in the front rank amongst the spiritual leaders of mankind. Who now will bring reproach against him, or do dishonour to the cross which he bears? Against that man God's displeasure will go forth. Some such thoughts were surely present to the Apostle's mind in writing these final words. They cannot but occur to us in reading them. Well done, we say, thou faithful servant of the Lord! Ill must it be for him who henceforth shall trouble thee.

"Troubles" indeed, and to spare, Paul had encountered. He has just passed through the darkest experience of his life. The language of the Second Epistle to Corinth is a striking commentary upon this verse. "We are pressed on every side," he writes, "perplexed, pursued, smitten down" (ch. iv. 8, 9). His troubles came not only from his exhausting labours and hazardous journeys; he was everywhere pursued by the fierce and deadly hatred of his fellow-countrymen. Even within the Church there were men who made it their business to harass him and destroy his work. No place was safe for him—not even the bosom of the Church. On land or water, in the throngs of the city or the solitudes of the desert, his life was in hourly jeopardy (1 Cor. xv. 30; 2 Cor. xi. 26).

Beside all this, "the care of the Churches" weighed on his mind heavily. There was "no rest" either for his flesh or spirit (2 Cor. ii. 13; vii. 5). Recently Corinth, then Galatia was in a ferment of agitation. His doctrine was attacked, his authority undermined by the Judaic emissaries, now in this quarter, now in that. The tumult at Ephesus, so graphically described by Luke, happening at the same time as the broils in the Corinthian Church and working on a frame already overstrung, had thrown him into a prostration of body and mind so great that he says, "We despaired even of life. We had the answer of death in ourselves" (2 Cor. i. 8, 9). The expectation that he would die before the Lord's return had now, for the first time it appears, definitely forced itself on the Apostle, and cast over him a new shadow, causing deep ponderings and searchings of heart (2 Cor. v. 1-10). The culmination of the legalistic conflict was attended with an inner crisis that left its ineffaceable impression on the Apostle's soul.

But he has risen from his sick bed. He has been "comforted by the coming of Titus" with better news from Corinth (2 Cor. vii. 6-16). He has written these two letters—the Second to the Corinthians, and this to the Galatians. And he feels that the worst is past. "He who delivered him out of so great a death, will yet deliver" (2 Cor. i. 10). So confident is he in the authority which Christ gave and enabled him to exercise in utter weakness, so signally is he now stamped as God's Apostle by his sufferings and achievements, that he can dare any one from this time forth to oppose him. The anathema of this Epistle might well make his opponents tremble. Its remorseless logic left their sophistries no place of refuge. Its passionate entreaties broke down suspicion and sullenness. Let the Circumcisionists beware how they slander him. Let fickle Galatians cease to trouble him with their quarrels and caprices. So well assured is he for his part of the rectitude of his course and of the Divine approval and protection, that he feels bound to warn them that it will be the worse for those who at such a time lay upon him fresh and needless burdens.

One catches in this sentence too *an undertone of entreaty*, a confession of weariness. Paul is tired of strife. "Woe is me," he might say, "that I sojourn in Meshech, that I dwell among the tents of Kedar! My soul hath long had her dwelling with him that hateth peace." "Enmities, ragings, factions, divisions"—with what a painful emphasis he dwells in the last chapter on these many forms of discord. He has known them all. For months he has been battling with the hydra-headed brood. He longs for an interval of rest. He seems to say, "I pray you, let me be at peace. Do not vex me any more with your quarrels. I have suffered enough." The present tense of the Greek imperative verb (παρεχέτω) brings it to bear on the course of things then going on: as much as to say, "Let these weapons be dropped, these wars and fightings cease." For his own sake the Apostle begs the Galatians to desist from the follies that caused him so much trouble, and to suffer him to share with them God's benediction of peace.

But what an argument is this with which Paul enforces his plea, — "for I bear the brand of Jesus in my body!"

"The *stigmata* of Jesus" — what does he mean? It is "in my body" — some marks branded or punctured on the Apostle's person, distinguishing him from other men, conspicuous and humiliating, inflicted on him as Christ's servant, and which so much resembled the inflictions laid on the Redeemer's body that they are called "the marks of Jesus." No one can say precisely what these brands consisted in. But we know enough of the previous sufferings of the Apostle to be satisfied that he carried on his person many painful marks of violence and injury. His perils endured by land and sea, his imprisonments, his "labour and travail, hunger and thirst, cold and nakedness," his three shipwrecks, the "night and day spent in the deep," were sufficient to break down the strength of the stoutest frame; they had given him the look of a worn and haggard man. Add to these the stoning at Lystra, when he was dragged out for dead. "Thrice" also had he been beaten with the Roman rods; "five times" with the thirty-nine stripes of the Jewish scourge (2 Cor. xi. 23-27).

Is it to these last afflictions, cruel and shameful they were in the extreme, that the Apostle specially refers as constituting "the brand *of Jesus*"? For Jesus was *scourged*. The allusion of 1 Pet. ii. 24 — "by whose *stripes* (literally, *bruise* or *weal*) ye were healed" — shows how vividly this circumstance was remembered, and how strongly it affected Christian minds. With this indignity upon Him — His body lashed with the torturing whip, scored with livid bruises — our Blessed Lord was exposed on the cross. So He was branded as a malefactor, even before His crucifixion. And the same brand Paul had received, not once but many times, for his Master's sake. As the strokes of the scourge fell on the Apostle's shuddering flesh, he had been consoled by thinking how near he was brought to his Saviour's passion: "The servant," He had said, "shall be as his Lord." Possibly some recent infliction of the kind, more savage than the rest, had helped to bring on the malady which proved so nearly fatal to him. In some way he had been marked with fresh and manifest tokens of bodily suffering in the cause of Christ. About this time he writes of himself as "always bearing about in his body the dying of the Lord Jesus" (2 Cor. iv. 10); for the corpse-like state of the Apostle, with the signs of maltreatment visible in his frame, pathetically imaged the suffering Redeemer whom he preached. Could the Galatians have seen him as he wrote, in physical distress, labouring under the burden of renewed and aggravated troubles, their hearts must have been touched with pity. It would have grieved them to think that they had increased his afflictions, and were "persecuting him whom the Lord had smitten."

His scars were badges of dishonour to worldly eyes. But to Paul himself these tokens were very precious. "Now I rejoice in my sufferings for you," he writes from his Roman prison at a later time: "and am filling up what is lacking of the afflictions of Christ in my flesh" (Col. i. 24). The Lord had not suffered everything Himself. He honoured His servants by leaving behind a measure of His afflictions for each to endure in the Church's behalf. The Apostle was companion of his Master's disgrace. In him the words of Jesus were signally fulfilled: "They have hated Me; they will also hate you." He was following, closely as he might, in the way that led to Calvary. All men may know that Paul is Christ's servant; for he wears His livery, the world's contempt. Of Jesus they said, "Away with Him, crucify Him;" and of Paul, "Away with such a fellow from the earth: for it is not fit that he should live" (Acts xxii. 22). "Enough for the disciple to be as his Master:" what could he wish more?

His condition inspired reverence in all who loved and honoured Jesus Christ. Paul's Christian brethren were moved by feelings of the tenderest respect by the sight of his wasted and crippled form. "His bodily presence is weak (2 Cor. x. 10): he looks like a corpse!" said his despisers. But under that physical feebleness there lay an immense fund of moral vigour. How should he not be weak, after so many years of wearying toil and relentless persecution and torturing pain? Out of this very weakness came a new and unmatched strength; he "glories in his infirmities," for there rests upon him the strength of Christ (2 Cor. xii. 9).

Under the expression "*stigmata* of Jesus" there is couched a reference to the practice of marking criminals and runaway slaves with a brand burnt into the flesh, which is perpetuated in our English use of the Greek words *stigma* and *stigmatize*. A man so marked was called *stigmatias, i.e.,* a branded scoundrel; and such the Apostle felt himself to be in the eyes of men of the world. Captain Lysias of Jerusalem took him for an Egyptian leader of banditti. Honourable men, when they knew him better, learned to respect him; but such was the reputation that his battered appearance, and the report of his enemies, at first sight gained for him.

The term *stigmata* had also another and different signification. It applied to a well-known custom of religious devotees to *puncture*, or tattoo, upon themselves the name of their God, or other sign expressive of their devotion (Isa. xiiv. 5; Rev. iii. 12). This signification may be very naturally combined with the former in the employment of the figure. Paul's *stigmata*, resembling those of Jesus and being of the same order, were signs at once of reproach and of consecration. The prints of the world's insolence were witnesses of his devotion to Christ. He loves to call himself "the slave of Christ Jesus." The scourge has written on his back his Master's name. Those dumb wounds proclaim him the bondman of the Crucified. At the lowest point of personal and official humiliation, when affronts were heaped upon him, he felt that he was raised in the might of the Spirit to the loftiest dignity, even as "Christ was crucified through weakness, yet liveth through the power of God" (2 Cor. xiii. 4.)

The words *I bear*—not united, as in our own idiom, but standing the pronoun at the head and the verb at the foot of the sentence—have each of them a special emphasis. *I*—in contrast with his opponents, man-pleasers, shunning Christ's reproach; and *bear* he says exultantly—"this is my burden, these are the marks I carry," like the standard-bearer of an army who proudly wears his scars (Chrysostom). In the profound and sacred joy which the Apostle's tribulations brought him, we cannot but feel even at this distance that we possess a share. They belong to that richest treasure of the past, the sum of

> "Sorrow which is not sorrow, but delight
>
> To hear of, for the glory that redounds
>
> Therefrom to human kind and what we are."

The *stigmatization* of Paul, his puncturing with the wounds of Jesus, has been revived in later times in a manner far remote from anything that he imagined or would have desired. *Francis of Assisi* in the year 1224 A.D. received in a trance the wound-prints of the Saviour on his body; and from that time to his death, it is reported, the saint had the physical appearance of one who had suffered crucifixion. Other instances, to the number of eighty, have been recorded in the Roman Catholic Church of the reproduction, in more or less complete form, of the five wounds of Jesus and the agonies of the cross; chiefly in the case of nuns. The last was that of Louise Lateau, who died in Belgium in the year 1883. That such phenomena have occurred, there is no sufficient reason to doubt. It is difficult to assign any limits to the power of the human mind over the body in the way of sympathetic imitation. Since St. Francis' day many Romanist divines have read the Apostle's language in this sense; but the interpretation has followed rather than given rise to this fulfilment. In whatever light these manifestations may be regarded, they are a striking witness to the power of the cross over human nature. Protracted meditation on the sufferings of our Lord, aided by a lively imagination and a susceptible physique, has actually produced a rehearsal of the bodily pangs and the wound-marks of Calvary.

This mode of knowing Christ's sufferings "after the flesh," morbid and monstrous as we deem it to be, is the result of an aspiration which however misdirected by Catholic asceticism, is yet the highest that belongs to the Christian life. Surely we also desire, with Paul, to be "made conformable to the death of Christ." On our hearts His wounds must be impressed. Along the pathway of our life His cross has to be borne. To all His disciples, with the sons of Zebedee, He says, "Ye shall indeed drink of My cup; and with the baptism that I am baptized withal shall ye be baptized." But "it is the Spirit that quickeneth," said Jesus; "the flesh profiteth nothing." The pains endured by the body for His sake are only of value when, as in Paul's case, they are the result and the witness of an inward communion of the Spirit, a union of the will and the intelligence with Christ.

The cup that He would have us drink with Him, is one of sorrow for the sins of men. His baptism is that of pity for the misery of our fellows, of yearning over souls that perish. It will not come upon us without costing many a pang. If we receive it there will be ease to surrender, gain and credit to renounce, self to be constantly sacrificed. We need not go out of our way to find our cross; we have only not to be blind to it, not to evade it when Christ sets it before us. It may be part of the cross that it comes in a common, unheroic form; the service required is obscure; it consists of a multitude of little, vexing, drudging sacrifices in place of the grand and impressive sacrifice, which we should be proud to make. To be martyred by inches, out of sight—this to many is the cruellest martyrdom of all. But it may be Christ's way, the fittest, the only perfect way for us, of putting His brand upon us and conforming us to His death.

Yes, conformity of spirit to the cross is *the mark of Jesus*. "If we suffer with Him" —so the Apostolic Churches used to sing—"we shall also be glorified together." In our recoil from the artificial penances and mortifications of former ages, we are disposed in these days to banish the idea of mortification altogether from our Christian life. Do we not study our personal comfort in an un-Christlike fashion? Are there not many in these days, bearing the name of Christ, who without shame and without reproof lay out their plans for winning the utmost of selfish prosperity, and put Christian objects in the second place? How vain for them to cry "Lord, Lord!" to the Christ who "pleased not Himself!" They profess at the Lord's Table to "show His death;" but to show that death in their lives, to "know" with Paul "the fellowship of His sufferings," is the last thing that enters into their minds. How the scars of the brave Apostle put to shame the self-indulgence, the heartless luxury, the easy friendship with the world, of fashionable Christians! "Be ye followers of me," he cries, "as I also of Christ." He who shuns that path cannot, Jesus said, be My disciple.

So the blessed Apostle has put his mark to this Epistle. To the Colossians from his prison he writes, "Remember my bonds." And to the Galatians, "Look on my wounds." These are his credentials; these are the armorial bearings of the Apostle Paul. He places the seal of Jesus, the sign-manual of *the wounded hand* upon the letter written in His name.

THE BENEDICTION

One benediction the Apostle has already uttered, in ver. 16. But that was a general wish, embracing all who should walk according to the spiritual rule of Christ's kingdom. On his readers specifically he still has his blessing to pronounce. He does it in language differing in this instance very little from that he is accustomed to employ.

"The grace of our Lord Jesus Christ" is the distinctive blessing of the New Covenant. It is to the Christian the supreme good of life, including or carrying with it every other spiritual gift. *Grace* is Christ's property. It descended with the Incarnate Saviour into the world, coming down from God out of heaven. His life displayed it; His death bestowed it on mankind. Raised to His heavenly throne, He has become on the Father's behalf the dispenser of its fulness to all who will receive it. There exalted, thence bestowing on men "the abundance of grace and of the gift of righteousness," He is known and worshipped as *our Lord Jesus Christ*.

What this grace of God in Christ designs, what it accomplishes in believing hearts, what are the things that contradict it and make it void, this Epistle has largely taught us. Of its pure, life-giving stream the Galatians already had richly tasted. From "Christ's grace" they were now tempted to "remove" (ch. i. 6). But the Apostle hopes and prays that it may abide with them.

"With your spirit," he says; for this is the place of its visitation, the throne of its power. The spirit of man, breathed upon by the Holy Spirit of God, receives Christ's grace and becomes the subject and the witness of its regenerating virtue. This benediction contains therefore in brief all that is set forth in the familiar three fold formula—"the grace of our Lord Jesus Christ, and the love of God, and the communion of the Holy Ghost."

After all his fears for his wayward flock, all his chidings and reproofs, forgiveness and confidence are the last thoughts in Paul's heart: "Brethren" is the last word that drops from the Apostle's pen,—followed only by the confirmation of his devout *Amen*.

To his readers also the writer of this book takes leave to address the Apostle Paul's fraternal benediction: The Grace of our Lord Jesus Christ be with your spirit, brethren. Amen.

FOOTNOTES:

[1] The text used in this exposition is, with very few exceptions, that of the Revised English Version, or its margin.

[2] Compare Acts xiv. 4, 14 (*Barnabas and Paul*); 1 Thess. ii. 6 (*Paul and his comrades*); Rom. xvi. 7 (*Andronicus and Junias*); 2 Cor. viii. 23 (*Titus and others*, "apostles of the churches"); 2 Cor. xi. 13 ("false apostles": *Judean emissaries*); also Rev. ii. 2; Heb. iii. 1; John xiii. 16. On the N.T. use of *apostle*, see Lightfoot's Galatians, pp. 92-101; but especially Huxtable's *Dissertation* in the Pulpit Commentary (Galatians), pp. xxiii.-l., the most satisfactory elucidation of the subject we have met with. Prebendary Huxtable however presses his argument too far, when he insists that St. Paul held his higher commission entirely in abeyance until the crisis of the Judaic controversy.

[3] 1 Cor. xv. 10; 2 Cor. iv. 2; vi. 3-10; xi. 5, 16-xii. 13.

[4] 2 Thess. i. 5-7; 2 Tim. iv. 18; Heb. x. 12, 13; 1 Pet. v. 10.

[5] 1 Cor. x. 11; Heb. ix. 26.

[6] 1 Cor. vii. 31; 1 John ii. 17.

[7] Rom. viii. 18; Eph. i. 13, 14.

[8] 1 Cor. iv. 9-13; xv. 30, 32; 2 Cor. vi. 4, 10; xi. 16, 33.

[9] 1 Cor. iv. 3, 4; 2 Cor. v. 9-12; xii. 19.

[10] 2 Cor. i. 8-10; ii. 12, 13; iv. 8-11; vii. 5-7.

[11] 2 Cor. x. 1-11; xiii. 1-10; 1 Cor. iv. 18-21.

[12] Session vi., Can. xii.

[13] Session xxii., Can. vi.

[14] Comp. Rom. ix. 22; 1 Cor. xii. 3; xv. 1; 2 Cor. viii. 1.

[15] See ch. ii. 6-14; 1 Cor. i. 12; iii. 22; iv. 9; ix. 1-5; xv. 8-10.

[16] This genitive is, however, open to the other construction, which is unquestionable in 1 Cor. i. 7; 2 Thess. i. 7; also 1 Pet. i. 7, 13. Rev. i. 1 furnishes a prominent example of the *subjective* genitive.

[17] Acts ix. 1-19; xxii. 5-16; xxvi. 12-18.

[18] Ἐπιφανεία, a supernatural appearance, such as that of the Second Advent.

[19] Φωτίζω, comp. 2 Cor. iv. 6.

[20] Ch. v. 11; comp. 1 Cor. ix. 20; Acts xvi. 3; xxi. 20-26; xxiii. 6.

[21] Acts vii. 58; viii. 1-3; ix. 1.

[22] *Les Apôtres*, p. 180, note 1.

[23] 1 Cor. xiv. 18; 2 Cor. xii. 1-6; Acts xvi. 9; xviii. 8, 9; xxii. 17, 18.

[24] ἡμέραι ἱκαναί, *a considerable time*. The expression is indefinite.

[25] Ver. 18: that is, parts of "three years," according to ancient reckoning—say from 36 to 38 A.D., possibly less than two in actual duration.

[26] 2 Cor. xi. 13; iii. 1-3. See the remarks on the word *Apostle* in Chapter I. p. 12.

[27] See Rom. ix. 1; 2 Cor. i. 17, 18, 23; 1 Thess. ii. 5.

[28] Acts xi. 27-30. It is significant that this ministration was sent "to the Elders."

[29] For the ministry alluded to in Acts xxvi. 20 there were other, later opportunities, especially in the journey described in Acts xv. 3; see also Acts xxi. 15, 16.

[30] Ver. 22. It is arbitrary in Meyer to exclude from this category the Church of Jerusalem.

[31] We follow Lightfoot in reading the ποτὲ as in ch. i. 23, and everywhere else in Paul, as a particle of *time*.

[32] The writer is compelled in this instance to depart from the rendering of the English Version, for reasons given in the sequel. See also a paper on *Paul and Titus at Jerusalem*, in The Expositor, 3rd series, vol. vi., pp. 435-442. The last three words within the brackets agree with the R.V. *margin*.

[33] These fourteen years probably amounted to something less in our reckoning,—say, from 38 to 51 A.D. Some six years elapsed before Paul was summoned to Antioch.

[34] Acts xiii. 2, 7, 13, 43, 45, 46, 50; xiv. 12, 14; xv. 2, 12.

[35] Comp. Rom. xi. 13; xv. 16, 17.

[36] *Hibbert Lectures*, p. 103. This testimony is the more valuable as coming from the ablest living exponent of the Baurian theory.

[37] Acts xv. 28: "It seemed good to the Holy Ghost and to us." This was in the Early Church no mere pious official form.

[38] For this use of ἀλλ' οὐδὲ compare Acts xix. 2 (here also after a question); 1 Cor. iii. 2; iv. 3. We observe a similar instance of the phrase in Æschylus, *Persæ*, l. 792. Ἀλλ' opposes itself to the expectation of the Judaistic "compellers," present to the mind of Paul and his readers.

[39] This particle is a serious obstacle in the way of the ordinary punctuation, which attaches the following clause to ver. 3. The δὲ is similar to that of ver. 6 (ἀπὸ δὲ τ. δοκούντων); not of κατ' ἰδίαν δὲ in ver. 2, nor of θανάτον δὲ σταύρου (Phil. ii. 8), which are parenthetical qualifications. And to say, "Because of the false brethren Titus was not compelled to be circumcised," is simply an inconsequence. Would he have been compelled to be circumcised if they had *not* required it? This is the assumption implied by the above construction.

[40] For this rendering of ποτὲ comp. ch. i. 13, 23; and see Lightfoot, or Beet, *in loc.*

[41] Comp. Rom. ii. 11; 1 Cor. i. 27-31; xv. 9, 10; Eph. vi. 9; Col. iii. 25.

[42] We cannot explain προσανέθεντο here by the ἀναθέμην of ver. 2, as though Paul wished to say, "I imparted to them my gospel; they imparted to me nothing *further*." Forπρος- implies *direction*, rather than *addition*. See Meyer on this verb in ch. i. 16.

[43] Ch. i. 18. See Chapter V.

[44] See Rom. i. 5; 1 Cor. xv. 10; Eph. iii. 2, 7, 8; 1 Tim. i. 13.

[45] *Zum Evangelien d. Paulus und d. Petrus*, p. 273. Holsten is the keenest and most logical of all the Baurian succession.

[46] Ch. i. 12; iii. 22; ix. 5.

[47] *The Acts of the Apostles critically investigated*, vol. ii., pp. 28, 30: Eng. Trans.

[48] *Paulus*, vol. i., p. 130: Eng. Trans.

[49] Rom. ii. 25-iii. 1.

[50] Rom. i. 16; ii. 9, 10; ix. 4, 5; xi. 1, 2.

[51] In his *L'apôtre Paul: esquisse d'une histoire de sa pensée*, an admirable work, to which the writer is under great obligation.

[52] See Chapter VII. pp. 109, 110.

[53] ἐὰν μὴ has the same partially exceptive force as εἰ μὴ in ch. i. 7, 19. Comp. Rom. xiv. 14; also Luke iv. 26, 27.

[54] For this emphatic *found*, describing a process of moral conviction and inward discovery, comp. Rom. vii. 10, 18, 21; the whole passage strikingly illustrates the reminiscence of our text.

[55] *Commentarii, in loc.*

[56] See Grimm's *Lexicon*, or Trench's *N. T. Synonyms*, on this word. Comp. ch. iii. 19; Rom. ii. 23-27; iv. 15; v. 14.

[57] The *I* of this sentence is quite indefinite. On the other hand ver. 19, with its emphatic ἐγώ γάρ, brings us into a new vein of thought.

[58] Comp. ch. iii. 10-12, 19; Rom. iii. 20; iv. 15.

[59] This verb has, as Schott suggests, a tinge of irony.

[60] Rom. vii. 7-viii. 1.

[61] Hofmann is so far right when he makes the Apostle turn to the Galatians in ch. ii. 15, and draws at this point the line between the historical and doctrinal sections of the Epistle.

[62] What is said of χάρις, applies also to its derivatives, χαρίζομαι, κ.τ.λ.

[63] Eph. i. 5-9; 2 Tim. i. 9; Rom. iii. 24; Heb. ii. 9; 2 Cor. v. 20-vi. 1; Gal. iv. 5; Tit. iii. 5-7; ii. 11-14; Rom. v. 21.

[64] Rom. vii. 12, 14; 2 Thess. ii. 4-8; comp. 1 John iii. 4.

[65] Rom. iii. 20; iv. 15; v. 20; vii. 5, 24; Gal. ii. 16; iii. 10, 11, 19.

[66] Rom. iii. 24, 25; Eph. ii. 8; etc.

[67] Rom. iv. 1-4; xi. 6; Gal. ii. 16; iii. 12.

[68] Rom. iv. 16; viii. 28-39; xi. 5; Eph. i. 4-6; Tit. iii. 7; Acts xx. 32; Gal. iii. 18: δι' ἐπαγγελίας κεχάρισται ὁ Θεός.

[69] 1 Cor. xv. 3, 4, 11; Rom. iv. 24, 25; x. 9; 1 Thess. iv. 14.

[70] Rom. v. 14; 1 Cor. xv. 22, 45-48; 1 Tim. ii. 5.

[71] 1 Cor. xv. 45-49; comp. Col. i. 15-17; John i. 4, 9, 15, 16.

[72] Pfleiderer, *Hibbert Lectures*, pp. 65, 6. Dr. Pfleiderer's delicate and sympathetic interpretation of Paul's teaching (in these *Lectures*, and still more in his *Paulinism*) has made all students of the Apostle his debtors, however much they may quarrel with his historical criticism.

[73] Ch. iii. 14; iv. 6, 7; v. 5; 1 Cor., vi. 17, 19; Rom. viii. 9-16.

[74] Ch. iii. 28; Col. iii. 11; Rom. xv. 5-7.

[75] The verb προεγράφη (*openly set forth*) probably means *painted up* rather than *placarded*. This more vivid meaning belongs to γράφω, and there is no sufficient reason why it should not attach to προ-γράφω. It is entirely in place here. "Jesus Christ crucified" is not an announcement to be made, but an object to be delineated.

[76] On βασκαίνω see the note in Lightfoot's Commentary *in loc.;* also Grimm's N. T. Lexicon. "The Scripture calleth envy an 'evil eye;' ... so there still seemeth to be acknowledged in the act of envy an ejaculation or irradiation of the eye. Envy hath in it something of witchcraft.... It is the proper attribute of the Devil, who is called 'The envious man, that soweth tares among the wheat by night.'" —(Lord Bacon: *Essay* ix.)

[77] Comp. 2 Cor. xi. 1-4, a passage closely parallel to this context, containing what is expressed here and in Gal. i. 6, 7; iv. 11, 17, 18.

[78] 2 Tim. ii. 10; Eph. vi. 24 (ἀφθαρσία is *incorruption* everywhere else in Paul: why not here?)

[79] Ch. iii. 26, 27; Rom. vi. 2-4; Col. ii. 11-13; Tit. iii. 5.

[80] Comp. 2 Thess. i. 4-6; Ph. i. 28-30; Rom. viii. 17; 2 Tim. i. 8.

[81] Matt. iii. 9; John viii. 33-59.

[82] Gen. xii. 3: the first promise to Abraham. In this text the Hebrew and the Greek (LXX) say, *All the tribes (families) of the earth.* The synonymous ἔθνη, with its special Jewish connotation, suited Paul's purpose better; and it is used in the repetition of the promise in Gen. xviii. 18.

[83] Rom. viii. 4; 1 Cor. vi. 9; Eph. v. 9; Tit. ii. 12-14; etc.

[84] *Of faith* qualifies *live* in the Hebrew of the prophet, and in the LXX, also in the quotation of Heb. x. 38. The presumption is that it does so in Rom. i. 17, and Gal. iii. 11. We can see no sufficient reason in these passages to the contrary.

[85] 2 Chron. xx. 7; Isai. xli. 8; comp. Jas. ii. 23.

[86] Deut. xxvii. 26; Jos. viii. 32-35. *All things,* given by the LXX in the former passage, is wanting in the Hebrew. But the phrase is true to the spirit of this text, and is read in the parallel Deut. xxviii. 15.

[87] Hab. ii. 4. For the construction, see *note* on p. 186.

[88] Lev. xviii. 5.

[89] The Hebrew of Deut. xxi. 23 reads "a curse *of God;*" the LXX, "cursed *by God*" (κεκαταρημένος however, not ἐπικατάρατος as in Paul's phrase). The Apostle omits the two last words, not inadvertently, as Meyer supposes, for he must have had a painfully vivid remembrance of the wording of the original, but out of a reverence that made it impossible to speak of the Redeemer as "accursed *by God.*"

[90] See the able and convincing elucidation of διαθήκη in Cremer's *Biblico-Theological Lexicon of N.T. Greek.*

[91] See Heb. ix. 16-18, where so much ingenuity has been expended to turn *testament* into *covenant*.

> "*Sweet is the memory of His name,*
> *Who blessed us in His will.*"

[92] Gen. xxii. 16-18; Heb. vi. 17.

[93] Comp. Rom. viii. 33, 34; Acts xi. 17; 2 Cor. i. 21, for a similar emphasis.

[94] We gain nothing, and we may lose much, in "trying to settle questions of Old Testament historical criticism by casual allusions in the New Testament." (See Mr. Beet's sensible observations, in his Commentary *ad loc.*)

[95] Gen. xii. 2, 3; xv. 2-6; xvii. 4-8, 15-21; xxii. 16-18.

[96] Ch. iv. 21-31; Rom. iv. 17-22; comp. Heb. xi. 11, 12.

[97] Rom. xi.

[98] Luke i. 54, 55, 68-73.

[99] Τῶν παραβάσεων: the definite article can scarcely mean less than this.

[100] Comp. the reference to this word in Chapter IX., p. 143.

[101] Acts vii. 53: comp. διαταγὰς ἀγγέλων and διαταγεὶς δι' ἀγγέλων. Stephen's last words may well have lingered in the ear of Saul. From the lips of Stephen, they were something of an *argumentum ad hominem*.

[102] A doubtful citation at the best: the reading of the LXX is more to the point than the Hebrew text.

[103] See the quotations from Jewish writers to this effect given by Meyer or Lightfoot.

[104] Comp. Heb. ii. 2-4; also Col. ii. 15: "(*scil.* God) having stripped off the principalities and powers"—the earlier forms of angelic mediation. The writer may refer on this latter passage to his note in the *Pulpit Commentary*, also to *The Expositor*, 1st series, x. 403-421.

[105] But the title "mediator" belongs to *Christ*, given by Paul himself—the "one mediator between God and men, the man Christ Jesus" (1 Tim. ii. 5). (Comp. Heb. viii. 6; ix. 15; xii. 24.) Christ is so styled however under an aspect very different from that in which the word appears here. "There is one mediator," the Apostle writes in 1 Timothy, "*who gave Himself a ransom for all*," the one *atoning* mediator. But Christ's manifestation of God was direct, as that of Moses was not. His Person does not come between men

and God, like that of the Sinaitic mediator; it brings God into immediate contact with men. Moses acted for a distant God: Christ is Immanuel, *God with us*. On the *human* side Christ is mediator (ἄνθρωπος Χριστὸς Ἰησοῦς); He acts for individual men with God. On the *Divine* side, He is more than mediator, being God Himself.

[106] Matt. xix. 8. Comp. Ezek. xx. 25.

[107] Comp. 1 Cor. viii. 6; 1 Tim. ii. 5; also Mark xii. 29, 30; Jas. ii. 19.

[108] Hence the *present* participle, συγκλειόμενοι (Revised reading of ver. 23), in combination with the *imperfect* of the foregoing verb, ἐφρονρουμεθα.

[109] The phrase *faith in Christ Jesus* is a link between this Epistle and those of the third and fourth groups. Comp. Col. i. 4; Eph. i. 15; 1 Tim. iii. 13; 2 Tim. i. 13; iii. 15. More frequently in this connection our "in" represents εἰς (*into*), not ἐν as here.

[110] Rom. vi. 1, 2; Tit. iii. 4-7 ("not of *works* ... that we had done)."

[111] Comp. Eph. ii. 15; iv. 13; but *neuter* in ii. 14.

[112] Surely *the world of men*, not the cosmical elements; comp. Col. ii. 8, 20 (where *rudiments of the world* is parallel to *tradition of men*); also Gal. vi. 14; Heb. ix. 1. 1 Cor. iii. 1-3 supplies an interesting parallel: those who are *babes in Christ*, are so far carnal and walk *according to man*, animated by *the spirit of this world* (1 Cor. ii. 12).

[113] Comp. Rom. i. 3, 4; ix. 5; 2 Cor. xiii. 4; Eph. iv. 9, 10; Ph. ii. 6-8; Col. i. 15, 18; ii. 9; 1 Tim. iii. 16.

[114] Matt. x. 20; Luke xi. 13; John xiv. 16; Acts i. 4, 5.

[115] John xiv. 17; the *present* (ἐστίν) is the preferable reading. See Westcott *ad loc.*

[116] Comp. Rom. viii. 31-35; Acts xi. 17.

[117] John xii. 26; xvii. 24; Rev. iii. 21; Phil. i. 23; Col. iii. 4; 1 Pet. v. 1.

[118] For the rendering of this clause, see the exposition which follows.

[119] Comp. 2 Cor. ii. 4; vii. 8.

[120] Comp. 1 Thess. i. 5; ii. 7, 8.

[121] 1 Cor. ii. 3; 2 Cor. iv. 7; x. 1, 10; xi. 6.

[122] Comp. 2 Cor. xii. 7-10, referring apparently to the first outbreak of this mysterious affliction.

[123] Comp. Matt. xviii. 9.

[124] Ζηλόω, *to have zeal* towards a person or thing, *to affect* (A.V.: in its older English sense of *seeking, paying regard to any one*).

[125] The *full stop* placed in the English Version at the end of ver. 18, on this view, is out of place.

[126] Kalisch, *Commentary*, on Genesis xxi. 9.

[127] Comp. Heb. xi. 11, 12; 1 Pet. iii. 6.

[128] Paul writes "the *Sinai* mountain" (τὸ Σινᾶ ὄρος) in tacit opposition to the other, familiar *Mount Zion* (Hofmann *in loc.*). In Heb. xii. 22 the same inversion appears, with the same significance.

[129] The reading of this clause is doubtful. The ancient witnesses disagree. Dr. Hort suggests that the Revised reading—the best attested, but scarcely grammatical—may be due to a primitive corruption, TH for EΠ (ἐλευθερίᾳ). This emendation gives an excellent and apposite sense: *for (with a view to) freedom Christ set us free.* The phrase ἐπ' ἐλευθερίᾳ is found in ver. 13, and would gain additional force there, if read as a repetition of what is affirmed here. The confusion of letters involved is a natural one; and once made at an early time in some standard copy, it would account for the extraordinary confusion of reading into which the verse has fallen. If conjectural emendation may be admitted anywhere in the N. T., it is legitimate in this instance.

[130] Comp. John xv. 5, 6, where in ἐβλήθη, ἐξηράνθη, there is a like *summary* aorist.

[131] Comp. 2 Pet. iii. 17; for the figure suggested, Eph. iv. 14; 1 Tim. i. 19.

[132] Acts xxiii. 6; xxiv. 15; xxvi. 6-8; comp. John vi. 39, 40, 44.

[133] "*Working* through love," not *wrought* (R.V. *margin*). The latter rendering of the participle is found in some of the Fathers, and is preferred by Romanist interpreters in the interest of their doctrine of *fides formata*. Paul's theology and his verbal usage alike require the *middle* sense of this verb, adopted by modern commentators with one consent. The middle voice implies that through love faith *gets into action, is operative, efficacious, shows what it can do*. Comp., for Pauline usage, Rom. vii. 5; 2 Cor. i. 6, iv. 12; Eph. iii. 20; Col. i. 29; 1 Thess. ii. 13; 2 Thess. ii. 7; and see Moulton's Winer's *N. T. Grammar*, p. 318 (note on *dynamic middle*).

[134] See Chapter I, on the *date* of the Epistle.

[135] Comp. ch. iii. 4: "*ye suffered so many things.*"

[136] Comp. Chapter XII.

[137] Compare Chapter IX. We refer this occurrence to the interval between the second and third of Paul's missionary journeys (Acts xviii. 22), A.D. 54.

[138] The rendering of the R.V. *margin* is that of all the Greek interpreters, and of Meyer, Lightfoot, Beet, and the strict grammatical commentators amongst the moderns. The form and usage of the verb do not allow of any other. Apart from its unseemliness, the expression is powerfully appropriate. This condemnation of the Old-Testament sacrament is not more severe than the language of Isa. lxvi. 3: "He that slaughtereth an ox is a man-slayer, he that bringeth a meal-offering—it is *swine's blood*."

[139] The construction of ch. vi. 16; Rom. iv. 12; Phil. iii. 16, is not strictly analogous.

[140] Comp. Jas. iv. 5: "The Spirit which He made to dwell in us, yearneth even unto jealous envy" (*R. V. margin*); also the double use of ζηλόω in ch. iv. 17, 18 (Chapter XVIII.).

[141] See Rom. vi. 6, 12; vii. 4, 5, 23, 24; viii. 10-13; Col. ii. 11-13; iii. 5.

[142] Comp., 1 Tim. ii. 13-15: *saved through the childbearing*—*i.e.*, surely, the bearing of the Child Jesus, *the seed of the woman.*

[143] For this pregnant force of ἐν see the grammarians: Moulton's *Winer*, pp. 514, 5; *A. Buttmann*, pp. 328, 9. (Eng. Ver.).

[144] 1 Tim. ii. 14: the expression is parallel in point of grammar, as well as sense; γέγονεν ἐν παραβάσει.

[145] 1 Cor. iv. 1-5; 2 Cor. i. 12; v. 10-12.

[146] See 2 Thess. iii. 17, 18; 1 Cor. xvi. 21-23. In ver. 22 of the latter passage we can trace a similar autographic message, on a smaller scale. Comp. also Philemon 19.

[147] οἱ περιτεμνόμενοι (*Revised Text*). On this idiom, see Winer's *Grammar*, p. 444; A. Buttmann's *N. T. Grammar*, p. 296. In ch. i. 23, and in ii. 2 (τ. δοκοῦσι), we have had instances of this usage.

[148] Στοιχήσουσιν; comp. ch. v. 25.